Sir Gawain and the Green Knight

Sir Gawain and the Green Knight:

A Reference Guide

by
Robert J. Blanch

The Whitston Publishing Company
Troy, New York
1983

For Sandi "swete"

and my knights — errant,

Bobby, Randy, Kevin, and David.

CONTENTS

INTRODUCTION 1

WRITINGS ABOUT *SIR GAWAIN*, 1824-1978 13

ADDENDA 267

INDEX 279

INTRODUCTION

Sir Gawain and the Green Knight, the rainbow crown of Middle English romances, appears in a single manuscript (British Museum MS., Cotton Nero A.x.)—a small quarto volume which also contains *Pearl,* an elegy in the form of a symbolic dream vision, and two Biblical homilies, *Purity* (or *Cleanness*) and *Patience.* Noted for their complex fusion of themes (purity, loyalty) and structure, their artistic use of symmetry and contrast, and their dynamic metrical patterns and alliterative diction, the Cotton poems—composed in the latter part of the fourteenth century (ca. 1350-1400) and preserved in an early fifteenth-century scribal hand—are usually attributed to one anonymous author, perhaps a member of an aristocrat's household in the Northwest Midland area of England. Although the precise identity of the *Pearl*-poet (or *Gawain*-poet, as he is often termed) cannot be established with certainty, his four works were included in the library of Henry Savile of Bank (1568-1617), a Yorkshire antiquarian. Ultimately, these poems came into the hands of Sir Robert Cotton, a seventeenth-century bibliophile, and miraculously survived the blaze (1731) at Cotton's Ashburnham House—a fire which scorched or destroyed numerous medieval manuscripts.

Remaining in a shadowy literary limbo for nearly a century, the Cotton poems—particularly *Sir Gawain*—flare into prominence in the early nineteenth century. With the publication of Richard Price's edition (1824.1) of Thomas Warton's *History of English Poetry, Gawain* is briefly highlighted, for Price includes the first passage (lines 20-36) from *Gawain* ever to appear in printed form. Noting the links between this "old romance" and the traditional Anglo-Saxon poetic mode, Price signalizes the employment of Old English vocabulary, formulas, and idioms in *Gawain.* Even more significant than the contribution of Price to the literary history of *Gawain* is the scholarly corpus of Sir Frederic Madden, the manuscript librarian for the British

Museum and the pre-eminent nineteenth-century editor of Arthurian texts. Scholars are indebted to Madden for unearthing, restoring, and cataloguing the Cottonian Library—those manuscripts not consumed by the fire at Ashburnham House. Furthermore, Madden assigned to *Gawain* its present-day title when he first read (July 9, 1829) this romance in Cotton Nero A.x. Ten years later, he produced a remarkably accurate transcription of *Gawain* for the first published edition (1839.1) of this poem—*Syr Gawayne; A Collection of Ancient Romance Poems by Scotish* [sic] *and English Authors Relating to that Celebrated Knight of the Round Table.*

With the publication of Madden's edition of *Gawain* and the subsequent editions (1864.2 and 1869.2) by Richard Morris for the Early English Text Society, critical interest in *Gawain* is slowly ignited, for, apart from editions and reprints of scholarly studies of *Gawain*, approximately thirty critical works—investigations of the poem's sources and analogues, diction, dialect, alliterative techniques, dating, and authorship—appear between 1869 and the close of the nineteenth century. While such works, reflecting early scholars' overriding concern with historical and literary background, philology, and authorship questions, may ultimately spark literary interpretations of *Gawain*, we cannot anticipate the explosion of critical activity in the twentieth century.

Detonated especially during the 1950's, 1960's, and 1970's, this scholarly charge generates numerous interpretations—including dissertations, articles, and book-length studies—of the theme, meaning, and structure of *Gawain* as well as many philological notes, editions, and translations. In fact, over eight hundred scholarly appraisals of *Gawain*, exclusive of reprints, have been published since 1900. Fortunately, however, the almost impossible task of tracing the contours of *Gawain* criticism is softened by the appearance of three bibliographic essays— Morton W. Bloomfield's "*Sir Gawain and the Green Knight:* An Appraisal" (1961.3), a judicious evaluation of critical treatments of *Gawain* published between 1883 and 1960 and a point of departure for future studies of the poem; Robert W. Ackerman's "*Sir Gawain and the Green Knight* and Its Interpreters" (1968.2), a survey of *Gawain* studies appearing between 1961 and 1967; and Donald R. Howard's "*Sir Gawain and the Green*

Knight," in *Recent Middle English Scholarship and Criticism: Survey and Desiderata* (1971.20), an extension through 1968 of Bloomfield's analysis of critical treatments, editions, and translations of *Gawain.* Inasmuch as Bloomfield, Ackerman, and Howard collectively span the terrain of *Gawain* scholarship through 1968, the purpose of this section of my introductory essay is to present a selective, albeit brief, chronological overview of *Gawain* studies between 1969 and 1977, including significant critical works and trends in interpretation, and to propose desiderata for future *Gawain* research. For the sake of convenience and clarity, I will divide *Gawain* scholarship into three periods—1969-1971, 1972-1974, and 1975-1977—periods which are nearly equivalent in the number of works published on *Gawain.*

In the early 1970's, moreover, three critical studies deserve special attention. A. C. Spearing's *The Gawain Poet: A Critical Study* (1970.29), a valuable discussion of all four Cotton Nero poems, explores the psychological realism and the style of *Gawain*—two relatively neglected elements—as well as the ambiguous nature of the Green Knight and the moral issues (*cortaysye,* chastity) pervading the poem. John A. Burrow's *Ricardian Poetry: Chaucer, Gower, Langland and the Gawain Poet* (1971.6), an ambitious effort to pinpoint "common characteristics" in the foremost poets of the Ricardian age (1377-99), also examines the style of *Gawain,* including the poet's artistic use of diction, irony, and structural divisions. Burrow discusses, likewise, the significance of the confession scenes, Gawain's confession to the priest at Castle Hautdesert and his "confession" to the Green Knight as lay confessor (Green Chapel), and the comic spirit informing *Gawain.* Manfred Markus's *Moderne Erzählperspektive in den Werken des Gawain-Autors* (1971.25), the last scholarly work under consideration, is especially useful because it scrutinizes the modern narrative style (perspective, composition, tone, and syntax) of *Gawain* through an elucidation of the points of view employed in this romance. Furthermore, Markus zeroes in on the pivotal role played by the narrator of *Gawain,* his spatial and temporal distance from narrative characters and events.

Apart from the broad focus of these three scholarly studies, *Gawain* criticism appearing between 1969 and 1971 is noted for

its variety, ranging from discussions of ironic reversals involving
the ambiguous concept of courtesy, the imprint of rule ritual,
and the impact of Northern topography upon *Gawain*'s structure
to well-traveled terrain—the poem's use of symmetry, the pentangle symbolism, the leitmotifs of *trawþe* and loyalty, and the
origins of the "alliterative revival." Perhaps the most illumi-
nating analyses produced in this period call attention to matters which have been overlooked or developed inadequately by
critics of earlier generations—the shaping influence of oral narrative and oral-formulaic techniques upon the interlaced pattern
of *Gawain;* the dramatic employment of time as a means of un-
veiling the behavior of characters or of particularizing a scene;
the function and meaning of Gawain's antifeminist tirade; and
the poet's artful shift from *þou* (thou) to *ȝe* (you) in the dia-
logues at Hautdesert and the Green Chapel. Finally, some useful studies of the multi-leveled *Gawain* concentrate upon its diction, including its realistic manipulation of Scandinavian loan-
words, and upon the collision between chivalric duties and
Christian ethics or the tension between the tinsel values of
knighthood and alliterative romance conventions. Other scholarly investigations, however, emphasize the game-like qualities of
Gawain—its theatricality, artifice imagery, and playful tone—
even though such critical efforts fail to designate what game-
playing really meant in the fourteenth century.

At least two books—a critical study and an edition of
Gawain—published between 1972 and 1974 represent important
contributions to scholarship. Charles Muscatine's *Poetry and
Crisis in the Age of Chaucer* (1972.20), a provocative analysis
of Chaucer, Langland, and the *Pearl*-poet, comments perceptive-
ly upon the variational style of *Gawain,* "the interplay between
formal unity and variation . . . at the core of both the style and
the meaning" (p. 45) of this romance. In the course of his discussion of diction, imagery, and descriptive detail, Muscatine
emphasizes the symmetrical patterns and contrasts threaded
throughout the poem as well as the interlinking of words through
sound. W. R. J. Barron's edition (1974.1), however, contains
on facing pages the text and a graceful prose translation, probably the best translation of *Gawain* since Marie Borroff's distinguished verse effort (1967.3). Barron's twenty-four page
Introduction to his edition of *Gawain* is also significant, for it
explores fully the conventions and materials of the romance

genre and the chivalric code and reveals how and why the occasional violation of such conventions in *Gawain* intensifies the
irony and suspense in the poem.

Such stylistic and ironic tones struck in the works of
Muscatine and Barron resonate throughout much of the *Gawain*
criticism produced between 1972 and 1974. While some studies
emphasize the poem's pounding rhythm and meter or the beat
of the alliterative long line, other works discuss the artistic
strokes of verbal ambiguity, the use of comic irony and sharply
defined images, the disoriented style of *Gawain*—a jarring mixture of formalized and discordant elements, or the employment
of syntax and style for the psychological revelation of character.
In addition to this recurrent concern with style, numerous new
strains are sounded in *Gawain*—topographical studies, including
the influence of Old Norse elements as well as the appearance
of two disparate *Gawain* landscapes, the rhetorical embellish-
ments of the "romance" country and the "realistic" *topos;*
the parallels between *Gawain* and *La Mule sans frein*, especially
in the works of D. D. R. Owen (1972.21 and 1973.17); the
emergence of patterns—linear, cyclical, numerological, and spatial
(enclosure); the reverberation of the *felix culpa* motif throughout
the poem; the ambiguous conclusion of *Gawain*, particularly the
meaning of Camelot's laughter; the visual techniques—repetition, variation, and blurring of details; and the echoes of Arabic
literary traditions in *Gawain* (1974.15), especially the Green
Knight as a fictional embodiment of the Persian and Islamic
figure, al-Khadir ('the green one').

In this final section of my review, the *Gawain* scholarship
published between 1975 and 1977, two books should be noted.
Although Edward Wilson's *The Gawain-Poet* (1976.37) devotes
a disproportionate number of pages to *Pearl, Patience,* and
Purity, his relatively brief discussion of *Gawain* provides a useful
analysis of the topographical allusions, particularly those traced
in Gawain's journey from the idealized world of romance to the
perils of the real world. Wilson examines, likewise, the elements
of play and game in the poem—especially the badinage between
Gawain and Lady Bercilak—and Gawain's isolation at the conclusion of his romance-quest. Charles Moorman's edition (1977.11)
of *The Works of the Gawain-Poet,* however, represents the first
complete scholarly compilation (one volume) of all four Cotton

Nero poems, for his edition contains full critical apparatus—medieval texts, explanatory and textual notes, general introduction, glossary, and select bibliography. While Moorman's Introduction to his edition is generally competent, it is not especially original because his study treads along familiar critical paths, particularly the characteristics of the "alliterative revival," the sources of *Gawain*, and *Gawain*'s artistic qualities (mythic elements, comedy, and the courtly love convention). Furthermore, Moorman's introductory commentary as well as his explanation of knotty passages and allusions are overshadowed by the scholarly breadth of Malcolm Andrew and Ronald Waldron's recent edition (1978.1), *The Poems of the Pearl Manuscript*.

The critical concern with style manifested in the early 1970's is sounded once again in *Gawain* scholarship published between 1975 and 1977. Although some analyses focus upon the link between metrical patterns and syntactic patterns, the tension between *Gawain*'s style and content, the poem's employment of alliterative verse techniques (formulaic and idealizing phrases), and the summarizing, anticipatory, ironic or symbolic functions of the bob and wheel stanzas, still other studies explore the diction in the temptation scenes, the ambiguous overtones of concrete situations, and Gawain's ironic affinity with Solomon, the Biblical figure enmeshed in the coils of passion. Apart from critiques of *Gawain*'s style, many new readings of the whole poem are produced within this period—archetypal analyses involving the initiation of the hero; liturgical investigations, including an elucidation of the religious feasts, formulas, and rituals at the core of *Gawain;* structuralist exposition, the view of the poem as a free-flying fictional romance which does not aim to mirror the real world; psychological interpretations, including the representation of Gawain's creative mind as the springboard for the poem's narrative events and characters or the application of Freudian terms and themes used in explicating folktales and dreams to the plot and characters of *Gawain;* and the significance of the Franciscan Exemplarist mode in the poem. Finally, three new critical stances—perhaps reflecting contemporary involvement with feminist issues and values, alienation, and the interplay between reader and creative artist—examine, respectively, the roles of women, especially Lady Bercilak, in the poem; the significance of the isolation motif; and the audience's initiation into Gawain's thought patterns and game world.

Despite the mushrooming of *Gawain* scholarship within the past ten years, many areas need further work. Once the *Middle English Dictionary* is finished and the analysis of English place-names and dialects is completely crystallized, significant philological study—the foundation of all critical interpretations of *Gawain*—may truly expand. In this vein, then, an investigation of *Gawain*'s style—its artistic employment of concrete verbs and nouns, tense switches, passive voice, figures of speech, and Scandinavian vocabulary—may yield promising results. Furthermore, *Gawain* should be scrutinized in terms of other Middle English alliterative romances, especially Northern Arthurian romances, and the apparent conflict or rapprochement between chivalric romance ideals and Christian goals should be precisely determined, especially through a careful study of fourteenth-century culture and English nationalism. While many aspects of *Gawain* have been discussed extensively, other important subjects need to be probed, including the reasons for the poem's aura of ambiguity; the thematic and symbolic interlacing between the Cotton Nero poems; the objective pose of the narrator and his aesthetic distance from his material; visual techniques; point of view and other narrative methods, particularly the *Gawain*-poet's reliance upon audience expectations and participation in Gawain's dilemmas; clothing and sound imagery; and the poet's constant fascination with extravagant adornments and trappings—emblems of worldliness—even in his depiction of Gawain's pentangle, the symbol of the hero's perfection. Several other areas, the apocalyptic judgement theme and the *Gawain*-poet's city imagery, also demand investigation. Fortunately, Professors Susan L. Clark and Julian N. Wasserman have initiated a study of city imagery, an analysis of the convergence of the poet's spatial (inclusion and exclusion) and temporal (linear and cyclical time) concerns, in an article ("The *Pearl*-Poet's City Imagery") published in volume 16 of *The Southern Quarterly* (Add. 9).

At the time of writing this introduction, several scholars have graciously provided me with information on their current research. R. E. Kaske, for example, views the governing motif of *Gawain* as *lewté* or troth, proposes a new interpretation of the pentangle, and perceives the Green Knight and the two ladies of Hautdesert as symbols, respectively, of Nature and Fortune with the double face. Such a critical commentary appears in

"*Sir Gawain and the Green Knight,*" soon to be published in Vol. 10 (1979) of *Medieval and Renaissance Studies: Proceedings of the Southeastern Institute of Medieval and Renaissance Studies.* W. R. J. Barron, however, examines a number of vexing problems in *Gawain* scholarship. In "Arthurian Romance: Traces of an English Tradition," *English Studies,* 61 (1980), 2-23, he investigates "common elements—nationalistic spirit, dynastic interest, and realism—in Layamon's *Brut,* the alliterative *Morte Arthure, Golagros and Gawane,* and *Sir Gawain and the Green Knight* as constituting the basis of an English tradition in the Arthurian romances," whereas in "Alliterative Romance and the French Tradition," in *The Alliterative Tradition,* ed. D. A. Lawton (Scolar Press, 1981), he considers "the various types of redactive process in *William of Palerne, Chevalere Assigne, Golagros and Gawane,* and the alliterative *Morte Arthure,* as casting light on the relationship of *Sir Gawain* to the French tradition and to its supposed French original." Barron, likewise, scrutinizes "the critical use of irony in the evaluation of chivalric ideals, as exemplified by an analysis of *Sir Gawain,* lines 1855-1921 and Chrétien's *Yvain,* lines 907-2171," and attempts to uncover the sources of this ironic method within the medieval social and literary milieu. Barron's final scholarly effort, '*Trawthe' and Treason: The Sin of Gawain Reconsidered* (Publications of the Faculty of Arts of the University of Manchester, No. 25), Manchester, England: Manchester University Press, 1980, represents a book-length study of *Gawain*'s "theme of chivalric idealism and human fallibility." Indebted to Thiébaux's *The Stag of Love* (1974.32) as well as to medieval legal, historical, and literary conventions and documents on sexual treason and its punishment, Barron offers a detailed explanation of fitts three and four, particularly the suggestion of "a metaphorical relationship between the hunting and wooing scenes," the legal and chivalric ramifications of Gawain's behavior during the temptations, the nature and significance of the green girdle, and the theological underpinnings of the confession scenes and Gawain's fault.

In compiling this volume of *Gawain* scholarship, I have consulted four important secondary bibliographies. The updated edition (May, 1979) of James Joyce's "Checklist of Materials on *Sir Gawain and the Green Knight,*" a bibliography in computer-readable form, attempts to cover "all printed material on *Sir Gawain.*" While Joyce's checklist is not an exhaustive survey, it provides many obscure citations, especially reviews and articles, unavailable elsewhere. In some cases, objective abstracts and sources of bibliographical items are supplied. Charles R. Courtney's "The *Pearl* Poet: An Annotated International Bibliography, 1955-1970" (1975.5), a work containing judicious interpretive commentary on the contents and scope of American and foreign *Gawain* scholarship, proposes to include all unpublished doctoral dissertations, books, essays, translations, modernizations, and editions of all four Cotton Nero poems and *St. Erkenwald.* The late Professor Francis Lee Utley and Richard Schrader's privately circulated checklist (unannotated) of writings on the *Pearl*-poet is reasonably complete, especially for American scholarship, through 1966, whereas William Vantuono's unannotated bibliography—a typescript which is part of a prospective omnibus edition of the *Pearl* poems—offers a select number of background studies and bibliographies as well as books and articles on the *Pearl*-poet.

Other standard reference tools, none of which are specifically noted in this volume, include the current listings of *Gawain* criticism in the *Annual Bibliography of English Language and Literature* (complete through 1975); in bibliographic-essay form in *The Year's Work in English Studies* (complete through 1976); in the annual volumes of the *MLA International Bibliography* (complete through 1978); in the annual survey of articles, notes, and critical reviews contained in the *International Medieval Bibliography* and in the quarterly numbers of *International Guide to Medieval Studies: A Quarterly Index to Medieval Literature;* and in the annotated lists of editions, translations, historical studies, criticism, and reviews appearing in the annual volumes of the *Bulletin Bibliographique de la Société internationale Arthurienne* (complete through 1976). In addition to these current bibliographical sources, less recent *Gawain* scholarship—especially unpublished doctoral dissertations—may be located easily in *Progress of Medieval and Renaissance Studies in the United States and Canada* (1923-60), John J. Parry and Margaret Schlauch's *Arthurian Bibliography* (1922-35), and "A Bibliography of Critical Arthurian Literature," published annually (1940-63) in the June issue of *Modern Language Quarterly.*

An extremely significant bibliographical guide which appeared too late for adequate evaluation in this volume is Malcolm

Andrew's *The Gawain-Poet: An Annotated Bibliography, 1839-1977* (New York: Garland Publishing, Inc., 1979). Inasmuch as Professor Andrew attempts to offer a comprehensive bibliography of writings (1313 items) on all four Cotton Nero works and does not restrict his citations only to interpretive or critical commentaries upon these poems, "all editions and translations of any of the four poems, and all books, articles, and notes specifically about one or more of them" (p. x) are included in his reference guide. Furthermore, Andrew's volume cites some brief commentaries in handbooks and anthologies and offers both a selective list of reviews and an unannotated list of doctoral dissertations and occasional M.A. theses. While Andrew's specific coverage of *Gawain* research—over 900 items—is quite comprehensive, especially in its treatment of the works of Japanese scholars, his annotations represent general, telegraphic summaries rather than detailed expositions of the contents of the critical works.

I hope that this reference work serves as a useful guide to past *Gawain* scholarship and stimulates future critical interest in this challenging medieval poem. Although the bibliographical coverage of substantive research on *Gawain* is intended to be reasonably comprehensive, especially through 1976, some items will not be included in this volume; brief commentaries in handbooks and anthologies will ordinarily be excluded, while editions, reviews, and translations lacking *interpretive* matter will not be listed. Furthermore, many important articles focusing on the Massey authorship controversy and the *Pearl*-poet's "signature" will not appear in this volume, for such critical pieces will be listed in a second reference guide, an annotated bibliography of criticism on *Pearl, Patience,* and *Purity.* Despite my attempt to be comprehensive in the coverage of *Gawain* scholarship, some lapses will undoubtedly occur because Japanese and other foreign dissertations, articles, and books are noted infrequently in the standard reference sources. Since the current listings of *Gawain* criticism contained in the *MLA International Bibliography, The Year's Work in English Studies,* and *Annual Bibliography of English Language and Literature* are not up-to-date, the bibliographic citations for 1977 and 1978 in the main body of this volume constitute an important sampling, not a comprehensive survey of the available *Gawain* criticism. Furthermore, items are placed in chronological order with the elimination of any year containing no references; items unseen by the editor are indicated by asterisks immediately preceding the numbers of the relevant citations. All annotations are represented as objective abstracts, whereas necessary editorial comments are enclosed in brackets appearing before the annotations. Items which were unseen until the main body of the bibliography was completed appear in an "Addendum" section near the end of the book. Finally, the Index, a selective listing of the most significant items, includes representative medieval works, authors, and themes; occasional Biblical figures and allusions; explanatory and textual notes; important topics explored in *Gawain* criticism; and the clearly identified authors of scholarly works on *Gawain,* but not the titles of their publications.

For providing me with bibliographical information, offprints, or notices of articles and books, I am grateful to Professors John Leyerle, R. E. Kaske, W. R. J. Barron, Eugene O. Young, Caroline D. Eckhardt, A. Kent Hieatt, Diana T. (Leo) Childress, Clifford J. Peterson, Edward Wilson, William Vantuono, William F. Woods, John M. Ganim, Anne H. Schotter, Susan L. Clark, Albert B. Friedman, Saburo Ohye, Yoshio Nagano, Gwyn Jones, Michael Foley, Paul Theiner, and James Joyce. Additional assistance—lists of obscure articles and dissertations as well as copies of bibliographies and checklists—was supplied by Professors Carl Berkhout, James Joyce, William Vantuono, Charles R. Courtney, and Richard Schrader. I am especially indebted to Professors Eiichi Suzuki, Tadahiro Ikegami, and Goichi Hoshiya for annotations for their articles in Japanese and for the addresses of Japanese scholars. I am grateful, likewise, to the inter-library loan staff of Northeastern University's Dodge Library—especially Louise Dennett, Beverly Slayton, Jay Glasthal, and Sarah Bourne—for their careful, efficient handling of my requests. Similarly, the libraries of Harvard University, particularly the Andover-Harvard Theological Library, Widener, Houghton, and Lamont, provided me with valuable research materials. Finally, financial support from the Arts and Sciences Research Grant Program of Northeastern University helped to defray the costs of preparing this book for publication.

A special note of appreciation should also be extended to my wife, Marjorie, for she patiently read the entire manuscript and offered numerous helpful suggestions on style and content. Any errors which remain, are of course, my own.

Boston, Massachusetts
June 1, 1980

R. J. B.

WRITINGS ABOUT *SIR GAWAIN*,
1824 - 1978

1824

1   WARTON, THOMAS. *The History of English Poetry, from the Close of the Eleventh to the Commencement of the Eighteenth Century.* Edited by Richard Price. Vol. 1. London: Thomas Tegg, 187-188.

[The editor includes the first passage (11. 20-36) from *Gawain* ever to appear in printed form.]

[Editor]   Notes that the alliterative verse from this "old romance" (unnamed) resembles the poetic diction of Anglo-Saxon verse and reveals an "exuberance of obsolete terms . . . attention to set phraseology and antique idioms" (p. 188).

1839

1   MADDEN, SIR FREDERIC. *Syr Gawayne; A Collection of Ancient Romance Poems by Scotish* [sic] *and English Authors Relating to that Celebrated Knight of the Round Table.* Edited by Sir Frederic Madden for the Bannatyne Club (Edinburgh). London: Richard and John E. Taylor, 500 pp.

[First published edition (pp. 3-92) of *Sir Gawain.* Contains lengthy Introduction (pp. ix-xlvi), Description of the Manuscripts (pp. xlvii-lxviii), Notes, and Glossary.]

"Introduction":   Attempts "to consider the history, character, and exploits assigned to our Hero Syr Gawayne in this phalanx of romance authorities" (p. xi).

"Description of the Manuscripts":   Depicts the Cotton MS. Nero A.x. as a "small quarto volume. . . . Prefixed is an imperfect list of contents, in the hand-writing of James, the Bodley Librarian. . . . The second portion [of the volume] . . . is described by James as 'Vetus poema Anglicanum, in quo sub insomnii figmento multa ad religionem et mores spectantia explicantur. . . .' This portion of the volume extends from fol. 37 to fol. 126, inclusive, and is written by one and the same hand, in a small, sharp, irregular character, which is often, from the paleness of the ink, and the contractions used, difficult to read. There are no titles or rubrics, but the divisions are marked by large initial letters of blue, florished [sic] with red, and several illuminations, coarsely executed, serve by way of illustration, each of which occupies a page" (p. xlvii).

"Notes": Assigns *Sir Gawain* (because of its illuminations and script) to Richard II's reign (p. 301).

1864

1   MORRIS, RICHARD, ed. "Preface," in *Early English Alliterative Poems in the West-Midland Dialect of the Fourteenth Century.* Early English Text Society, Original Series 1. London: Trübner and Company, pp. v-ix, xxxvii-xxxix.

[Revised edition: 1869.1.] Notes the inclusion of *Gawain, Pearl, Patience,* and *Purity* in the Cotton Nero A.x. manuscript and rejects the Huchowne theory of authorship for *Gawain.* Includes, with slight alterations, Madden's discussion (1839.1) of the manuscript—its contents, foliation, and illuminations.

2   MORRIS, RICHARD, ed. *Sir Gawayne and the Green Knight: An Alliterative Romance-Poem.* Early English Text Society, Original Series 4. London: N. Trübner, 144 pp.

[This edition, the second printed version of *Gawain,* is almost completely dependent upon Madden's work (1839.1). *See also* 1869.2.]

1869

1   MORRIS, RICHARD, ed. "Preface," in *Early English Alliterative Poems in the West-Midland Dialect of the Fourteenth Century.* Second edition. Early

English Text Society, Original Series 1. London: Trübner and Company, pp. v-ix, xli-xliii.

[Revised edition of 1864.1; no substantive changes in the discussion of *Gawain* are included. Reprinted: 1965.18.]

2   MORRIS, RICHARD, ed. *Sir Gawayne and the Green Knight: An Alliterative Romance-Poem.* Revised edition. Early English Text Society, Original Series 4. London: N. Trübner, 144 pp.

[Revised edition of 1864.2. Contains a full glossary and narrative sidenotes, but no helpful introduction. For full description of the manuscript, authorship, and dialect, *see* 1864.1.]

1876

1   TRAUTMANN, MORITZ. *Ueber Verfasser und Entstehungszeit einiger alliterierender Gedichte des Altenglischen.* Halle: Max Niemeyer, pp. 25-33.

[In German.]   Examines the word and phrase usage as well as the versification in *Gawain*, *Purity*, and *Patience*, and concludes that these poems were written (ca. 1370-1380) by one author. Contends, likewise, that the long lines of *Gawain* are composed of seven-stress verses.

1877

1   BRINK, BERNHARD TEN. *Geschichte der Englischen Litteratur.* Vol. 1. Berlin: Robert Oppenheim, 422-435.

[In German. *See also* 1889.1 and 1899.2.]

1878

1   ROSENTHAL, F. "Die alliterierende englische Langzeile im 14. Jahrhundert." *Anglia,* 1:414-459.

[In German.] Metrical analysis (accented and unaccented syllables) of the alliterative long line in English poetry of the fourteenth century. Examines, among other works, *Gawain*,

Piers Plowman, and *William of Palerne.*

2   TRAUTMANN, MORITZ. "Der Dichter Huchown und
      seine Werke." *Anglia,* 1:115-121.
          [In German.]   Refutes the Huchown authorship theory
      for *Gawain* and the other Cotton Nero Poems. Demonstrates
      that the Cotton Nero poems were written by one author by
      noting common words in all four poems as well as similar
      treatment of the alliterative rhymes.

1882

1   TRAUTMANN, MORITZ.   Review of Carl Horstmann's
      Altenglische Legenden. Anglia, 5, no. 2: "Anzeiger,"
      21-25.
          [In German.]   Examines the vocabulary and alliteration
      of the Cotton Nero MS poems and of *St. Erkenwald.* Because
      the vocabulary of *Erkenwald* is virtually identical to that of
      the Cotton poems, concludes that all five poems bear the im-
      print of one author.

1883

1   THOMAS, MARTHA CAREY. *Sir Gawayne and the
      Green Knight: A Comparison with the French Per-
      ceval, Preceded by an Investigation of the Author's
      Other Works and Followed by a Characterization of
      Gawain in English Poems.* Zurich: Orell Füssli, 105
      pp. [Doctoral dissertation, University of Zurich.]
          Argues that *Pearl* may be attributed to the author of
      Gawain, Patience, and *Cleanness* because of verbal similarities
      (the last line of each poem as an echo of its first line) and the
      common use of pearl imagery and moral ideals. Claims that
      the *Gawain*-poet's material is rooted in the *Livre de Caradoc*
      as found in the verse *Perceval;* this discussion includes an
      analysis of color symbolism employed by both poets.

1884

1   SCHWAHN, FRIEDRICH. *Die Conjugation in Sir Ga-
    wayn and the Green Knight und den sogenannten
    Early English Alliterative Poems: Ein Beitrag zur
    mittelenglischen Grammatik.* Strassburg: Johann
    Heinrich Eduard Heitz, 27 pp.
        [In German.] Grammatical analysis of verbs (strong,
    weak, and irregular) and their endings in the works of the
    Pearl-poet. Argues that *Gawain* is rooted in the Northwest
    Midlands, perhaps Lancashire.

1885

1   KNIGGE, FRIEDRICH. "Die Sprache des Dichters von
    Sir Gawain and the Green Knight der sogenannten
    Early English Alliterative Poems, und *De Erken-
    walde.*" Doctoral dissertation, University of Marburg.
        [In German. *See also* 1886.2.]

2   STEINBACH, PAUL. *Über den einfluss des Crestien de
    Troies auf die altenglische literatur.* Leipsig: Metzger
    & Wittig, pp. 48-50. [Inaugural dissertation, Leip-
    sig.]
        [In German.] Portrays the influence of Chrétien de
    Troyes, especially his *Perceval,* on *Gawain.*

1886

1   FUHRMANN, JOHANNES. *Die alliterierenden Sprach-
    formeln in Morris' Early English Alliterative Poems
    und im Sir Gawayne and the Green Knight.* Ham-
    burg: William Hintel's Buchdruckerei, 82 pp. [In-
    augural dissertation, University of Kiel.]
        [In German.] Focuses on the German speech forms (al-
    literative words, formulas, and phrases) in the works of the
    Pearl-poet.

2   KNIGGE, FRIEDRICH. *Die Sprache des Dichters von
    Sir Gawain and the Green Knight, der sogenannten*

Early English Alliterative Poems, und De Erkenwalde. Marburg: N. G. Elwert'sche Verlags-Buchhandlung, 120 pp.

[In German. *See also* 1885.1.] Analyzes the vocabulary and phonological aspects of *Gawain, Pearl, Cleanness, Patience,* and *St. Erkenwald.* Concludes that these poems, the product of one author, are written in the Northwest Midland dialect.

1887

1 VEITCH, JOHN. *The Feeling for Nature in Scottish Poetry.* Two vols. Edinburgh: William Blackwood and Sons, I, 129-139.

Terms *Gawain* a Scottish poem containing "probably the earliest surviving descriptions of the scenes of nature in the Scottish language." The poet who depicted the winter terrain "had as true and fine an eye for his native scenery as any subsequent Scottish poet, down even to our own time."

1888

1 BRADLEY, HENRY. "The English *Gawain*-Poet and *The Wars of Alexander.*" *The Academy: A Weekly Review of Literature, Science, and Art,* 33, no. 819 (14 January), 27.

Assigns *Wars* to the *Gawain*-poet because of similarities of diction, tone, and style in *Wars* and the Cotton Nero poems.

2 PARIS, GASTON. "Gauvain et le Vert Chevalier," in *Histoire littéraire de la France,* Vol. 30. Paris: Académie des Inscriptions et Belles-Lettres, pp. 71-78.

[In French.] Finds it very probable that *Gawain* is derived from a lost French poem. Considers *Gawain* the jewel of medieval English literature.

1889

1   BRINK, BERNHARD TEN. *History of English Litera-
     ture (to Wiclif)*. Translated by Horace M. Kennedy.
     Vol. 1. New York: Henry Holt, 337-351.

     [Translation from the German (1877.1). Contains discus-
     sion of *Pearl, Purity*, and *Patience*.] Suggests that the *Gawain*-
     poet, perhaps a scribe of some aristocrat, knew Latin, French,
     the Bible, hunting lore, and chivalric exercises.   Claims that
     the poet, likewise, reshaped in an original way his story ma-
     terial, rooted in Chrétien de Troyes's *Perceval* (*Conte del
     Graal*). Terms *Gawain* a carefully structured "art of composi-
     tion . . . a symmetrical and attractive whole."

2   HENNEMAN, JOHN BELL. *Untersuchungen über das
     mittelenglische Gedicht Wars of Alexander*. Berlin:
     G. Bernstein, pp. 30-36.   [Inaugural dissertation,
     Berlin.]

     [In German.]   Employs linguistic evidence in order to
     prove that no common author exists for both the *Wars of
     Alexander* and the works of the *Gawain*-poet.

3   LUICK, KARL. "Die englische Stabreimzeile im XIV.,
     XV. und XVI. Jahrhundert. IV." *Anglia*, 11:572-585.

     [In German.]   Examination of the metric character and
     the position of words in *Gawain*. Also contains a brief discus-
     sion of *Patience, Cleanness,* and *St. Erkenwald*. Concludes
     that the *Gawain*-poet is the author of *Erkenwald*.

1891

1   GOLLANCZ, ISRAEL. "Introduction," in his edition
     and modern rendering of *Pearl: An English Poem of
     the Fourteenth Century*. London: David Nutt, pp.
     xx-xxi, xxxiii-lii.

     Describes the history and contents of the Cotton Nero
     manuscript and the metrical scheme of *Gawain* as well as the
     significance of the illustrations accompanying *Gawain*. Dis-
     cusses, furthermore, Gawain's knightly character and his role
     in medieval romances, the link between Gawain's exploits
     with Lady Bercilak and King Edward III's dalliance with the

Countess of Salisbury, and the connection between the dating of *Gawain* (1345-60) and the founding of the Order of the Garter (1345). Claims that one poet—perhaps Ralph Strode—wrote the four Cotton poems and offers an hypothetical biography of the poet and the order of his works (*Gawain, Pearl, Cleanness, Patience*).

2   KALUZA, MAX. "Strophische Gliederung in der mitte-lenglischen rein alliterirenden Dichtung." *Englische Studien*, 16 (November), 177-179.

[In German.] Examines strophic divisions in Middle English alliterative poetry, including the works of the *Gawain*-poet. Claims that such strophes are based on multiples of four lines although not necessarily on true quatrains.

1892

1   LAWRENCE, JOHN. "Chapters on Alliterative Verse." Doctoral dissertation, University of London.

[*See also* 1893.2.]

1893

1   BRANDL, ALOIS. "Der *Gawain*-Dichter und seine Schule," in *Grundriss der germanischen Philologie*, Vol. 2, part 1, ed. Hermann Paul. Strassburg: Karl J. Trübner, pp. 661-665.

[In German.] Attributes the four poems in the Cotton Nero MS. and *St. Erkenwald* to the same author. Views the *Roman de Perceval* as the immediate source of *Gawain*, and claims that *Gawain*, although more original, sceptical, and penetrating than *Ywain and Gawain*, represents a development of the Middle English romance of chivalric virtue initiated by *Ywain and Gawain*.

2   LAWRENCE, JOHN. *Chapters on Alliterative Verse.* London: Henry Frowde, pp. 89-90, 93-98.

[*See* 1892.1. Also contains discussion of vowel alliteration in *Cleanness* and *Patience*.] Provides detailed tables indicating all the various examples of vowel alliteration in *Gawain*. Notes that "words with initial *h*" appear in *Gawain:* "69 times out of a total of 102 verses with vowel alliteration."

3 SKEAT, W. W. "Notes on English Etymology," *Transactions of the Philological Society of London* (1891-1894), part 1. London: Kegan Paul, Trench, Trübner and Company, pp. 138, 141, 143, 146.

Interprets difficult words, including *fewte* as "track"; *pentacle,* "a six-pointed star-shaped figure" which is "formed by two equal and equilateral triangles, one above the other," as equivalent to *pentangel* (*Gawain,* 1. 627), a "five-angled" figure formed by continuous lines; *quilt* (1. 877) as "counterpane"; and *vewters* (1. 1146) as "keepers of hounds."

4 SKEAT, W. W. "Rare Words in Middle English," *Transactions of the Philological Society of London* (1891-1894), part 2. London: Kegan Paul, Trench, Trübner and Company, pp. 364, 370-373.

Interprets difficult words, including *ker* (1. 1431) as "marsh"; *aker syde* (1. 1421), emended to *ker-syde,* "at the side of the marsh"; *touch* (1. 1301) as "touch, deed"; *teneling,* emended to *teueling* ("sport"); *thulged* (1. 1859) as "bore patiently"; *treieted* (1. 960), emended to *trejeted* ("adorned"); and *troched* (1. 795), a hunting term connoting "the clustered and shorter projections on the other [side of a hart's horn], near the tip," as "adorned with small pointed pinnacles."

1894

1 ANON. "Philological [Society]—Nov. 2." *The Athenaeum: Journal of English and Foreign Literature, Science, the Fine Arts, Music and the Drama,* No. 3498 (10 November), p. 646.

[Report on paper read by Israel Gollancz—"On Puzzling Words and Passages in Alliterative Poems—*Patience, Cleanness,* and *Gawain and the Grene Knyght.*" Gollancz interpets *sere fyve sythes* (1. 632 of *Gawain*) as "five times five."

2 McLAUGHLIN, EDWARD TOMPKINS. "The Mediaeval Feeling for Nature," in his *Studies in Mediaeval Life and Literature.* New York: G. P. Putnam's Sons,

pp. 18-19, 30.

Claims that the *Gawain*—poet, the noble forerunner of Spenser, is superior to Chaucer in his vivid depiction of winter scenes. *Gawain* contains "moral dignity, romantic interest, simplicity, and directness, united with deep seriousness of style, creative imagination in dealing both with character and with nature."

1895

1   TRAUTMANN, MORITZ. "Zur Kenntniss und Geschichte der mittelenglischen Stabzeile." *Anglia,* 18 (September), 83-100.

[In German.] Examines the nature and arrangement of alliterative verse in Middle English. Notes that *Gawain* contains seven stresses per line.

1897

1   F. [OSTER], T. G. "The Revised Text of *Sir Gawayne and the Green Knight.*" *The Modern Language Quarterly* (London), 1 (November), 53-55.

Reviews Gollancz's edition (*EETS,* OS 4, 4th ed. rev.) of *Gawain.* Contains technical commentary on restored MS readings, Gollancz's emendations, and Foster's own readings of words.

2   NAPIER, ARTHUR S. "Old and Middle English Notes." *The Modern Language Quarterly* (London), 1 (November), 52.

Interprets difficult words and phrases, including *& ay þe lady let lyk, a hym loued mych* (1. 1281) as "And ever the lady acted (feigned) as though she loved him much"; *lowe* (1. 1399) as "an aphetized form of the common M.E. verb *alowen,* 'to praise, commend' "; and *Inn-melle* (1. 1451) as "at the same time." Omits *felle* (1. 427), an editorial addition, and interprets *hit* (1. 427) as "came."

3   WESTON, JESSIE L. *The Legend of Sir Gawain: Studies upon its Original Scope and Significance.* Grimm

Library, No. 7. London: David Nutt, pp. 85-102.
[Reprinted: 1900.5; 1972.28.] Notes that the story narrated in *Gawain* is found in other romances—*Diu Krône* and
La Mule sans frein—perhaps suggesting that all three works
spring from a common source. Claims, however, that "the
oldest version [of the Gawain story] now accessible is that
of the *Fled Bricrend* (Bricriu's Feast), an Irish Tale preserved
in MSS. written toward the end of the eleventh or beginning of
the twelfth century. . . ." Concludes that various details connected with the Celtic hero Cuchulinn, including his magic
girdle, link him with Gawain.

1899

1   AMOURS, F. J. *"Capados."* Notes and Queries, 4, 9th
     Series (14 October), 308.
         Interprets the difficult word *capados* in *Gawain* (11. 186,
     572) as "a gambison reaching up to, and fitting close round,
     the neck." The gambison was probably fashioned from Cappa-
     docian leather.

2   BRINK, BERNHARD TEN. *Geschichte der Englischen
     Litteratur.* Revised edition, ed. Alois Brandl. Vol. 1.
     Strassburg: Karl J. Trübner, 393-406, and as indexed.
         [In German. *See* 1877.1. Contains an Index and Appen-
     dices on various Anglo-Saxon works.]

3   KUHNKE, BRUNO. *Die Allitterierende* [sic] *Langzeile
     in der mittelenglischen Romanze Sir Gawayn and
     the Green Knight I.* Weimar: Emil Felber, 46 pp.
     [Part of inaugural dissertation, Königsberg.]
         [In German. For the complete version of this work, *see*
     1900.2.] Surveys the scholarship on the alliterative long line
     and examines the alliterative patterns in *Gawain.*

1900

1   FISCHER, JOSEPH. *Die Stabende Langzeile in den Wer-
     ken des Gawaindichters.* Darmstadt: G. Otto's Hof-
     buchdruckerei, 32 pp.   [Part of inaugural disserta-

tion, Bonn.]

[In German. For the complete version of this work, *see* 1901.2.] Scrutinizes the verse form of the works of the *Pearl*-poet and claims that seven stresses may be found in each line of poetry.

2 KUHNKE, BRUNO. *Die alliterierende Langzeile in der mittelenglischen Romanze Sir Gawayn and the Green Knight.* Studien zum germanischen Alliterationsvers, No. 4, ed. Max Kaluza. Berlin: Emil Felber, 88 pp.

[In German. Abridged 1899.3.] Complete examination of the alliterative patterns (both the first-half and the second-half lines) in *Gawain*.

3 PATON, LUCY ALLEN. "Morgain la Fée, a Study in the Fairy Mythology of the Middle Ages." Doctoral dissertation, Radcliffe College.

[*See* 1903.3.]

4 WEICHARDT, CARL. *Die Entwicklung des Naturgefühls in der mittelenglischen Dichtung vor Chaucer (einschliesslich des Gawain-Dichters).* Kiel: P. Peters, pp. 83-92. [Inaugural disseration, Kiel.]

[In German. Also discusses (pp. 77-83) *Pearl, Patience,* and *Purity*.] Praises *Gawain* for its descriptions of nature, especially the hunting scenes and the passages on winter. Sees the poet as a precursor of Shakespeare.

5 WESTON, JESSIE L. *The Legend of Sir Gawain: Studies upon its Original Scope and Significance.* London: David Nutt, pp. 85-102.

[Reprint of 1897.3.]

1901

1 BILLINGS, ANNA HUNT. *A Guide to the Middle English Metrical Romances Dealing with English and Germanic Legends, and with the Cycles of Charlemagne and of Arthur.* Yale Studies in English, Vol. 9. New York: Henry Holt, pp. 160-168.

[Reprinted: 1965.4; 1975.2.] Provides an account of

critical commentaries on *Gawain* while tracing the outlines of the poem's story, sources, metre, dialect, date, and author.

2 FISCHER, JOSEPH. "Die Stabende Langzeile in den Werken des Gawaindichters." *Bonner Beiträge zur Anglistik,* 11:1-64.

[In German. Abridged 1900.1.] Examines the nature and scope of the alliterated words (substantives, adjectives, adverbs), especially in *Gawain.* Claims that accentual verse in *Gawain* consists of alternately weak and strong syllables. Contends, furthermore, that a caesura divides the *Gawain*-line into on-verses (four feet) and off-verses (three feet).

3 FISCHER, JOSEPH and FRANZ MENNICKEN. "Zur mittelenglischen Stabzeile." *Bonner Beiträge zur Anglistik,* 11:139-154.

[In German.] Comments upon the use of the alliterative long line, especially in *Sir Gawain.*

4 GOLLANCZ, SIR ISRAEL. "Huchown." *The Athenaeum: Journal of English and Foreign Literature, Science, the Fine Arts, Music and the Drama,* No. 3842 (15 June), p. 760.

Notes that "Huchown was a disciple of the school of the West-Midland author of *Gawain*. . . ."

5 NEILSON, GEORGE. "Huchown: II. The *Parlement of the Thre Ages.*" *The Athenaeum: Journal of English and Foreign Literature, Science, the Fine Arts, Music and the Drama,* No. 3861 (26 October), pp. 559-560.

Points out parallels between the phraseology of *Gawain* and that of the *Parlement of the Thre Ages.* Claims that *a bende of a bryght grene* (1. 2517) is "expressly declared . . . a settled badge of the Round Table."

6 NEILSON, GEORGE. *Sir Hew of Eglintoun and Huchown off the Awle Ryale: A Biographical Calendar and Literary Estimate. Proceedings* of the Philosophical Society of Glasgow, No. 32. Glasgow: Philosophical Society, 40 pp.

Notes (pp. 31 and 33) the use of legal terminology and the phraseology of courtly regulations—especially "hyrdman,

or man of the court circle" and "speaking reason"—in *Gawain,*
a poem attributed to Huchown.

7   STUCKEN, EDUARD. *Gawân, ein Mysterium.* Berlin:
     Verlag Dreililien, 100 pp.
     [In German. A five-act dramatization of *Sir Gawain.*]

1902

1   BROWN, J. T. T. *Huchown of the Awle Ryale and his
     Poems, Examined in the Light of Recent Criticism.*
     Edinburgh: Lorimer and Chalmers, pp. 1-2, 15-16,
     19, 24-26.
     [Read to the Royal Philosophical Society, Glasgow on
     April 21, 1902.] Argues that although *Gawain* and the other
     Cotton poems have been attributed to Huchown (Sir Hew
     of Eglinton), the evidence is skimpy. Denies on metrical
     grounds the common authorship of *Gawain* and *St. Erken-
     wald,* and disputes the claim that *Gawain* was written by a
     Scot.

2   KULLNICK, MAX. *Studien über den Wortschatz in Sir
     Gawayne and the grene kny3t.* Berlin: Mayer &
     Müller, 54 pp. [Inaugural dissertation, Berlin.]
     [In German.] Analyzes the vocabulary in *Gawain* and
     claims that the words are derived from Anglo-Saxon (49%),
     Old Norse (17.8%), German (4.6%), Old French (28%), and
     Celtic (0.6%). Investigates, likewise, the particular words
     employed by both the *Gawain*-poet and other medieval
     writers.

3   NAPIER, ARTHUR S. "Notes on *Sir Gawayne and the
     Green Knight.*" *Modern Language Notes,* 17 (March),
     85-87.
     Interprets difficult words and phrases, including *Bot* in
     Bot his wombe & his wast (1. 144) as "both."; *and reled hym
     up & doun* (1. 229) as "and rolled them (his eyes) up and
     down"; *hadet* (read *hacked, hakked*) in 1. 681 as "hacked to
     pieces"; *gedere3* (read *gerde3*) in 1. 777 as "strikes"; *sawes*
     (read *sawses*) in 1. 893 as "sauces"; *knitten* (read *kitten*) in
     1. 1331 as "cut"; *boute spyt more* (1. 1444) as "without

further delay"; and "Þe *day dryueȝ to* þe *derk* (read Þe *day to-dryues* þe *dark*) in 1. 1999 as "the day disperses the darkness."

4   NEILSON, GEORGE. *Huchown of the Awle Ryale, the Alliterative Poet: A Historical Criticism of Fourteenth Century Poems Ascribed to Sir Hew of Eglintoun.* Glasgow: James Mac Lehose and Sons, pp. 7, 71-74, 80-81, 120-122, and as indexed.

[Revised version (including index) of 1901.6. Includes discussion of *Patience, Cleanness,* and *Pearl.*] Attributes the authorship of *Gawain* to Huchown. Notes parallels between *Gawain* (the deer hunt) and the opening hunting scene in *Parlement of the Thre Ages,* thereby pointing to "identity of workmanship." Suggests further parallels between *Gawain* and *The Wars of Alexander, Titus* and *Vespasian,* and the alliterative *Morte Arthure,* and emphasizes *Gawain*'s connection with the Order of the Garter, especially its motto—*Honi soit qui mal y pense.*

1903

1   BRUCE, J. DOUGLAS. "The Breaking of the Deer in *Sir Gawayne and the Green Knight.*" *Englische Studien,* 32 (January), 23-36.

Notes the graphic descriptions of the chase in the *Parlement of the Thre Ages* (11. 65-91) and in *Gawain* (11. 1323 ff.). Employs various French hunting manuals—*Chace dou Cerf* (13th century), *Le livre du Roy Modus et de la Royne Racio* (14th century)—in order to elucidate the passage in *Gawain.*

Interprets difficult words in *Gawain,* including *asay* (1. 1328) as an allusion to "taking the depth of the fat [of the deer]"; *sesed* þe *erber* (1. 1330) as "the first step in the process of disembowelling"; þe *slot* (1. 1330) as "the hollow above the breast-bone"; *Schaued wyth a scharp knyf* (1. 1331) as "removing the flesh from about the erber [the passage leading to the stomach]"; *Syþen rytte* þay þe *foure lymmes* (1. 1332) as "the skinning of the legs of the deer"; & *bere of* þe *knot* (1. 1334) as "the removal of the erber tied up"; *gargulun* (1. 1335) as "throat"; *wesaunt* (1. 1336) as "eso-phagus"; and *rymeȝ* (1. 1343) as "strips."

2   CHAMBERS, E. K. *The Mediaeval Stage.* Vol. 1. London: Oxford University Press, 185-186.

   Suggests that the Green Knight in *Gawain* is identified with a central figure in medieval folk drama and art—the Green Man, the Jack-in-the-Green or village "wild man" who is the victim of a mock beheading ceremony.

3   PATON, LUCY ALLEN. *Studies in the Fairy Mythology of Arthurian Romance.* Radcliffe College Monographs, No. 13. Boston: Ginn and Company, pp. 133, 136.

   [Revised version of 1900.3. *See also* 1960.10.] Claims that Morgan la Fée, the sister of King Arthur, assumes the guise of a "loathly lady" in *Gawain*.

1904

1   BROWN, CARLETON F. "The Author of *The Pearl,* Considered in the Light of his Theological Opinions." *Publications of the Modern Language Association of America,* 19:115-119, 127.

   Discusses the various theories (Huchown and Ralph Strode) regarding the identity of the *Pearl*-poet. Claims that the poet's moral character, as exemplified by his fondness for Biblical references and his concern with purity, colors *Gawain*.

2   GOLLANCZ, ISRAEL. "Philological—March 4." *The Athenaeum: Journal of English and Foreign Literature, Science, the Fine Arts, Music and the Drama,* No. 3985 (12 March), p. 343.

   [Summary of papers read (March 4) to the Philological Society.] Claims that *on lyt* and *on lyte* in *Gawain* mean "slightly."

1905

1   LUICK, KARL. "Der mittelenglische Stabreimvers," in *Grundriss der germanischen Philologie,* Vol. 2, part 2, ed. Hermann Paul. Second edition. Strassburg:

Karl J. Trübner, pp. 164-167.

[In German.] Examines the metrical patterns—the use of caesura and the alliterated syllables—in *Gawain*. Claims that the works of the *Gawain*-poet include *Gawain, Purity, Patience,* and *St. Erkenwald.*

2   MOORMAN, FREDERIC W. *The Interpretation of Nature in English Poetry from Beowulf to Shakespeare.* Quellen und Forschungen zur Sprach-und Culturgeschichte der germanischen Völker, Vol. 95. Strassburg: Karl J. Trübner, 95-102, and as indexed.

[Contains discussion of *Pearl* (pp. 102-104), *Cleanness* (pp. 104-106) and *Patience* (p. 106).] Notes that *Gawain* exhibits "the primitive love for winter scenes" so characteristic of Old English poetry. Places *Gawain* squarely within the context of the "alliterative revival" since this romance is "strictly Saxon in its verse, its diction, and its interpretation of Nature." Notes, further, that "in his pictures of winter among the craggy ice-bound fells of the north of England, the *Gawayne*-poet is without rival. . . . There is no placidity here: everything is in turbulent movement." *See also* 1972.19.

3   WESTON, JESSIE L. "Preface," in *Sir Gawain and the Green Knight: A Middle-English Arthurian Romance Retold in Modern Prose.* New York: New Amsterdam Book Company, pp. v-xii.

[Reprinted: 1970.36.] Discusses the Cotton Nero A.x. MS as well as the West Midland dialect (perhaps Lancashire) of *Gawain*. Notes the *Gawain*-poet's fondness for nature and his refined tone as well as the unique fusion of the challenge and temptation motifs in *Gawain*. Argues that the figure of Bercilak's wife evokes memories of Queen of the Magic Castle, the blood relative of a magician, and that the character of Gawain, the exemplar of chivalry and courtesy, is drawn according to his original conception in Arthurian legend.

1906

1   COOK, ARTHUR BERNARD. "The European Sky-God; VI., The Celts (continued)." *Folk-Lore,* 17 (September), 338-341, 347.

Claims that the figure of the Green Knight stems from the ancient tree-god Virbius (p. 340).

2   GOLLANCZ, SIR ISRAEL. "Gringolet, Gawain's Horse." *Saga Book of the Viking Club* (London, Viking Society for Northern Research), 5:104-109.

Claims that Gringolet was originally the name of Wade's boat (Gringalet or Guingalet) in the legendary exploits of the Scandinavian hero. "The Horse of *Gawain* represents the necessary change from the sea character of the *Vilkinasaga* to the chivalrous character of the mediaeval romance; the ship was the 'horse of ocean' both in Anglo-Saxon and Old Norse" (p. 106).

3   REICKE, CURT. *Untersuchungen über den Stil der mittelenglischen alliterierenden Gedichte Morte Arthure, The Destruction of Troy, The Wars of Alexander, The Siege of Jerusalem, Sir Gawayn and the Green Knight.* Königsberg: Hartungsche Buchdruckerei, 85 pp. [Inaugural dissertation, Königsberg.]

[In German.] A contribution to the solution of the Huchown authorship theory through a stylistic analysis of *Morte Arthure, The Destruction of Troy, The Wars of Alexander, The Siege of Jerusalem,* and *Sir Gawayn and the Green Knight.* Focuses largely upon the tags found in the second-half lines of such poems and concludes that no common author wrote the five poems.

4   SAINTSBURY, GEORGE. *A History of English Prosody from the Twelfth Century to the Present Day.* Vol. 1. London: Macmillan, 105, 373.

Comments on the "bob and wheel" stanza in *Gawain.*

5   SCHOFIELD, WILLIAM HENRY. *English Literature from the Norman Conquest to Chaucer.* New York: Macmillan, pp. 23, 215-217, 220, 383, 451.

[Reprinted: 1914.2; 1921.7; 1925.5.] Contends that the *Gawain*-poet was a native of the West Midland district, perhaps Cheshire. Suggests, moreover, that the poet was the first to fuse two separate motifs—the Beheading Game (also found in *Bricriu's Feast* and in the verse *Perceval*) and the Chastity Test. Notes that the end of *Gawain* probably stems from the creation (1348) of the Order of the Garter.

SKEAT, W. W. "Notes on English Etymology," in *Transactions of the Philological Society of London* (1903-1906), part 3. London: Kegan Paul, Trench, Trübner and Company, pp. 359-360.

Suggests that *enbaned* (1. 790), "a derivative of the O. F. *bane,* a horn," is a term describing "horn-work" or projections in fortifications. Also discusses use of this word and *bantel* in *Pearl* and *Purity.*

WRIGHT, ELIZABETH MARY. "Notes on *Sir Gawayne and the Green Knight.*" *Englische Studien,* 36 (April), 209-227.

Uses the *English Dialect Dictionary* to interpret difficult words, including *baret* (1. 752) as "strife"; *barlay* (1. 296) as "claim"; *capados* (11. 186,572) as "of superior quality or appearance," especially the exquisite material from Cappadocia; *chymbled* (1. 958) as "twisted in ungainly fashion"; *devaye* (1. 1497) as "desist"; *drechch* (1. 1972) as "delay"; *dreȝly* (1. 1026) as "incessantly"; *foul* (1. 717) as "ugly"; *grayn* (1. 211) as "the thick end of the head [of an axe], into which the handle is fixed"; *gryed* (1. 2370) as "shuddered"; *ker* (1. 1421) as "marshy ground"; *knot* (11. 1431, 1434) as "a mound of rough boulders . . . forming a projection at the foot of [a] cliff"; *lyte* (1. 2303) as "waiting in expectation"; *molaynes* (1. 169) as "trappings of the horse's bridle"; *muged* (1. 2080) as "drizzling"; *mused* (1. 2404) as "walked": *mynt* (11. 2274, 2290) as "to make a feigned attempt at [striking]"; *nirt* (1. 2498) as "the little scar"; *to þe note* (1. 420) as "to the axe"; *no-bot* (1. 2182) as "nothing but"; *raged* (1. 745) as "hoar-frosted"; *rande* (1. 1710) as "border"; *roche* (1. 2294) as "hard, gravelly"; *rocher* (11. 1427, 1432, 1698) as "rocky bank"; *rykande* (1. 2337) as "noisy"; *skyued* (1. 2167) as "precipitous [banks]"; *slentyng* (1. 1160) as "flashing slantwise through the air"; *bot slokes* (1. 412) as "without stops"; *snitered* (1. 2003) as "blew on the biting blast"; *sprent* (1. 1896) as "darted forward with a spring or sudden motion"; *sprit* (1. 2316) as "ran off suddenly"; *stad* (1. 2137) as "furnished with a staff"; *strothe* (1. 1710) as "narrow strip"; *titleres* (1. 1726) as "coupled [wearing collars] hounds"; *toppyng* (1. 191) as "forelock"; *traunt*

(1. 1700) as "trick"; *trochet* (1. 795) as "ornamented with little turrets"; *wrast* (1. 1663) as "anger"; and *wysty* (1. 2189) as "empty."

1907

1   CHAMBERS, R. W. *"Sir Gawayne and the Green Knight, lines 697-702."* *Modern Language Review,* 2 (January), 167.

      Focuses on the geography in *Gawain,* specifically Holyhead on the way to Wirral. Feels that Holywell, not Holyhead, would be more logically consistent. "But to swim from Holyhead to Liverpool seems too great a feat to expect even from a knight of the Table Round."

2   GOLLANCZ, ISRAEL. *"Pearl, Cleanness, Patience,* and *Sir Gawayne,"* in *Cambridge History of English Literature.* Edited by A. W. Ward and A. R. Waller. Vol. 1. New York: G. P. Putnam's Sons, 357-373.

      Suggests that the Cotton Nero manuscript, probably in a hand of the end of the fourteenth century, contains major divisions indicated by large blue capitals, "flourished with red." Contends, moreover, that *Gawain,* an artistic fusion of the alliterative long line and a lyrical burden (bob and wheel), includes one MS. illustration depicting a scene between a knight and a courtly woman; appended to this illustration is a couplet, "Mi mind is mukel on on, that wil me noght amende: / Sum time was trewe as ston, and fro schame couthe her defende" (p. 363).

      Discusses, likewise, the probable original source of the "beheading game"—*Fled Bricrend*—and the parallels between *Gawain* and Gautier de Doulens's first continuation of Chrétien's *Conte del Graal* as well as the link between *Gawain* and the establishment of the Order of the Garter (ca. 1345). Praises *Gawain* for its graphic descriptions of primitive nature, its symmetry, and its artistry and conjectures that *Gawain* was composed before the other three Cotton Nero poems. Offers, finally, a hypothetical biography of the *Pearl*-poet, traces the various theories of authorship (with Ralph Strode his personal choice), and notes the parallels (hunting passages) between *Gawain* and *Parlement of the Thre Ages.*

3   KER, W. P. "Metrical Romances I, 1200-1500," in *Cambridge History of English Literature.* Edited by A. W. Ward and A. R. Waller. Vol. 1. New York: G. P. Putnam's Sons, 330-331.

Notes that the "beheading game" motif in *Gawain* appears in *Bricriu's Feast* and in *La Mule sans Frein.* Suggests that the *Gawain*-poet artfully employs his imagination so as to compel his audience to accept bizarre exploits as a reasonable part of human existence. Praises *Gawain* for its skillful use of winter landscapes and for its symmetrical elements (hunts and temptations).

4   MAYNADIER, HOWARD. *The Arthur of the English Poets.* Boston: Houghton Mifflin, pp. 205-210.

Claims that the Cotton Nero poems were probably composed (1350-1375) by the same poet. Praises *Gawain* for its moral tone without sermonizing, its depiction of nature, and its realistic portrayal of "country-house life."

1908

1   HAMILTON, GEORGE L. " 'Capados' and the Date of *Sir Gawayne and the Green Knight.*" *Modern Philology,* 5 (January), 365-376.

Interprets *capados* (11. 186 and 572) as a headdress, the lower part of which "covered the shoulders and upper chest" (p. 367), and links the furlined hood of the Order of the Garter (the reign of Edward III) with the *blaunner* of Gawain. Concludes that *Gawain* should be dated "between the foundation of the Order of the Garter, and the death of Edward III (1348-77)" (p. 375).

2   SCHMITTBETZ, KARL ROLAND. *Das Adjectiv im Verse von Syr Gawayn and þe Grene Knyȝt.* Bonn: Emil Eisele, 49 pp. [Part of inaugural dissertation, Bonn.]

[In German. For the complete version of this work, *see* 1909.2.] Offers a linguistic analysis of the adjectives in *Gawain*—their number, arrangement, and function in alliterative verse.

3   THOMAS, JULIUS. *Die alliterierende Langzeile des Gawayne-Dichters.* Coburg: Druck von A. Rossteutscher, 70 pp. [Inaugural dissertation, University of Jena.]

     [In German.] Analyzes the alliterative long line (tone, prosody, verse endings) employed by the *Gawain*-poet in *Sir Gawain, Patience,* and *Cleanness.*

1909

1   KALUZA, MAX. *Englische Metrik in historischer Entwicklung.* Normannia: Germanisch-Romanische Bucherei, Vol. 1. Edited by Max Kaluza and Gustav Thurau. Berlin: Emil Felber, pp. 183-198, 202-203.

     [In German.] Analyzes alliterative techniques—rhythmical constructions, accented words, strophic divisions, vocabulary, and concatenation—in *Gawain, Purity, Patience,* and *Pearl.*

2   SCHMITTBETZ, KARL ROLAND. "Das Adjektiv in *Syr Gawayn and the Grene Knyȝt.*" *Anglia,* 32:1-60, 163-189, 359-383.

     [In German. Abridged 1908.2.] Offers a linguistic analysis of the adjectives in *Gawain*—their number, arrangement, and function in alliterative verse. Study includes a discussion of the substantive use of adjectives.

1910

1   MacCRACKEN, HENRY NOBLE. "Concerning Huchown." *Publications of the Modern Language Association of America,* 25:532.

     Refutes the Huchown authorship theory for *Gawain.* Contends that the alliterative *Morte Arthure* and *Gawain* were written by two different authors: "The two most important differences seem . . . to be the metrical tests of the 'w' and 'v' rime, regular in the *Morte Arthure* and never occurring in the four poems of the Gawayne group, while, on the other hand, 'wh' rimes with 'w' continually in the Gawayn group and very rarely in the *Morte Arthure.*"

1911

1   KALUZA, MAX. *A Short History of English Versification from the Earliest Times to the Present Day.*
Translated by A. C. Dunstan. London: George Allen, pp. 191-223 passim.

    Comments on the rhythmical and stanzaic structure of
Gawain as well as the poem as an example of unrhymed alliterative verse.

1912

1   HENDERSON, GEORGE. "Arthurian Motifs in Gadhelic
Literature," in *Miscellany Presented to Kuno Meyer.*
Edited by Osborn Bergin and Carl Marstrander.
Halle: Max Niemeyer, pp. 18, 26-27.

    Claims that *Fled Bricrend* (*Feast of Bricriu*), a possible
source for the Beheading Game motif in *Gawain* (p. 27),
depicts the *green* challenger as the human counterpart of the
oak tree (p. 26), thereby underscoring Cook's claim (1906.1)
that the Green Knight is a tree-god.

2   KER, W. P. *English Literature: Medieval.* Home University Library, No. 45. New York: Henry Holt, pp.
137-141.

    [Reprinted: 1969.14, as *Medieval English Literature.*]
Gawain, "one of the most original works in medieval romance," employs the romance convention of the "beheading
game" in order to test the hero's loyalty and courage. Claims
that it is likely that the *Gawain*-poet composed the other
Cotton Nero poems.

3   KIRTLAN, ERNEST J. B., trans. "Introduction" to his
*Sir Gawain and the Green Knight: Rendered Literally
into Modern English from the Alliterative Romance
Poem of A.D. 1360, from Cotton MS. Nero A.x. in
British Museum.* London: Charles H. Kelly, pp. 1-50.

    [Prose translation, except for the bobs and wheels. Re-
printed: 1913.3.] Provides a literary history of King Arthur
and the knights of the Round Table, and outlines the manuscript, dialect, and sources of *Gawain.*

4   WESTON, JESSIE L., trans. *Romance, Vision & Satire: English Alliterative Poems of the Fourteenth Century.* Boston: Houghton Mifflin, pp. 331-332.
     [Reprinted: 1965.25. Contains verse translation (pp. 3-106) of *Gawain.*] Comments upon *Gawain*—its manuscript, dialect (West Midland), and date (ca. 1370)—and contends that *Gawain* stems from a lost French poem, especially because of the numerous French names in this Arthurian romance. Traces the Challenge/Beheading Game motif back to *Bricriu's Feast* (*Fled Bricrend*) and suggests other works which employ this theme. Claims, however, that the Temptation motif cannot be found in other versions of the Gawain story.

1913

1   BRETT, CYRIL. "Notes on *Sir Gawayne and the Green Knight.*" *Modern Language Review,* 8 (April), 160-164.
     Interprets difficult words and phrases, including *angarde3* (1. 681) as "arrogance" or "pride . . . exultation," perhaps stemming from the use of *angarde* as "a watch-tower or elevation of the mind"; *bay* (1. 967) as "jutting out, rounded"; and *quyle myd ouer vnder* (1. 1730) as " 'till midoverundern,' i.e. about 10.30 a.m."

2   JACKSON, ISAAC. "*Sir Gawain and the Green Knight* Considered as a 'Garter' Poem." *Anglia,* 37 (December), 393-423.
     Focuses on the motto of the Order of the Garter—*Hony soyt qui mal pence*—appearing at the end of *Gawain.* Inasmuch as 11. 552-3 of *Gawain* mention *Lionel* and the *Duke of Clarence,* and King Edward III made his son Lionel "the first English Duke of Clarence on the King's birthday, November 13th, 1362," Jackson claims that *Gawain* was composed in 1362. Notes, furthermore, that the topography of *Gawain* suggests Beeston Castle (Cheshire)—a castle belonging to the Black Prince—as the prototype for Bercilak's castle, and that *Gawain* depicts a Garter feast. Emphasizes, also, heraldic patterns common to both King Arthur's banner in the *Morte Arthure* and Gawain's shield (*gules* and the image of the

Virgin): such patterns link *Gawain* with the Order of the Garter and identify Gawain with the Black Prince.

Views green, the emblem of inconstancy and the color of the girdle, as germane because of Gawain's weaknesses although blue, "the color of constancy," is the color of the Garter. "Also Sir Gawain's 'token of truth,' the pentangle, was replaced by the true-blue ribbon of the Garter."

3   KIRTLAN, ERNEST J. B., trans. "Introduction" to his *Sir Gawain and the Green Knight: Rendered Literally into Modern English from the Alliterative Romance Poem of A.D. 1360, from Cotton MS. Nero A.x. in British Museum.* London: Every Age Library, pp. 1-50.

[Reprint of 1912.3.]

4   SCHUMACHER, KARL. "Studien über den Stabreim in der mittelenglischen Alliterationsdichtung. I. Teil." [Part of inaugural dissertation, Bonn, 96 pp.]

[In German. For the complete version of this work, *see* 1914.3.]

5   THOMAS, P. G. "The Middle English Alliterative Poem *Sir Gawayne and the Green Knight.*" *Englische Studien,* 47 (December), 311-313.

Interprets numerous difficult words and phrases, including *selly in siȝt* (1. 28) as "a wondrous sight"; *pane* (1. 154) as "fur"; *scholes* (1. 160) as "little soles"; *in fere* (1. 267) as "in array"; *trochet* (1. 795) as "crowded"; *quyle þe messequyle* (1. 1097) as "until dinner-time"; *blessed* (1. 1296) as "made happy"; *to-wrast* (1. 1663) as "awry"; *prowe* (1. 1680), emended to *prowes;* and *loke* (1. 2438) as "lock."

6   WRIGHT, ELIZABETH MARY. *Rustic Speech and Folk-Lore.* London: Humphrey Milford, Oxford University Press, pp. 68-71.

[Includes comments on *Pearl, Patience,* and *Cleanness.*] Suggests that the *Pearl*-poet was probably "a literary country gentleman, born and bred in Lancashire, a man equally at home in his study, pen in hand, describing armed knights, and embattled castles," Biblical tableaux, or graphic hunting scenes. "He was a lover of nature and outdoor life, with extraordinary powers of accurate observation, and an artist's eye for picturesque detail."

Claims, likewise, that many words found in *Gawain* are unique although they appear "in the North-country dialects of to-day." Examples of such words include *molaynes*, identified with *Mullen*, "the head-gear of a horse"; *toppyng*—"a horse's forelock"; *mynt*—"to make a feigned attempt at" striking a blow; and *wysty*—"empty, bare, large."

1914

1   BALDWIN, CHARLES SEARS. *An Introduction to English Medieval Literature.* New York: Longmans, Green, pp. 154-161, and as indexed.

[Reprinted: 1922.1.] Considers the *Gawain*-poet—the author of two carefully structured works (*Gawain* and *Pearl*), and possibly, of two less artistic works (*Purity* and *Patience*)— to be renowned for his originality and narrative skill as well as for his luminous depiction of chivalric life.

Notes, furthermore, that the *Gawain*-stanzas—types of "narrative paragraphs"—are not precise in length. "The average is about twenty-four lines; but the stanzas vary from twenty lines, or even less, to forty or more."

2   SCHOFIELD, WILLIAM HENRY. *English Literature from the Norman Conquest to Chaucer.* New York: Macmillan, pp. 23, 215-217, 220, 383, 451.

[Reprint of 1906.5.]

3   SCHUMACHER, KARL. *Studien über den Stabreim in der mittelenglischen Alliterationsdichtung.* Bonner Studien zur englischen Philologie, No. 11, ed. K. D. Bülbring. Bonn: Peter Hanstein, Verlagsbuchhandlung, 213 pp.

[In German. Abridged 1913.4.] Detailed analysis of alliterative patterns (distribution and quality) in numerous medieval works, including *Gawain, Patience, Cleanness, St. Erkenwald, Parlement of the Thre Ages, Wynnere and Wastoure,* and *Piers Plowman.*

1915

1   BRETT, CYRIL. "Notes on *Cleanness* and *Sir Gawayne.*" *Modern Language Review,* 10 (April), 189-195.

Interprets difficult words and phrases, including *scholes* (1. 160) as "some leather or other protections, under and inside the thighs, 'where the man rides' "; *grayn* (1. 211) as "the thick part of the head of the axe" or "a spike at the back [of the axe]"; *schale* (1. 1240) as "I shall (be)"; and *devaye* (1. 1497) as "refuse," "deny," or "hinder."

2   HULBERT, J. R. *"Syr Gawayn and the Grene Kny3t."* *Modern Philology,* 13 (December), 433-462.

[*See also* 1916.3.]   Examines the origins of the "beheading game" motif in *Gawain* and finds that the beheading game represents a test for the hero in order to win the love of a fairy mistress.   Interprets the greenness of the Green Knight and the Chapel as well as the whiteness of Castle Hautdesert as the colors of fairies and the Otherworld.

3   KNOTT, THOMAS A. "The Text of *Sir Gawayne and the Green Knight.*" *Modern Language Notes,* 30 (April), 102-108.

[Review of Madden (1839.1) and several *EETS* editions of *Gawain.*]   Offers a technical commentary upon manuscript readings, errata in various editions, and editorial emendations.

1916

1   CURRY, WALTER CLYDE. *The Middle English Ideal of Personal Beauty; as Found in the Metrical Romances, Chronicles, and Legends of the XIII, XIV, and XV Centuries.*   Baltimore: J. H. Furst, pp. 41, 50, 59-60, 93, and as indexed.

Suggests that *beaver-hued* (*Gawain,* 1. 845) is an epithet used to describe the beards of strong, handsome knights and that green—the Green Knight's clothing and eyebrows—link the Knight with the devil.   Comments, likewise, upon the physiognomic association of the Knight's red eyes (304) with ferocity and upon the mixture of white and red in the lady's complexion (1204) as a conventional sign of ideal feminine beauty.

2   EMERSON, OLIVER FARRAR. "More Notes on *Patience.*" *Modern Language Notes,* 31 (January), 2-3.

Claims that the *Gawain*-poet does not employ a rigid four-line structure in all of the poems attributed to him, for *Gawain* contains irregular stanzas, many of which fail to include an even number of lines; only the "wheel" at the end of each stanza can be termed a quatrain.

3   HULBERT, J. R. "*Syr Gawayn and the Grene Kny3t.*" *Modern Philology,* 13 (April), 689-730.

[Continuation of 1915.2.]   Reiterates his view that *Gawain* was "originally a fairy-mistress tale" (p. 691), transformed by the *Gawain*-poet into a loyalty test.   Scrutinizes the Green Chapel, Bercilak's wife, and the green girdle and maintains that the sources of these objects and characters spring from Celtic fairy lore.

Repudiates *Gawain*'s alleged connection with the Order of the Garter because of the poem's emphasis upon a green baldric and the Yuletide festivities.   Traces the origins and history of the pentangle, a symbol of truth and a protection against evil: the pentangle is usually linked with Solomon ("Solomon's seal").

4   KITTREDGE, GEORGE LYMAN. *A Study of Gawain and the Green Knight.*   Cambridge, Massachusetts: Harvard University Press, 331 pp.

[Reprinted: 1960.4.]   Claims that the immediate source of *Gawain* is a lost French romance and that *Gawain* is the only romance to interlace two separate Celtic motifs—the Challenge/Beheading Game and the Temptation—in a single narrative.   Offers an exhaustive analysis, moreover, of possible sources for the Challenge, including *Fled Bricrend* (*Bricriu's Feast*); *Le Livre de Caradoc;* the first continuation of Chrétien's *Perceval; La Mule sanz Frain; Perlesvaus;* and *Humbaut.*   Investigates, likewise, sources for the Temptation, including *Ider; The Carl of Carlisle; Le Chevalier à l'Épée;* and *Humbaut.*

Examines particular folk-motifs, such as the "returning

of surviving head" and "disenchantment by decapitation."
Claims that the Green Knight may have assumed the qualities of a "Demon of Vegetation" because of his greenness,
for green men appear frequently in folklore. Comments
briefly on the Knight's possible affinity with a "wild man"
although he ultimately debunks these mythological and folk-
lore theories as not being germane to *Gawain*.

1917

1   SCUDDER, VIDA D. *Le Morte Darthur of Sir Thomas
    Malory and its Sources.* New York: E. P. Dutton,
    pp. 169-173, and as indexed.

    Emphasizes the fairy elements in *Gawain*—the fairy green
    of the challenger and the Green Chapel, "a hollow fairy
    mound." Claims that despite "the supernatural elements . . .
    Gawain . . . owes its chief quality to its direct appeal to plain
    honorable manhood." Rooted, in part, in the *Feast of Bri-
    criu, Gawain* is the best English romance before Malory.

2   TAYLOR, RUPERT. "Some Notes on the Use of *Can*
    and *Couth* as Preteritive Auxiliaries in Early and
    Middle Scottish Poetry." *Journal of English and
    Germanic Philology,* 16 (October), 574, 587.

    Notes that *can* is used as a preteritive auxiliary four
    times ("with *studie, onsware, enclyne,* and *roun*") in *Gawain,*
    probably as a metrical technique for placing the needed word
    into a rhyming position.

3   WEBSTER, K. G. T. "Introduction" to *Sir Gawain and
    the Green Knight, Piers the Ploughman.* Translated
    and edited by K. G. T. Webster and W. A. Neilson.
    Cambridge, Massachusetts: Riverside Press, pp. v-viii.

    Claims that of all Arthur's knights Gawain occupies a pre-
    eminent position in medieval literature, especially because he
    is the exemplar of courtesy and bravery. Discusses briefly the
    Cotton Nero MS. and its contents; the origins and nature of
    the "alliterative revival"; the sources of *Gawain* and its use of
    the Challenge and Temptation motifs; and the *Gawain*-poet, a
    religious, albeit urbane, man, who probably resided in Lanca-
    shire.

1918

1   BRETT, CYRIL. "Introduction" to *Sir Gawayne and the Green Knight: A Fourteenth-Century Poem Done into Modern English*. Translated by Kenneth Hare. Stratford-upon-Avon: Shakespeare Head Press, pp. v-ix.

[*See also* the revised edition (1948.7).] Notes that *Gawain* was composed (1360) in the North Lancashire dialect and is comparable in many ways to Chaucer's finest literary achievements. Focuses on *Gawain*'s sharp visual images—dress, hunting scenes, banquets, and winter terrains—as well as on the skillful employment of both forms of the second person pronoun.

2   EKWALL, EILERT. "A Few Notes on English Etymology and Word-History." *Anglia Beiblatt*, 29 (July), 200-201.

Interprets *strothe* (1. 1710) as "wood," derived from O. N. *storð*. Notes that *storth*, probably identified with the word *strothe*, is a "common place-name" in Lancashire.

1919

1   BRETT, CYRIL. "Notes on Passages of Old and Middle English." *Modern Language Review*, 14 (January), 7-8.

Interprets " 'Now sir, heng vp þyn ax, þat hatz in-nogh hewen' " (1. 477) as both "the literal command (literally obeyed), and the jesting proverb," employed to assuage the fear of Guinevere and her entourage. Suggests that *Mused* (1. 2423) denotes "were lost in thought of, in gazing at, women."

2   DAY, MABEL. "The Weak Verb in the Works of the *Gawain*-Poet." *Modern Language Review*, 14 (October), 413-415.

Notes numerous examples of the omission "of the final -d of weak preterites and past participles" in *Purity*, *Pearl*, *Patience*, and *Gawain*.

3   EMERSON, OLIVER FARRAR. "Middle English *Clannesse.*" *Publications of the Modern Language Association of America,* 34:499, 515, 518-520.

Interprets *wrathed* (*Gawain,* 1. 2420) as "be deceived"; *enbaned* (*Gawain,* 1. 790) as "surrounded, encompassed, *girt,* bordered"; *wykes* (*Gawain,* 1572) as "the corners of a boar's mouth"; *paume* (*Gawain,* 1155) as "antlers"; and *in þede* (*Gawain,* 1499) as "among the people."

1920

1   BRINK, AUGUST. *Stab und Wort im Gawain: Eine stilistische Untersuchung.* Studien zur Englischen Philologie, Vol. 59, ed. Lorenz Morsbach. Halle: Verlag von Max Niemeyer, 65 pp. [Doctoral dissertation, Goettingen.]

[In German.] Offers a stylistic analysis of substantives (including designations for people) and adjectives in *Gawain.* Contends that many "metrical irregularities" in *Gawain* are erroneously viewed as irregular and that fourteenth-century alliterative poems often preserve antiquarian phrases and words for metrical purposes. Focuses largely upon the link between words and their use in the alliterative long line and their stylistic qualities.

2   JACKSON, ISAAC. "Sir Gawain's Coat of Arms." *Modern Language Review,* 15 (January), 77-79.

Comments on lines 619-20 and 648-50, especially the image of Mary painted on the inside of Gawain's shield. Claims that the lines portraying Mary are rooted in an episode of an Irish tale, *An T'ochtar Gaedhal;* this tale focuses on Cuillean, "the 'ceard' or smith who gave his name to Cuchullain, i.e., 'hound of Cuillean' " (p. 78), placing "the image of Tiobhal [goddess of the sea] on Conchubar's [identified with King Arthur] shield" (p. 78).

3   LEONARD, WILLIAM ELLERY. "The Scansion of Middle English Alliterative Verse," in *Studies by Members of the Department of English: Series 2.* University of Wisconsin Studies in Language and Literature, No. 11. Madison: University of Wisconsin, pp. 58-63.

Advocates a four-accent theory of Middle English alliterative verse, specifically "a first half of four stresses, a second half of three" (p. 63), in the alliterative long line. Notes that the four-line rhymes concluding the *Gawain* stanzas contain three stresses.

4   SUNDÉN, K. F. "Några förbisedda skandinaviska lånord i *Sir Gawayne and the Grene Kny3t,*" in *Minnesskrift utgiven av Filologiska Samfundet i Göteborg.* Göteborgs Högskolas Årsskrift, Vol. 26. Göteborg: Wettergren & Kerber, 140-153.

[In Swedish.] Offers a technical philological discussion of Scandinavian words in *Gawain,* including *nirt* (1. 2498); *snyrt* (1. 2312); *skayued* (1. 2163); *spenne* (1. 1074); and *for3* (1. 2173).

1921

1   EMERSON, OLIVER FARRAR. "Imperfect Lines in *Pearl* and the Rimed Parts of *Sir Gawain and the Green Knight.*" *Modern Philology,* 19 (November), 139-141.

Suggests emendation of metrically imperfect lines in *Gawain* by adding "an inflectional or syntactical final [unstressed] *e*" (p. 139).

2   EMERSON, OLIVER FARRAR. Review of Robert J. Menner's *Purity: A Middle English Poem. Journal of English and Germanic Philology,* 20 (April), 239.

Interprets *palays* (*pyked palays*) in line 769 of *Gawain* as "enclosure."

3   EMERSON, OLIVER FARRAR. "Two Notes on *Sir Gawain and the Green Knight.*" *Modern Language Notes,* 36 (April), 212-215.

Interprets *scholes* (1. 160), an allusion to the Green Knight, as "shoeless" and Þe *ver, by his visage* (1. 866) as "The spring, compared with his appearance."

4   GOLLANCZ, SIR ISRAEL, ed. "Introduction," in *Pearl: An English Poem of the XIVth Century.* Edited,

with modern rendering, together with Boccaccio's
Olympia. London: Chatto and Windus, pp. xiii-xv,
xxxii-xxxviii, xlii-xliii.

Contends that *Gawain* is the forerunner of Spenser's
Faerie Queene. Comments at length on the Cotton Nero
MS.—its contents, history, divisions, illuminations, and hand-
writing—and focuses on the fusion of alliterative verse and
rhyming verse common to romances in *Gawain* as well as the
poem's illustrations and the history of *Gawain* in English
poetry.

Contends that *Gawain* was composed after 1345, "the
probable date of the foundation of the Order of the Garter"
(p. xxxvi). Treats the authorship problem (Ralph Strode
being his favored choice), and provides an imaginary biography
of the *Gawain*-poet.

5   GOLLANCZ, SIR ISRAEL. "The Middle Ages in the
     Lineage of English Poetry," in *Mediaeval Contribu-
     tions to Modern Civilisation.* Edited by F. J. C.
     Hearnshaw. London: George G. Harrap, pp. 181,
     183-184, 187.

     Focuses on the technical skill and artistry of the *Gawain*-
     poet, a West Midland writer who represents the harbinger of
     Spenser's *Faerie Queene.*

6   HULBERT, JAMES ROOT. "The 'West Midland' of the
     Romances." *Modern Philology,* 19 (August), 1-16.

     Questions the validity of assigning *Gawain* and other al-
     literative poems (including the remaining Cotton Poems) to
     the West Midland dialect. Claims that these poems were
     "probably written in some place which possessed a mixed
     Northern and Midland dialect" (p. 16).

7   SCHOFIELD, WILLIAM HENRY. *English Literature
     from the Norman Conquest to Chaucer.* New York:
     Macmillan, pp. 23, 215-217, 220, 383, 451.

     [Reprint of 1906.5.]

1922

1   BALDWIN, CHARLES SEARS. *An Introduction to*

English Medieval Literature. New York: Longmans, Green, pp. 154-161, and as indexed.
[Reprint of 1914.1.]

2   EMERSON, OLIVER FARRAR. "Notes on *Sir Gawain and the Green Knight.*" *Journal of English and Germanic Philology,* 21 (July), 363-410.

Interprets difficult words and phrases, including *selly in siȝt* (1. 28) as "a marvel in appearance to the sight"; *stad & stoken* (33) as "fixed and established"; *glaumande gle* (46) emended to *glaum ande gle* ("noisy joy and glee"); *on sille* (55) as "on earth"; *þe chauntre* (63) as "the mass"; *ȝeȝed ȝeres ȝiftes on hiȝ* (67) as "loudly cried new year's gifts" and the gifts (65, 67) lost by ladies and happily won by men as "kisses"; *lenge* (88) as "long"; *leve* (98) as "leave"; *Nwe nakryn noyse* (118) as "and ever the kettledrums resound"; *fade* (149), derived from Old English **faed,* as "decorous"; *pane* (152ff.) as "skirt or outside of the mantle"; *heme* (157) as "close-fitting"; *haled* (157) as "drawn up"; *halched* (185) as "turned"; *reled hym* (229) as "rolled it [his eye] up and down"; *preve* (262) as "friendly"; *in fere* (267) as "had come here (together with you here)"; *were* (271) as "protection"; *rous rennes of* (310) as "the boasting runs of"; *stel bawe* (435) emended to *stele-bowe* ("stirrup"); *bluk* (440) as "headless body"; *be-com* (460) as "attained to"; *layking of enterludes* (427) as "playing of interludes"; *doser* (478) as "tapistry, curtain, hanging as for ornament"; *woþe þat þou me wonde* (488) as "shrink not from the danger"; *þrepeȝ* (504) as "strives"; *raweȝ* (513) as "hedge-rows"; *no sage* (531) as "no wise man"; *fare on þat fest* (537) as "good time in farewell"; *tule tapit* (568) as "a carpet of tulle (fine silk net)"; *knoteȝ of golde* (577) as "knotted, gilded straps attached to the knee-cops (caps?) of Gawain's armor"; *Ay quere* (599) emended to *ayquere* ("everywhere"); *As mony burde* (613) as "as if many a maiden"; *mote* (635) as "village, city, castle"; *hadet* (681) as "beheaded"; *angardeȝ pryde* (681) as "pride of position"; *aneled* (723) as "raged at"; *yrnes* (729) as "arms, armor"; *raged* (745) as "ragged"; *carande for his costes* (750) as "anxious for his hard lot"; *kever* (750) as "gain, get"; *servy* (751) as "sorrow"; *ȝarked up* (820) as "thrown up"; *he hem raysed rekenly* as "he raised (bestirred) himself promptly," with *hem* emended to *hym; lee* (849) as "shelter"; *charge*

(863) as "wearing"; *tapit* (884) emended to *tablet* ("little table"); *double felde* (890) as "double fold (portion)"; *hersum* (932) as "noble"; *lyre* (943) as "body"; *chés* (946) as "chose to go"; *Chymbled* (958) as "fastened"; *mene* (985) as "bring"; *kyng* (992) as a reference to Bercilak, the starter of games and thus "the king of Christmas"; *ly3t* (992) as "cease (the play)"; *grome* (1006) emended to *gome; wayned* (1032) emended to *wayved* ("turn aside"); *steven* (1060) as "agreement"; *terme* (1068f.) as "goal (of your endeavor)"; *Quyle forth daye3* (1072) as "later days"; *spenne* (1074) as "space, interval"; *messe-quyle* (1096) as "mass-time"; *daylyeden* (1114) as "bandying pleasantries"; *unty3tel* (1114) as "bold bantering"; *frenkysch fare* (1116) as "French manners, politeness"; *quethe* (1150) as "song" or "promise"; *stablye* (1153) as "huntsmen"; *mene* (1157) as "subdue" or "give hard chase unto"; *wende under wande* (1161) as "turn in hesitation"; *at-wapped* (1167) as "rush through"; *þe resayt* (1168) as the last division of greyhounds in the chase; *taysed* (1169) as "driven"; *launce* (1175) as "utter forcibly"; *upon* (1183) as "open"; *space* (1199) as "do"; *lete* (1206) as "appear"; *true* (1210) as "agreement, truce"; *3e3e* (1215) as "cry out"; *happe yow here* (1224) as "make you even more my prisoner"; *won* (1238) as "pleasure"; *littel daynte* (1250) as "little importance"; *louue* (1256) as "praise"; lines 1265-66 (translated) as "And others full commonly of other people take their actions (follow what other people do or think), but the nice things they say in regard to my deserts are of no value"; lines 1283-87 (translated) as " 'Though I were the fairest woman,' the lady thought to herself, 'the less love [there would be] in his conduct on account of the perilous adventure he has sought without ceasing—the stroke that must overcome him—and it must needs be finished' "; *fire* (1304) as "further"; *fowlest* (1329) as "leanest"; *out token* (1333) emended to *outtaken* ("except"); *lystily* (1333) as "cunningly"; *Evenden* (1345) as "cut evenly"; *wayth* (1381) as "game [hunting term] "; *walle* (1403) as "boiled" or "mulled"; *Sone þay calle of a quest* (1421) as "Soon they [the uncoupled hounds] indicate by their call (or cry) the quest, or pursuit of the game"; *menged* (1422) as "disturbed"; *glaverande glam* (1426) emended to *glaver ande glam* ("clamor and din"); *boute spyt more* (1444) as "without further outrage"; *onlyte drogen* (1463) as "few advanced (drew-on)"; *schafted* (1467) as "shot out in

rays like shafts"; *layde . . . wordeȝ* (1480) as "remonstrate";
tevelyng (1514) as "adventuring"; *tytelet* (1515) as "titular,
entitled"; *Felle* (1566) as "fiercely"; *rasse* (1570) as "rising
or perpendicular slope (of a cliff)"; *nye* (1573) as "annoy";
By stoden (1573) as "surrounded"; *upon hepeȝ* (1590) as "together"; *slot* (1593) as "hollow above the breast bone";
Chargeaunt (1604) as "burdensome"; *þe lorde ful lowde*
(1623) as emended to *þe lorde watȝ ful lowde; largesse* (1627)
as "gift"; *lodly* (1634) emended to *ledly* ("in princely manner"); *Now þrid tyme þrowe best* (1680) as "Now the third
time . . . throw (succeed) best"; 1699-1700 (translated) as
"Some fell in with the scent where the fox had rested . . . ,
trailed often a traitoress [vixen] by trick of her wiles"; *fyskeȝ*
(1704) as "wandered about" or "ran here and there";
wreȝande (1706) as "denounced"; *weterly* (1706) as "clearly";
strothe rande (1710) as "edge or margin of wood"; *clatered
on hepes* (1722) as "clattered together"; *out rayked* (1727) as
"wandered out"; *mery* (1736) as "bright"; *dreȝ* (1750) as
"long"; *draveled* (1750) as "dragged out"; *mare* (1769) as
"Mary"; *leke* (1830) as "closed, fastened"; *beten* (1833) as
"embroidered"; *þuldged with hir þrepe* (1859) as "became
patient with her rebuke"; *on þrynne syþe* (1868) as "a third
time"; *boldely* (1875) as "loyally"; *forfaren* (1895) as "out-
stripped"; *arered* (1902) as "escaped"; *mute* (1915) as "pack
of hounds"; *pertly* (1941) as "openly"; *seȝen* (1958) as "ar-
rived"; *ȝef* (1964) as "beg"; *dele* (1968) as "discern"; *rede*
(1970) as "counsel"; *drechch* (1972) as "hindrance, delay";
dryveȝ to (1999) as "drove on"; *cote* (2026) as the *"cote
armure* of 586"; *balȝe* (2032) as "bulging"; *byled* (2082) as
"roared"; *Welawylle* (2084) emended to *Wela wylle* ("alas,
the wild"); *skweȝ* (2167) as "steep sides of the projecting
rocks"; *forȝ* (2173) as "channel"; *glodes* (2181) emended to
glades ("bright open space"); *grwe* (2251) as "horror"; *dreȝ*
(2263) as "enduringly"; *myntest* (2274) as "intended"; *fyked*
(2274) as "fidgeted"; *kest no cavelacion* (2275) as "made no
caviling"; *rapeled* (2294) as "fixed"; *þe hyȝe hode* (2297) as
"high hood," identified with the *capados* (572); *on lyte*
(2305) as "at fault"; *snyrt* (2312) as "touch"; *sprit* (2316)
as "start, spring"; *rykande* (2337) as "commanding"; *rove*
(2346) as "scratched"; *gryed* (2370) as "felt horror"; *sadly*
(2409) as "satisfactorily"; *saynt* (2431) as "sash"; *gomen*
(2461) as "magical device, trick"; and *gopnyng* (2461) emend-

ed to *glopnyng* ("fright").

3   EMERSON, OLIVER FARRAR. "Some Notes on the *Pearl.*" *Publications of the Modern Language Association of America,* 37 (March), 53-62, 64-65, 67, 72, 77, 79-84, 86-87, 89, 91.

Comments upon the errors made by the copyist in producing the Cotton Nero MS. and alludes often to *Gawain* in his analysis (linguistic) of the rhymes in *Pearl.*

4   GOLLANCZ, SIR ISRAEL, ed. "Introduction" to his *St. Erkenwald (Bishop of London 675-693): An Alliterative Poem, Written about 1386, Narrating a Miracle Wrought by the Bishop in St. Paul's Cathedral.* Select Early English Poems, Vol. 4. London: Humphrey Milford, Oxford University Press, pp. lvi-lxii.

Assigns the authorship of *Erkenwald* to the *Gawain*-poet.

5   MENNER, ROBERT J. *"Sir Gawain and the Green Knight* and the West Midland." *Publications of the Modern Language Association of America,* 37 (September), 503-526.

[Refutes Hulbert's argument (1921.6).]   Attempts to prove that particular "phonological and inflectional characteristics" of *Gawain* and of the other Cotton Nero works clearly link these poems with the West (Northwest) Midland dialect.

1923

1   BRUCE, JAMES DOUGLAS. *The Evolution of Arthurian Romance: From the Beginnings Down to the Year 1300.* Vol. 1. Baltimore: Johns Hopkins Press, 125-126.

[Revised edition (bibliography): 1928.1. Reprint of revised edition: 1958.2.]   Notes that the most distinguished Middle English Arthurian romances, including *Gawain,* were composed in northern England, "the most backward part of the kingdom, where the old feudal ideals and the literary tastes corresponding were least changed" (p. 125). Discusses the pre-

ponderance of French and Scandinavian vocabulary in *Gawain*
as well as the original elements in *Gawain*.

2   DAY, MABEL. "The Word 'Abloy' in *Sir Gawayne and
the Green Knight.*" *Modern Language Review,* 18
(July), 337.
  [Reply to Wright (1923.9).]   Concurs with Wright's
interpretation, but notes that *abloy* "is not adapted directly
from the French past participle, but is an example of the
poet's habit of occasionally omitting *-ed* in the pret. and p.p.
of weak verbs."

3   GOLLANCZ, ISRAEL.   "Introduction" to his *Pearl,
Cleanness, Patience and Sir Gawain: Reproduced in
Facsimile from the Unique MS. Cotton Nero A.x. in
the British Museum.*   Early English Text Society,
Original Series #162.   London: Oxford University
Press, pp. 7-11.
  [Reprinted: 1931.3; 1955.4; 1971.14. *See also* 1924.3.
Contains a list of the scribal errors and emendations for
Gawain (pp. 32-39) as well as the *Gawain* manuscript (folios
90b-126a).]   Notes that the manuscript, part of the library
of Henry Savile of Bank (1568-1617), eventually came into
the hands of Sir Robert Cotton: "The MS., a small quarto
volume, was bound up by Cotton between two other MSS.
in no way connected with the poems . . . " (p. 7).   Points out,
further, that Cotton's librarian, Richard James, compiled a list
of contents for the Cotton Nero poems, wherein he states:
"Vetus poema Anglicanum, in quo sub insomnii figmento
multa ad religionem et mores spectantia explicantur" (p. 7), a
description which is applicable to *Pearl*.
  Contends that the MS. hand may be linked with the close
of the fourteenth century, that no names are given to the
Cotton poems, and that "Large letters of blue, flourished with
red, and illustrations mark off the poems and their main divisions" (p. 8).   Claims, likewise, that the extant MS., a scribal
copy, is not a precise reproduction of the original.   Comments,
finally, on the illustrations contained in the MS., including
the beheading of the Green Knight at the Yuletide feast, a
visit of Bercilak's wife to the sleeping Gawain, the Green
Chapel scene, and Gawain—wearing a high helmet (1. 607)—
upon his return to Camelot.

4   HARE, KENNETH. *"Sir Gawain and the Green Knight."* *The Times Literary Supplement* (6 September), p. 588.

    [Reply to Onions (1923.6).]   Argues that the original MS. reading, *no sage* ("no wise man"), be retained.

5   HULBERT, JAMES R.   "The Name of the Green Knight: Bercilak or Bertilak," in *The Manly Anniversary Studies in Language and Literature.* Chicago: University of Chicago Press, pp. 12-19.

    Notes that the Cotton scribe wrote "Bercilak," a name which is probably rooted in Bertelak of the Vulgate Arthurian romances.   Contends, moreover, that the *Gawain*-poet's portrayal of Morgan and his allusion to the Duke of Clarence (1. 552) suggest the poet's familiarity with the Vulgate romances.

6   ONIONS, C. T.   *"Sir Gawain and the Green Knight."* *The Times Literary Supplement* (16 August), p. 545.

    [Emends 11. 530-531.]   Proposes to change *no sage* to *no fage* ("deceit"); thus *no fage* denotes "certainly" or "indeed," as in the Lancashire dialect.

7   ONIONS, C. T.   *"Sir Gawain and the Green Knight."* *The Times Literary Supplement* (20 September), p. 620.

    [Reply to Hare (1923.4).]   Demonstrates that phrases expressed in the form of *no fage* were used in the fourteenth century.   Offers syntactical and grammatical evidence to prove that *no fage* is the correct phrase.

8   VON SCHAUBERT, ELSE.   "Der englische Ursprung von *Syr Gawayn and the Grene Kny3t.*" *Englische Studien,* 57 (August), 330-446.

    [In German.]   Rejects Hulbert's "fairy-mistress" theory and supports Kittredge's views on the challenge and beheading motifs in *Gawain.*   Claims that the atmosphere permeating *Gawain* evokes the spirit of the *chansons de geste* rather than Arthurian legend.   Concludes that *Gawain* is an original poem, for it neatly fuses two separate motifs (challenge-beheading and temptation) so as to achieve structural unity.

9   WRIGHT, ELIZABETH M. "The Word 'Abloy' in *Sir Gawayne and the Green Knight,* 1. 1174." *Modern Language Review,* 18 (January), 86-87.
    [*See also* 1923.2.] Suggests that *abloy,* derived from the Old French *esbloy,* means "dazed, transported, reckless."

1924

1   BAKER, ERNEST A. *The History of the English Novel: From the Beginnings to the Renaissance.* Vol. 1. London: H. F. & G. Witherby, 152-153, 172, 311.
    [Reprinted: 1950.1; 1957.2.] Notes the mythic origins (Celtic nature worship) of the figure of Gawain and links the Green Knight with a Celtic tree-deity.

2   FÖRSTER, MAX. "Der Name des Green Knight." *Archiv für das Studium der neueren Sprachen und Literaturen,* 147 (November), 194-196.
    [In German.] Examines the geography of *Gawain,* including the location of the Green Chapel. Offers, likewise, a linguistic analysis of the name (Bercilak de Hautdesert) of the Green Knight, and identifies the Chevalier Vert, perhaps Count Amadeus VI of Savoy (1334-83), with the legendary Knight.

3   GREG, W. W. Review of Gollancz facsimile reproduction of the Cotton Nero MS. *Modern Language Review,* 19 (April), 223-228.
    [*See also* 1923.3.] Provides helpful comments on the "quatrain" structure of the poems, textual emendations, folio numberings, and the manuscript illustrations.

4   HOLTHAUSEN, FERDINAND. "Zu *Sir Gawain and the Green Knight.*" *Anglia Beiblatt,* 35 (January), 32.
    [In German.] Interprets lines 530-531 of *Gawain* as "and winter returns, as the world (nature) requires, in deed."

5   LOOMIS, ROGER SHERMAN. "The Story of the Modena Archivolt and its Mythological Roots." *Romanic Review,* 15, nos. 3-4 (July-December), 272, 275-276.

Claims that the figure of Bercilak/Green Knight springs both in name and in function from the disguised Curoi, a *bachlach*, in *Bricriu's Feast.*

6   MENNER, ROBERT J. "Notes on *Sir Gawain and the Green Knight.*" *Modern Language Review,* 19 (April), 204-208.

Interprets difficult words and passages, including *sturtes* (1. 171) as "projecting metal knobs or ornamental nails" (part of a horse's equipment); *ver* (1. 866) as "fur-trimming"; and *nysen* (1. 1266)—emended to *uysen*—as "devise."

7   ONIONS, C. T. "Notes on *Sir Gawain and the Green Knight.*" *Notes and Queries,* 146 (22 March), 203-204.

Interprets difficult words and phrases, including *in si3t* (1. 28) as "to look upon"; *Agrauayn a la dure mayn* (1. 110) as paralleling an epithet in Chrétien de Troyes' *Perceval* (11. 9509-10); *blaunner* (lines 155, 573, 1931) as an altered form of *blauncnere,* or possibly, as "ermine" (white fur with black tails); *Euesed al vmbe-torne* (1. 184) as "clipped all round about"; *Preue* (1. 262) as "valiant, doughty"; and *A þwarle knot* (1. 194) as "A tight knot."

8   ONIONS, C. T. "Notes on *Sir Gawain and the Green Knight.*" *Notes and Queries,* 146 (5 April), 244-245.

[Continuation of 1924.7.] Interprets *bluk* (1. 440) as a misreading of *bulk* ("trunk of the body"); *sperred* (1. 670) as "darted, thrust (with a spear)"; *saynt Gilyan* (1. 774) as St. Julian, the patron of hospitality; and *mylke-quyte vayles* (1. 958) as emended to *chalk-quyte* in order to perfect the alliteration.

9   ONIONS, C. T. "Notes on *Sir Gawain and the Green Knight.*" *Notes and Queries,* 146 (19 April), 285-286.

[Continuation of 1924.8.] Interprets *in vayres* (1. 1015) as a variant of the Anglo-Norman *en veirs* ("in truth"); *Dos* (1. 1533) as equivalent to the Latin *Age* ("Come!"); *coste3* (11. 1695-96) as "goes along the sides of"; and *Hestor* (1. 2102) as "Hestor des Mares . . . one of the Knights of the Round Table, brother of Sir Lancelot."

1925

1   EMERSON, OLIVER FARRAR. "Shakespearean and Other Feasts." *Studies in Philology*, 22 (April), pp. 166, 175, 178, 181, 183.

Discusses the Green Knight's Challenge which takes place after the first course of a Yuletide feast, interprets *mes* (1. 999) as "course or part of meal" and *messes* as "portions for one or more people at a feast," and analyzes the significance of "after-suppers" (desserts) in *Gawain* (11. 977-80, 1402, 1664) as well as the practice of group serving ("messmates") at meals (11. 107-13, 128-29, 1001-04).

2   GARRETT, ROBERT MAX. "The Lay of *Sir Gawayne and the Green Knight*." *Journal of English and Germanic Philology*, 24 (January), 125-134.

Focuses on the connection between *Gawain*—its verse form, diction, and pride in England's past—and the "alliterative revival." Emphasizes, likewise, the links between *Gawain*, a lay (11. 30-36), and the Breton lais: both *Gawain* and the lais suggest "a refined theory of love; a scrupulous courtliness; an atmosphere of antiquity; a connection [greenness of the Knight] with the Celtic otherworld; a love of the picturesque; a high degree of artistry and polish; and a comparative brevity" (p. 132).

3   HULBERT, J. R. Review of the Tolkien-Gordon edition of *Gawain. Modern Philology*, 23 (November), 246-249.

[*See also* 1925.8.] Discusses the Introduction, Select Bibliography, Glossary, and Notes to the edition. Offers alternative notes, glosses, and emendations for difficult words, phrases, and passages; criticizes the editors for failing to credit the scholarly sources of their notes and emendations.

4   McKEEHAN, IRENE PETTIT. "St. Edmund of East Anglia: The Development of a Romantic Legend." *University of Colorado Studies*, 15 (September), 18-20.

Notes that both *Gawain* and the legend of St. Edmund employ the "speaking head" motif. "Each depends . . . on the same primitive belief that after decapitation both head and body may retain life and, under certain circumstances, be reunited."

5   SCHOFIELD, WILLIAM HENRY. *English Literature from the Norman Conquest to Chaucer.* New York: Macmillan, pp. 23, 215-217, 220, 383, 451.
[Reprint of 1906.5.]

6   SELF-WEEKS, WILLIAM. *"Gawayne and the Green Knight: Harled."* *Notes and Queries,* 148 (14 February), 122.
Suggests that *harled* (1. 744) means " 'to be knotted' or 'entangled' " as well as "a state of general confusion."

7   SNELL, BEATRICE SAXON. "Four Notes on *Gawayne and the Green Knight."* *Notes and Queries,* 148 (31 January), 75.
Interprets difficult words and passages, including *sturtes* (1. 171) as "knob" or "nail"; *harled* (1. 744) as "twisted" (like a fiber); and 11. 1292-1298 as a parallel to the prose *Perceval.* Also perceives a *double entendre* in lines 11-19: *"Wynne* has the double sense of 'toil, labour,' and 'joy, happiness, felicity'; and 'bliss and blunder' reflects the contradiction of the name *Felix Brutus."*

8   TOLKIEN, J. R. R. and E. V. GORDON, eds. "Introduction," in their edition of *Sir Gawain and the Green Knight.* Oxford: Clarendon Press, pp. vii-xxiv.
[For the revised second edition of this book, see Davis (1967.6). *See also* 1925.3; 1927.1 and 3; 1928.5; 1930.1.] Discusses the Cotton Nero manuscript (history, date, scribal hand, dialect, oversized and smaller capitals, and illustrations), the power of magic in *Gawain,* and the poem's artistic unity. Examines, likewise, the analogues and sources of the challenge/beheading game and temptation motifs. Portrays, furthermore, the *Gawain*-poet's originality, the use of traditional alliterative formulas, the stylistic, thematic, and "moral" parallels between *Gawain* and the other Cotton poems, and the character of the poet, perhaps a priest or an aristocrat. Concludes with a summary of the evidence regarding the date (1375-1400) and dialect (south Lancashire) of *Gawain.*

9   VAN DER VEN-TEN BENSEL, ELISE F. W. M. *The
      Character of King Arthur in English Literature.*
      Amsterdam: H. J. Paris, pp. 115, 136-137.

> Observes that *Gawain*, "the gem of mediaeval Arthurian
> poetry," represents "a very typical example of this large
> class of poems in which Arthur himself has withdrawn into the
> background . . . while the exploits of his knights have become
> the centre of interest" (p. 115). Suggests that Arthur is de-
> picted in *Gawain* as youthful, vibrant, and fun-loving. Notes
> that Arthur's conduct demonstrates graciousness and courage;
> yet, when the Green Knight leaves the court abruptly, "Arthur
> evinces a kind of naive courtesy, not devoid of a little manly
> pride and vanity . . ." (p. 137).

1926

1   MENNER, ROBERT J. "Four Notes on the West Mid-
      land Dialect." *Modern Language Notes,* 41 (Novem-
      ber), 455-456.

> Claims that it is significant that "final *i, y* . . . is written
> *é* in the West Midland of the late fourteenth and early fif-
> teenth centuries . . ." (p. 455).

2   ONIONS, C. T. *"No fage."* *The Times Literary Supple-
      ment* (11 February), p. 99.

> [Provides further substantiation for Onions's interpreta-
> tion of *no fage* (1923.6 and 7).] Points out another example
> of *no fage* in line 3811 of Lydgate's *Reson and Sensuallyte.*

3   RAY, B. K. *The Character of Gawain.* Dacca University
      Bulletin, No. 11. London and Bombay: Oxford Uni-
      versity Press, 13 pp.

> [Pamphlet which traces the portrayal of Gawain from
> early medieval writings through Tennyson. Claims that
> Gawain is not delineated as a villain in English literature be-
> fore Malory.] Claims that *Gawain* "owes its chief quality to
> its direct appeal to plain honourable manhood" (p. 5).

4   SAVAGE, HENRY L., ed. "Introduction" to his *St.
      Erkenwald: A Middle English Poem.* Edited with
      Introduction, Notes, and Glossary. Yale Studies in

English, Vol. 72. New Haven: Yale University Press,
pp. xlviii-lxv.

[Extensive bibliography (pp. 85-91) containing many
items which are directly applicable to *Gawain* and the other
Cotton poems.] Discusses the various poems of the alliterative
school, and, after an investigation of vocabulary, alliterative
patterns, and stylistic characteristics of both *Erkenwald*
and the Cotton MS. poems, concludes that one author wrote
all five poems.

1927

1   BRETT, CYRIL. Review of Tolkien-Gordon edition of
Gawain. Modern Language Review, 22 (October),
451-458.

Contains a thorough discussion of the edition (1925.8),
including the introduction and the text proper. Offers numerous textual notes, glosses, and emendations.

*2   CHAPMAN, COOLIDGE O. "A Lexical Concordance to
the Middle English *Pearl, Cleanness, Patience* and *Sir
Gawain and the Green Knight."* Ph.D. dissertation,
Cornell University.

[Cited in Metcalf (1976.22).]

3   EMERSON, OLIVER FARRAR. Review of Tolkien-
Gordon edition of *Gawain. Journal of English and
Germanic Philology,* 26 (April), 248-258.

[*See also* 1925.8.] Contains valuable textual notes and
glosses. Criticizes the editors for their insubstantial "Select
Bibliography" and for their failure to acknowledge the scholarly sources of their notes.

4   LOOMIS, ROGER SHERMAN. *Celtic Myth and Arthurian Romance.* New York: Columbia University
Press, pp. 16, 33, 59-60, 69-84, 88, 91, 114-115, 165,
192.

Contends that Gawain and Bercilak/Green Knight play the
same roles in the Beheading Game as Cuchulinn and Curoi of
Bricriu's Feast. Claims, further, that the challenger in both
Gawain and in the *Livre de Caradoc* is garbed in green: "This

transformation is entirely explicable by the fact that one of the Irish words for gray, *glas,* also may mean green" (p. 59). Notes, also, that the name Bercilak is rooted in the Irish word *bachlach* (churl, herdsman), the conventional designation for the disguised Curoi. Views the Green Knight as host (Bercilak) as the old Celtic sun god because of Bercilak/Green Knight's association with fire imagery; Gawain, then, would be identified with the young sun god.

5   ONIONS, C. T. *"Fade* in *Sir Gawain and the Green Knight." The Times Literary Supplement* (20 January), p. 44.

Suggests that the word *fade,* as found in the modern Cheshire dialect, means "mold" or "green mold," especially since *fade* (1. 149) appears in the description of the greenness of the Knight.

6   ONIONS, C. T. *"Fade* in *Sir Gawain and the Green Knight." The Times Literary Supplement* (3 February), p. 76.

[Reply to Sisam (1927.8).] Suggests that the meaning of *fade* ("valiant, bold") in line 149 of *Gawain* is uncertain and that *fade* denotes, perhaps, "overgrown with (green) mold."

7   SERJEANTSON, MARY S. "The Dialects of the West Midlands in Middle English." *Review of English Studies,* 3 (July), 327-328.

[Also discusses *Pearl, Patience,* and *Purity.*] Notes that all four poems, preserved in the Cotton Nero MS., are "in the same hand . . . of the late fourteenth or early fifteenth century" (p. 327). Examines place-name evidence as well as dialect forms and concludes that the manuscript should be assigned to Derbyshire and that *Pearl, Patience,* and *Purity* may be rooted "in an area rather to the east of that in which *Sir Gawayne* was written" (p. 327).

8   SISAM, KENNETH. *"Fade* in *Gawain,* line 149." *The Times Literary Supplement* (27 January), p. 60.

[Reply to Onions (1927.5).] Interprets *fade* as "fierce, bold, valiant."

9   SISAM, KENNETH. *"Fade* in *Gawain,* line 149." *The*

Times Literary Supplement (17 March), pp. 193-194.
[Reply to Onions (1927.6).] Reiterates his interpretation of *fade* as "bold" and suggests that *fade* as "overgrown with mold" is inconsistent and ridiculous.

1928

1 BRUCE, JAMES DOUGLAS. *The Evolution of Arthurian Romance: From the Beginnings Down to the Year 1300.* Vol. 1. Baltimore: Johns Hopkins Press, 125-126.
[Revised edition (with bibliography) of 1923.1. Reprinted: 1958.2.]

2 CARGILL, OSCAR and MARGARET SCHLAUCH. *"The Pearl* and Its Jeweler." *Publications of the Modern Language Association of America,* 43 (March), 118-123.
Contends that *Gawain* is linked with the Order of the Garter and with the St. George legend, for the poem contains many references to the Garter—the motto, the pentangle, the girdle, and the narrative proper. Claims that "The production of a poem especially suited for a feast of the Garter on St. George's day, in 1370, suggests in the poet a person closely associated with the English court. . ." (p. 122); such an individual could be John Donne (a valet) or John Prat ("King's minstrel").

3 GOLLANCZ, SIR ISRAEL. "Chivalry in Medieval English Poetry," in *Chivalry: A Series of Studies to Illustrate Its Historical Significance and Civilizing Influence.* Edited by Edgar Prestage. New York: Alfred A. Knopf, pp. 175-178.
The poet of *Sir Gawain,* "the very gem of medieval English romance," is second only to Chaucer in poetic artistry. Maintains that *Gawain,* "the glorification of English chivalry," may be linked with the Order of the Garter, founded by Edward III (1344-47).

4 LOOMIS, ROGER SHERMAN. "Gawain, Gwri, and Cuchulinn." *Publications of the Modern Language*

Association of America, 43 (June), 393.

Contends that Bercilak represents the "solar aspect" of Curoi and that the Green Knight suggests the storm-god aspect of Curoi.

5   MAGOUN, FRANCIS P., JR. "Anmerkungen zum Glossar des Tolkien—Gordonschen *Sir Gawain and the Green Knight." Anglia,* 52 (March), 79-82.

[In German.]   Calls attention to particular omissions in the glossary of the Tolkien-Gordon edition (1925.8), and examines some etymologies and meanings presented in this glossary.

6   SAVAGE, HENRY L.   "The Significance of the Hunting Scenes in *Sir Gawain and the Green Knight." Journal of English and Germanic Philology,* 27 (January), 1-15.

[Reprinted (with some revisions): 1956.10.]   Claims that the behavior of the animals in the three hunts and the heraldic meaning of such animals parallel Gawain's conduct during the three temptations.   Emphasizes the link between the object of the third day's chase, the duplicitous fox which attempts to forestall death through his artful movements, and the crafty Gawain who accepts and hides the girdle in order to avoid certain death at the Green Chapel.

1929

1   ANDREW, S. O., trans.   "Introduction" to his *Sir Gawain and the Green Knight: A Modern Version of the XIV Century Alliterative Poem in the Original Metre.*   New York: E. P. Dutton, pp. vii-xiv.

Discusses the artistic fusion of the temptation motif and the beheading motif in *Gawain* as well as sources for the beheading—*Diu Krone, La Mule sans Frein,* and *Fled Bricrend (Bricriu's Feast).*   Focuses on the dialect, rhythm, alliteration, and date of composition (1370-1380).

Claims that "Out of the raw material of folk-lore and the elements of crude magic he [the poet] has conceived a human story with human motives, without sacrificing anything of the real magic which is the atmosphere in which his story lives" (p. xi).

2   ANDREW, S. O. "The Preterite in North-Western Dialects." *Review of English Studies,* 5 (October), 431-436.

Employs many examples from the works of the *Gawain*-poet in concluding that "in classes IV and V of the strong verbs the plural type of the preterite with a long close e was the prevailing one in the North-Western dialects" and that "there was a tendency to extend it [the ē-preterite] by analogy to verbs in which there was no good historical ground for it. . . ."

3   ANON. "Nature in Medieval Poetry." *The Times Literary Supplement* (1 August), pp. 597-598.

Praises *Gawain* for its "original" depictions of nature, especially its graphic portrayal of winter landscapes.

4   BANKS, THEODORE HOWARD, JR., trans. "Introduction" to his translation of *Sir Gawain and the Green Knight.* New York: F. S. Crofts, pp. 5-8.

Suggests that the *Gawain*-poet was probably a native of Lancashire because he was well acquainted with North Wales. Comments upon the four poems in the Cotton Nero MS., the literary fruits of one author. Notes that *Gawain* fuses two separate Celtic motifs—the Challenge and the Temptation.

5   EVERETT, DOROTHY. "A Characterization of the English Medieval Romances." *Essays and Studies by Members of the English Association,* 15:102-103, 105, 111-112.

[Reprinted: 1955.3.] Claims that the *Gawain*-poet was familiar with contemporary fashion (architecture and women's clothing) and with the activities of noblemen (hunting). Suggests that *Gawain* revitalizes the familiar with unique imaginative force and lends verisimilitude to the Green Knight, an Otherworld being.

6   KING, R. W. "Notes on *Sir Gawain and the Green Knight.*" *Review of English Studies,* 5 (October), 449-452.

Interprets numerous difficult words and phrases, including *auinant* (1. 806) as "pleasantly"; *Wich spede is in speche* (1. 918) as "What is success in conversation we may learn without asking"; *Who bryngez vus þis beuerage* (1. 1112) as "Ho! bring us the drink"; *gruchyng* (1. 2126) as "murmuring"; *I hope þat þi hert arze wyth þyn awen seluen* (1. 2301) as "I reckon that thy heart is afraid for thine own self"; *vnder* (1. 2318) as "under his left arm"; and *stylle* (1. 2385) as "quietly, without protest or outcry" or "humbly."

7   SAVAGE, HENRY L.   *"Sir Gawain and the Green Knight,* 1. 1704."   *Modern Language Notes,* 44 (April), 249-250.

       Interprets *And he fyskez hem byfore; þay founden hym sone: he* refers to a "kennet"; *fyskez,* derived from the Swedish *fjaska,* denotes "bustles"; and *hym* means "the fox."

8   SUNDÉN, K. F. "The Etymology of ME. *trayþ(e)ly* and *runisch, renisch." Studia Neophilologica,* 2:41-55.

       [Notes the unique appearance of *traypely* in *Purity,* of *runisch* in *Purity* and *Patience,* and of *renisch* in *Purity.*] Interprets *runisch* (1. 457) as "violent" and *runischly* (1. 304) as "fiercely." Postulates that *runisch* is derived from the Old English substantive *hreones(s),* meaning "roughness, fierceness."

1930

1   ANDREW, S. O. "The Text of *Sir Gawayn and the Grene Knyzt." Review of English Studies,* 6 (April), 175-182.

       Examines the accuracy of the *Gawain* text edited by Tolkien and Gordon (1925.8). Focuses especially on the poem's alliteration, rhythm, and sense.

*2   BUTLER, NORBERT P. "An Analysis of the Metrics of *Sir Gawain and the Green Knight."* Ph.D. dissertation, University of Wisconsin.

       [Cited in *Progress of Medieval Studies in the United States of America.* Compiled by James F. Willard. Bulletin No. 8 (1930). Boulder: University of Colorado.]

3   MATHEWS, J. C. *"Sir Gawain,* Line 133: An Emendation." *Philological Quarterly,* 9 (April), 215-216.

Attempts to make lines 130-136 more intelligible and dramatic by inserting *ne* before *myȝt* in line 133, *þat þe lude my t haf leue liflode to cach* ("so that the people might [not] have leave to take food").

4 OAKDEN, J. P. *Alliterative Poetry in Middle English: The Dialectal and Metrical Survey.* Vol. 1. Manchester, England: Manchester University Press, 72-89, 154-156, 177, 179-180, 251-255, 257-263, and passim.

[Reprinted: 1968.22. *See also* Oakden (1935.3).] Examines the linguistic and dialectal aspects of *Gawain* and the other Cotton Nero poems and finds no substantive dialectal variations in the four poems. Contends that the dialect is probably that of South Lancashire, especially because there is a large number of Old Norse words in the Cotton poems. Discusses, furthermore, the continuity of the alliterative tradition from Anglo Saxon poetry through Middle English works composed during the "alliterative revival" and focuses on *Gawain*—its stanzaic pattern of unrhymed lines followed by the "bob and wheel" and its employment of unique alliterative license and ornamental alliteration.

Argues, moreover, for the theory of common authorship of the Cotton Nero poems and, probably, *Erkenwald* and postulates seven scribes for the Cotton poems. Claims, finally, that *Gawain* was composed in the vicinity of the Ribble Valley, that Castle Hautdesert was patterned after Clitheroe Castle—a castle owned by John of Gaunt (1360-1398) who joined (1370) the Order of the Garter, that the Green Chapel may be localized at Downham Mill near Downham Green, and that the *Gawain*-poet was, perhaps, a member of Gaunt's household.

5 RÓHEIM, GÉZA. *Animism, Magic, and the Divine King.* London: Kegan Paul, Trench, Trübner and Company, pp. 290-297.

Suggests that Gawain's exploits with the Green Knight are linked with "one of those New Year or Whitsuntide Kings . . . who represent vegetation. . . ." Notes that holly is both a Christmas emblem and a symbol of fertility and death: "Holly brought into the room means death within a year and a day in Wales. . . ." So when Gawain appears at the Green Chapel one year and a day after he "beheaded" the Green Knight, Gawain's "deathday" must be at hand. Views Gawain as a "phallic hero" preserved from death by a girdle ("love of woman" or sexual intercourse); coitus as a form of sovereignty; and kingship as a penis.

6   SAVAGE, HENRY L. *"Fnasted* in *Sir Gawain,* 1702." *Philological Quarterly,* 9 (April), 209-210.
    Claims that *fnasted ful þike* denotes "sniffed frequently, or in quick succession."

7   SUNDÉN, K. F. "The Etymology of the ME. Verbs *Roþe, Roþele,* and *Ruþe,*" in *A Grammatical Miscellany Offered to Otto Jespersen on His Seventieth Birthday.* Edited by N. Bogholm, Aage Brusendorff, and C. A. Bodelsen. Copenhagen: Levin & Munksgaard, pp. 117-122.
    [Also discusses the use of *roþele* and *ruþe* in *Cleanness.*] Focuses on *ruþe,* a verb in the Northwest Midland dialect of the fourteenth century, in *Gawain* (1. 1558). Interprets the word as meaning "to shake," especially in the sense of "rouse or awaken." Concludes that "the ME. weak verb *ruþe* . . . is a Scandinavian loan-word, an adoption of the ON. weak verb *hryðja* 'to fling, empty, unload, etc.' "

8   TAYLOR, A. B. *An Introduction to Medieval Romance.* London: Heath Cranton, pp. 78-85, and as indexed.
    Argues that *Gawain,* written for a sophisticated medieval audience, portrays Gawain as the exemplar of chastity and courtesy.

9   WHITEHALL, HAROLD. "A Note on North-West Midland Spelling." *Philological Quarterly,* 9 (January), 1-6.
    Notes that most scholars argue that "the spelling *qu* should be equated with a pronunciation (XW) or (kw), and taken, on the whole, as a distinctively Northern dialect feature" (p. 1), as, for example, in the *Gawain* poems. Contends, however, that *qu* may be a feature of the Northwest Midland dialect, especially if "the North West Midland scribes, in adapting Northern texts to their own dialect, gradually became accustomed to use this symbol themselves to indicate

the corresponding, but dissimilar sound of their own dialect-area" (p. 5).

1931

1   BECKER, P. A. "Der grüne Ritter." *Archiv für das Studium der neueren Sprachen,* 159 (June), 275-276.

Notes the existence of several historical green knights on the Continent, and claims that Jean le Maire's work, the first *Epistre de l'Amant verd* (lines 265ff.), may signalize his familiarity with *Gawain.*

2   CHAPMAN, COOLIDGE OTIS. "The Musical Training of the *Pearl* Poet." *Publications of the Modern Language Association of America,* 46 (March), 177-181.

Notes that the *Pearl*-poet gives evidence in all of his works of his appreciation of secular and ecclesiastical music. Points out the sounds made by the pipes and other instruments in lines 116-118 of *Gawain* and the hunting music reverberating throughout the three chase scenes (lines 1141, 1165-66, 1362-64, and 1465-67). Notes the poet's depiction of indoor music—carolling, minstrelsy, and dancing—in lines 484, 1654-56, and 1952-53.

3   GOLLANCZ, ISRAEL. "Introduction" to his *Pearl, Cleanness, Patience and Sir Gawain: Reproduced in Facsimile from the Unique MS. Cotton Nero A.x in the British Museum.* Early English Text Society, Original Series #162. London: Oxford University Press, p. 7-11.

[Reprint of 1923.3.]

4   HEATHER, P. J. "Precious Stones in the Middle-English Verse of the Fourteenth Century, I." *Folk-Lore,* 42 (September), 241, 260-262.

Notes the poet's use of gems and precious metals in *Gawain,* including the gem-studded *vrysoun,* the circle of his helmet (diamonds), and the constant references to gold. Emphasizes "the foundation of magic" underlying the green girdle and the association of gold and gems within *Gawain.*

5   HULBERT, JAMES R. "A Hypothesis Concerning the Alliterative Revival." *Modern Philology,* 28 (May), 405-422.

Theorizes that a group of barons opposed to the court served as wealthy patrons for a number of poets (alliterative) who sought to re-establish the original alliterative metre in English poetry, to adopt a courtly tone, and to choose a dialect (Northwest Midland) rich in archaic poetic diction. Mentions the artistry and urbanity of *Gawain,* composed for a courtly audience familiar with the historical traditions of England.

6   MENNER, ROBERT J. "Middle English 'Lagmon' (*Gawain* 1729) and Modern English 'Lag'." *Philological Quarterly,* 10 (April), 163-168.

Claims that *lagmon* is associated with the "modern English *lagman* derived from *lag* 'last or hindmost person' " (p. 165) and that "to lead one by lagman" may be an idiomatic expression or an aphorism springing from some game.

7   ONIONS, C. T. *"No fage." The Times Literary Supplement* (5 February), p. 99.

[Further substantiation for *no fage* (1. 531). See 1923.6; 1923.7; 1926.2.] Points out two more examples of *no fage* ("no lie") in Lydgate's *Siege of Thebes.*

8   PLESSOW, GUSTAV L. *Gotische Tektonik im Wortkunstwerk, Künstlerisches im Bau der mittelenglischen Romanze von Gawain und dem Grünen Ritter: Eine eidologische Literaturbetrachtung.* Munich: Max Hueber, pp. 68-189.

[In German.] Analyzes the artistic employment of Gothic structure, including the nature of symmetry and the function of the "wheel," in *Gawain.* Discusses the dynamics of each fitt, especially the poet's use of musical elements (verse rhythm and the alliterative long line) and of rhetorical "descriptio" in his depiction of nature.

9   SAVAGE, HENRY L. "A Note on *Sir Gawain and the Green Knight* 700-2." *Modern Language Notes,* 46 (November), 455-457.

Claims that the *Gawain*-poet, probably a native of Lancashire or Cheshire, was acquainted with Wirral—a forest district overrun by outlaws and marauders in the late fourteenth century.

10   SAVAGE, HENRY L. "Notes on *Sir Gawain and the Green Knight.*" *Publications of the Modern Language Association of America,* 46 (March), 169-176.

Offers interpretive notes and commentary, including *barlay* (1. 296), ironically applied to the "beheading game," as an interjection—"Call truce!"; *rous* (1. 310), derived from Old Norse *raus,* denotes "big, loud talk"; *bulleȝ* (1. 722) as "Males of the semi-wild cattle"; *wende on his way þat watȝ wyȝe stronge* (1. 1028) as a reference to sober men who could make their way (without any assistance) to bed; *Couples huntes of kest* (1. 1147) as running hounds which are cast off; *hertteȝ* (1. 1154) as "males of the red deer"; *hindeȝ* (1. 1158) as "females of the red deer"; *bukkeȝ* (1. 1155) as "males of the fallow deer"; *does* (1. 1159) as "females of the fallow deer"; *wende under wande* (1. 1161) as "pathway of the forest"; *þonk þurȝ my craft serued* (1. 1380) as an allusion to the lord's expertise in the "breaking" of the deer; *ȝarrande* (1. 1595) as "crying, shouting"; *ȝed ouer* (1. 1595: MS. *ȝedoū*) as emended to *ȝed doun; chef huntes* (1. 1604) as a reference to two hunters, "the Lord and the 'master of game' "; *kenet* (1. 1701), springing from Old French *chenette* ("a small dog"), suggests a beagle; *titleres* (1. 1726), an allusion to the hounds, as "babblers" or, more probably, as "greyhounds . . . wearing collars"; *Alle þat euer her bugle* (1. 1913) as bugle-carriers—the noblemen; and *grwe* (1. 2251), derived from Old French *gru* ("grain"), denotes "not a whit."

11   WHITING, ELLA KEATS. *The Poems of John Audelay.* Early English Text Society, Original Series, No. 184. London: Oxford University Press, pp. xxiv-xxv, xxvii.

Compares the vocabulary of the largely alliterative poem, *De tribus regibus mortuis,* with the diction of *Gawain.*

1932

1   BUCHANAN, ALICE. "The Irish Framework of *Gawain and the Green Knight.*" *Publications of the Modern*

Language Association of America, 47 (June), 315-338.

Examines two versions of the Beheading Game—*The Champion's Bargain* and the *Yellow and Terror* story—in *Bricriu's Feast* as well as *Curoi's Castle* and the *Carl of Carlisle*. Perceives four versions in Arthurian literature of the interlaced Beheading Game and Temptation motifs. ". . . in every one there survives . . . the old tradition that the temptress and the ax-bearer were in collusion" (p. 337).

2   CHAPMAN, COOLIDGE OTIS. "The Authorship of the *Pearl.*" *Publications of the Modern Language Association of America*, 47 (June), 346-353.

Notes that the *Gawain*-poet was well acquainted with the Bible, theological writings, religious and secular literature, and the life and customs of the nobility. Suggests that John of Erghome, an Augustinian Friar of York and the author of the Latin *Prophecy of John of Bridlington,* may have been the *Gawain*-poet and briefly compares *Gawain* and *Prophecy.*

3   GORDON, E. V. and C. T. ONIONS. "Notes on the Text and Interpretation of *Pearl.*" *Medium Aevum*, 1 (September), 128-131.

[*See also* 1933.1.] Interprets *strothe* (*Gawain*, 1. 1710) as "patch of long herbage or bushes"; *strothe* is probably derived from the Old Norse *storð*.

4   GREG, W. W. "A Bibliographical Paradox." *The Library: A Quarterly Review of Bibliography*, 4th Series, 13 (September), 188-191.

Repudiates Oakden's theory (1930.4) of seven scribes, "each with his own dialectal peculiarities and individual types of error" (p. 188), for the Cotton Nero MS. Finds Oakden's palaeographical evidence singularly weak.

5   KOZIOL, HERBERT. *Grundzüge der Syntax der mittelenglischen Stabreimdichtungen.* Wiener Beiträge zur englischen Philologie, Vol. 58. Vienna: Wilhelm Braumüller, 188 pp.

[In German. Covers many Middle English works, including the Cotton poems and *Morte Arthure.*] Detailed analysis of syntactical features of Middle English alliterative poetry.

6 KOZIOL, HERBERT. "Zur Frage der Verfasserschaft einiger mittelenglischer Stabreimdichtungen." *Englische Studien,* 67 (November), 169-171.
   [In German. Covers *Gawain, Pearl, Patience,* and *Purity.*] Employs syntactical approach in his examination of alliterative poetry. Concludes that the poems in the Cotton group and *St. Erkenwald* have a common author.

1933

1 GORDON, E. V. and C. T. ONIONS. "Notes on the Text and Interpretation of *Pearl* (concluded)." *Medium Aevum,* 2 (October), 185.
   [Continuation of 1932.3.] Interprets *Enbaned* (*Gawain,* 1. 790) as " 'provided with bantels,' which in these castles are placed just under the battlements: the bantels are in fact the *tablez* of *Sir Gawain* 789. . . ."

2 LIPPMANN, KURT. *Das ritterliche Persönlichkeitsideal in der Mittelenglischen Literatur des 13. und 14. Jahrhunderts* [Inaugural dissertation, Leipzig]. Meerane: E. R. Herzog, pp. 4-5, 13-14, 16-18, 31, 38-40, 44-45, 64-65, 119-123.
   [In German.] Claims that the romance version of a courtesy book is embodied in *Gawain,* a work emphasizing such chivalric virtues as steadfastness, truth, loyalty, and magnanimity. Discusses the temptation scenes—scenes involving the delicate chivalric problem of the conflict between love and true morality and courtesy. Examines Gawain's pentangle as well as his knightly courtesy and views Gawain as the exemplar of the perfect knight.

3 LOOMIS, ROGER SHERMAN. "The Visit to the Perilous Castle: A Study of the Arthurian Modifications of an Irish Theme." *Publications of the Modern Language Association of America,* 48 (December), 1003-1004, 1023-1024, 1026-1027, 1029-1030.
   [Reprinted: 1970.20.] Claims that *Gawain,* "composed by an anonymous author in Cheshire or Lancashire about 1375," employs the Champion's Bargain episode of *Bricriu's Feast* and closely parallels in numerous details, especially

Kingrimursel's challenge, Wolfram's *Parzival*. Notes that the greenness of the Green Knight may be rooted in an ambiguous word, *glas* ("gray" or "green"), found both in Irish and in Welsh. With this ambiguity in mind, then, the Green Knight may be a representation of Curoi, traditionally depicted as "the man in the gray mantle" (p. 1030).

4   OAKDEN, J. P. "The Continuity of Alliterative Tradition." *Modern Language Review*, 28 (April), 233.

Examines metre, especially alliterative enjambment in 11. 509-10 of *Gawain* and other Middle English alliterative poems, in order to prove the continuity of the alliterative tradition from the Anglo-Saxon period through the Middle Ages.

5   OAKDEN, J. P. "The Scribal Errors of the MS. Cotton Nero A.x." *The Library: A Quarterly Review of Bibliography*, 4th Series, 14 (December), 353-358.

[Reply to Greg (1932.4).] Speculates that the Cotton Nero scribe may have arranged "the poems in what *he* may have thought a more suitable order—the three religious poems first and the secular romance last" (p. 354). Claims that parallels in vocabulary and ideas between the Cotton Nero group and other alliterative poems suggest that "the works in question [Cotton Nero poems] were copied more than once and eventually gathered together as a collection in a single MS" (p. 354). Concludes by reiterating his view of scribal transmission in order to understand "the confused dialectal and paleographical forms in the sole surviving manuscript" (p. 358).

6   OLSZEWSKA, E. S. "Illustrations of Norse Formulas in English." *Leeds Studies in English and Kindred Languages*, 2:82-83.

Notes that *leie wordes* (*Gawain*, 1. 1480), a phrase bearing Old West Norse imprint (*leggja orð*), means "to urge" and that *mare* (*more*) *and minne* in line 1881 is rooted in OWN. *meiri ok minni.*

7   SAVAGE, HENRY L. "Hunting in the Middle Ages." *Speculum*, 8 (January), 35-38, 40.

Notes that the Old Southern Hound, a scenting-hound,

was rather slow in *Gawain*: "it took all day to finish off the boar, and, despite an early start, it was 'nigh night' before the fox, the quarry on the succeeding day, was finished off" (p. 37). Claims that the greyhound was employed in *Gawain*, and generally in medieval hunts, in order to expedite the chase. Views the medieval hunt as a game with particular rules and sportsmanship.

1934

1 DICKINS, BRUCE. "A Yorkshire Chronicler (William of Newburgh)." *Transactions of the Yorkshire Dialect Society,* 5, part 35 (November), 19.

Suggests a parallel between the Green Knight in *Gawain* and the green children in a narrative recorded by William of Newburgh, a twelfth-century chronicler. Inasmuch as green is the color of fairies, the "two children completely green in their persons" are inhabitants of fairyland.

2 KING, R. W. "A Note on *Sir Gawayn and the Green Knight,* 2414 ff." *Modern Language Review,* 29 (October), 435-436.

Claims that lines 2414-2419 of *Gawain,* a commentary on men (Biblical) victimized by women's wiles, stems from traditional prose homilies (p. 435). Argues that the *Gawain*-poet may have been familiar with lines 7709-15 of the rhymed *Alisaunder* romance, for this passage closely parallels lines 2414-2419 of *Gawain* (p. 435).

3 SAVAGE, HENRY L. "A Note on *Sir Gawain and the Green Knight* 2035." *Modern Language Notes,* 49 (April), 232-234.

Interprets *gay* ("rather") as an adverb modifying *wel* in *þat gay wel bisemed* and this entire clause as a commentary upon the artistic positioning of the girdle over Gawain's red surcoat.

4 SMITH, JOHN HARRINGTON. "Gawain's Leap: *G. G. K.* 1. 2316." *Modern Language Notes,* 49 (November), 462-463.

Interprets *spenne-fote* as "joined feet" or "with the feet close together."

1935

1 GEROULD, GORDON HALL, trans. "The Author of *The Pearl* and *Sir Gawain*," in *Beowulf and Sir Gawain and the Green Knight: Poems of Two Great Eras with Certain Contemporary Pieces.* New York: Ronald Press, pp. 126-127.

[Reprinted: 1953.3. Contains prose translation (pp. 132-99) of *Gawain*.] Notes that the *Gawain*-poet was acquainted with literature—Latin, French poetry, and the works of Dante and Boccaccio—as well as with courtly manners and ideals. Claims that *Gawain*, an artistic fusion of marvelous adventure and the urbane manners of courtesy, emphasizes suspense, realistic human behavior, and the interlacing of setting with narrative effect.

2 MACDONALD, ANGUS. *"Sir Gawain and the Green Knight,* 11. 14 ff." *Modern Language Review,* 30 (July), 343-344.

Interprets *wonder* (1. 16) as "destruction."

3 OAKDEN, J. P. *Alliterative Poetry in Middle English: A Survey of the Traditions.* Vol. 2. Manchester, England: Manchester University Press, 46-48, 89-93, 167-168, 179-181, 183-193, 263-312, passim, 381-391, passim, 392-399.

[Reprinted: 1968.23. *See also* Oakden (1930.4).] Emphasizes the realism of *Gawain*, especially in its depiction of natural scenes, and notes the common links in phraseology between *Erkenwald* and the Cotton poems. Discusses the diction of *Gawain*, including nominal compounds; alliterative words; poetic, archaic, technical, dialectal, rare, and Old Norse vocabulary; alliterative phraseology; and the stylistic employment of tags, substantival use of adjectives, and similes.

4 OSGOOD, CHARLES GROSVENOR. "Renaissance of the Fourteenth Century," in his *The Voice of England: A History of English Literature.* New York: Harper and Brothers, pp. 96-99, and as indexed.

[Also covers the other works of the *Gawain*-poet: *Patience, Purity, Pearl,* and perhaps, *St. Erkenwald.*] *Gawain*, a romance written about 1360-80, is "a masterpiece, a first-

rank specimen not of romance only, but of all medieval literature." Notes that *Gawain* fuses together two famous chivalric
motifs—temptation and challenge.

5   SAVAGE, HENRY. "A Note on *Sir Gawain and the
     Green Knight,* 1. 1700." *Medium Aevum,* 4 (Octo-
     ber), 199-202.
        Interprets *trayleȝ,* derived from Old French *traillier,* as a
     hunting term linked with the modern *draw*—"to search (a
     wood, covert, etc.) for game."

6   WRIGHT, ELIZABETH M. *"Sir Gawain and the Green
     Knight." Journal of English and Germanic Philology,*
     34 (April), 157-179.
        Contains notes on difficult words and phrases, including
     aboute (1. 1986) as "busy about" or "occupied with"; *watȝ
     hym ate* (1474) as "with him"; *bare* (465) as "openly"; *baret*
     (752) as "strife"; *big* (554) as "strong"; line 1283 as emended
     to Þaȝ *ho were burde bryȝtest þe burne in mynde hade; byde*
     (2041) as "withstand"; *cacheres* (1139) as "huntsmen";
     capados (572) as (citing Hamilton) "a hood"; *cauclaciounȝ*
     (683) as "disputes"—"the sham fights and mock quarrellings
     of knights in mumming plays" (p. 167); *charge* (863) as "to
     put on"; *chastysed* (1143) as "guided"; *chepe* (1940) as
     "goods"; *cheuisaunce* (1. 1939) as "proceeds"; *chepeȝ* (1939)
     as "wares, merchandise"; *costes, costes of care* (750, 2495) as
     "hardships"; *a deuys* (617) as "choice"; *drechch* (1972) as
     "delay"; *drowpyng* (1748, 1750) as "a state of relaxation";
     dryȝe (1460) as "continual"; *forfaren* (1895) as "intercepted";
     forȝ (2173) as "channel"; *com gayn* (1621) as "came to-
     wards"; *for gode* (1822) as "for my own behoof"; *gruchyng*
     (2126) as "indignantly"; *gryed* (2370) as "shuddered"; *upon
     heȝe* (48) as "aloft"; *heȝly* (983) as "aloft"; *as hende* (896) as
     "with equal courtesy"; *keped* (1312) as "awaited"; *lent*
     (1319) as "engaged in"; *lettrure of armes* (1513) as "literature
     of knightly warfare"; *loupe þat louked* (792) as "loop-hole—
     which formed together"; *lufly* (1606) as "willingly"; *on lyve*
     (2054) as an alliterative tag; *in mornyng of* (1751) as "in the
     morning full of"; *þus much* (447) as "all this"; *mused* (2424)
     as "existed"; *nobelay* (91) as "nobility of nature"; *olde*
     (1124) as "eminent"; *orpedly* (2232) as "truculently"; *ouer-
     take* (2387) as "take control of"; and *prys* (1. 1247) as "es-

teem."

Comments on *Gawain* as literature and suggests that the *enterludeȝ* (1. 472); pseudo-disputes between knights in a Yuletide *gomen* (11. 682-683); and the Green Knight's double role may point to "an admirable description of play-acting" (p. 158) by an essentially urbane gentleman, Bercilak. Contends that the Green Knight's explosive entrance into Arthur's court is a type of "mumming-play."

7   WRIGHT, ELIZABETH M. *"Sir Gawain and the Green Knight."* Journal of English and Germanic Philology, 34 (July), 339-350.

[Continuation of Wright (1935.6).] Explains difficult words and phrases, including *may þe, knyȝt, rede* (1. 2111) as "I may warn you, knight," a reflection of a change in pronoun of address; *rekenly* (39) as "nobly"; *reled* (229) as "rolled"; *rimed* (308) as "drew up"; *rurde* (2219) as "utterance"; *bi ryȝt* (274) as "grant me"; *Rys* (1698) as "brushwood"; *Saȝe* (1202) as "speech"; *soiourned sauerly* (2048) as "richly stabled"; *schyre* (506, 2083) as "mightily"; *soberly* (2051) as "earnestly"; *much spelleȝ* (2140) as "speak so much"; *stalle, stale* (104, 107) as connoting Arthur, both standing and assuming the place of honor; *tene* (2075) as "dangerous"; *tayles* (1377) as "hindquarters"; *tayt* (1377) as "in good condition"; *token* (1486) as "sign"; *trwe* (1637) as "agreement"; *þrich* (1713) as "narrow passage or gorge"; *vnhap* (2511) as "to uncover"; *wayued* (984) emended to *wayned* ("called upon"); *wonder* (16) as "distress"; *wrake* (16) as "vengeance"; *wylle* (2084) as "desolate, dreary"; and *wynne* (2420) as "struggle."

1936

1   ANON. Editorial correction. *The Times Literary Supplement* (31 October), p. 887.

[Correction of Savage (1936.11).] Notes that "the word 'scrape' was wrongly given as 'scraþe'."

2   ANON. (A., L. E.) *"Sir Gawain and the Green Knight and Pearl."* Notes and Queries, 170 (11 January), 27.

[Query.] Wonders whether *Gawain* and *Pearl* are still attributed by scholars to the same poet.

3   ANON. (F., J. R.) "The Five Wounds." *Notes and Queries,* 171 (7 November), 335-336.

   [Reply to Anon. (1936.5), to Bayley (1936.7), and to Forse (1936.8).]   Offers a detailed account of devotion to the Five Wounds.

4   ANON. (L., O. E.) "The Inner Side of the Shield." *Notes and Queries,* 170 (4 January), 8.

   [Query.] Notes that Mary's image is depicted on the inside of both Gawain's and Arthur's shields. "Was it a prevalent custom to have images so painted, or only one belonging to Arthurian romance?"

5   ANON. (M., T. O.) "The Five Wounds." *Notes and Queries,* 171 (24 October), 301.

   [Reply to Anon. (1936.6) and to Bayley (1936.7).] Concurs with the argument offered by R.: "Even if only one *nail* was used at the foot of the cross, two *wounds* would be made in His feet, and the crown of thorns would make many small wounds, not one."

6   ANON. (R.) "The Five Wounds." *Notes and Queries,* 171 (26 September), 227.

   [Query.] Read in some notes on *Gawain* that Christ's wounds include "those made by the thorns on His head; one in each hand; one through the two feet and the wound made by the spear-thrust." Thought, however, that Christ's feet-wounds were two separate entities. Wonders what is the ordinary meaning of the phrase, "the five wounds."

7   BAYLEY, A. R. "The Five Wounds." *Notes and Queries,* 171 (10 October), 266.

   [Reply to Anon. (1936.6).] Contends that the wounds of Christ are "usually represented as one in each hand; one in each foot; and the pierced side."

8   FORSE, EDWARD J. G. "The Five Wounds." *Notes and Queries,* 171 (24 October), 300-301.

   [Reply to Anon. (1936.6) and to Bayley (1936.7).] Ad-

mits that the conventional representation of the wounds includes Christ's hands, feet, and side, but alludes, nevertheless,
to the iconographical association of His side and devotion to
His Sacred Heart.

9   GEROULD, GORDON HALL. "The *Gawain* Poet and
     Dante: A Conjecture." *Publications of the Modern
     Language Association of America,* 51 (March), 31-36.
         Argues that Dante's stirring apologia (*Convivio*) for his
     native speech may have prompted the *Gawain*-poet to write in
     his native Northwest Midland dialect rather than in the Lon-
     don dialect.

10   NITZE, WILLIAM A. "Is the Green Knight Story a
     Vegetation Myth?" *Modern Philology,* 33 (May),
     351-366.
         Suggests that the Green Knight tale in *Perlesvaus* em-
     bodies a vegetation myth and that fertility rites may be sig-
     nificant in determining the origins of a story like *Gawain.*
     Focuses on the numerous vegetation images and motifs in
     Gawain and claims that the Green Knight may represent, in
     opposition to Kittredge's views (1916.4), "the annual death
     and rebirth of the embodied vital principle" (p. 358).

11   SAVAGE, HENRY L. "*Scrape* in *Sir Gawain.*" *The
     Times Literary Supplement* (26 September), p. 768.
         Interprets *scrape* (1. 1571) in the depiction of the boar's
     actions as "sharpen."

12   STRACHAN, L. R. M. "The Five Wounds." *Notes and
     Queries,* 171 (10 October), 266.
         [Reply to Anon. (1936.6).] Refers to Tolkien's note on
     line 642 of *Gawain,* and advises the reader to investigate Vol.
     15, p. 714 of the *Catholic Encyclopedia* (1913 ed.) for a
     complete history of the devotion.

13   WRIGHT, ELIZABETH M. "*Sir Gawain and the Green
     Knight.*" *Journal of English and Germanic Philology,*
     35 (July), 313-320.
         [Additional notes on *Gawain.*] Interprets difficult words,
     including *of þe best* (11. 889, 1000) as "(those) of the best
     quality"; *blame* (1. 2506) as "punishment, hurt"; *busken up*

(1128) as "begin"; *Coste₃* (1696) as "gives quality to" or "colors"; *daynté* (1250, 1889) as "delight, pleasure"; *dryuez to* (1999) as "moves on towards"; *fare* (409, 2494) as "journey"; *fare* (694) as "hospitality"; *gafe* (1861) as "surrendered"; *gaudi of grene* (167) as "verdant hue of green"; *lete* (1206) as "have (a particular) appearance"; *nobelay* (91) as "nobility of nature"; *nysen* (1266) as "are foolish"; *race* (2076) as "blow"; *spede* (918) as "excellence"; *sturne* (143, 846) as "massive"; *sturne* (2099, 2136) as "fiercely brave"; *swypely* (1479) as "at once"; *takles* (1129) as "arrows"; *tas to ille* as "comes to no ill"; and *vnþryuande* (1499) as "unworthy".

1937

1   BAKER, SISTER IMOGENE. "The King's Household in the Arthurian Court from Geoffrey of Monmouth to Malory." Doctoral dissertation, Catholic University of America.

Notes that Gawain maintains a preeminent position in Arthur's household and that "None of the officers of the household are given titles. . . ." (p. 116) in *Sir Gawain*. In this poem, "The nearest approach to a traditional court is found in the opening scenes . . . wherein a Christmas feast is celebrated for fifteen days" (p. 144).

2   KAISER, ROLF. *Zur Geographie des mittelenglischen Wortschatzes.* Palaestra 205: Untersuchungen und Texte aus der deutschen und englischen Philologie. Leipzig: Mayer & Müller, pp. 154-168.

[In German.] Examines the "geographical" terms in the Cotton poems and concludes that these poems should be assigned to the outermost Northeast section of Lancashire.

3   MAGOUN, FRANCIS P., JR. "Kleine Beiträge zu *Sir Gawain.*" *Anglia*, 61 (January), 129-135.

[In German.] Offers interpretive notes on the final *-us* in the MS. as well as comments on the punctuation, diction, and nomenclature used in *Gawain*.

4   MAGOUN, FRANCIS P., JR. "*Sir Gawain* and Medieval

Football." *English Studies,* 19 (October), 208-209.
Views lines 427-428 as an intimation of the Camelot knights playing football with the severed head of the Green Knight.

5 OLSZEWSKA, E. S. "Norse Alliterative Tradition in Middle English I." *Leeds Studies in English and Kindred Languages,* 6:59-61.
Contends that *glaum ande gle* (1. 46 of *Gawain*), a phrase suggesting "the noise of merrymaking," is probably derived from the Old West Norse *glaumr ok gleði.*

6 PERRY, L. M. "*Sir Gawain and the Green Knight,* Line 2511." *Modern Language Review,* 32 (January), 80-81.
Notes that *n* and *m* are often confused in the manuscript. Suggests that *non* in *For non may hyden his harme but unhap ne may hit* be emended to *mon* ("one").

7 SAVAGE, HENRY L. "*Brow* or *Brawn?*". *Modern Language Notes,* 52 (January), 36-38.
[Discusses 11. 1454-61 of *Gawain.*] Claims that the Tolkien-Gordon emendation of the MS. reading *browe* (1. 1457) to *browen,* a variant form of *brawen* ("boar's flesh"), is erroneous (pp. 36-37). The ferocious boar is covered with thick bristles above the eyebrows, and the upper portion of his body is insulated from the cold by a coarse mane. "In his rage the beast has erected the bristles of the aforesaid mane, so that he appears a hand-breadth larger than he actually is . . ." (p. 37).

1938

1 COLGRAVE, BERTRAM. "Sir Gawayne's Green Chapel." *Antiquity,* 12 (September), 351-353.
Contends that the chapel depicted in *Gawain* closely parallels the typical "Neolithic or Early Bronze Age round or long barrow" (p. 351). Argues that since the *Gawain*-poet's barrow contains a hole at the end and in either side of the mound, the Green Chapel may be identified with a chambered tomb, the Bridestones, in the hilly Peak district of Derbyshire.

2   C.[RAWFORD], O. G. S. Editorial note. *Antiquity: A Quarterly Review of Archaeology,* 12 (September), 353.

[Expansion of Colgrave (1938.1).] Contends that Colgrave's description of the "holes" of the Green Chapel is equally applicable to "a partially ruined chambered mound, the 'holes' being burial-chambers that had been exposed." Suggests for consideration some barrows in Derbyshire.

3   HOPPER, VINCENT FOSTER. *Medieval Number Symbolism: Its Sources, Meaning, and Influence on Thought and Expression.* Columbia University Studies in English and Comparative Literature, No. 132. New York: Columbia University Press, pp. 123-125.

Suggests that the magic qualities attributed to "five" are rooted in Persian religion and that "Solomon's Seal," the pentangle or five-pointed star, represents the conventional magic emblem of this number. "The properties of this figure [pentangle] coincide perfectly with the attributes of the number 5, for, like the lover's knot, it is endless and thus corresponds to the "circular" [one which repeats its last digit when raised to the second power] property of the number" (p. 124). Claims that the pentangle, a figure invested primarily with magical properties, is linked more with the magic of the Green Knight than with the spiritual meanings attached to its depiction on Gawain's shield.

4   KRAPPE, A. H. "Who *Was* the Green Knight?" *Speculum,* 13 (April), 206-215.

Identifies the Green Knight with the personification of Death. Views greenness as an emblem of death and interprets Gawain's quest for the Green Knight as a journey to the land of the dead (Hades) for the purpose of overpowering Death. Contends that the Green Knight's holly sprig is a symbol of death as well as a Yuletide token.

5   LÖHMANN, OTTO. *Die Sage von Gawain und dem Grünen Ritter.* Schriften der Albertus-Universität: Geisteswissenschaftliche Reihe, Vol. 17. Königsberg: Ost-Europa-Verlag, 101 pp.

[In German.] Summarizes the numerous theories con-

cerning the poet's employment of Celtic analogues (the beheading game, the "exchange of winnings" motif, and the
fairy mistress tale) and traces parallels between *Gawain* and
numerous other works, including *Livre de Caradoc* and *Fled
Bricrend*. Contends that *Gawain* springs from English sources
and that the lady's amorous overtures represent a test of the
hero's loyalty.

6 LOOMIS, ROGER SHERMAN and LAURA HIBBARD
LOOMIS. *Arthurian Legends in Medieval Art.* Mod-
ern Language Association of America Monograph
Series. New York: Modern Language Association of
America, pp. 7, 10, 138-139.

Terms the illustrations to the Cotton Nero poems "carica-
tures" and "infantile daubs." Reproduces three of the four
Gawain pictures—(1) the decapitated Green Knight holding his
head in his hands (fig. 389); (2) the lady's visit while Gawain
lies in bed (fig. 390); and (3) the Green Chapel scene wherein
Gawain prepares for the blow from the Knight's ax (fig. 391).
Claims that the lady's "headdress and high-collared gown"
(fig. 390) and Gawain's armor (fig. 391) closely establish the
dating of *Gawain* (near 1400).

Contends that the *Gawain*-illustrator shows a familiarity
with contemporary English miniaturists; finds analogies between the *Gawain* pictures and the *Lydgate Troy Book* (Ry-
lands Library, Manchester) pictures—especially in their use of
"bunched lines" or "shores indicated by dark green banks, cut
by sharp brown gashes" (p. 138). Suggests that Upper Rhine
art shaped late medieval English miniatures and that clear
parallels exist between the Cotton MS. illustrations and particular German MS. pictures (fifteenth century).

7 OBRECHT, DENISE. "Le thème et la langue de la chasse
dans *Sir Gawain and the Green Knight.*" *Bulletin
de la Faculté des Lettres de Strasbourg,* 17 (November), 22-23.

[In French. Summary of thesis.] Illustrates the originality of *Gawain* through a close examination of medieval treatises
on hunting—the *Book of St. Albans*, the *Master of Game*, and
the *Booke of Hunting*—and medieval literary works (English
and French). Argues that the *Gawain*-poet is more concerned
with symbols and moral meanings than with a precise depic-

tion of medieval hunting traditions and terminology.

8   SAVAGE, HENRY L. *"Sir Gawain* and the Order of the Garter." *Journal of English Literary History,* 5 (June), 146-149.
     Surveys the numerous critical attempts to determine the identity of the *Gawain*-poet. Conjectures that *Gawain* was composed either on the occasion (1365) of the wedding ceremony for "Enguerrand de Coucy, seventh Sire de Coucy, and Isabella, eldest daughter of Edward III" (pp. 148-149) or upon de Coucy's relinquishing (1377) his manorial estates (Lancashire and Yorkshire) as well as the Garter offered to him by Edward III once Coucy reaffirmed his allegiance to the French throne.

1939

1   WRIGHT, ELIZABETH M. "Additional Notes on *Sir Gawain and the Green Knight." Journal of English and Germanic Philology,* 38 (January), 1, 3-9, 11-12, 14-18, 20, 22.
     [Erroneous title, for the article deals with *Pearl.*] Contains numerous references to words in *Gawain.*

1940

1   DAY, MABEL. "Introduction" to *Sir Gawain and the Green Knight.* Edited by Sir Israel Gollancz. Early English Text Society, Original Series, No. 210. London: Oxford University Press, pp. ix-xxxix.
     [This book also contains an analysis (pp. xli-lxvi) by Mary S. Serjeantson of the language of the Cotton Nero poems as well as a comprehensive bibliography (through 1938) of *Gawain* scholarship.] Presents an extensive discussion of the Cotton Nero manuscript—foliation, illustrations, order of composition and metrical system of the Cotton poems, and dating—and argues that one author probably wrote the Cotton poems and *Erkenwald.* Discusses the various theories regarding the identity of the *Gawain*-poet and links the topographical description of the Green Chapel in *Gawain* with the cave at

Wetton Mill, Staffordshire. Examines the possible analogues and sources of the beheading game, temptation, and exchange of winnings.

2   SAVAGE, HENRY L. "A Note on *Sir Gawain* 1795." *Modern Language Notes,* 55 (December), 604.

Interprets *may* in *as may þat much lovyes* as "woman."

3   SAVAGE, HENRY L. "The Historical Background of the 14th Century English Poem *Sir Gawain and the Green Knight,*" in *Year Book 1939 of the American Philosophical Society.* Philadelphia: American Philosophical Society, pp. 281-282.

Contends that *Gawain,* written in the dialect of "Yorkshire West Riding or that of S. E. Lancashire," is somehow linked with the Order of the Garter. Claims that the arms depicted in *Gawain* may be linked with "those of the Anglo-French house of Coucy-Guisnes," a member of whom was a Knight of the Garter and possessed land in York and Lancashire.

*4   STEPHENS, G. ARBOUR. *Carmarthen and the Green Knight.* Carmarthen: Privately printed.

[Cited in John J. Parry, "A Bibliography of Arthurian Critical Literature," *Modern Language Quarterly,* 2 (June, 1941).]

5   VOGEL, HENRY. "Étude du personnage de Gauvain dans *Sir Gawayn and the Green Knight.*" *Bulletin de la Faculté des Lettres de Strasbourg,* 18 (February), 77-81.

[In French. Summary of thesis.] Rebuts the traditional view of *Sir Gawain* and its hero as reflections of French prototypes (ca. 1150-1350). Underscores the poet's originality in his depiction of Gawain's fear and reactions to the chastity tests, and especially, in his portrayal of Gawain as the perfect Christian knight.

1941

1   BATESON, F. W., ed. *The Cambridge Bibliography of*

English Literature. Vol. 1, 600-1660. Cambridge, England: Cambridge University Press, 135-136.
[Reasonably comprehensive bibliography of early editions, translations, and scholarly studies of *Gawain. See also* Watson (1974.34).]

2   CLARK, JOHN W. "The Authorship of *Sir Gawain and the Green Knight, Pearl, Cleanness, Patience,* and *Erkenwald* in the Light of the Vocabulary." Ph.D. dissertation, University of Minnesota.
[*See Summaries of Ph.D. Theses, University of Minnesota,* 4 (1949), 107-112. *See also* Clark (1949.2), (1950.4 and 5), and (1951.3).] Discusses dialect, prosody, syntax and style, and parallel passages in the Cotton Nero poems plus *Erkenwald* as well as favorite words in *Gawain* and *Cleanness* and Old French/Old Norse diction in the five poems. Argues that the evidence supporting the common authorship theory is weak and circumstantial and that "the five poems . . . represent the work of at least three men," if not five separate authors.

3   GREG, W. W. *"Sir Gawain and the Green Knight." The Times Literary Supplement* (8 February), p. 67.
[Corrects an error in the review (25 January, *TLS*) of the Gollancz edition of *Gawain.*] Claims that the Green Knight's other name is Bercilak or Bertilak.

4   RICHARDSON, M. E. "A Note on *Sir Gawain and the Green Knight,* 1. 877." *Notes and Queries,* 180 (8 February), 96-97.
Uses the will of Sir Thomas Ughtred, who died in 1401, to explain the meaning of *koynt*—" of subtle or curious workmanship" (p. 96).

1942

1 . KÖKERITZ, HELGE. "Two Interpretations." *Studia Neophilologica,* 14, no. 2:279-280.
Interprets *bordes* (1. 1954) as a variant form of *burdes,* derived from the Old English *byrde* ("maiden"). Translates the second half of 1. 1954, therefore, as "with the gay chatter

(or laughter) of the maidens (young ladies)" (p. 280).

2   OWINGS, MARVIN ALPHEUS. "The Fine and Applied
      Arts in the Middle English Romances." Doctoral dis-
      sertation, Vanderbilt University.
      [*See also* 1952.6.]

1943

1   KÖKERITZ, HELGE. *"Sir Gawain and the Green
      Knight,* 1954." *Modern Language Notes,* 58 (May),
      373-374.
      Interprets *"with lotez of bordes"* as "With the gay chatter
      (or laughter) of the maidens" (p. 374).

2   LOOMIS, ROGER SHERMAN. "More Celtic Elements
      in *Gawain and the Green Knight." Journal of English
      and Germanic Philology,* 42 (April), 149-184.
      [*See also* 1956.6 and 1969.16.] Claims that the green
      girdle, the pentangle, and the character of Morgan le Fay stem
      from Celtic tradition. Contends, further, that the narrative
      framework of *Gawain* may have been carved by "a French-
      man, perhaps a contemporary of the architects of Amiens and
      Rheims cathedrals" (p. 184).

3   ROBBINS, ROSSELL HOPE. "A Gawain Epigone."
      Modern Language Notes, 58 (May), 361-366.
      Notes parallels in phraseology between *Gawain* and a
      poem ("On clife þat castell so knetered") by Humfrey Newton
      (1466-1536), and suggests that Newton may have consciously
      imitated *Gawain* in his poem.

4   SAVAGE, HENRY. " 'Methles' in *Sir Gawain and the
      Green Knight,* 2106." *Modern Language Notes,* 58
      (January), 46-47.
      Contends that *methles* denotes "without principle," for
      the Green Knight represents "a conscienceless 'thug,' heedless
      of compassion or any ideal held sacred by his order" (p. 47).

1944

1   BOWEN, E. G. and GWYN JONES. Review of the Gollancz edition of *Gawain. Medium Aevum,* 13:58-65.

[*See also* 1940.1.] Examines the cultural origins of *Gawain* in the Highland region of Britain and proposes a hypothetical hagiographical source—the life of St. Samson of Dol—for *Gawain.* Discusses the Green Chapel, the Green Knight's axe, and the meanings of difficult words in *Gawain.*

2   COOMARASWAMY, ANANDA K. "*Sir Gawain and the Green Knight*: Indra and Namuci." *Speculum,* 19 (January), 104-125.

Employs Indian mythology, particularly mythical motifs involving the psychic appeal of sacrifice as well as decapitation (the dissolution of a spell binding the victim), in order to shed light upon the "beheading game" in *Gawain.*

3   RIDLEY, M. R., trans. "Preface" to *The Story of Sir Gawain and the Green Knight in Modern English.* Leicester: Edmund Ward, pp. 5-11.

[Modern Prose translation. Reprinted: 1950.11; 1962.17.] Contends that the *Gawain*-poet, probably a native of South Lancashire and a chaplain in an aristocratic household, composed his work during Richard II's reign. Comments in detail upon the poet's particular use of alliterative metre, a vital force in Northern and Western Midlands, even though *Gawain* is mostly French in substance.

1945

1   CHAPMAN, COOLIDGE OTIS. "Virgil and the *Gawain*-Poet." *Publications of the Modern Language Association of America,* 60 (March), 16-23.

Suggests that the *Gawain*-poet was familiar with the *Aeneid,* for the works of the *Gawain*-poet and the *Aeneid* share similar figures of speech and mannerisms. Claims that the *Gawain*-poet borrowed particular lines in his works from the *Aeneid:* Ticius (1. 11) may allude to Titus Tatius in the *Aeneid* (VIII. 637-38), whereas Felix Brutus (1. 13), especially the term *felix,* may be derived from the *infelix* Roman Brutus

(*Aeneid* VI. 817-22) who condemns his sons to death.

2   SAVAGE, HENRY L. *"Lote, Loteʒ* in *Sir Gawain and the Green Knight." Modern Language Notes,* 60 (November), 492-493.

[Also discusses the use of these words in *Pearl* and *Patience.*] Interprets these words in line 639 and other passages as meaning "bearing," "din," "uproar," and "jests," not just their conventional editorial glosses—"word(s)" or "speech."

3   SAVAGE, HENRY L. *"Sir Gawain and the Green Knight,* lines 875-877." *The Explicator,* 3, no. 7 (May), no. 58.

Suggests that chairs in the *Gawain*-poet's age, especially chairs with cushions, were normally owned by aristocrats. Contends that Gawain's chair, counterpanes, and cushions (*whyssynes*) at Hautdesert are emblematic of luxury—"a summons to lowered standards of conduct."

4   WHITBREAD, L. "A Reading in *Sir Gawayne." Notes and Queries,* 189 (3 November), 189-190.

For the sake of clarity, transposes þaʒ ("though") in 1. 350 with þat ("that") in 1. 352.

5   WHITE, BEATRICE. " 'Chevisaunce' as a Flower Name." *Review of English Studies,* 21 (October), 317-319.

Notes that the word *chevisaunce* appears often in *Gawain* —"once in the sense of 'achieving' (1. 1939), and in the other three instances as 'booty,' 'spoils'." Claims that Spenser may have been familiar with *Gawain,* and suggests that Spenser employs *chevisaunce* as "flowery spoils" in the April Eclogue of *Shepheardes Calender.*

1946

1   DE BRUYNE, EDGAR. *Études d'esthétique médiévale.* Vol. 2. Brussels: De Tempel, 348-350.

[In French.] Claims that five represents the "human number" because it represents the five senses and the union of the male number (3) with the female number (2) as well as the endlessness of mankind. Notes that five is a circular number because when one multiplies five, the product always includes a five; five also suggests the earthly sphere and man as microcosm. Calls attention to the link between the redemptive power of Christ's five wounds and Gawain's virtues embedded in his pentangle.

2   HILL, LAURITA LITTLETON. "Madden's Divisions of *Sir Gawain* and the 'Large Initial Capitals' of *Cotton Nero A.X." Speculum,* 21 (January), 67-71.

Contends that Madden's division of *Gawain* into four *fyttes,* sections which are marked by four oversized colored capitals, is not substantiated by the manuscript; the manuscript contains nine large capitals, all of which demarcate clearly stages in the progression of the narrative. Suggests that the MS. divisions serve a narrative function as they do in the other Cotton Nero poems.

3   PONS, EMILE, ed. "Introduction" to *Sire Gauvain et le Chevalier Vert: Poème Anglais du XIVe Siècle.* Translated by Emile Pons. Bibliothèque de Philologie Germanique, Vol. 9. Paris: Editions Montaigne, pp. 15-95.

[In French. Contains French translation and Middle English text of *Gawain* on facing pages plus an extensive "Select Bibliography" (pp. 96-99).] Discusses romance elements (clothing, armor, architecture, hunting terminology); the links between *Gawain* and the founding of the Order of the Garter; "biographical" elements in and the meaning of *Pearl;* the "Beheading Game" and the "Fairy Mistress" legend; the symbolic use of green and of the Pentangle; the quest-theme; and the symbolism underlying the three temptation scenes. Questions whether the four poems in the Cotton Nero MS were necessarily written by a single author.

4   SAVAGE, HENRY L. *"Sir Gawain and the Green Knight,* lines 206-07." *The Explicator,* 4, no. 6 (April), no. 41.

Comments on the *Gawain*-poet's graphic depiction of winter vegetation, the dark green holly sprig.

5   SMITH, ROLAND M. "Guinganbresil and the Green Knight." *Journal of English and Germanic Philology,*

45 (January), 1-25.

Claims that an Irish source—the Finn cycle—may be found for Bercilak's role as hunter and for the hunting episodes in *Gawain*. Focuses, likewise, on the Irish elements in the Guinganbresil episode in Chrétien de Troyes's *Conte del Graal*. Suggests that the name Bercilak in *Gawain* may stem from *Bresalach* ("contentious").

1947

1   CEBESOY, AYŞE, trans. "Introduction," in *Sir Gawain ve Yeşil Şövalye (Sir Gawain and the Green Knight)*. English Classics, No. 53. Istanbul: Millî Eğitim Basimevi, pp. I-III.

[In Turkish. Assistance with the Turkish translation of this work was provided by Mrs. Bedia Odkan.] Contends that the precise date of composition for *Gawain* is unknown although the motto (*Hony soyt qui mal pence*) following the poem—the motto of Edward III's Order of the Garter—and references to fourteenth-century architecture and clothing suggest 1345 as a *terminus a quo* for dating the poem. Discusses the *Gawain*-poet's deeply religious character and his delight in learning and aristocratic life; the poem's dialect, probably that of Cheshire or Lancashire; the French origins of *Gawain* and its use of the challenge and temptation motifs; and the poet's original treatment of romance conventions and materials.

2   LANHAM, MARGARET. *Chastity: A Study of Sexual Morality in the English Medieval Romances.* Nashville: Joint University Libraries (Ph.D. dissertation, Vanderbilt University).

[Available as a fifty-page summary of the dissertation.] Focuses primarily on "ideal and acceptable sexual behavior" (continence and abstinence) in English chivalric romances composed before 1400. Perceives *Gawain* as representing an ideal fusion of Christian and chivalric behavior—"courtly manners used in the service of a firm but not inflexible standard of morality, conventionality without vulgarity" (p. 49).

3   WHITING, B. J. "Gawain: His Reputation, His Courtesy

and His Appearance in Chaucer's *Squire's Tale*." *Mediaeval Studies*, 9:189-234.

[Traces Gawain's reputation, especially as a lover and a courteous knight, in English and French poetry. Reprinted (in part) in Fox (1968.6).] Notes that Gawain is an exemplar of chivalry in *Sir Gawain*. Contends that "in the late *Sir Gawain* . . ., Gawain is characterized not by chastity, but by a continence induced by his sense of social and personal obligation. The test is not of Gawain's chastity, but of his honor . . ." (p. 203, n. 49). Discusses, finally, the similarities between the initial scenes of *Gawain* and Chaucer's *Squire's Tale* as well as the function and significance of courtesy in *Gawain* (pp. 230-234).

1948

1   BAUGH, ALBERT C. "The Middle Ages," in his *A Literary History of England*. Vol. 1. New York: Appleton-Century-Crofts, 190, 236-238.

[*See also* the revised edition (1967.1) of this book.] Emphasizes *Gawain*'s dynamic scenes, descriptions analogous to tapestries, and dialogue. Claims that *Gawain* is not narrated in order to substantiate a moral element.

2   BREWER, D. S. "Gawayn and the Green Chapel." *Notes and Queries*, 193 (10 January), 13.

[*See also* 1948.4.] Suggests that the Green Chapel is identified with a long barrow—a detail not normally found in Arthurian romances.

3   CHAPMAN, COOLIDGE OTIS. "Ticius to Tuskan, *GGK*, line 11." *Modern Language Notes*, 63 (January), 59-60.

Argues that *Ticius* should be emended to *Turnus*, the legendary founder of Tuscany.

4   DAVIES, R. T. "Gawayn and the Green Chapel." *Notes and Queries*, 193 (1 May), 194.

[Reply to Brewer (1948.2).] Contends that it is very probable "that it is a cave or fissure in the hillside which forms the Green Chapel."

5   MATHEW, GERVASE. "Ideals of Knighthood in Late
     Fourteenth-Century England," in *Studies in Medieval
     History Presented to Frederick Maurice Powicke.*
     Edited by R. W. Hunt, W. A. Pantin, and R. W.
     Southern. Oxford: Clarendon Press, pp. 354-362.
          [Reprinted in Fox (abridged) 1968.6.] Examines ideals
     of knighthood, as illustrated by the herald of Sir John Chan-
     dos (Worcester College MS. 1) and the Cotton Nero MS. in
     order to shed light on the development of medieval social
     theory.   Suggests a northern provenance for the Cotton
     poems because the MS. was passed on by the "Yorkshire
     antiquarian Henry Savile of Bank (1568-1617)" to Sir Robert
     Cotton and claims that such works were delivered orally,
     perhaps for the edification of a nobleman's family.   Claims
     that the scribal hand points to the early fifteenth century
     and the manuscript illuminations signalize a lost original for
     the MS., perhaps "a repertory book commissioned by a
     magnate of wealth not much before 1390" (p. 356).
          In attempting to establish the contemporary meaning of
     various chivalric virtues, claims that two virtues—prowess
     (skill at arms and "indomitability") and loyalty (faithfulness
     to one's word, loyalty in a guest-host relationship, or *lewté*
     stemming from friendship)—were especially esteemed.   Notes
     that other virtues—franchise (generosity of spirit) and courtesy
     (good breeding)—are stressed also in *Gawain*.

6   SAVAGE, HENRY L. "Sir Gawain 'fer ouer þe French
     flod'." *Journal of English and Germanic Philology,*
     47 (January), 44-52.
          [Review article based on Pons's edition (1946.3) of
     Gawain.] Notes that although *Gawain*-scholarship has elu-
     cidated many aspects of the poem, such criticism has been
     primarily "technical" rather than "literary" in its treatment.
     Traces the possible sources of *Gawain* and emphasizes Ga-
     wain's responsibility for his own actions and his ultimate fate
     at the Green Chapel.   Offers valuable comments upon the
     Gawain-poet's use of hunting terms and techniques and reaf-
     firms the argument for common authorship of the Cotton
     Nero poems. Includes numerous textual comments.

7   WILSON, R. M. "Introduction" to *Sir Gawayne and the
     Green Knight: A Fourteenth-Century Poem Done*

into Modern English. Translated by Kenneth Hare. Second Edition. London: Eyre & Spottiswoode, pp. 7-14.

[Revised edition of 1918.1. Contains verse translation (Hare) as well as notes and select bibliography (pp. 82-84) by Wilson.] Comments upon the manuscript (history, nature, contents, and illustrations) and the NW Midland dialect of the Cotton poems. Claims that the poet is a native of Cheshire or, more probably, South Lancashire. Discusses, moreover, the Celtic motifs—Beheading Game and the Temptation—found in *Gawain* as well as the sources of this poem; suggests that in all the early romances, Gawain is the exemplar of chivalry. Concludes with an examination of the artistry of *Gawain* and of the qualities possessed by the *Gawain*-poet.

8   ZIMMER, HEINRICH. *The King and the Corpse: Tales of the Soul's Conquest of Evil.* Edited by Joseph Campbell. Bollingen Series, Vol. 11. New York: Pantheon Books, 67-95.

[Reprinted in Fox (1968.6). For a German version of Zimmer's theories, see 1953.10. Revised edition: 1956.13.] Notes that pale green is the hue of "livid corpses" and that Buddhist art links green with death. Interprets Bercilak's wife as life, the wife of death, and Gawain's quest for the Green Knight as a journey to the land of the dead for the purpose of overpowering Death.

1949

1   BERRY, FRANCIS. "The Sublime Ballet: An Essay on *Sir Gawain and the Green Knight.*" *The Wind and the Rain,* 6, no. 3 (Winter), 165-174.

Contends that *Gawain* represents a fusion of three artistic traditions: the native English tradition with its vigorous alliterative verse and graphic descriptions of nature; the French courtly tradition; and the Celtic (Welsh) tradition with its emphasis on magic as well as on the Challenge-Beheading Game motif. Maintains that *Gawain* is rooted in seasonal mythology, especially the principle of the "Life Force" pulsating throughout the poem and shaping the work into an unified whole.

2   CLARK, JOHN W. "Observations on Certain Differences
     in Vocabulary between *Cleanness* and *Sir Gawain
     and the Green Knight.*" *Philological Quarterly,* 28
     (April), 261-273.

> [*See also* Clark (1941.2).] Attempts through a statistical
> study of vocabulary to illuminate the question of common or
> multiple authorship of *Gawain* and *Cleanness.* Restricts his
> linguistic examples to "impressive instances of differences"
> in diction and concludes that one poet did not compose both
> *Gawain* and *Cleanness.*

3   CUTLER, JOHN LEVI. "A Manual of Middle English
     Stanzaic Patterns." Ph.D. dissertation, Ohio State
     University.

> [Partly on *Gawain. See Ohio State University Abstracts
> of Doctoral Dissertations 1948-49,* 60:61-66.] Investigates
> rhyme, especially rhyme as a structural device in poetry from
> the eleventh through the fifteenth centuries. Examines the
> numerous examples of the "wheel" stanza in Middle English
> poetry, including *Gawain*'s bizarre mixture of "non-riming
> stave with riming wheel."

4   DOWDEN, P. J. *"Sir Gawayne and the Green Knight."*
     Modern Language Review, 44 (April), 229.

> Comments on the sources of the pentangle symbolism,
> especially the pentangle as a sign of Solomon, in lines 620
> and 625. Notes that John Erghome, "prior of the York house
> in 1385," includes among his books on the occult—"*Tractatus
> de penthagono salomonies/Vinculim salomonies.*"

5   EAGAN, JOSEPH F. "The Import of Color Symbolism
     in *Sir Gawain and the Green Knight.*" *Saint Louis
     University Studies,* Series A (Humanities), 1, no. 2
     (November), 11-86.

> In the first part (pp. 11-42), discusses the symbolism per-
> vading medieval culture; the origins of medieval color sym-
> bolism; the rules governing color symbolism; and the symbolic
> meaning of individual colors as they are reflected in heraldry,
> Christian art, precious gems, church liturgy and vestments, and
> literature. Examines (second part of the essay), however, how
> color symbolism shapes the theme and meaning of *Gawain*—
> "a satire on contemporary romances in their glorification of

the adulterous and sentimental code of courtly love and of
degenerate chivalry" (p. 53).

6   LOOMIS, ROGER SHERMAN. *Arthurian Tradition &
    Chrétien de Troyes.* New York: Columbia University
    Press, pp. 41-42, 46, 85, 126, 278-282, 284, 288,
    367, 406, 418, 420.

    Perceives parallels between the Welsh *Owain, Gawain,* and
    the Irish *Bricriu's Feast,* for all three narratives are rooted in
    the Yellow and Terror episode of *Bricriu's Feast.* Claims that
    Bercilak may be identified with the Storm-Knight (*Owain*) be-
    cause of the allusions to lightning (1. 199) and to the Green
    Knight's ax, a conventional emblem of lightning; Bercilak is
    also linked with the Hospitable Host figure (radiant castle,
    bright beard, and a countenance as fierce as fire). Contends
    that Bercilak assumes two roles—"solar Host and Storm-
    Knight." Notes that the Celtic god Curoi is metamorphosed
    into the Green Knight and Hospitable Host in *Gawain* and that
    various elements in *Gawain* (challenge and temptations) mirror
    Chrétien's Guingambresil episode.

7   PONS, EMILE. "Note sur *Gauvain et le Chevalier Vert:*
    790, embaned," in *Mélanges de Philologie Romane et
    de Littérature Médiévale offerts a Ernest Hoepffner
    par ses élèves et ses amis.* Edited by Paul Imbs.
    Paris: Les Belles Lettres, pp. 71-75.

    [In French.] Suggests that *embaned* denotes "horn," as
    applied to the wall of a castle or fortress.

8   SAVAGE, HENRY L. "The Green Knight's *Molaynes,*"
    in *Philologica: The Malone Anniversary Studies.*
    Edited by Thomas A. Kirby and Henry Bosley Woolf.
    Baltimore: Johns Hopkins Press, pp. 167-178.

    Interprets the *molaynes* (1. 169) of the Green Knight's
    horse as the visible ends of the bit, specifically the bosses at
    both ends of the bitbar. Suggests that *molaynes* is derived
    from Old French *molein.*

9   SPEIRS, JOHN. *"Sir Gawain and the Green Knight."*
    Scrutiny, 16 (Winter), 274-300.

    [Reprinted with minor revisions in Speirs (1957.12) and
    (in part) in Fox (1968.6).] Offers a "fertility myth" interpre-

tation of *Gawain,* for the resurgent Green Man of the peasantry is viewed as a descendant of the traditional vegetation or nature god, a god "whose death and resurrection mythologizes the annual death and re-birth of nature—in the East the dry and rainy seasons, in Europe winter and spring" (pp. 277-278). Emphasizes *Gawain*'s sophisticated comedy as well as the energy and vitality pulsating throughout the poem.

10   WATSON, MELVIN R. "The Chronology of *Sir Gawain and the Green Knight." Modern Language Notes,* 64 (February), 85-86.
Focuses on lines 995-1125 of Fitt II and the initial lines of Fitt III. Argues that the poet carefully "telescoped" December 27th and 28th so that "an extra day has seemed to pass and the three days of the hunt seem to bring the poem to New Year's Day" (p. 86).

11   WILLIAMS, MARGARET, ed. and trans. *Glee-Wood: Passages from Middle English Literature from the Eleventh Century to the Fifteenth.* New York: Sheed & Ward, pp. 360-363.
Suggests that the anonymous *Pearl*-poet composed "pearl-poetry." "His work is brilliant, clean-cut, precious, and it catches fire" (p. 360). Focuses, in part, upon the common authorship theory concerning the four Cotton Nero poems and upon a possible background for the poet—an aristocratic Lancashire family. Maintains that *Gawain* emphasizes the quality of courtesy, fuses romance traditions with reality, and offers an amalgam of Old English accentual verse (alliterative long lines) and of French patterned verse (bob and wheel).

1950

1   BAKER, ERNEST A. *The History of the English Novel: From the Beginnings to the Renaissance.* Vol. 1. New York: Barnes and Noble, 152-153, 172, 311.
[Reprint of 1924.1.]

2   BAUGHAN, DENVER EWING. "The Role of Morgan le Fay in *Sir Gawain and the Green Knight." Journal of English Literary History,* 17 (December), 241-251.

Suggests that Morgan successfully employs magic, especially in the beheading episode, in order to scare Guinevere and to humiliate Camelot. Contends that through the testing of Gawain's chastity the beheading episode imparts meaning to *Gawain*.

3 BAYLEY, JOHN. "Correspondence." *Scrutiny*, 17 (Summer), 128-130.
[Reply to Speirs (1949.9).] Criticizes Speirs for his mythic interpretation of *Gawain* and argues that *Gawain* in its final literary form is an artistic poem, not a myth.

4 CLARK, JOHN W. "Paraphrases for 'God' in the Poems Attributed to 'the *Gawain*-Poet'." *Modern Language Notes*, 65 (April), 232-236.
[*See also* Clark (1941.2).] Notes the presence of paraphrases for God, usually with the pronoun "he that," in *Gawain, Patience, Purity,* and *Erkenwald* as well as in other alliterative poems. Contends that three distinct paraphrases for God—a term designating "Lord" or a nobleman, a personal pronoun, or a word denoting "man"—and the sharp divergence between paraphrases for God in *Erkenwald* and the terms found in the Cotton poems may suggest a "multiple authorship" theory.

5 CLARK, JOHN W. " 'The *Gawain*-Poet' and the Substantival Adjective." *Journal of English and Germanic Philology*, 49 (January), 60-66.
[*See also* Clark (1941.2).] Analyzes the employment of the substantival adjectives (seventeen of which appear in *Gawain*) in poems often attributed to the *Gawain*-poet—the four Cotton Nero poems and *Erkenwald*. Claims that the evidence adduced fails to support the hypothesis of the common authorship of these poems.

6 GOLLANCZ, ISRAEL. "Ralph Strode," in *Dictionary of National Biography*. Edited by Sir Leslie Stephen and Sir Sidney Lee. Vol. 19. London: Oxford University Press, 57-59.
Contends that Strode (1350-1400) may be the *Pearl*-poet.

7 JACKSON, ISAAC. "*Gawain and the Green Knight* (A

Note on *fade*, line 149)." *Notes and Queries*, 195 (21 January), 24.

> Claims that *fade*, signifying "elvish," is a Breton word. Translates 11. 149-50 as "He fared as an elvish person, (clad) in fairy green."

8   LEAVIS, Q. D. *"Sir Gawain and the Green Knight Again."* *Scrutiny*, 17 (Autumn), 253-255.

> [Part of the "Correspondence" section.] Mentions R. S. Loomis's mythic source studies as further support for Speirs's argument and methodology. Conjectures that the Norwegian settlers in England brought with them a vision of the end of the world through winter devastation, a possible explanation for the description of the winter landscape in *Gawain*.

9   ONG, WALTER J. "The Green Knight's Harts and Bucks." *Modern Language Notes*, 65 (December), 536-539.

> Claims that the *Gawain*-poet employs precise hunting terminology, especially with respect to deer (11. 1154-59). "The high heads identify the 'hertteʒ' precisely as male red deer, the broad palms [of] the 'bukkeʒ' as male fallow deer" (p. 538). Notes the poet's differentiation between hinds, female red deer, and does, female fallow deer.

10   PATCH, HOWARD ROLLIN. *The Other World, According to Descriptions in Medieval Literature.* Cambridge, Massachusetts: Harvard University Press, pp. 292, 318.

> [Reprinted: 1970.25.] Views the mound (Green Chapel) and the stream as of Celtic provenance. Claims that the hollow hill stems from Other World tradition.

11   RIDLEY, M. R., trans. "Preface" to *Sir Gawain and the Green Knight.* London: Edmund Ward, pp. 5-11.

> [Reprint of 1944.3.]

12   ROBBINS, ROSSELL HOPE. "The Poems of Humfrey Newton, Esquire, 1466-1536." *Publications of the Modern Language Association of America*, 65 (March), 258-259, 276-279.

> [*See also* Robbins's note (1943.3).] Refers to one poem

(No. XXII), "On clife þat castell so knetered," which is composed in "three-stress alliterative cross-rimed quatrains" (p. 258) and parallels *Gawain* in some phraseology. Contends that "either Newton himself or some professional minstrel had an intimate acquaintance with *Sir Gawain and the Green Knight*" (p. 259).

13   SISAM, KENNETH. *"Sir Gawain,* lines 147-50." *Notes and Queries,* 195 (27 May), 239.
     [Reply to Jackson (1950.7) and Smithers (1950.14).] Contends that *fade,* a Middle English word, signifies "valiant" in line 149.

14   SMITHERS, G. V. "A Crux in *Sir Gawain and the Green Knight." Notes and Queries,* 195 (1 April), 134-136.
     [Expands Jackson's note (1950.7).] Notes that the main ideas of lines 147-50 are echoed in lines 232-40, that green is linked with fairies in the Middle Ages, and that the Green Knight is "a being of the otherworld (since he is a shape-shifter" (p. 135). Claims that the *Gawain*-poet may have been familiar with a Latin text, Gervase of Tilbury's *Otia Imperialia,* in which the word *fadus* ("fairy") appears.

15   SPEIRS, JOHN. "Correspondence." *Scrutiny,* 17 (Summer), 130-132.
     [Reply to Bayley (1950.3).] Defends his interpretation and methodology.

1951

1   BONJOUR, ADRIEN. " 'Werre and wrake and wonder' (*Sir Gawain,* 1. 16)." *English Studies,* 32 (April), 70-72.
    Claims that line 16 must be analyzed within the context of the entire stanza. Contends that *wonder* ("marvel, wondrous deed") contrasts with *werre and wrake* just as *blysse* deviates sharply from *blunder.*

2   CHAPMAN, COOLIDGE OTIS. *An Index of Names in Pearl, Purity, Patience, and Gawain.* Cornell Studies in English, No. 38. Ithaca: Cornell University Press, 76 pp.

Includes a list—together with line references and biographical, literary, and historical background—of the proper names contained in the four poems. Notes Biblical allusions and explanatory summaries of Biblical stories when relevant to the Cotton Nero poems.

3   CLARK, JOHN W. "On Certain 'Alliterative' and 'Poetic' Words in the Poems Attributed to 'The *Gawain*-Poet'." *Modern Language Quarterly,* 12 (December), 387-398.

[*See also* Clark (1941.2).] Examines "poetic" words, synonyms expressing movement, and diction infrequently found in non-alliterative poetry in order to shed light upon the question of common or multiple authorship of the four Cotton Nero poems and *Erkenwald.* Suggests that the use of such vocabulary in the five poems runs counter to the common authorship theory, especially a common author for both *Gawain* and *Purity.*

4   HOSHIYA, GOICHI. *"Sir Gawain* and *Pearl." Eigo Seinen (The Rising Generation),* 97, no. 9 (1 September), 391-394.

[In Japanese. Annotation provided by the author.] Focuses on the "season-sense" in *Gawain,* specifically the *Gawain*-poet's sensitive depiction of the beauty of winter and moral chivalry.

5   KANE, GEORGE. *Middle English Literature: A Critical Study of the Romances, the Religious Lyrics, Piers Plowman.* London: Methuen, pp. 9, 45, 52, 66, 70-71, 73-76, 189-190.

Contrasts *Gawain,* a poem set on or near the turf of the fairy world, with the heroic *Alliterative Morte Arthure.* Focuses on the "visual quality" of *Gawain,* particularly the lucid, well-defined descriptions, as well as the idealized portrayal of reality, and delineates the role played by magic in this romance.

6   KOBAYASHI, ATSUO. "Traits of Medieval Romances and the Formative Grace of *Sir Gawain and the Green Knight." The Annual Reports of the Faculty of Arts and Letters, Tohoku University* (Sendai, Japan),

2:110-150.

[In Japanese. English summary on pp. 5-6 of the issue.] Discusses the chief features of the medieval romance—the knight's quest, supernatural or marvelous elements, and the emphasis upon ornamentation, feasting, and hunting. Analyzes the artistic fusion of the challenge/beheading game and temptation motifs in *Gawain* as well as the poem's use of symmetry and parallelism (hunts, temptations, and "blows" at the Green Chapel). Praises the poem for its graphic description, its portrait of chivalric life and courtly love, and its dramatic pace.

7   LUTTRELL, C. A.   " 'Sooth' in Johnson's *Dictionary* and in Keats." *Notes and Queries,* 196 (15 September), 406.

   Suggests (in agreement with Gollancz) that *sothly* (*Gawain*, 1. 673) means "gently, softly, quietly."

8   PONS, EMILE.   "Y a-t-il une psychologie proprement anglaise du caractère de Gauvain?". *Bulletin Bibliographique de la Société Internationale Arthurienne,* 3:103.

   [In French, abstract.]   Notes that *Gawain* fuses two important motifs—the beheading and the "fairy mistress" story and that the courtly love language in *Gawain* bears the imprint of both English humor and theological concepts.

9   SAVAGE, HENRY L.   "Hunting Terms in Middle English." *Modern Language Notes,* 66 (March), 216.

   [Reply to Ong (1950.9).] Praises Ong for his perceptive comments on the significance of hunting in *Gawain* and alludes to another article (1931.10) wherein the technical terms for deer are clarified. Interprets the *oþer dere* (1322) as "prickets, three-year olds (of fallow deer), and brockets, staggards, stags . . . and hinds of the red deer."

10   SPEIRS, JOHN.   "Correspondence." *Scrutiny,* 18
 •   (Winter), 193-196.

   [Reply to Watson (1951.11).] Defends his remarks impugning scholarship, especially "conjectural" scholarship with no real substantive proof.

11   WATSON, JOHN GILLARD. "Correspondence." *Scrutiny,* 18 (Winter), 191-193.

    Criticizes Speirs (1949.9) for his debunking of scholarship.

1952

1   BAZIRE, JOYCE. "ME. ẹ̄ and ẹ̄ in the Rhymes of *Sir Gawain and the Green Knight.*" *Journal of English and Germanic Philology,* 51 (April), 234-235.

    Claims that the poet has generally composed "perfect rhymes, but in two examples the power of making tense a preceding slack *ē* has to be allowed to *n* and possibly to *r* before perfect rhymes can be admitted" (p. 235).

2   BRADDY, HALDEEN. "Sir Gawain and Ralph Holmes the Green Knight." *Modern Language Notes,* 67 (April), 240-242.

    Notes that *Gawain* was composed between 1345 and 1400. Identifies the Green Knight of *Gawain* with Ralph Holmes, a man who was commonly termed the Green Squire before he was inducted into knighthood. Notes a parallel between the decapitation of the Green Knight in *Gawain* and the beheading of Holmes by Henry of Trastamara in 1369.

3   CUTLER, JOHN L. "The Versification of the 'Gawain Epigone' in Humfrey Newton's Poems." *Journal of English and Germanic Philology,* 51 (October), 562-570.

    [Expansion of Robbins's comments (1943.3) and (1950.12).] Claims that an analysis of the metre of the "Epigone," probably copied—not composed—by Newton, buttresses "the view that this poem is indebted to *Sir Gawain* . . . and the poetry of the alliterative 'Revival' in general" (p. 562). Suggests that the stanzaic form of the poem is complex, and reconstructs the poem into one 17-line bob-wheel stanza followed by "a single thirty-seven-line wheel stanza" (p. 566). Concludes by quoting *De tribus regibus mortuis,* a fifteenth-century poem, and by noting the verbal and metrical parallels between this poem and the "Epigone" (pp. 568-70).

4   JONES, GWYN, trans. "Introduction," in *Sir Gawain and the Green Knight: A Prose Translation with an Introductory Essay.* London: Golden Cockerel Press, pp. 1-20.

[Contains six color engravings by Dorothea Braby.] Discusses the Cotton Nero MS as well as the date (1375-1400) and place of composition (perhaps south Lancashire) of *Gawain* and contends that all four Cotton poems, but not *Erkenwald,* were probably composed by one person. Examines the fusion of three motifs in *Gawain*—the "beheading game," temptation, and exchange of winnings—as well as the poem's analogues and amalgamation of disparate traditions (Irish-Welsh, English, and French).

Contends that the Green Chapel is the vestige of a "megalithic barrow" and that the Green Knight is vaguely linked with the vibrating energy of nature. Comments upon the poem's symmetry; Gawain's testing (loyalty); the parallels between the hunts and temptations; the circular form (the links between the beginning and end of the poem); the metrics; and the humanity of Gawain.

5   MOSSÉ, FERNAND. *A Handbook of Middle English.* Translated by James A. Walker. Baltimore: Johns Hopkins Press, pp. 237-239, 248, 380-383.

Discusses the artistry of *Gawain* as well as the manuscript, dialect, orthography, phonology, vocabulary, and alliterative verse. Claims that *Gawain* was composed during the poet's youth.

6   OWINGS, MARVIN ALPHEUS. *The Arts in the Middle English Romances.* New York: Bookman Associates, pp. 55, 59, 66, 70, 75, 80, 92, 104-106, 108-109, 111, 113, 133.

[Revised version of 1942.2.] Claims that *Gawain* depicts "realistically" the fine and applied arts (castle towers, battlements, gates, windows, fireplaces, halls, and chapels; and furnishings—curtained beds, dining tables and tablecloths, chairs, and trumpets heralding the serving of meals), thereby mirroring "contemporary civilization and taste."

7   SAVAGE, HENRY L. "The Feast of Fools in *Sir Gawain and the Green Knight.*" *Journal of English and*

Germanic Philology, 51 (October), 537-544.

Argues that lines 62-65 allude to the mass celebrating the feast of the subdeacons (January 1) as well as the Circumcision of Christ (pp. 537-539); such a feast—the feast of fools—conducted by subdeacons represented a noisy burlesque of the sacred rites. Claims that the *Loude crye . . . of clerke3* (1. 64) connotes the shouts made by minor orders at the "feast of fools" (p. 542) and that *Nowel* (1. 65) suggests a public acclamation of joy, not Christmas (pp. 542-543).

1953

1   AKKARTAL, T. "A Point of Syntax in *Sir Gawain and the Green Knight.*" *Notes and Queries,* 198 (August), 322.

Interprets *theroute* (11. 518, 2000, 2481) as "out of it"; and *therwyth* (11. 121, 980, 1610) as "together with, with."

2   CHAPMAN, COOLIDGE OTIS. "Chaucer and the *Gawain*-Poet: A Conjecture." *Modern Language Notes,* 68 (December), 521-524.

Contends that the first section of Chaucer's *Squire's Tale* was influenced by Fit I of *Gawain.*

3   GEROULD, GORDON HALL, trans. "The Author of *The Pearl* and *Sir Gawain,*" in *Beowulf and Sir Gawain and the Green Knight: Poems of Two Great Eras with Certain Contemporary Pieces.* New York: Ronald Press, pp. 126-127.

[Reprint of 1935.1.]

4   HIGHFIELD, J. R. L. "The Green Squire." *Medium Aevum,* 22, no. 1:18-23.

Raises the possibility that Simon Newton (1363-80), a West Midland man termed the "Green Squire" or "scutifer viridis," may be linked with the Green Knight.

5   ONIONS, C. T. "Middle English *Gawne:* A Correction, with Some Notes." *Medium Aevum,* 22, no. 2:111-113.

Contends that *gawne,* an offshoot of the Norse *gegn*-stem,

is employed in *Gawain* as a noun for "nearness," "convenience," or "advantage." Notes the appearance of the *gayn-*
stem (9 times) in *Gawain.*

6   REINHOLD, HEINZ. *Humoristische Tendenzen in der
    englischen Dichtung des Mittelalters.* Tübingen: Max
    Niemeyer, pp. 19, 42-43, 59, 64-65, 71, 84, 117-131,
    134-135.
        [In German.] Attempts to elucidate the nature of humor
    in Old English and Middle English poetry and gives numerous
    illustrations from *Gawain.* Divides humor into various types,
    including scorn and mockery, irony, fierce or grim humor
    (the beheading of the Green Knight), macabre and indecent
    humor, courtly humor (the lively, sophisticated repartee,
    "love-talk," between Gawain and Bercilak's wife), and humor
    of character and situation.

7   RIX, MICHAEL M. "A Re-examination of the Castleton
    Garlanding." *Folk-Lore,* 64 (June), 342-344.
        Suggests a parallel between sections of *Gawain* and the
    Castleton Garlanding ritual, wherein "A Jack-in-the-Green
    mounted on horseback parades through the village, . . . towers
    above the rest of the performers and looks super-human"
    (p. 343). Notes the Green Knight's primitive ax and the Green
    Chapel ("chambered tomb") as evidence for linking the Knight
    with the Jack-in-the-Green. Claims that the Knight's physical
    description and accouterments, especially the emphasis on
    green, identifies him with a fertility figure, while the removal
    of the "quane," a collection of flowers, in the Garlanding
    ceremony is analogous to the ritual decapitation of the Green
    Knight.

8   SMITHERS, G. V. "Story-Patterns in Some Breton
    Lays." *Medium Aevum,* 22, no. 2:89-92.
        Interprets *in londe so hatჳ ben longe* (1. 36) as "an expli-
    cit contemporary affirmation of the persistence of the allitera-
    tive medium continuously into the 14th century" (p. 89) and
    claims that line 31, juxtaposed with lines 33-36, suggests that
    there was an alliterative English source for *Gawain.* More pro-
    bably, however, "the whole passage has been written *for the
    minstrel or narrator,* and it is therefore he who is represented
    as speaking in the first person" (p. 90). Concludes by noting

that the reference to *laye* (1. 30) is appropriate because *Gawain* alludes to Britain's past, marvels, and adventures—themes normally found in literary Breton lays, and that the immediate source of *Gawain* may be "a literary Breton lay either in OF or ME" (p. 91).

9   WHITE, BEATRICE. "Two Notes on Middle English." *Neophilologus*, 37 (April), 114-115.

Suggests that further analysis of Edmund Gibson's gloss, *bardla-ictus, verber*, on *Christ's Kirk on the Green* may help interpret *barlay* (1. 295, *Gawain*).

10   ZIMMER, HEINRICH. "Gawan beim grünen Ritter," in *Deutsche Beiträge zur geistigen Überlieferung*. Edited by Arnold Bergsträsser. Chicago: Henry Regnery, pp. 46-56.

[In German.] Perceives *Gawain* as rooted in Celtic, pre-Celtic, and Indian myth. Suggests that the Green Knight represents the God of Death who permits Gawain to return to the earthly sphere and that the girdle is an emblem of release from death.

1954

1   HEATHER, P. J. "Divination." *Folk-Lore*, 65 (September), 89.

Contends that *Gawain* is linked with the ordeal, a form of divination: ". . . having sought the adventure, and having been accepted as a champion, Gawayne underwent a very real ordeal; the point at issue was the reputation for prowess of Arthur's court; and this Gawayne effectually sustained. . . ."

2   MACDONALD, ANGUS. "A Note on *Sir Gawain and the Green Knight*." *English Studies*, 35 (February), 15.

Contends that *wyth no wyȝ elleȝ on lyue* (1. 385), if examined within the context of Gawain's entire statement (11. 381-385), suggests a reiteration of the agreement between him and the Green Knight and a demand for the Knight's physical presence.

3 ROBERTSON, D. W., JR. "Why the Devil Wears Green." *Modern Language Notes,* 69 (November), 470-472.

[Explicitly denies any identification of the Green Knight with the devil. Yet many scholars employ this essay as a source for their critical commentaries on the demonic nature of the Green Knight.] Employs Pierre Bersuire's *Reductorium Morale* in order to determine why the devil wears green clothing, particularly in Chaucer's *Friar's Tale.* Suggests that just as green is protective coloration worn by hunters in their quest for game, so the devil is garbed in green because he is the eternal hunter of human souls.

1955

1 CLARK, CECILY. "The Green Knight Shoeless: A Reconsideration." *Review of English Studies,* New Series 6 (April), 174-177.

Reconsiders the argument for glossing *scholes* (line 160) as the adjective "shoeless." Rejects the syntactic argument for terming *scholes* a noun and notes that the *Gawain*-poet frequently interchanges parts of speech in his descriptive passages. Employs illustrations from English and French manuscripts, including the Ellesmere Manuscript of Chaucer's *Canterbury Tales* and *Les Très Riches Heures du Duc de Berry,* to demonstrate that "in the later fourteenth century at least dandies often wore hose alone without shoes" (p. 175).

2 ENGELHARDT, GEORGE J. "The Predicament of Gawain." *Modern Language Quarterly,* 16 (September), 218-225.

[Reprinted in Vasta (1965.24).] Examines Gawain's predicament in terms of courage (military sphere), piety (religious sphere), and courtesy (courtly sphere). Outlines the association between Gawain's pentangle and his complete virtue and analyzes the function and significance of the green girdle. Demonstrates how the moral and comedy of *Gawain* spring from the hero's numerous dilemmas.

3 EVERETT, DOROTHY. "The Alliterative Revival," in *Essays on Middle English Literature.* Edited by Patricia Kean. Oxford: Clarendon Press, pp. 48, 51-

52, 68-69, 73-85, 87, 93.

[Reprinted, in part, in Fox (1968.6). This book, likewise, contains a reprint of 1929.5.] Discusses the *Gawain*-poet's possible acquaintance with an aristocratic family, perhaps one opposed to the king, the hunting parallels between *Gawain* and *The Parlement of the Thre Ages,* and the Cotton Nero MS—its hand, dialect, date, authorship, and stylistic devices common to the Cotton poems.

Examines the *Gawain* stanza, including the nature and aims of the "bob and wheel"; the motifs underlying *Gawain; Gawain* as a test of chivalric virtue and as an anti-courtly love poem; the characters of Gawain and the Knight; the use of the second-person singular (*þy*); the employment of descriptions of nature and of parallel structure; and the use of "high style."

4   GOLLANCZ, ISRAEL. "Introduction" to his *Pearl, Cleanness, Patience and Sir Gawain: Reproduced in Facsimile from the Unique MS. Cotton Nero A.x. in the British Museum.* Early English Text Society, Original Series #162. London: Oxford University Press, pp. 7-11.
     [Reprint of 1923.3.]

5   HODGART, M. J. C. "In the Shade of the Golden Bough." *The Twentieth Century* (London), 157 (February), 116-117.
     Discusses Speirs's (1949.9) indebtedness to the Cambridge "anthropologists" and to Jessie Weston for his interpretation of *Gawain.* Questions the stance adopted by "mythological" critics: "If a poem can be shown to be based consciously on primitive myth and ritual (or even unconsciously), is it thereby a better poem than one which is not so based?" (p. 117).

*6   HOWARD, DONALD R. "The Contempt of the World: A Study in the Ideology of Latin Christendom with Emphasis on Fourteenth Century English Literature." Ph.D. dissertation, University of Florida (Gainesville).
     [Cited in *Doctoral Dissertations Accepted by American Universities,* 22 (1954-1955). *See also* Howard (1966.14).]

7   KELLEY, GERALD B. "Graphemic Theory and Its Application to a Middle English Text: *Sir Gawain and*

the Green Knight." Ph.D. dissertation, University of Wisconsin.

[*See Summaries of Doctoral Dissertations . . . University of Wisconsin,* 16 (1955), 542-543.] Claims that a study of the graphemes of *Gawain* underscores an ordered structure of oppositions "indicated either by physical differences between letters or by limitations in their distribution."

8   LUTTRELL, C. A. "The *Gawain* Group: Cruxes, Etymologies, Interpretations." *Neophilologus,* 39 (July), 209-211.

Interprets difficult words, including an argument for the retention of the MS. reading *caryeʒ* (1. 734, "rides, goes"), not the emendation to *cayreʒ; raged* (1. 745) as "shaggy, tufted"; and *rout* (1. 457) as "jerk."

9   MARKMAN, ALAN MOUNS. "Sir Gawain of Britain: A Study of the Romance Elements in the British Gawain Literature." Ph.D. dissertation, University of Michigan.

[Partly on *Gawain. See Dissertation Abstracts,* 15 (1955), 1613.] Focuses on Gawain's human qualities as disclosed in the various depictions of this hero in British literature (12th-15th centuries). Contends that the hero of *Gawain* is the ideal chivalric knight, not a servant of courtly love. Examines Gawain within the context of the "marvelous."

*10   MELTON, JOHN L. "Aspects of Comedy in the English Chivalric Romances." Ph.D. dissertation, Johns Hopkins University.

[Cited in *Doctoral Dissertations Accepted by American Universities,* 22 (1954-1955).]

11   PEARSALL, DEREK A. "Rhetorical *Descriptio* in *Sir Gawain and the Green Knight.*" *Modern Language Review,* 50 (April), 129-134.

Applies the rhetorical principles of Geoffrey of Vinsauf and Matthew of Vendôme on poetic description to the descriptive passages in *Gawain.* Claims that the depiction of the Green Knight and his horse is indebted to Vendôme's precept of "description through enumeration of detail" (p. 130) and that the description of ideal female beauty, a famous rhetori-

cal convention, is refurbished through the contrast of Bercilak's wife and the old woman (11. 950-69). Notes that Vendôme's description of the four seasons is echoed in *Gawain*
(500-30), wherein the poet emphasizes the struggle between
winter and summer as well as the evanescent nature of life.
Focuses on the description of landscape in *Gawain* and its
link with Gawain's psychological state.

1956

1   ANON. (J., G. P.) "The Author of *Sir Gawain and the
      Green Knight.*" *Notes and Queries,* New Series, 3
      (February), 53-54.
            Contends that only local people would have known of
      the fords leading from Flint to the Wirral. Claims that the
      Gawain-poet was a native of Lancashire, perhaps a resident of
      Whalley Abbey.

2   BARNET, SYLVAN. "A Note on the Structure of *Sir
      Gawain and the Green Knight.*" *Modern Language
      Notes,* 71 (May), 319.
            Contends that the Challenge is employed as a "frame" in
      order to suggest a tripartite structure—"Challenge, Tempta-
      tion, conclusion of Challenge"—reflected in Gawain's three
      prayers (1. 763) as well as in the three hunts, temptations, and
      kisses. Argues that "Each of the three hunts is narrated as a
      frame for each of the three temptations . . . exploits in arms
      make a frame for each game of love, even as the central story,
      with its sexual theme, is framed by the battle-like exchange of
      blows."

3   BORROFF, MARIE E. "The Style of *Sir Gawain and the
      Green Knight.*" Ph.D. dissertation, Yale University.
            [*See also* 1962.1.] Attempts to analyze critically the
      style and metrics of *Gawain* in order to discern the poet's
      comic art.

4   GREENWOOD, ORMEROD. "Introduction" to his *Sir
      Gawain and the Green Knight: A Fourteenth-Century
      Alliterative Poem now Attributed to Hugh Mascy.*
      Translated in the Original Metre by Ormerod Green-
      wood, with Twelve Lithographs by Roy Morgan.

London: The Lion and Unicorn Press, pp. 3-16.

Terms the treatment of Gawain's adventures "epic" in nature and scope, yet "realistic" in that the *Gawain*-poet employs details (beds, doors, fireplaces) of his own age. Focuses on the "beheading game" as a Yuletide interlude, on the double nature of the Green Knight—a fairy creature and a man—and on the use of language in *Gawain*. Emphasizes (pp. 5-6) the circular form of *Gawain,* and, employing Nicolas of Cusa's *De Docta Ignorantia* and other medieval/renaissance sources, interprets the circle, a geometrical figure, as an emblem of the world, universe, and God—a symbol of perfect unity and simplicity.

Discusses (pp. 6-12), also, the provenance, nature, and contents of the Cotton Nero MS and attempts to identify the author of the Cotton poems plus *Erkenwald* (common authorship argument): notes that the words *Thomas Masse(y) Esquier* and *Eesybyt Bothe of Dunham in the comytye of Chester* appear twice in the *Erkenwald* MS, and, after explaining the relationship between Massey and Elizabeth Booth, claims that the *Gawain/Erkenwald*-poet was Hugh Mascy.

Elucidates, then, the *Gawain*-poet's use of numerology (five and twelve), especially in *Pearl,* and illustrates the significance of numbers in the *Apocalypse,* Boethius's *De Musica,* and Pythagorean and Platonic thought. Identifies three, a "male" number, as "the first number with beginning, middle, and end, the number of magical incantation" (p. 8) and links five—a fusion of the first male (3) and female (2) numbers— with "love and harmony, and . . . mankind" (p. 9). Offers, then, a complex linguistic and numerological argument involving a pun (*Margery Mascy*) as well as the meaning of 101 in *Pearl* and notes the appearance of "Hugo de" at the head of *Gawain.* In the concluding sections of the essay, examines *Gawain* as an artistic blend of Celtic, English, and Norse cultures; its diction; its parody of courtly love traditions; and its use of alliterative verse.

*5   KEE, KENNETH O. "Gawain: A Study in Epic Degeneration."   Ph.D. dissertation, University of Toronto (Canada).

[Cited in *Comprehensive Dissertation Index, 1861-1972.* Vol. 29 (Language and Literature).   Ann Arbor: Xerox University Microfilms, 539.]

6   LOOMIS, ROGER SHERMAN. *Wales and the Arthurian Legend.* Cardiff: University of Wales Press, pp. 20, 77-90, 100, 163, 216.

[Entire volume reprinted: 1969.16. Pp. 77-90 represent a revised version (updated footnote references and some sections deleted) of 1943.2; pp. 77-90 reprinted: 1970.19.]

Claims that four elements in *Gawain*—Bercilak as hunter; the lady's temptations; the passage of a year, according to an agreement, between the two meetings of Gawain and the Green Knight; and the Green Chapel encounter set near a brook—are derived from the initial episode of the Welsh *Pwyll.* Suggests that Morgan le Fay and Bercilak's wife are "doublets," for Morgan is traditionally both an evil sorceress and a beautiful temptress.

7   LUTTRELL, C. A. "The *Gawain* Group: Cruxes, Etymologies, Interpretations—II." *Neophilologus,* 40 (October), 290-301.

Questions whether *swe3e* (1. 1796, *Gawain*) and *nay* (1. 1836) are strong preterites, interprets *barbe* (1. 2310) as "projection of the blade [of an ax]," and interprets *lauce, lause* (1. 526) as "loose." Emends *Lystily forlancyng, and lere of þe knot* (1. 1334) to *Lystily for laucyng & lere of þe knot,* interpreting *lere* as *lure* ("loss, destruction") and *laucyng* as "undoing"; translates this line as "deftly, for fear of undoing and destroying the knot." Glosses *swey* (1. 1796) as "fall down."

8   MOORMAN, CHARLES. "Myth and Mediaeval Literature: *Sir Gawain and the Green Knight.*" *Mediaeval Studies,* 18:158-172.

[Reprinted in Blanch (1966.4) and, in a revised version, in Moorman (1967.18). Castigates Zimmer (1948.8) and Speirs (1949.9) for focusing on the mythic underpinnings of *Gawain* and for neglecting it as an artistic work. Argues that the *rite de passage* ritual, wherein the innocent hero must undertake a journey in order to gain awareness of himself and of the values which should order his life, plays a significant role in *Gawain*— a testing of the chivalric ideals of Camelot.

9   RIGBY, MARJORY. "The Green Knight Shoeless Again." *Review of English Studies,* New Series 7

(April), 173-174.

Employs passages from Chrétien de Troyes's *Erec et Enide* and from *Athis et Prophilias* to substantiate Cecily Clark's interpretation (1955.1) of *scholes* (1. 160) as "shoeless."

10   SAVAGE, HENRY LYTTLETON. *The Gawain-Poet: Studies in His Personality and Background.* Chapel Hill: University of North Carolina Press, 254 pp.

[Chap. 2 is a reprint, with some revision, of 1928.6.] Discusses the Cotton Nero MS—its contents, date, dialect, and locality—and suggests that it is likely that the *Gawain*-poet composed *Erkenwald.* Offers conjectural information on the identity of the poet's patron—perhaps John of Gaunt or his brother-in-law, Enguerrand de Coucy—and the poet's familiarity with aristocratic life and learning. Comments on the poet's use of water and hunting imagery, legal terms, artistic style, and metrics. Examines medieval hunting and heraldic treatises in his analysis of the three hunts and temptations in *Gawain.*

Hypothesizes that the *Gawain*-poet's depiction of the hero is patterned after the adventures of de Coucy, a French Knight of the Garter who deserted his English wife, Princess Isabella, and repudiated his oath (Garter). Discusses the poet's place of origin (Lancashire); the date of *Gawain* (1376-1380); de Coucy and the Order of the Garter; and the meaning of the word *ver* (1. 866), derived from *vair*—"that arrangement of small shields or bells alternately argent and azure (white and blue)" (p. 180). In an extended analysis (Appendix E, pp. 158-68) of the pentangle, describes the association of this symbol with Pythagorean rites, Solomon, astrological and magical practices of the Neoplatonist and Alexandrian schools, and Freemasonry. "Within the five points of the Pentangle we find sometimes written the five letters SALUS ["Completeness or Soundness"], one at each point" (p. 159). Identifies the pentangle, moreover, with the five wounds of Christ, the five joys of Mary, the star followed by the Magi, completion and unity, and a source of protection against the ensnarement of evil powers. Conjectures that the *Gawain*-poet may have employed the pentangle to honor the complete Knight, Enguerrand de Coucy.

11   SCHLAUCH, MARGARET. *English Medieval Literature and Its Social Foundations.* Warsaw: Państwowe

Wydawnictwo Naukowe, pp. 218-221.

[Also discusses *Pearl, Patience,* and *Purity.*] Praises *Gawain* for its masterful use of "polychromatic vocabulary," skillful alliterative verse, and the "tail-rhyme" stanza. Comments upon Gawain's two tests—the Beheading Game and the Chastity Test. Notes, moreover, that *Fled Bricrend (The Feast of Bricriu)*, a possible source for the Beheading Game motif, is rooted in a nature myth involving yearly death and renewal—associations which are evoked, perhaps, by the Green Knight's color, holly sprig, and decapitation. Concludes by noting the *Gawain*-poet's graphic depiction of nature.

12   SHIELDS, ELLIS GALE. "Rhetoric and the *Gawain* Poet." Ph.D. dissertation, University of Southern California.

[*See Abstracts of Dissertations, University of Southern California* (1956), pp. 35-37.] Attempts to demonstrate the *Gawain*-poet's indebtedness to Latin and Germanic rhetorical traditions, especially Cicero's *Rhetorica ad Herennium.*

13   ZIMMER, HEINRICH. *The King and the Corpse: Tales of the Soul's Conquest of Evil.* Edited by Joseph Campbell. Second edition. Bollingen Series, Vol. 11. New York: Pantheon Books, 67-95.

[*See also* 1948.8. Reprinted (in part) in Fox (1968.6). Essay remains essentially the same, but an index is now included in the book.]

1957

1   ACKERMAN, ROBERT W. " 'Pared out of Paper': *Gawain* 802 and *Purity* 1408." *Journal of English and Germanic Philology,* 56 (July), 410-417.

Suggests that the description of Bercilak's castle in *Gawain* and of the platters of food at Belshazzar's feast in *Purity* are reflected in a painted paper castle leaning on a dish of food (Chaucer's *Parson's Tale*), a courtly table decoration employed in the fourteenth century.

2   BAKER, ERNEST A. *The History of the English Novel: From the Beginnings to the Renaissance.* Vol. 1.

New York: Barnes and Noble, 152-153, 172, 311.
[Reprint of 1924.1.]

3   CONLEY, JOHN. "The Meaning of 'Fare' in *Sir Gawain and the Green Knight* 694." *Notes and Queries,* New Series, 4 (January), 2.
Interprets *fare* as "going, way."

4   BURROW, J. A. "The Audience of *Piers Plowman.*" *Anglia,* 75, no. 4:373-374, 378, 384.
Contends that the "alliterative revival" of the fourteenth century was restricted, for the most part, to the West and Northwest of England. Conjectures that *Gawain* was composed in a "baronial court" of the area.

5   ENKVIST, NILS ERIK. *The Seasons of the Year: Chapters on a Motif from Beowulf to the Shepherd's Calendar.* Societas Scientiarum Fennica, Commentationes Humanarum Litterarum, Vol. 22, no. 4. Helsinki: Finska Vetenskaps-Societeten, 85-87, 134.
Praises the *Gawain*-poet's depiction of the turning of the seasons, an artistic fusion of traditional rhetorical formulae and dynamic language emphasizing conflict. Inteprets *Colde clenge3 adoun* (1. 505) as a technical allusion: "the frost draws itself deeper into the ground and away from the surface" (p. 86). Views the realistic winter landscape as linked with Gawain's emotional bleakness at the start of his journey to meet the Green Knight.

6   FRYE, NORTHROP. *Anatomy of Criticism: Four Essays.* Princeton: Princeton University Press, pp. 196-197, 199-200.
Examines nature spirits in the romance mode—those who represent "partly the moral neutrality of the intermediate world of nature and partly a world of mystery which is glimpsed but never seen, and which retreats when approached" (p. 196); views a green man—the Green Knight of *Gawain*—as one of these nature figures. Contends that the life cycle of the romance hero includes an age of youthful innocence, usually set in an Edenic atmosphere; the traditional colors of this romance paradise are green and gold, emblems of "vanishing youth" (p. 200).

7   IKEGAMI, TADAHIRO. "Gawain and the Arthurian
     Legend," *Eibungaku* (Keio University Centennial
     Essays, Department of Literature). Tokyo: Keio Uni-
     versity, pp. 143-170.
     [In Japanese. English summary on p. 171.] Traces the
     history and progress of the figure of Gawain in Arthurian
     legends and romances. Emphasizes *Sir Gawain*, an artistic
     creation which depicts the hero as the flower of courteous
     speech and deeds.

8   LONG, CLARENCE EDWARD. "Shapeshifting and As-
     sociated Phenomena as Conventions of the Middle
     English Metrical Romances." Ph.D. dissertation, Uni-
     versity of New Mexico.
     [Partly on *Gawain*. See *Dissertation Abstracts*, 17 (1957),
     2260.] Analyzes the motif of shapeshifting (origins and sym-
     bolism) in *Gawain* and views this poem as a fusion of Christian
     exemplum and preternatural episode.

9   LOOMIS, LAURA HIBBARD. "Foreword" to *Gawain*,
     in *Medieval Romances*. Edited by Roger Sherman
     Loomis and Laura Hibbard Loomis. New York:
     Modern Library, pp. 324-328.
     [This book reprints the Ridley translation (1944.3, 1950)
     of *Gawain*.] Discusses the *Gawain*-poet's zestful depiction of
     courtly life as well as his realistic evocation of winter's chilling
     blasts and contrasts the warmth and exuberance of indoor life
     with the coldness and isolation of nature. Examines the fusion
     of three motifs in *Gawain*—the "beheading game," springing
     ultimately from *Bricriu's Feast;* the temptations; and the "ex-
     change of winnings." Claims that the theme of *Gawain* is
     rooted in "a failure, even in the best of knights, to keep a per-
     fect integrity" (p. 327).

10   MARKMAN, ALAN M. "The Meaning of *Sir Gawain and
     the Green Knight.*" *Publications of the Modern
     Language Association of America,* 72 (September),
     574-586.
     [Reprinted in Blanch (1966.4).] Perceives *Gawain* as a
     romance, a genre which fuses the realistic and the marvelous
     and focuses upon the moral test of a real human being. Argues
     that Gawain represents both the perfect chivalric knight and a

fine man and that his primary test involves loyalty.

11   RANDALL, DALE B. J. "A Note on Structure in *Sir Gawain and the Green Knight.*" *Modern Language Notes,* 72 (March), 161-163.

Offers a "schematic outline" of the poem's structure and contends that the initial elements—fall of Troy, Felix Brutus, and Camelot—are echoed in inverted order at the end of *Gawain.* Analyzes the two journeys of Gawain and the division of each hunting tableau into two sections, sections which are interrupted by the inclusion of the temptation scenes at Bercilak's castle.

12   SPEIRS, JOHN. *Medieval English Poetry: The Non-Chaucerian Tradition.* London: Faber, pp. 215-251.

[Reprint (with only minor revisions) of 1949.9.]

13   WALDRON, RONALD A. "Oral-Formulaic Technique and Middle English Alliterative Poetry." *Speculum,* 32 (October), 792-804.

Applies the oral-formulaic theory of Old English poetry to *Gawain* and other fourteenth-century unrhymed alliterative poems (*Patience, Purity,* etc.). Perceives a continuous tradition of alliterative verse between the eleventh and the fourteenth centuries in England and finds that the alliterative style is basically oral in nature. Contends that the poems analyzed employ "a common diction" pointing to "the use of formulaic phrases fulfilling metrical, rather than stylistic or aesthetic, requirements" (p. 794).

1958

1   ACKERMAN, ROBERT W. "Gawain's Shield: Penitential Doctrine in *Gawain and the Green Knight.*" *Anglia,* 76, no. 2:254-265.

Traces the importance of penitential doctrine, as found in numerous vernacular works, as a possible source for the passage on the pentangle (11. 619-65); links the "five wits" with confession. Argues that the girdle is an emblem of Gawain's departure from the virtues of the pentangle.

2   BRUCE, JAMES DOUGLAS. *The Evolution of Arthur-
     ian Romance: From the Beginnings Down to the
     Year 1300.* Vol. 1. Gloucester, Massachusetts: Peter
     Smith, 125-126.
     [Reprint of 1928.1.]

3   EBBS, JOHN DALE. "Stylistic Mannerisms of the *Ga-
     wain*-Poet." *Journal of English and Germanic Phil-
     ology,* 57 (July), 522-525.
         Offers additional stylistic evidence for the common au-
     thorship of the Cotton Nero poems: the employment of a
     framing technique involving identical diction at the beginning
     and conclusion of *Gawain, Patience,* and *Pearl;* the representa-
     tion of an oral narrative device in *Gawain, Patience,* and
     Purity; and "the poet's habit . . . of often expressing his in-
     ability to describe some feature or detail [*Gawain,* 11. 165-66,
     718-19, 1007-08], or to give a satisfactory count [*Gawain,*
     11. 58-59] of a large group of people" (p. 524).

4   ELLIOTT, RALPH W. V. "Sir Gawain in Staffordshire:
     A Detective Essay in Literary Geography." *London
     Times* (21 May), p. 12.
         [Reprinted in Fox (1968.6).] Attempts to localize Berci-
     lak's castle and finds links between the terrain near the castle,
     situated *on a lawe,* in *Gawain* and Swythamley Park in the
     wilds of North Staffordshire. Identifies Ludchurch, set in the
     area of the Castle Cliff Rocks, with the Green Chapel.

5   GOLDHURST, WILLIAM. "The Green and the Gold:
     The Major Theme of *Gawain and the Green Knight.*"
     College English, 20 (November), 61-65.
         Views the major theme underlying *Gawain* as the concept
     that the elemental powers of nature are revealed to all men,
     including those who protect themselves with the thin insula-
     tion of chivalric life. "It [*Gawain*] tells us of man's struggle
     against tendencies which would draw him back to the state of
     nature, and of his uncertain efforts to maintain a hold on the
     comforts and codes of civilization" (p. 64). Interprets the
     poet's juxtaposition of green and gold as a symbolic represen-
     tation of an untamed natural force (green) and the urbane life
     of the court or civilization (gold).

6   GRAY, D. *"Sir Gawain and the Green Knight."* Notes
      and Queries, New Series, 5 (November), 487-488.

      Contends that *more* should be emended to *innore* in *In*
      þe more half of his schelde hir ymage depaynted (1. 649).

7   GUIDI, AUGUSTO, ed. "Introduction" to *Galvano e il*
      Cavaliere Verde. Translated by Augusto Guidi.
      Firenze: Casa Editrice Sansoni, pp. 9-17.

      [In Italian. Contains Italian prose translation and Middle
      English text of *Gawain* plus textual notes.] Discusses the
      poet's use of alliterative verse; the significance of the three
      temptations and hunts; the symbolism of green and of the
      pentangle; courtly and Christian elements; and the structure of
      Gawain.

8   HENDERSON, HAMISH. "The Green Man of Knowl-
      edge." *Scottish Studies,* 2, no. 1:47-85.

      Examines "The Green Man of Knowledge"—folktale
      number 313 in the Aarne-Thompson classification—and its
      possible links with *Gawain.* Suggests parallels between the
      "beheading game" (probably derived from *Fled Bricrend*) in
      Gawain and the game of skittles in *Green Man* as well as ties
      between the "temptation" in *Gawain* and the "Tasks" inci-
      dent in *Green Man;* similarly, the green girdle in *Gawain* is
      identified with the green scarf in folktale no. 313. Theorizes
      that this folktale type springs from some English folk version—
      one of the sources of *Gawain*—and discusses the symbolic
      thread tying *Gawain* and folktale no. 313 with the green man
      depicted in fertility ritual.

9   MUSKER, FRANCIS. *"Sir Gawain and the Green*
      Knight," in *Papers of the Manchester Literary Club*
      (1955-1957), Vol. 70. Manchester, England: H. Raw-
      son and Company, pp. 7-19.

      Provides a general survey of *Gawain* and its background,
      including the sources, the dialect (South Lancashire or West
      Cheshire), the authorship problems, the character of Gawain,
      and the geographical milieu of the poem. Praises the *Gawain*-
      poet for his imaginative descriptions of nature (the passing of
      the seasons and the hunt scenes) as well as for his Christian
      spirit which pervades, often in symbolic terms, his narrative.

10   RENOIR, ALAIN. "Descriptive Technique in *Sir Gawain and the Green Knight.*" *Orbis Litterarum,* 13, nos. 3-4:126-132.

Contends that the poet's descriptive method—the pulling of "a single detail out of a uniformly illuminated scene which is then allowed to fade out in obscurity and of which we may be given an occasional dim glimpse at psychologically appropriate moments" (p. 127)—is analogous to the spatial techniques used in modern cinematography. Analyzes the poet's cinematic techniques in his depiction of the beheading of the Green Knight, particularly the arc-like movement of the ax, and in his presentation of movement and space in the boar hunt scene.

1959

*1   BENSON, LARRY D. "The Art and Meaning of *Sir Gawain and the Green Knight.*" Ph.D. dissertation, University of California (Berkeley).

[Cited in *Bulletin bibliographique de la Société internationale Arthurienne,* 12 (1960). *See also* 1965.1.]

2   BERRY, FRANCIS. "*Sir Gawayne and the Grene Knight,*" in *The Age of Chaucer.* The Pelican Guide to English Literature, Vol. 1, edited by Boris Ford. Baltimore: Penguin, 148-158.

[This book also contains the Berry edition (pp. 351-430) of *Gawain.*] Calls attention to the "muscular images and rhythms . . . the firm grasp of concrete particulars" (p. 149) in *Gawain* as well as the conflict between the urbane and primitive. Emphasizes the seasonal rhythm in the poem and the creative energy of the Green Knight.

3   BURROW, JOHN. "The Two Confession Scenes in *Sir Gawain and the Green Knight.*" *Modern Philology,* 57 (November), 73-79.

[Reprinted in Blanch (1966.4).] Discusses Gawain's "fault" and the importance of the penance theme, especially in Gawain's confession to the priest (11. 1876-84). Claims that Gawain's confession is invalid and that this confession scene anticipates a second "valid" confession at the Green

Chapel, for Gawain as penitent reveals there his faults to the Green Knight as lay confessor.

4   D'ARDENNE, S. R. T. O. " 'The Green Count' and *Sir Gawain and the Green Knight.*" *Review of English Studies,* New Series 10 (May), 113-126.

Claims that the model for the Green Knight in *Gawain* may be Amadeus VI, Count of Savoy (1334-83)—a man who was called the Green Count (*Il Conte Verde*) and was noted for "his magnificence, his rich hospitality, his gallant deeds, and the splendor of his garments" (p. 113). In order to buttress his claim, notes that Amadeus's niece married Lionel, the first duke of Clarence (see *Gawain*, 1. 552) and that Amadeus established (1364) the Order of the Collar, an order whose characteristic costume includes a collar of green and gold enamel, knots (Savoy knots), and the image of the Virgin Mary (*Gawain*, 11. 646-647).

5   EVANS, WILLIAM W., JR. "The Second-Person Pronoun in *Sir Gawain and the Green Knight.*" Ph.D. dissertation, University of Florida (Gainesville).

[*See Dissertation Abstracts*, 24 (1964), 4184.] Focuses on the poet's use of *thou*, the normal pronoun employed in addressing inferiors, and *you*—the normal pronoun of address to superiors. Claims that the *Gawain*-poet occasionally departs from contemporary social customs by using *thou* dramatically.

6   GUIDI, AUGUSTO. "Un brano del 'Galvano' inglese," in *Studi in Onore di Angelo Monteverdi.* Vol. 1. Modena: Società Tipografica Editrice Modenese, 313-317.

[In Italian. Contains a modernized version of 11. 498-535 of *Gawain* and a translation (Italian) of these lines.] Comments briefly upon the poet's artistic use of language and courtly traditions as well as upon the major editions of *Gawain*.

7   HABICHT, WERNER. *Die Gebärde in englischen Dichtungen des Mittelalters.* Verlag der bayerischen Akademie der Wissenschaften, N. F., no. 46. Munich: C. H. Beck, pp. 11, 31, 60-61, 83, 86, 93, 98, 105-107, 124-125, 132, 148-157, 159.

[In German. Contains discussion of the other Cotton Nero poems. Examines the origin and nature of gestures (emotional, theatrical gestures which characterize the hero, and ceremonial—oaths, greetings, etc.) as they appear in medieval narrative poetry.] Contends that gestures in *Gawain* are artistically linked with characterization (Gawain) and with the plot, increase the sense of dramatic movement, and add force to the dialogue.

Examines the significance of gestures in the beheading scene and the poet's use of the bob and wheel, a device which may convey information. Argues that the poet's employment of description in some passages is analogous to the artistic techniques used by Giotto.

8   HAWORTH, MARY. "Barlay—*Sir Gawain and the Green Knight* (line 296)." *Notes and Queries,* New Series, 6 (March), 104.

Claims that the word "barlay," the signal made by the winner of the children's game "Creep Mouse," represents "a shout of triumph, and also a claim—'My Turn now!' " in *Gawain.*

9   KREUZER, JAMES R. "Introduction," in his edition of *Sir Gawain and the Green Knight.* Translated by James L. Rosenberg. New York: Rinehart, pp. vii-lxxi.

Discusses humorous elements in and the analogues and sources of *Gawain,* especially the beheading game and temptation motifs. Includes a running commentary on each stanza of *Gawain;* an evaluation of the plot, theme, characters, and ironic overtones; an examination of *Gawain*'s literary milieu; an explanation of the origins and development of romance; and a discussion of courtly love.

10   LEWIS, JOHN S. *"Gawain and the Green Knight." College English,* 21 (October), 50-51.

Views the main colors attributed to the Green Knight—green and gold—as emblematic of vanishing youth and as a reminder to Camelot that their joy and vitality are ephemeral.

11   LOOMIS, LAURA HIBBARD. *"Gawain and the Green Knight,"* in *Arthurian Literature in the Middle Ages:*

A Collaborative History. Edited by Roger Sherman Loomis. Oxford: Clarendon Press, pp. 528-540.

[Reprinted in Howard and Zacher (1968.8); Newstead (1968.20); and L. H. Loomis (1962.11). The footnotes for this essay provide a helpful bibliography of select editions, translations, and scholarly studies of *Gawain*.] Discusses briefly the Cotton Nero MS—its works, scribal hand, date, dialect, and illustrations—as well as the authorship problem and the poet's use of alliterative verse. Examines in detail, moreover, the various analogues and sources of the challenge/ beheading game, temptation, and exchange of winnings motifs.

Concludes with a discussion of the artistry of *Gawain*—its depiction of courtly life; its allusions to genres (lay and interlude); its portrayal of cold wintry terrains; its representation of the Knight's play-acting; its skillful use of parallelism and contrast (Camelot vs. Hautdesert, the three hunts and temptations, indoor festivities vs. harsh outdoor realities); and its spiritual tone and meaning.

12   McKISACK, MAY. *The Fourteenth Century: 1307- 1399.* The Oxford History of England, Vol. 5. Oxford: Clarendon Press, 525-526.

Suggests that most of the poetry of the "fourteenth-century revival," written in unrhymed alliterative lines, springs from the North Midland and the Northwestern provinces; such poetry is heard, perhaps, by the knightly and noble households located in those geographical areas. Contends that the Cotton Nero poems, probably composed by one author, bear the imprint of France and that *Gawain,* in particular, includes vocabulary rooted in Scandinavian sources.

13   MUSTANOJA, TAUNO F. "The Middle English Syntactical Type *His own hand(s)* 'with his own hands, himself'." *Neuphilologische Mitteilungen,* 60 (September), 271, 274, 280.

Notes the use of the Old English "synthetic instrumental dative" in connection with "naming," such as *nevenes hit his aune nome* (*Gawain,* 1. 10). Interprets *cors* (*Gawain,* 1. 1236) as meaning both "body" and "person."

14   RENOIR, ALAIN. "Gawain and Parzival." *Studia Neophilologica,* 31, no. 2:155-158.

Notes a parallel between the description of the winter landscape (11. 740-62) as Gawain journeys towards Hautdesert and the depiction of Parzival's travels in Book IX of Wolfram von Eschenbach's *Parzival.*

15   SCHNYDER, HANS. "Aspects of Kingship in *Sir Gawain and the Green Knight.*" *English Studies,* 40 (August), 289-294.

Examines the socio-political implications of *Gawain,* particularly the role of Gawain as one of Arthur's knights. Focuses in detail on Arthur's qualities—his restlessness, youthful zest for life, immaturity, and pride. Contends that Arthur's "boyish" nature (*childgered*) serves as a role model for his boastful knights and that his pride, the medieval version of *superbia,* precipitates his jeopardizing of Gawain's life as well as his own potential fall on Fortune's wheel. Links two emblems of pride, Belshazzar's feast in *Purity* and Arthur's Yuletide banquet in *Gawain.*

16   STONE, BRIAN. "Sir Gawain." *The Spectator* (London), 6848 (25 September), p. 411.

Justifies his translation, ". . . the brave knight, embarrassed,/Lay flat with fine adroitness . . . ," when Gawain lies cowering in bed and spots Bercilak's wife as she latches the door (first temptation). Affirms that his translation of lines 1842-45 capture the spirit of *amour courtois* permeating the original text.

17   STONE, BRIAN, trans. *Sir Gawain and the Green Knight.* Baltimore: Penguin, 144 pp.

[Reprinted (with some corrections): 1964.17; *see also* 1974.28. Contains an Introduction (pp. 7-15) and nine Appendices (pp. 127-44).]

"Introduction": Discusses language, courtly elements, sources, hunts and temptations, and characterization (Bercilak/Green Knight) as well as the Christian foundations of *Gawain.*

"Appendices": Focuses on the manuscript (writing, dialect, and illustrations); authorship theories; the history and progress of Gawain in Arthurian narratives; the traditional depiction of Arthur; the legendary origins of Camelot; and the origin, nature, and significance of both Merlin and Morgan le

Fay. Discusses the origin and meaning of the pentangle, perhaps the most crucial magical emblem: "The Pythagoreans used it [pentangle], probably because five is the perfect number, being the marriage of the first masculine number, three, with the first feminine number, two (unity not being a true number)" (p. 135). Suggests that the pentangle plays a role in Tarot symbolism and in Freemasonry, was termed "The Druid's Foot" in folk ritual, and takes the form of the Star of David in late Jewish tradition.

1960

1   FRIEDMAN, ALBERT B. "Morgan le Fay in *Sir Gawain and the Green Knight.*" *Speculum,* 35 (April), 260-274.

[Reprinted in Blanch (1966.4).] Rejects Baughan's contention (1950.2)) that chastity is an integral theme of *Gawain* while noting that the lady's girdle may represent an amulet as well as a "sexual trophy." Claims that Morgan le Fay is not the precipitator of the whole plot of *Gawain,* but rather more of a *dea ex machina.*

2   IKEGAMI, TADAHIRO. "The Green Knight and the Beheading Game." *Geibun-kenkyu (Journal of Art and Letters,* Keio University), No. 11:1-14.

[In Japanese. Annotation provided by the author.] Employs the source studies of Kittredge and Loomis in order to explain the characteristics of the Green Knight and the "beheading game" motif.

3   JONES, R. T., ed. "Introduction" to his *Sir Gawain and the Grene Gome: A Regularized Text.* Pietermaritzburg: Natal University Press, pp. 1-6.

[*See also* 1972.13. Reflects the interpretation of *Gawain* by Speirs (1949.9 and 1957.12).] Suggests that the challenger in *Gawain* is linked with "the vegetation god whose annual death and resurrection are manifest in the annual decline and upsurge of green life; the god who is still impersonated by Jack-in-the-Green in village festivals" (p. 3). Claims that the Christian and chivalric ethos of Camelot is tested by nature—a "green man" who lives "in an incompletely Christianized court in the North of England" (p. 3).

4 KITTREDGE, GEORGE LYMAN. *A Study of Gawain and the Green Knight.* Gloucester, Massachusetts: Peter Smith, 331 pp.
[Reprint of 1916.4.]

5 MATTHEWS, WILLIAM. *The Tragedy of Arthur: A Study of the Alliterative Morte Arthure.* Berkeley: University of California Press, pp. 33, 144, 156-157, 160-163, 169-170, 178, 208-209.

Views the hero of *Gawain* as a "Christlike figure" (p. 162) although he displays the weakness of the flesh. Perceives Arthur as arrogant, immature, and devoid of good judgment in the Challenge scene.

6 MOODY, PHILIPPA. "The Problems of Medieval Criticism." *Melbourne Critical Review,* No. 3:94-103.

Contends that many modern interpretations of *Gawain* ignore its creative vision and vitality or distort its values. Discusses the passage depicting the Green Knight's sudden appearance at Camelot and suggests that the Knight is more intensely real (physically) than the extravagant romance world of Arthur's court. "The drama in this passage . . . is enacted through contrasting images—the court contrasted with the knight; the juxtaposition of the colouring [the Knight's greenness] and the realistic detail—so that ordinary ideas of reality are exploded or expanded" (p. 101). Emphasizes the description of the turning seasons as an intimation of the alternation between "bliss" and "blunder" in *Gawain.*

7 MORTON, A. L. "The Matter of Britain: The Arthurian Cycle and the Development of Feudal Society." *Zeitschrift für Anglistik und Amerikanistik,* 8 (January), 6, 17-18.

Traces the transformation of the figure of Arthur into the energizing force underlying numerous romances and legends; such an influential force is ordinarily linked with the efflorescence and ultimate death of feudal society. Claims that Gawain—at least by the close of the thirteenth century— is usually portrayed as a corrupt knight; yet, strangely enough, *Sir Gawain and the Green Knight* delineates Gawain as the exemplar of knighthood.

8   OPPEL, INGEBORG. "The Endless Knot: An Interpretation of *Sir Gawain and the Green Knight* through Its Myth." Ph.D. dissertation, University of Washington.
[*See Dissertation Abstracts*, 21 (1961), 3092-93.] Offers various caveats to be observed in interpreting medieval poetry through myth. Examines a number of myth motifs—"beheading game," pentangle, journey, chase, green chapel, and green girdle—in her "mythic" analysis of *Gawain*. Suggests that irony and humor are employed in *Gawain*, a Yuletide poem, in order to poke fun at human weakness and to disclose Gawain's humanity.

*9   PAGANONI, MATILDE. *"Sir Gawayn and the Green Knight."* Ph.D. dissertation, Università del Sacro Cuore, Facoltà di Magistero, Milan.
[Citation provided by Professor Carl Berkhout.]

10   PATON, LUCY ALLEN. *Studies in the Fairy Mythology of Arthurian Romance.* Second Edition. New York: Burt Franklin, pp. 133, 136.
[Revised edition of 1903.3. Contains a "Survey of Scholarship on the Fairy Mythology since 1903" (pp. 280-304) and a "Bibliography" (pp. 305-307) by Roger Sherman Loomis.]

11   RANDALL, DALE B. J. "Was the Green Knight a Fiend?" *Studies in Philology,* 57 (July), 479-491.
Examines the various symbolic meanings attributed to green in the Middle Ages—death, life, fairyland, Otherworld, and the color of the devil as hunter of human souls. Contends that the Green Knight is a devil-hunter and that *Gawain* may represent the testing of a Christian knight by a hellish fiend.

12   RENOIR, ALAIN. "A Minor Analogue of *Sir Gawain and the Green Knight.*" *Neophilologus,* 44 (January), 37-38.
Claims that the twelfth-century work, *Miles Gloriosus,* may represent an analogue for the Hautdesert events in *Gawain.*

13   RENOIR, ALAIN. "The Progressive Magnification: An Instance of Psychological Description in *Sir Gawain*

and the Green Knight." Moderna Språk, 54, no. 3:245-253.

Suggests that as Gawain becomes more fearful of his imminent death at the Green Chapel, spatial elements—especially the magnification (height and depth) of the physical setting in proportion to the dwarfing of Gawain—play a significant role. Contends that the poet's visual description, particularly his depiction of the Green Knight standing on a high hill above Gawain, emphasizes Gawain's feelings of impotence and insignificance.

14   UTLEY, FRANCIS LEE. "Folklore, Myth, and Ritual," in *Critical Approaches to Medieval Literature: Selected Papers from the English Institute, 1958-1959.* Edited by Dorothy Bethurum. New York: Columbia University Press, pp. 86-92.

Reviews the various "mythic" interpretations of *Gawain* and adds a corrective to the "anthropological" theories of Speirs (1949.9 and 1957.12) and to Jungian criticism of *Gawain.* Claims that "the irrationality of *Gawain* is violence, the disruption of courtly and individual order, rather than fertility ritual" (p. 88). Interprets the three hunts in *Gawain* as suggestive of "the noble tastes of the audience" (p. 90).

1961

1   BARBER, R. W. *Arthur of Albion: An Introduction to the Arthurian Literature and Legends of England.* London: Barrie and Rockliff with Pall Mall Press, pp. 71, 85, 95-107, 111, 119, 121.

[Reprinted: 1971.2; 1973.1.] Claims that *Gawain,* perhaps composed between 1370 and 1390, is a masterpiece of Middle English Arthurian literature and the high point of English alliterative poetry. Traces the two Celtic motifs underlying *Gawain*—the Beheading Game, perhaps rooted in the Irish work *Fled Bricrend;* and the Temptation story, paralleled somewhat in *Pwyll,* an episode in the Welsh *Mabinogi.* Praises the *Gawain*-poet's description of nature, especially the passage on the turning of the seasons and the graphic portrayal of winter's fury. Views the theme of *Gawain* and of *Parzival* as the quest for perfection.

2   BENSON, LARRY D. "The Source of the Beheading
      Episode in *Sir Gawain and the Green Knight.*" *Mod-
      ern Philology,* 59 (August), 1-12.

         Examines the three versions (long prose, long metrical,
      and short metrical) of the beheading story in *Le Livre de
      Caradoc,* part of the first continuation of the *Perceval,* and
      perceives clear parallels (return blow, outcome of the Be-
      heading Game) between *Gawain* and *Caradoc.* Claims that
      the Irish features of *Gawain,* including the Green Knight's
      red eyes, bear the imprint of poetic invention, that *Caradoc*
      and *Gawain* do not spring from a common source, and that
      the beheading motif in *Gawain* is ultimately rooted in a long
      prose version of *Caradoc.*

3   BLOOMFIELD, MORTON W. "*Sir Gawain and the
      Green Knight*: An Appraisal." *Publications of the
      Modern Language Association of America,* 76
      (March), 7-19.

         [Reprinted in Howard and Zacher (1968.8) and in Bloom-
      field (1970.2).] Evaluates the significant *Gawain* scholarship
      published between 1883 and 1959 and offers *desiderata* for
      future studies of Gawain; such *desiderata* include philological
      analyses, studies of the social and historical background of
      Gawain, investigation of the fourteenth-century outlook upon
      style, rhetoric, and poetic theory, elucidation of the poem's
      Christian and moral elements, attention to *Gawain* as comedy,
      and studies of the poem's structure and of the romance genre.

4   BRUNNER, KARL. "Middle English Metrical Romances
      and Their Audience," in *Studies in Medieval Litera-
      ture in Honor of Professor Albert Croll Baugh.* Edit-
      ed by MacEdward Leach. Philadelphia: University of
      Pennsylvania Press, p. 226.

         Conjectures that *Gawain* and the other Cotton Nero
      poems were linked with an upper class family (northwest
      England), "and the poet may have had such a person as his
      patron," especially since "The MS. was in the possession of
      Henry Saville (1568-1617) of Banke in Yorkshire."

5   ELLIOTT, RALPH W. V. "Landscape and Rhetoric in
      Middle-English Alliterative Poetry." *Melbourne Criti-
      cal Review,* 4:67, 69, 71-76.

Discusses the *Gawain*-poet's indebtedness to Matthew of Vendôme's rhetorical principles of *descriptio,* especially the functional use of landscape depictions for evoking the mood and theme of the poem. Views landscapes (Wirral, Hautdesert, and the Green Chapel) and seasonal descriptions (winter) as indispensable parts of *Gawain* and as emblems of Gawain's testing. Notes the employment of "topographical" diction in *Gawain* in order to particularize the setting, especially because traditional rhetorical devices and the conventions of the *Roman de la Rose* did not allow the *Gawain*-poet to articulate the vision he experienced.

6   FISHER, JOHN H. "Wyclif, Langland, Gower, and the *Pearl* Poet on the Subject of Aristocracy," in *Studies in Medieval Literature in Honor of Professor Albert Croll Baugh.* Edited by MacEdward Leach. Philadelphia: University of Pennsylvania Press, pp. 140, 150-152.

[Also discusses *Pearl.*] Claims that the *Pearl*-poet "removed from the city and unconcerned with its social developments, continued to maintain a mystical conception of hierarchy that was at the same time equality." Notes that the *Pearl*-poet, "a writer with predominantly theological interests . . . wrote about and for the aristocracy." While the poet may not criticize the aristocratic system, the depiction of Arthur in *Gawain* may represent an oblique reflection on the nature of kingship, especially the concept of childishness (11. 86-89 of *Gawain*).

7   FRANKIS, P. J. *"Sir Gawain and the Green Knight,* line 35: *With lel letteres loken." Notes and Queries,* New Series, 8 (September), 329-330.

Claims that *With lel letteres loken* does not represent an allusion to alliterative verse composition, but rather "embodied in truthful words."

8   HALSTEAD, W. L. "Artifice in *Sir Gawain,*" in *A Chaucerian Puzzle and Other Medieval Essays.* Edited by Natalie Grimes Lawrence and Jack A. Reynolds. University of Miami Publications in English and American Literature, No. 5. Coral Gables: University of Miami Press, pp. 63-70.

Emphasizes *Gawain* as a fine illustration of literary artistry; the native alliterative verse would appeal to traditionalists, and the "bob and wheel" would delight those entranced by the sounds of French courtly poetry.

9   JAMES, BRIDGET. *"Pernyng* in *Sir Gawain and the Green Knight,* line 611." *Notes and Queries,* New Series, 8 (January), 9.

Contends that *pernyng,* associated with the dialect *pirn* ("reel, bobbin"), connotes "flitting."

10   KITELEY, J. F.   "The *De Arte Honeste Amandi* of Andreas Capellanus and the Concept of Courtesy in *Sir Gawain and the Green Knight." Anglia,* 79, no. 1:7-16.

Discusses the connection between the conduct recommended in *De Arte* and the conduct of Bercilak's wife. Perceives the temptation scenes in *Gawain* as a reversal of the courtly love tradition, for Bercilak's wife assumes the role of the aggressive male lover rather than that of the beloved lady. Identifies the Lady's particular brand of courtesy with the courtliness of *amour courtois*—a conception which is repudiated by the *Gawain*-poet—and associates Gawain with Christian courtesy.

11   LEIBLE, ARTHUR BRAY.   "The Character of Gawain in English Literature." Ph.D. dissertation, University of Missouri (Columbia).

[Partly on *Gawain. See Dissertation Abstracts,* 22 (1962), 3648.] Notes the link between Gawain and Celtic solar gods. Emphasizes that the hero of Gawain is the traditional Gawain —the exemplar of courtesy, nobility, and chastity—probably because *amour courtois* exerted little influence upon Middle English literature.

*12   LUTTRELL, C. A.   "The Scandinavian Element in Some North-West Midland Alliterative Poems." Ph.D. dissertation, University College, Leicester (England).

[Cited in *Index to Theses Accepted for Higher Degrees in the Universities of Great Britain and Ireland.* Edited by P. D. Record. Vol. 11 (1960-61). London: ASLIB.]

*13   McALINDON, T. E. "The Treatment of the Supernatural in Middle English Legend and Romance, 1200-1400." Ph.D. dissertation, Cambridge University (Fitzwilliam House).
        [Cited in *Dissertations in English and American Literature: Theses Accepted by American, British and German Universities, 1865-1964*. Edited by Lawrence F. McNamee. New York: R. R. Bowker, 1968.]

14   McLAUGHLIN, JOHN C.   "A Graphemic-Phonemic Study of a Middle English Manuscript: MS. Cotton Nero A.x." Ph.D. dissertation, Indiana University.
        [*See also* 1963.10.]

15   SCHNYDER, HANS. *Sir Gawain and the Green Knight: An Essay in Interpretation.* Cooper Monographs on English and American Language and Literature, No. 6. Bern: A. Francke Verlag, 81 pp.
        Views *Gawain* "against the background of its own time and within the context of its genuine cultural climate" (p. 7), and interprets the poem totally as allegory. Such an allegorical reading is ultimately rooted in St. Augustine's doctrine of charity (*De Doctrina Christiana*). Perceives Gawain's quest to represent "that journey through inner realities which are symbolically mirrored in the elements of the outside world" (p. 36).
        Identifies the Green Knight with the Word of God, and anagogically, with Christ (p. 41). Notes that green ("in malo") is the color of the devil, but interprets the greenness of the Green Knight as "being spiritually alive in faith and hope and charity, being fertile in the production of good works" (p. 42). Concludes his allegorical study of *Gawain* with comments upon the green girdle: once Arthur and his court garb themselves in green, they recognize "the former corruption of their court through sinful pride" (p. 73).

16   STEVENS, JOHN. "The 'Game of Love'," in *Music and Poetry in the Early Tudor Court.* London: Methuen, pp. 154-202, passim.
        Examines love-talking and the exchange of New Year's gifts, perhaps a version of the game "Handy-Dandy," in *Gawain*.

17   ZESMER, DAVID M. "The Alliterative Revival," in his *Guide to English Literature from Beowulf through Chaucer and Medieval Drama.* College Outline Series, No. 53. New York: Barnes & Noble, pp. 154-162.

[This book also contains a select, albeit extensively annotated, bibliography (pp. 322-323, 332, 342-344) of editions, translations, and scholarly studies of *Gawain;* the bibliography was compiled by Stanley B. Greenfield.] Discusses the *Gawain* stanza; the fusion of the beheading game and temptation motifs in the poem; the parallels between the hunts and temptations; the pentangle; the characterization of Gawain and the Knight; and a survey of critical interpretations of the Green Knight (sun god, vegetation figure, death, devil).

1962

1   BORROFF, MARIE. *Sir Gawain and the Green Knight: A Stylistic and Metrical Study.* Yale Studies in English, Vol. 152. New Haven: Yale University Press, 307 pp.

[Revised version of Borroff (1956.3). Reprinted (in part) in Howard and Zacher (1968.8) and in Fox (1968.6).] Discusses various historical notions of style, the link between style and meaning in communication, and the role of style in poetry. Provides a detailed analysis of the style of *Gawain,* particularly the diction of this romance and the relationship between traditional vocabulary and the alliterative verse form. Examines ("The Criticism of Style"), moreover, the diction and attitudes of the narrator. Investigates the meter of *Gawain,* especially the normal and extended forms of the alliterative long line.

2   CARSON, MOTHER ANGELA. "Morgain la Fée as the Principle of Unity in *Gawain and the Green Knight.*" *Modern Language Quarterly,* 23 (March), 3-16.

Examines the pivotal role in *Gawain* of Morgan, a character who artistically links the Green Knight, Gawain's quest, Bercilak's castle, and the three temptations, and scrutinizes Morgan and the text of *Gawain* in the light of "the general tradition of myth and folklore known to the author and his audience" (p. 3). Perceives the ugly crone at Hautdesert and

Lady Bercilak as traditional aspects (enchantress and seductress) of Morgan's dual nature and views Bercilak as a type of
Urien, a character associated with Morgan in Otherworld tradition. Links Hautdesert with the Otherworld and explicates
Morgan's traditional antipathy toward Camelot.

3 CAWLEY, A. C. "Introduction," in his edition of *Pearl
   and Sir Gawain and the Green Knight.* Everyman's
   Library, No. 346. London: Dent, pp. ix-x, xvi-xxii.
   [Reprinted in Cawley and Anderson (1976.5). Contains
   a select bibliography of editions, translations, literary histories,
   and scholarly studies (mainly articles) of *Gawain.*] Traces
   briefly the main outlines of the Cotton manuscript—its works
   and dialect—as well as the authorship problem and *Gawain*'s
   role in and reasons for the "alliterative revival." Examines the
   beheading and temptation motifs; the employment of suspense and mystery in *Gawain;* the significance of triplicities;
   Gawain's humanity; the Green Knight's association with the
   natural world; the contrast between the civilized world of the
   court and the harshness of nature; *Gawain*'s diction, a blending
   of Anglo-Saxon and French traditions; and the thematic pattern underlying this poem—"the journey or quest, the test or
   purgation, and the spiritual renewal" (p. xxii).

4 DONALDSON, E. TALBOT. *"Sir Gawain and the Green
   Knight,"* in *The Norton Anthology of English Literature.* Edited by M. H. Abrams *et al.* Vol. 1. New
   York: Norton, 183-184.
   [Reprinted, in part, in Fox (1968.6). This essay appears
   (pp. 218-219) in the revised edition (1968) of *The Norton Anthology* and in all subsequent editions; Borroff's translation
   (1967.3) appears in the revised edition (1968) of the *Anthology* and in all subsequent editions.] Discusses the Chris-
   tianization in *Gawain* of the theme of the green man's beheading and the poem as a "comedy of manners" as well as a satire
   on the chivalric ideals and reputation of Arthur's court.
   Examines Gawain's predicament, his dangerous entanglement
   in situations which emasculate his two main virtues, courtesy
   and valor. Contends that the poem is infused with comic
   irony and that the green baldric represents "a reminder that
   what God asks of men is not primarily courtly or martial
   prowess, but a humble and a contrite heart" (p. 184).

5   GREEN, RICHARD HAMILTON. "Gawain's Shield and the Quest for Perfection." *Journal of English Literary History,* 29 (June), 121-139.

[Reprinted in Blanch (1966.4) and Vasta (1965.24).] Perceives Gawain, in part, as the knight *par excellence,* a true representative of chivalric and Christian values, and discerns a sharp vein of humor which undercuts *Gawain*'s noble theme and reduces the hero to somewhat human size. Focuses particularly upon the relationship between the poem's comic tone and "the ideal of secular perfection."

Discusses the significance of the pentangle on Gawain's shield as Solomon's sign of truth and a symbol (in *Gawain*) of both perfection and possible failure; the link between Gawain's fault and the weakness of Solomon who, although traditionally associated with perfection, forsakes God because of the temptations of women; and the significance of the number five and the pentangle as emblems of natural perfection, not supernatural perfection.

6   HENRY, P. L.   "A Celtic-English Prosodic Feature." *Zeitschrift für Celtische Philologie,* 29:91, 95, 97.

Claims that a feature of Celtic poetry (*dúnadh*)—the repetition of the same word, phrase, or line at the beginning and end of a poem—appears in *Gawain* and other works of the *Pearl*-poet. Contends that the *Pearl*-poet's familiarity with the topography of North Wales suggests the imprint of Welsh literature upon his works.

7   IKEGAMI, TADAHIRO. "The Temptation in *Sir Gawain and the Green Knight.*" *Geibun-kenkyu (Journal of Art and Letters,* Keio University), Nos. 14-15:62-75.

[In Japanese.   Annotation provided by the author.] Examines *The Green Knight* (Percy Folio MS.) and analyzes the temptation theme in *Sir Gawain.* Contends that Gawain is a truly courteous knight despite the antifeminist element reflected in the poem.

8   KITELEY, J. F.   "The Knight Who Cared for his Life." *Anglia,* 79, no. 2:131-137.

[Reprinted in Howard and Zacher (1968.8).]   Claims that Gawain's apparent failure in his adventure and his acknowledgment of cowardice (2374,2508) may spring from the poet's indebtedness to other depictions of Gawain in Middle English romances, particularly the traditional romance portrayal of Gawain as a "knight who cared for his life." Conjectures that Gawain's concern with self-preservation may be rooted in the original solar myth emphasizing "the fluctuating nature of his strength" (p. 137).

9   LEVY, BERNARD S. "Style and Purpose: A Reconsideration of the Authorship of the Poems in MS. Cotton Nero A.x." Ph.D. dissertation, University of California at Berkeley.

Supports the common authorship theory. Maintains that the four Cotton poems share common elements of style and moral objective—to demonstrate man's need to accept humbly God's will.

10   LEWIS, C. S. "The Anthropological Approach," in *English and Medieval Studies Presented to J. R. R. Tolkien on the Occasion of his Seventieth Birthday.* Edited by Norman Davis and C. L. Wrenn. London: George Allen & Unwin, pp. 219-223.

[Reprinted in Fox (abridged) 1968.6; in Howard (complete) 1968.8.] Criticizes the anthropological approach, especially an approach which emphasizes mythic and ritual origins of symbols and literary motifs, because it fails to illuminate the romances. Singles out Speirs (1957.12) for his advocacy of seasonal gods and the Jack-in-the-Green as keys to the mysteries of *Gawain.* Maintains that Bercilak is a unique creation, "a living *coincidentia oppositorum*"—a vivacious half-giant, yet a courtly knight.

11   LOOMIS, LAURA HIBBARD. *"Gawain and the Green Knight,"* in *Adventures in the Middle Ages: A Memorial Collection of Essays and Studies.* Selected Papers in Literature and Criticism, No. 1. New York: Burt Franklin, pp. 293-308.

[Reprint of 1959.11.]

12   LUTTRELL, C. A. "A *Gawain* Group Miscellany." *Notes and Queries,* New Series, 9 (December), 449-450.

Interprets *child-gered* (1. 86) as "full of boyish high spirits" (p. 450) and *bytwene hem* (1. 977) as suggesting "the idea of privacy" (p. 450).

13   MEHL, DIETER. *"Zu* Sir Gawain and the Green
     Knight.*"* *Germanisch-Romanische Monatsschrift,*
     Neue Folge, 12 (October), 414-417.
     [In German.]   Claims that lines 1237-38 of *Gawain* do
     not suggest an overt sexual invitation by Bercilak's wife; she
     is actually informing Gawain that she enjoys his company.

14   NAGANO, YOSHIO. "Old Icelandic Loan-Words in *Sir
     Gawayne and the Grene Knight.*" *Studies in English
     Literature and Language* (Kyushu University, Fukuo-
     ka, Japan), No. 12: pp. 55-66.
     [Part I of the essay. *See also* 1966.25.]   Notes that
     Gawain was composed in the Northwest Midland dialect
     (south Lancashire or northwest Derbyshire) between 1375
     and 1400.   Discusses the influence of the invasions of the
     Northmen upon the speech patterns of the North Midlanders:
     ". . . in *Sir Gawayne* the form of words borrowed from those
     dialects [of the Northmen] is in many cases exactly the same
     [as], or for the rest directly traceable back to, the original
     Icelandic as preserved in written records" (p. 56).   Contends
     that the exigency of alliterative verse often demanded an Ice-
     landic form (like *sk* in *skyfted,* line 19) and that formulaic
     phrases, such as þe *more and* þe *mynne* ("the more and the
     less") of line 1881, bear the imprint of foreign (Icelandic)
     literary tradition.   Concludes with a summary of the morpho-
     logical features of Old Icelandic and the phonology of Old
     Icelandic loan-words.

15   OHYE, SABURO. "Metrical Influences in the Grammar
     of the Four Poems Preserved in MS. Cotton Nero
     A.x." *St. Paul's Review* (St. Paul's (or Rikkyo) Uni-
     versity, Tokyo), 11 (March), 75-97.
     [Contains a discussion of all four Cotton Nero poems.]
     Examines the verse form of *Gawain,* including the unrhymed
     alliterative lines and the rhymed "bob and wheel"; the rhyth-
     mic patterns; and the alliterative patterns.   Analyzes fully the
     metrical influences (grammar) upon the *Gawain*-poet's choice
     of language; claims that the linguistic differences among the
     Cotton poems may be attributed to the poem's employment
     of two distinct verse techniques—the unrhymed alliterative
     line and "the rimed line with alliteration added" (p. 93).

16   RENOIR, ALAIN. "An Echo to the Sense: The Patterns
      of Sound in *Sir Gawain and the Green Knight.*"
      English Miscellany, 13:9-23.
           [Reprinted in Howard and Zacher (1968.8).] Argues that
      sounds illuminate the tone of particular scenes and signalize
      Gawain's psychological state at key junctures in the story.
      Points out the trumpet calls at Camelot when Gawain is seated
      next to Guenevere, perhaps an intimation of Gawain's pride.
      Notes the grinding noise at the Green Chapel (11. 2199-2204),
      a suggestion of Gawain's anxiety as he confronts the prospect
      of death.

17   RIDLEY, M. R., trans. "Preface" to *Sir Gawain and the
      Green Knight.* London: Edmund Ward, pp. 5-11.
           [Reprint of 1944.3.]

18   SAPERSTEIN, J. "Some Observations on *Sir Gawain
      and the Green Knight.*" *English Studies in Africa,* 5
      (March), 29-36.
           Notes that *Gawain* examines in a probing, critical way the
      chivalric ideal and discloses through the use of irony the weak-
      nesses of this ideal. Views the courtly sophistication of *Ga-
      wain* as almost Renaissance in tone.

19   TAYLOR, ANDREW. "*Sir Gawain and the Green
      Knight.*" *Melbourne Critical Review,* 5:66-75.
           Emphasizes the contrast between the sophisticated milieu
      of Camelot-Hautdesert and the mutable world of nature—its
      dynamism, conflicts (seasons), and vitality. Views the Green
      Knight as "the embodiment of inextinguishable and com-
      pletely amoral vitality" (p. 68). Contends that Gawain "dra-
      matizes the relation between the moral world of Man and the
      amoral vitality of Nature" (p. 74) in order to reveal how man
      may harness the power of nature.

20   WALDRON, R. A. "*Sir Gawain and the Green Knight,*
      1046-51.*" *Notes and Queries,* New Series, 9 (Octo-
      ber), 366-367.
           Interprets *derue dede* (1. 1047) as "terrible act com-
      mitted"; "Bertilak, who as yet does not wish to admit openly
      any knowledge of Gawain's purpose, mischievously suggests to
      him that it must be as an outlaw because of some terrible

crime that he has left Arthur's court at such an unlikely time and alone" (p. 367). Suggests that Bercilak is playfully aware of Gawain's past *derue dede*—the beheading of the Green Knight.

1963

1   BOWERS, R. H. *"Gawain and the Green Knight* as Entertainment." *Modern Language Quarterly,* 24 (December), 333-341.

[Reprinted in Howard and Zacher (1968.8).] Chastizes Markman (1957.10), Moorman (1956.8), and Burrow (1959.3) for their overly solemn interpretations of *Gawain.* Perceives *Gawain* as a *jeu d'esprit,* an entertaining romance which emphasizes comic irony, laughter, and high-spirited fun.

2   BROOK, G. L. *English Dialects.* London: Andre Deutsch, pp. 68, 185.

Notes that *Gawain* was composed, perhaps, in the South Lancashire dialect. Explains the meaning of numerous words in *Gawain,* including *molaynes* (1. 169) as "the headgear or bridle of a horse"; *toppyng* (1. 191) as "a horse's forelock"; *wysty* (1. 2189) as "spacious bare"; *mynteȝ* (1. 2290) as "aims a blow"; and *barlay* (1. 296), a word frequently found in children's games, as "I claim."

3   CARSON, MOTHER ANGELA. "The Green Chapel: Its Meaning and Its Function." *Studies in Philology,* 60 (October), 598-605.

[Reprinted in Howard and Zacher (1968.8).] Attempts to explain why the Green Chapel is a hollow mound rather than a Christian sanctuary. Maintains that the Green Knight's "Chapel" springs from a twelfth-century French word, *chapler* ("to cut down"); this word suggests a place where blows are exchanged and killing may occur. Argues that Gawain's perception of the Green Chapel as a "burial mound" is ironic and that "the contrast between what Gawain expects and what he encounters" (p. 604) is intertwined with the ambiguous connotation of "chapel."

4   CARSON, MOTHER ANGELA. "The Green Knight's

Name." *English Language Notes,* 1 (December), 84-90.

Contends that the name (lines 2445-47) "Bercilak de Hautdesert," created by the *Gawain*-poet, is linked with Bercilak's roles as challenger and as host, particularly with his roles as springing from the magical power of Morgan le Fay. Suggests that "Bercilak" is a compound name derived from *bercer* ("to hunt," "to shoot arrows," and "to strike") and from *lak* ("sport, fun, contest" and "a small stream of running water"). Notes that "De Hautdesert" is a compound, fusing *haut* ("high, lofty, great") and *desert* ("merit" and "a wilderness").

5   COOK, ROBERT G. "The Play-Element in *Sir Gawain and the Green Knight." Tulane Studies in English,* 13:5-31.

Employs Johan Huizinga's *Homo Ludens* as the basis of an analysis of games and play in *Gawain,* elements which produce both comedy and seriousness in this romance. Claims that once *Gawain* as *gomen* is completed, Gawain is the only player who comprehends the significance of the game; "and for that one—Gawain—the meaning is such a disturbing self-awareness that the fun is gone" (p. 30).

6   DODGSON, JOHN McNEAL. "Sir Gawain's Arrival in Wirral," in *Early English and Norse Studies: Presented to Hugh Smith in Honour of his Sixtieth Birthday.* Edited by Arthur Brown and Peter Foote. London: Methuen, pp. 19-25.

Focuses on the geography found in lines 697-702 of *Gawain,* specifically *And fareʒ ouer þe fordeʒ by þe forlondeʒ, /Ouer at þe Holy Hede* (11. 699-700)—perhaps the three crossings of Dee or a legendary constable's ford at the mouth of the estuary. Claims that the geographical underpinnings of Gawain's entrance into Wirral create an air of mystery appropriate to a romance landscape.

7   GÖLLER, KARL HEINZ. *König Arthur in der Englischen Literatur des Späten Mittelalters.* Palaestra, Vol. 238. Göttingen: Vandenhoeck & Ruprecht, 95, 99-101, 103, 127, 168.

[In German.] Maintains that the best example of the

Middle English romance is *Gawain,* a work of real artistic merit; in its intellectual-religious power and subtle structure, *Gawain* may be compared with the best medieval French works. Notes that Arthur here is young and revels in youth in the same childlike manner.

8   HILLS, DAVID FARLEY. "Gawain's Fault in *Sir Gawain and the Green Knight.*" *Review of English Studies,* New Series 14 (May), 124-131.

> [Reprinted in Howard and Zacher (1968.8).] Argues that the alleged discrepancy between Gawain's recognition and confession of his fault to the Green Knight and the Knight's perception of this flaw may be resolved through an analysis of covetousness. Views Gawain's *couetyse* (2374-83) as a type of *cupiditas,* an unreasonable self-love and a desire for worldly objects; such *cupiditas* is displayed once Gawain accepts the girdle in order to preserve his life. Contends that the Green Knight and Arthur's court are not inclined to judge Gawain's fault harshly because they are well acquainted with the impact of fear upon men.

9   McINTOSH, ANGUS. "A New Approach to Middle English Dialectology." *English Studies,* 44 (February), 5-6.

> Analyzes the language of *Gawain* and concludes that this work "can only *fit* with reasonable propriety in a very small area either in SE Cheshire or just over the border in NE Staffordshire" (p. 5). Claims that *Gawain's* "dialectal characteristics *in their totality* are reconcilable with those of other (localised) texts in this and only this area" (pp. 5-6).

10   McLAUGHLIN, JOHN C. *A Graphemic-Phonemic Study of a Middle English Manuscript.* The Hague: Mouton, 162 pp.

> [*See also* his dissertation (1961.14).] Represents a technical linguistic analysis of the writing system of the Cotton Nero manuscript in order to accurately reproduce the written dialect of the Cotton poems. Attempts "to reconstruct a phonemic system of the language basing critical assumptions on all available evidence from sound patterns, spelling, earlier and later expressions of the dialect . . . , known scribal peculiarities of the period and locale . . ." (p. 7).

11   PEARCE, T. M. "Sir Gawain and the Hostess." *American Notes and Queries*, 1, no. 5 (January), 70-71.

Contends that Guilielmus Peraldus's "Treatise on the Vices" may have shaped, in part, the temptation scenes in *Gawain*. Notes a parallel between the *Bestiary* account of the deceitful fox, a type of the devil, and the third hunt/temptation, wherein Bercilak offers fox skin to the sly Gawain and Bercilak's wife is garbed in fox skins when she visits Arthur's knight. Suggests a possible parallel between Jonah and his three days in the whale's belly and Gawain's three days at Hautdesert.

12   SCHLAUCH, MARGARET. *Antecedents of the English Novel, 1400-1600.* Warsaw: Polish Scientific Publishers, pp. 23-28.

Emphasizes the *Gawain*-poet's artistic descriptions of nature, the comedy underlying the temptations, the skillful use of gesture, the poet's probing into Gawain's thoughts, and the use of "unity of point of view"—an anticipation of modern narrative techniques.

13   SCHROEDER, HENRY A., JR. "*Sir Gawain and the Green Knight*: An Essay in Criticism." Ph.D. dissertation, Yale University.

Traces the poem's use of romance convention, alliterative techniques, concepts of courtly love, chivalry, and courtesy, and descriptive techniques. Contends that *Gawain* represents "an imaginative progression away from simplicity toward actuality."

14   SMITHERS, G. V. "What *Sir Gawain and the Green Knight* is About." *Medium Aevum*, 32, No. 3:171-189.

Discusses the Green Knight's link with a chapel and the *raison d'être* of Gawain's confession to the Green Knight and finds parallels for these elements in *Perlesvaus* and *La Queste del saint Graal*. Suggests that the name of the Green Knight (Bertilak de Hautdesert), "of the high hermitage," and the spiritual and chivalric ideals portrayed in *Gawain* may be rooted in the *Queste*. Examines the temptation scenes in *Gawain*.

15　SOLOMON, JAN. "The Lesson of Sir Gawain." *Papers of the Michigan Academy of Science, Arts, and Letters*, 48:599-608.

[Reprinted in Howard and Zacher (1968.8).] Focuses, in part, on the structural unity of *Gawain*—the thread which ties together the green girdle, a central element, and Gawain's chivalric virtues—loyalty, courtesy, and chastity—which are tested; the poem as a series of concentric circles is discussed. Argues that the theme of *Gawain* hinges upon a lesson in *mesure* (humility, moderation, balance), for Gawain must recognize his human frailty, his immoderate pride (*surfet*, 1. 2433) in his knightly accomplishments and reputation.

1964

1　BRANFORD, WILLIAM. "Bercilak de Hautdesert: An Interrogation of the Green Knight." *English Studies in Africa*, 7 (March), 54-64.

Notes in his attempt to identify the symbolic nature and significance of the Green Knight that green is linked with vegetation and otherworld creatures. Suggests that "the Green Knight's primary function is to bring home to Gawain, through long and varied experience, the full implications of *trawthe*" (p. 57).

2　BURROW, J. A. "*Cupiditas* in *Sir Gawain and the Green Knight.*" *Review of English Studies*, New Series 15 (February), 56.

[Reply to Hills (1963.8). Reprinted in Howard and Zacher (1968.8).] Suggests that Gawain refers (1. 2374f.) to the specialized meaning of *couetyse* ("love of riches")—a quality which is naturally opposed to *larges*. Contends that cowardice precipitated Gawain's covetous action, the deliberate retention and concealment of the girdle.

3　DEAN, CHRISTOPHER. "*Sir Gawain and the Green Knight*, 2231-2232." *The Explicator*, 22, no. 8 (April), no. 67.

Focuses on traditional folklore material—the Green Knight's use of his axe as a vaulting pole in order to cross the stream near the Green Chapel. Claims that the Knight avoids

contact with water because water would render this supernatural creature completely powerless.

4   EMBLER, WELLER B. "The Sanity of True Literature."
      CEA Critic, 26, no. 8 (May), 1, 3-4.
         Claims that Gawain's behavior after he receives the blow
      from the Green Knight is psychologically "realistic" although
      this romance employs supernatural and magical elements.
      Perceives the audience and all the characters, except for
      Gawain, as spectators to Gawain's testing and views this
      romance as "more orderly, more sane than life, more rational,
      more reasonable, healthier, as literature very nearly always
      is" (p. 4).

5   FARLEY—HILLS, DAVID L. "The *Roman de la Rose*
      and the Poems of MS Cotton Nero Ax, 4." *Journal
      of the Faculty of Arts* (Royal University of Malta), 2,
      no. 3:229-235.
         Argues that a link exists between the poems of the Cotton
      MS. and the *Roman de la Rose* because of the repetition of the
      words *clene* and *clannes* in the works of the *Pearl*-poet. In
      Gawain, for example, Gawain's conclusions regarding the pre-
      cise relationship between the Christian moral code and courtly
      behavior are analogous to the solutions posed by Jean de
      Meun—". . . the art of love is greatly to be respected, but . . .
      it is itself subservient to Christian morality."

6   HOWARD, DONALD R. "Structure and Symmetry in
      Sir Gawain." Speculum, 39 (July), 425-433.
         [Reprinted in Blanch (1966.4), Fox (1968.6), and
      Howard and Zacher (1968.8).] Examines the structural paral-
      lels in *Gawain;* the juxtaposition of the shield and girdle,
      emblematic of Gawain's chivalric perfection and worldliness,
      respectively; the parallel contrasts between the incidents at
      Hautdesert and the events at the Green Chapel; the narrative
      structure rooted in the four oversized capitals of the Cotton
      Nero manuscript; and the poet's employment of suspense
      and comic irony.

7   IKEGAMI, TADAHIRO. "Nature in *Sir Gawain and the
      Green Knight." Studies in English Literature* (English
      Literary Society of Japan), 40 (February), 1-15.

[In Japanese. English synopsis of article (pp. 100-101).]
Suggests that the *Gawain*-poet depicts graphically the numbing
cold of a winter landscape. Appearing "almost as if it were a
character" (p. 100) in *Gawain,* winter tests the physical
aspects of the hero's character. Notes that the outdoor world
of nature mirrors Gawain's psychological state.

8   LEWIS, C. S. *The Discarded Image: An Introduction to
      Medieval and Renaissance Literature.* Cambridge,
      England: Cambridge University Press, pp. 126, 130,
      147, 198.
           Discusses briefly the Green Knight as a fairy creature and
      the fall of Troy passage as an integral part of *Gawain.*

9   LOOMIS, ROGER SHERMAN. *The Development of
      Arthurian Romance.* Harper Torchbook 1167. New
      York: Harper and Row, pp. 24, 133, 152-165.
           Theorizes that the *Gawain*-poet was linked with a noble
      household and contends that the "bob and wheel" acts like
      a conclusion to a paragraph. Claims that the turning of the
      seasons passage in *Gawain* emphasizes the transitory nature of
      life and that the poet interweaves the beheading game, temp-
      tation, and exchange of winnings motifs. Notes the link be-
      tween Curoi (a shapeshifter) and Cuchulainn of *Bricriu's Feast*
      and the Knight and Gawain of *Gawain.* Calls attention to the
      use of suspense in *Gawain;* the character of the Green Knight,
      an amalgam of Curoi and Arawn (the Wild Huntsman in folk-
      lore); the humanity of Gawain; and the parallels between
      Gawain and Wolfram von Eschenbach's *Parzival,* especially in
      each author's treatment of the hero.

10   MALARKEY, STODDARD and J. BARRE TOELKEN.
      "Gawain and the Green Girdle." *Journal of English
      and Germanic Philology,* 63 (January), 14-20.
           [Reprinted in Howard and Zacher (1968.8).] Argues that
      the poet zooms in on Gawain's state of mind as Gawain con-
      fronts the Green Knight at the Green Chapel, especially if one
      translates line 2226 as "It [the axe] was no smaller by reason
      of that girdle [*lace*] that gleamed so brightly" (p. 16). Notes
      that the green girdle is termed "lace" in eight other examples
      from *Gawain,* that the girdle is lustrous (11. 2037-39), and
      that Gawain wears the shining *luf-lace* over his surcoat (2032-

36). Contends that when Gawain wraps his girdle over the surcoat, he is overtly, albeit unconsciously, rejecting the virtues of the pentangle and that Gawain's apparent lack of faith in the girdle precipitates his shrinking away from the Knight's axe.

11   MANNING, STEPHEN. "A Psychological Interpretation of *Sir Gawain and the Green Knight.*" *Criticism*, 6 (Spring), 165-177.

[Reprinted in Howard and Zacher (1968.8).] Offers a Jungian analysis of *Gawain*, wherein Gawain (ego) confronts and recognizes the shadow or "personal unconscious" (Bercilak)—the evil aspect of his psyche. Views Bercilak/Green Knight as somewhat ambivalent because of his greenness, for green is an emblem of spiritual rebirth and hope as well as a sign of "chthonic (i.e., earthly or material) life as opposed to the life of the spirit" (p. 170). Perceives Bercilak's wife as the anima, a destructive force often linked with the shadow, and Morgan le Fay as the Terrible Mother.

12   MARKMAN, ALAN. "A Computer Concordance to Middle English Texts." *Studies in Bibliography: Papers of the Bibliographical Society of the University of Virginia,* 17:55-75.

Discusses the textual and technical operations, including the problems of non-uniform texts, the choice of base texts, editorial variants, proper names, and the choice of headwords, in preparing a computer concordance (1966.17) to the printed texts of *Gawain, Pearl, Patience, Purity,* and *St. Erkenwald.*

13   MEHL, DIETER. " 'Point of View' in Mittelenglischen Romanzen." *Germanisch-Romanische Monatsschrift, Neue Folge* 14 (January), 38, 41, 44.

[In German.] Offers a brief commentary on the *Gawain*-poet's modern use of scenic techniques and his subtle handling of narrative point of view.

*14   MILLS, A. D. "A Comparative Study of the Versification, Vocabulary, and Style of *Pearl, Patience, Purity* and *Sir Gawain and the Green Knight.*" Ph.D. dissertation, University of Manchester (England).

[Cited in Foley (1974.5).]

15   SILVERSTEIN, THEODORE. "The Art of *Sir Gawain and the Green Knight.*" *University of Toronto Quarterly,* 33 (April), 258-278.

> [Reprinted in Howard and Zacher (1968.8).] Employs Geoffrey de Vinsauf and other writers on medieval poetic in his analysis of the *topoi* and verbal devices forming the substratum of the turning of the seasons (*Gawain,* 11. 491-535). Discusses the aphorisms in 11. 495-99, especially their literary origins and histories, and the links between the description of the seasons in *Gawain* and *conflictus* poems, medieval cosmologies, and formal *descriptiones loci* in rhetorical handbooks.

16   SPEARING, A. C. "*Sir Gawain and the Green Knight,*" in his *Criticism and Medieval Poetry.* London: Edward Arnold, pp. 26-45.

> [Pp. 38-45 are reprinted in Howard and Zacher (1968.8) as "Gawain's Speeches and the Poetry of 'Cortaysye'."] Discusses the graphic sense of concreteness in *Gawain* and refutes critical theories which represent the Green Knight, not Gawain, as the focus of the poem. Examines the "beheading game" and the chastity test which is rooted in the bedroom scenes at Hautdesert. Analyzes the meaning of *cortaysye,* a concept which ranges "from politeness . . . through elegant conversation about love . . . to the conduct of a real-love affair" (p. 35), and perceives a real conflict between Gawain's *cortaysye* and chastity in the poem; scrutinizes Gawain's speeches as signposts leading to the hero's *cortaysye.*

17   STONE, BRIAN, trans. *Sir Gawain and the Green Knight.* Baltimore: Penguin, 144 pp.

> [Reprint of 1959.17.]

1965

1   BENSON, LARRY D. *Art and Tradition in Sir Gawain and the Green Knight.* New Brunswick, New Jersey: Rutgers University Press, 332 pp.

> [Reprinted, in part, in Howard and Zacher (1968.8) and in Fox (1968.6).] Contends that the ultimate subject of *Gawain* is the romance genre, especially the conflict between

chivalric ideals and the claims of the real world. Examines the sources and structure of *Gawain* as well as the relationship between the poem's style and meaning; demonstrates how and why *Gawain* employs traditional materials (alliterative style and the convention of ideal feminine beauty) or deviates sharply from the expected conventions. Discusses the ambivalent nature of the Green Knight and the ambiguous implications of his greenness; claims that the *Gawain*-poet's description of the Green Knight fuses characteristics of two figures—the Green Man, generally associated with spring, youth, and vitality; and the Wild Man, linked with winter and old age.

2   BENSON, LARRY D. "The Authorship of *St. Erkenwald.*" *Journal of English and Germanic Philology,* 64 (July), 393-405.

Contends that *St. Erkenwald* should not be attributed to the *Gawain*-poet because the stylistic similarities (diction, parallel phrases, verse style) between *Erkenwald* and the Cotton Nero poems are non-existent. Notes that the appearance of similar lines in two or more poems points to a common tradition of alliterative formulas, that periphrases for God are represented in many alliterative poems, and that the employment of synonyms in the Cotton Nero poems is radically different from the use of synonyms in *Erkenwald*.

3   BERCOVITCH, SACVAN. "Romance and Anti-Romance in *Sir Gawain and the Green Knight.*" *Philological Quarterly,* 44 (January), 30-37.

[Reprinted in Howard and Zacher (1968.8).] Examines the dualistic structure of *Gawain,* the employment of playful and realistic scenes which comically puncture romance conventions and still energize and support romance ideals. Assigns this dualistic view to each scene as well as to the figures of Bercilak and his wife; claims that the lord's anti-romance characteristics contrast with Gawain's chivalric behavior.

4   BILLINGS, ANNA HUNT. *A Guide to the Middle English Metrical Romances Dealing with English and Germanic Legends, and with the Cycles of Charlemagne and of Arthur.* New York: Haskell House, pp. 160-168.

[Reprint of 1901.1.]

5   BROES, ARTHUR T. *"Sir Gawain and the Green Knight*: Romance as Comedy." *Xavier University Studies,* 4, no. 1 (March), 35-54.

Claims that the *Gawain*-poet employs comic elements and ironic humor in order to poke fun at Gawain, Arthur, the chivalric code, and the medieval romance.

6   BURROW, J. A. *A Reading of Sir Gawain and the Green Knight.* London: Routledge & Kegan Paul, 207 pp.

[Pp. 96-104 are reprinted in Fox (1968.6).] Provides a "linear reading," fitt by fitt, of the meaning and plot of *Gawain.* Claims that the thematic focus of Gawain is *trawþe* and that the test of Gawain's *trawþe* is rooted in the game element of the poem, specifically the "exchange of winnings" agreement. Notes that since Gawain fails to honor completely his *forwarde* with Bercilak, the poem will emphasize the importance of confession and penitence. Offers comments upon the poem's use of color and number symbolism, patterns of time, symmetry, seasonal motifs, realism, and pentangle symbolism.

7   CLERK, JAYANA J. *"Sir Gawain and the Green Knight*: An Appreciation." *Bulletin of the Chunilal Gandhi Vidyabhavan,* 12-13:74-84.

[The actual date of publication is listed as 1965-66.] Emphasizes the artistic descriptions in *Gawain,* descriptions which blend the realm of magic and the realm of real human life into a unified whole. Focuses on the crucial chastity theme, the circular pattern underlying *Gawain,* the fusion of the Beheading and Temptation motifs, and the parallels between the animals hunted by Bercilak and Gawain's behavior during the lady's temptations. Notes the *Gawain*-poet's rejection of *amour courtois* and adherence to Christian ideals.

Concludes with a commentary upon the contrast between the warmth of courtly life and the coldness of nature; the visual effects evoked—effects which are reminiscent of modern cinematic techniques; and the bob and wheel. *Gawain* is like "Gothic architecture with ornamentation and pointed arches and spires which converge on the point which suggests the moral of the poem" (p. 84).

8   DELANY, PAUL. "The Role of the Guide in *Sir Gawain and the Green Knight." Neophilologus,* 49 (July),

250-255.

[Reprinted in Howard and Zacher (1968.8).] Views the guide, a character who often appears in mythology, as a tester of Gawain's chivalric virtues (courage, loyalty, truth); the guide's moral temptation contrasts with the physical tests which Gawain undergoes on his journey to Hautdesert and represents a device of dramatic suspense "by showing the perceptive reader that from his arrival at the Castle Gawain can never escape surveillance by the powers that rule the magic world" (p. 254).

9   DONNER, MORTON. "Tact as a Criterion of Reality in *Sir Gawain and the Green Knight.*" *Papers on English Language and Literature,* 1 (Autumn), 306-315.

Focuses on the psychological complexity of people in their relationships with others, particularly Gawain's tact in dealing with the challenge of the Green Knight and the temptations offered by Bercilak's wife. Contends that Gawain's tact points to the poet's "sophisticated conception of social reality, subtly demonstrating how the normality of civilized society is achieved only by imposing an overlay of pretense upon actuality" (p. 315).

10   GARDNER, JOHN. "Introduction and Commentary," in his translation of *The Complete Works of the Gawain-Poet.* Woodcuts by Fritz Kredel. Chicago: University of Chicago Press, pp. 3-16, 19-20, 22-26, 28-29, 35-36, 38-41, 44-45, 50, 52, 70-84, 87-90.

[Includes background discussions and translations of all four Cotton poems plus *Erkenwald.*] Discusses numerous aspects of *Gawain,* including the background of the poet; parallels between *Gawain* and Chaucer's *Troilus and Criseyde;* parallels between the Green Knight and the figure of youth in *Parlement of the Thre Ages;* symbolism (Green Knight, color, number, and pentangle); the importance of the bob and wheel and alliterative tradition; and the poem's use of comic and courtly love elements.

Argues that the dramatic force of *Gawain* springs from "the conflict between human selfishness and the ideal of selfless courtesy" (p. 70) and that such a conflict stems from "mutability, the implications of man's existence within nature" (p. 70). Emphasizes the significance of order in *Gawain,* the Yuletide aspects of the poem, the meaning of Hautdesert, and the relationship between the hunting and temptation scenes.

11   GILLIE, CHRISTOPHER. *Characters in English Literature.* London: Chatto & Windus, pp. 33-40.

Claims that *Gawain,* a romance pervaded by characters who are depicted graphically and cogently, is cast in a symbolic mold. Suggests that Arthur's youthful spirits energize Camelot and that Guinevere "sits in an aura of rich fabrics and blazing gems, because she is representatively the magnet of virile ardour and a lofty code [of chivalry]" (p. 34). Perceives Gawain's quest as a test of his chivalric virtues and the order and richness of Camelot as a challenge to the forces of disarray, death, and primitivism.

Views the Green Knight as half-fairy, half-real as well as an amalgam of nature and humanity, whereas the hunted animals at Hautdesert—the deer (cowardice), the boar (aggressiveness), and the fox (deceit)—symbolize the human weaknesses which jeopardize Gawain's position as an exemplar of knighthood. Focuses on the need for Arthurian civilization to be resuscitated by nature, and yet, to overcome nature's challenge.

12   LASS, ROGER GEORGE. "Gawain's Apprenticeship: Myth and the Spiritual Process in *Gawain and the Green Knight.*" Ph.D. dissertation, Yale University.

[*See Dissertation Abstracts,* 26 (1965), 2185.] Emphasizes the spiritual nature of *Gawain* and compares its narrative to the first half of Dante's *Divine Comedy.* Employs patristic and mystical commentaries in order to demonstrate that Gawain aims at Christian perfection through a maturely Christian self-awareness.

13   LEVY, BERNARD S. "Gawain's Spiritual Journey: *Imitatio Christi* in *Sir Gawain and the Green Knight.*" *Annuale Mediaevale,* 6:65-106.

Perceives in *Gawain* a Scriptural pattern—a "spiritual circumcision" (New Year's Day and the feast of the Circumcision of Christ) linked with the journey motif as depicted in St. Augustine's *Confessions* and Dante's *Divine Comedy.* Contends that Gawain learns to forsake the sin of pride in his spiritual pilgrimage, to act as a Christian knight in imitation of Christ. Analyzes the multiple symbols (color, holly branch, axe, Green Chapel, girdle) pervading *Gawain,* including an identification of Bercilak/Green Knight with the devil, the hunter of human souls.

14   McALINDON, T. "Comedy and Terror in Middle English Literature: The Diabolical Game." *Modern Language Review,* 60 (July), 329-332.
　　　　Notes that *Gawain* is characterized by "a sardonic intermingling of grimness and jest. The diabolical parodies the religious, and horror is ritualized in sportive forms" (p. 329). Contends that Bercilak/Green Knight evokes the memory of a demon and that the game motif is linked with the caustic comedy of the diabolical characters in religious drama and legend (pp. 331-332).

15   McALINDON, T. "Magic, Fate, and Providence in Medieval Narrative and *Sir Gawain and the Green Knight.*" *Review of English Studies,* New Series 16 (May), 121-139.
　　　　Examines the fatalistic spirit underlying Celtic pagan literature, the distinction between the pagan and the Christian world's employment of magic as well as their fusion in *Gawain,* and the function and the significance of the Christian tradition in *Gawain.* Explores the *Gawain*-poet's subtle use of magic, pact stories, and Gawain's employment of free will in order to accede to the Divine Will.

16   MILLS, M. "Christian Significance and Romance Tradition in *Sir Gawain and the Green Knight.*" *Modern Language Review,* 60 (October), 483-493.
　　　　[Reprinted in Howard and Zacher (1968.8).] Compares *Gawain* and the *Queste del Saint Graal* in order to determine whether *Gawain* represents a Christian allegory of spiritual progress. Traces parallels between the Green Chapel and the chapels in *Perlesvaus,* between Hautdesert and the Perilous Castle. Concludes by interpreting *couetyse* as "lustful desire," Gawain's imagined reason for failing his quest.

17   MOON, DOUGLAS M. "Clothing Symbolism in *Sir Gawain and the Green Knight.*" *Neuphilologische Mit-*

teilungen, 66, no. 3:334-347.

Claims that the *Gawain*-poet employs the chastity test motif commonly found in Arthurian romances by transforming some of its traditional elements into "functional symbols." Examines four particular symbols—the mantle (11. 153-56, 878-81, 1736-37, 1831), *capados* (11. 185-86, 572, 2297), hood, and *bleaunt*—and contends that these symbols mirror the moral state of the individuals who wear them.

18   MORRIS, RICHARD, ed. "Preface," in *Early English Alliterative Poems in the West-Midland Dialect of the Fourteenth Century.* Second edition. Early English Text Society, Original Series 1. Oxford: Oxford University Press, pp. v-ix, xli-xliii.
[Reprint of 1869.1.]

19   NICKEL, GERHARD. "Die Begleiterepisode in *Sir Gawain and the Green Knight.*" *Germanisch-Romanische Monatsschrift, Neue Folge,* 15 (October), 355-365.
[In German.] Claims that although the themes of temptation and warning appear in various medieval works linked with *Gawain,* the *Gawain*-poet's method of thematically fusing warning and temptation, namely in the guide's warning scene (11. 2074-2159) is unique in medieval literature.

20   SAVAGE, HENRY L. "Hang Up Thine Axe." *Notes and Queries,* New Series, 12 (October), 375-376.
Claims that *heng vp þyn ax* (*Gawain,* 1. 477), a Middle English proverb connoting "cease from activity, call quits," persists in language even today.

21   SCHELP, HANSPETER. "Nurture: Ein mittelenglischer Statusbegriff." *Anglia,* 83, no. 3:253-254, 260.
[In German.] Focuses on the concept of *nurture* (good breeding), a form of courtesy in *Gawain* (lines 917, 919, 927).

22   SCHLAUCH, MARGARET. "Arthurian Material in Some Late Icelandic Sagas." *Bulletin Bibliographique de la Société Arthurienne,* 17:90-91.
Examines the hero of *Gawain* and the protagonist of the late Icelandic *Vilhjálms saga sjóds* (IV) and notes particular

parallels between the two works—a potential forfeit for the hero "in the deepest winter season" and the hero's attempt to break a spell precipitated by supernatural forces.

23   SILVERSTEIN, THEODORE. *"Sir Gawain,* Dear Brutus, and Britain's Fortunate Founding: A Study in Comedy and Convention." *Modern Philology,* 62 (February), 189-206.

Scrutinizes the first two stanzas of *Gawain* (the fall of Troy and the founding of Britain by Felix Brutus)—stanzas which are cast in a serious, heroic mold but disclose humorously Gawain's legacy of glory and guilt from Troy to Camelot. Examines syntactic ambiguity in the opening stanzas and discusses Aeneas, Ticius (Tuscus or Tirrus), and Felix Brutus.

24   VASTA, EDWARD, ed. *Middle English Survey: Critical Essays.* Notre Dame: University of Notre Dame Press, pp. 57-92.

[Reprint of Engelhardt (1955.2) and Green (1962.5).]

25   WESTON, JESSIE L., trans. *Romance, Vision & Satire: English Alliterative Poems of the Fourteenth Century.* Gloucester, Massachusetts: Peter Smith, pp. 331-332.

[Reprint of 1912.4.]

26   WHITE, BEATRICE. "The Green Knight's Classical Forbears." *Neuphilologische Mitteilungen,* 66, no. 1: 112-119.

Traces the classical origins (Latin poetry) of the "severed, living head" motif and claims that Joseph of Exeter's *De Bello Troiano* may represent the work which links together the Latin and medieval illustrations of this motif. Suggests that the "severed head" theme in *Gawain,* rooted in folklore yet rhetorically shaped by the *Gawain*-poet into a dramatic oxymoron, ultimately springs (stylistically) from Latin poetry.

27   WHITE, ROBERT B., JR. "A Note on the Green Knight's Red Eyes (*GGK,* 304)." *English Language Notes,* 2 (June), 250-252.

[Reprinted in Howard and Zacher (1968.8).] Uses handbooks of physiognomy (*Secreta Secretorum*) in order to determine the symbolic values assigned to the Green Knight's red eyes—strength, courage, virility (especially in battle).

28   YAMAGUCHI, HIDEO. "A Lexical Note on the Language of *Sir Gawain and the Green Knight.*" *Philologica Pragensia* (Prague), 8, nos. 2-3:372-380.

Terms *Gawain* "a lively, rugged form of sprung rhythm, alive with force and meaning" (p. 372), a poem which artistically fuses the harsh vocabulary of the North with the musical French beat and diction. Notes the Northern influence upon the winter scenes in *Gawain* as well as upon the depiction of the hero's journey through Wirral. Focuses technically upon the Old Norse, Old English, and Old French linguistic elements and underscores the poet's employment of "alliterating synonyms" for "man"; religious, psychic, and moral terms; social qualities; verbal and nominal actions; and nature.

1966

1   ACKERMAN, ROBERT W. "Middle English Literature to 1400," in *The Medieval Literature of Western Europe: A Review of Research, Mainly 1930-1960.* Edited by John H. Fisher. New York: New York University Press, pp. 75-77, 91-92, 94-95, 98-100.

[Provides an annotated list of bibliographical aids and a select annotated bibliography of *Gawain* scholarship.]

2   ALJUBOURI, A. H. "The Treatment of Chivalric Ideals in *Sir Gawain and the Green Knight.*" *Baghdad Bulletin of the College of Arts,* 9:37-49.

Claims that the *Gawain*-poet intentionally focuses upon chivalric ideals (even though such ideals were obsolescent) in order to underscore his central concern—the challenge to knightly perfection. Depicting Gawain as the knight *par excellence,* the poet humanizes Gawain by portraying his weaknesses.

3   BENSON, LARRY D. Review of Gardner's *The Complete Works of the Gawain-Poet. Journal of English and Germanic Philology,* 65 (July), 580-583.

[*See also* 1965.10.] Criticizes Gardner's translation of *Gawain* for its "jarring colloquialisms" and for its distortions (through imprecise renditions of speeches and characterizations) of Gawain and the Green Knight. Notes that Gardner's introduction, primarily theological in nature and scope, seems to be intended for graduate students, not undergraduates.

4   BLANCH, ROBERT J., ed. *Sir Gawain and Pearl: Critical Essays.* Bloomington: Indiana University Press, pp. 123-235.

[Contains reprints of Burrow (1959.3); Friedman (1960.1); Markman (1957.10); Green (1962.5); Howard (1964.6); and Moorman (1956.8).]

5   BREUER, ROLF. "Die Funktion des Naturschilderungen in den mittelenglischen Versromanzen." Doctoral dissertation, University of Göttingen.

[In German. English abstract provided by the author.] Notes that the *Gawain*-poet artfully fuses his plot and his descriptions of nature so that "the inner state and development of the hero are reflected in the descriptions of the seasons and of the landscape." Argues that the nature descriptions parallel Gawain's psychological fears as well as signalize the structure of this romance, especially the poet's use of spatial and time patterns.

6   BREWER, D. S. "Courtesy and the *Gawain*-Poet," in *Patterns of Love and Courtesy: Essays in Memory of C. S. Lewis.* Edited by John Lawlor. Evanston: Northwestern University Press, pp. 54-56, 67-78, 81-85.

[Reprinted: Newstead (1968.20).] Attempts to consider the concept and use of courtesy in the Cotton Nero poems, works probably composed by one author. Views courtly life in *Gawain*—particularly Camelot and Hautdesert—as representations of courtesy and the diction of courtesy, especially *hende* and *cortays* as pervading the poem. Claims that courtesy is often equated with "verbal good manners" in *Gawain* and that Gawain's own courtesy is interlaced with the five virtues of the pentangle. Examines in detail the courteous speech, "love-talking," in the lady's seductive advances made toward Gawain (pp. 70-76) and views Gawain's antifeminism (lines 2414-19) as the human chink in his armor.

Claims, in an appendix ("The Character of Gawain") to his essay, that two versions of Gawain—the lady's version, "the character of a man who simply cannot resist any young and pretty woman" (p. 84); and the poet's portrayal of a Gawain renowned for his courtly speech and behavior—exist in this romance.

7   BRUTEN, AVRIL. "Gawain's Green Girdle as a 'Sign'." *Notes and Queries*, New Series, 13 (December), 452-454.

Employs St. Augustine's theory of signs, as outlined in his *De Magistro*, as a means of explaining Camelot's reaction to Gawain's tale of the green girdle: "A relation is proposed first between *res* (physical reality) and *verba* (conventional language); and it is argued that unless a man has had previous experience through the senses of a particular physical reality, a word used to signify it will have no meaning for him" (p. 453). Argues that Gawain underscores the realities (11. 2506-10) lurking behind the sign (girdle); yet Arthur and his court fail to reflect upon such "realities" (p. 453), thereby calling attention to "the impossibility of one man teaching others . . . to know the truth, since all true knowledge is from within" (p. 454).

8   CLARK, CECILY. *"Sir Gawain and the Green Knight*: Characterisation by Syntax." *Essays in Criticism*, 16 (October), 361-374.

[Reprinted in part (1968.6).] Employs Spearing's argument (1964.16) that for Gawain as well as for the Green Knight, ". . . character is expressed through syntax rather than through imagery" (p. 45, Spearing). Demonstrates how variations in syntax signalize each individual "character and tone of voice" (p. 362).

Suggests that the poet employs brief sentences and the imperative mood and avoids conditional clauses in order to create the brusque, imperial tone of the Green Knight. Notes that Bercilak's wife uses conditional clauses frequently as well as the familiar form of the second person; her tone of voice is thus complex and suspenseful.

9   DAVIS, NORMAN. *"Sir Gawain and the Green Knight*
     611-612." *Notes and Queries,* New Series, 13 (De-
     cember), 448-451.
     Emends the manuscript reading *pernyng* (1. 611) to
     peruyng ("periwinkle"), the stylized depiction of which often
     appears in medieval decorative design (p. 449). Interprets
     trulofez (1. 612) as "quatrefoils," not "true lovers' knots."

10   DICKINS, BRUCE. "Going at Gawain." *The Times
     Literary Supplement* (6 January), p. 10.
     Argues that foxes were not always viewed as "vermin" in
     medieval England. Suggests that "when the fox is taken, it is
     first flayed (as in *SGGK* 1920-1) and its case . . . hung up as a
     trophy in the hall." Interprets *fule* (*Gawain,* 1. 1944) as
     "stinking," an allusion to the odor emitting from an impro-
     perly cured fox.

11   GARDNER, JOHN. Review of Benson's *Art and Tradi-
     tion in Sir Gawain and the Green Knight. Journal of
     English and Germanic Philology,* 65 (October), 705-
     708.
     [*See also* 1965.1. Reprinted: Howard and Zacher
     (1968.8).] Praises Benson for his elucidation of romance
     conventions and of the artistic techniques employed in *Gawain*
     as well as for his analysis of rhetoric and the "alliterative re-
     vival." Contends that Benson overlooks the importance of
     Christian allegory and myth in *Gawain.*

12   GUIDI, AUGUSTO. "Il meglio di *Pearl." Annali Isti-
     tuto Orientale di Napoli, Sezione Germanica,* 9:199-
     200, 203.
     [In Italian.] Claims that *Gawain* and *Pearl* were not writ-
     ten by the same author although both works employ elaborate
     descriptive passages. Notes that *Gawain* does not use descrip-
     tion in a symbolic manner.

13   HEISERMAN, ARTHUR. "Gawain's Clean Courtesy, or,
     the Task of Telling of True Love." *Modern Language
     Quarterly,* 27 (December), 449-457.
     [Review of Benson (1965.1) and Burrow (1965.6).] Of-
     fers an appreciative analysis of the authors' works, albeit with
     some caveats, and emphasizes the importance of medieval

conventions of courtesy and love as well as of troth in *Gawain.*

14   HOWARD, DONALD R. *The Three Temptations: Medi-
       eval Man in Search of the World.* Princeton: Prince-
       ton University Press, pp. 6, 8, 13-14, 38, 65, 148,
       215-254, 261, 264, 266-268, 270-271, 274-275, 278-
       279, 284-287, 290, 295.

    Examines a number of aspects of *Gawain,* including the
basic chivalric dilemma, "that it [chivalry] was a worldly in-
stitution founded upon otherworldly ideals" (p. 223). Claims
that Gawain—like Adam—falls prey to "pride of life," the emblem of which is the green girdle. Discusses the style and the
game-like tone of *Gawain;* the use of structural parallelism;
the employment of symbolism, irony, and realism; and the
roles played by space and time.

15   JONES, SHIRLEY JEAN. *"Sir Gawain and the Green
       Knight:* Its Magic, Myth, and Ritual." Ph.D. disserta-
       tion, University of Oklahoma.

    [*See Dissertation Abstracts,* 26 (1966), 6696-97.] Ex-
plores the ambiguous characters of Gawain, Bercilak/Green
Knight, and Morgan le Fay in terms of myth and magical belief. Analyzes the use of symbolism in *Gawain.*

16   KELLOGG, ALFRED L. "The Location of the Green
       Chapel in *Sir Gawain and the Green Knight." Year
       Book of the American Philosophical Society:* 652-
       654.

    [Reprinted: 1972.14.] Identifies the Green Chapel with
the Chapel of the Grune, located in Skinburness, Cumber-
land. Substantiates his case by noting that *grune* (*grene* or
green) suggests Satan's snare of temptation as well as a trap for
catching wild animals and by pointing out the malevolent
connotations linked with north, west, and green.

17   KOTTLER, BARNET and ALAN M. MARKMAN. *A
       Concordance to Five Middle English Poems: Clean-
       ness, St. Erkenwald, Sir Gawain and the Green
       Knight, Patience, Pearl.* Pittsburgh: University of
       Pittsburgh Press, 795 pp.

    [*See also* 1967.2; 1969.20.] Describes the format and the
methodology employed in compiling this concordance, includ-

ing the use of one base text (published edition) and at least
one variant text (published edition) of each of the five poems.

18   LASS, ROGER. " 'Man's Heaven': The Symbolism of
       Gawain's Shield." *Mediaeval Studies,* 28:354-360.
       Offers a numerological and theological analysis of the
       shield symbolism and explains the association of this symbol
       with the theme of perfection. Suggests that the pentangle is
       five, the number of physical man, and one—a sign of mutable
       "self-sufficiency" (p. 357)—and that three pentads—physical,
       religious, and courtly—fused together form a perfect Christian
       knight. Views the pentangle as a "representation of possible
       perfection of man in Christ" (p. 359), counterbalanced by
       Mary, the fleshly source of divine perfection. ". . . the two
       emblems on the shield [pentangle and image of Mary] repre-
       sent 'mannys heuene,' man perfected and the flesh glori-
       fied . . ." (p. 359).

19   LAWRENCE, R. F. "The Formulaic Theory and Its Ap-
       plication to English Alliterative Poetry," in *Essays on
       Style and Language: Linguistic and Critical Ap-
       proaches to Literary Style.* Edited by Roger Fowler.
       London: Routledge and Kegan Paul, pp. 171, 180,
       183.
       Comments upon R. A. Waldron's application (1957.13) of
       oral-formulaic theories and techniques to Middle English alli-
       terative poetry, including *Gawain* (1. 2251). Notes that such
       formulas poetically fuse alliterative and rhythmical elements.

20   LEWIS, C. S. *Studies in Medieval and Renaissance Litera-
       ture.* Collected by Walter Hooper. Cambridge, Eng-
       land: Cambridge University Press, pp. 11-14.
       Criticizes Speirs (1957.12) for his concentration on the
       mythical origins of literature, particularly the character of
       Bercilak as stemming from the Jack-in-the-Green figure or the
       Eniautos Daimon. ". . . the poem [*Gawain*] is illuminating
       the myth; the myth is not illuminating the poem" (p. 11).

21   McINTOSH, ANGUS. "Middle English *upon schore* and
       Some Related Matters," in *Studies in Language and
       Literature in Honour of Margaret Schlauch.* Edited
       by Mieczyslaw Brahmer, Stanislaw Helsztyński, and

Julian Krzyżanowski. Warsaw: Polish Scientific Publishers, pp. 255-260.

Claims that *vpon schore* (1. 2332) in *Gawain* refers to the Green Knight's axe placed "at a slant" or "deviating from the vertical (or horizontal)" (p. 256).

22   MATHEW, GERVASE. "Ideals of Friendship," in *Patterns of Love and Courtesy: Essays in Memory of C. S. Lewis.* Edited by John Lawlor. Evanston: Northwestern University Press, pp. 50-51.

Suggests that *franchise,* a kind of generosity of spirit, was intertwined with fellowship in *Gawain* (1. 652).

23   MATONIS, ANN THERESE. *"Sir Gawain and the Green Knight:* Characterization and Structural Motifs." Ph.D. dissertation, University of Pennsylvania.

[See *Dissertation Abstracts,* 27 (1967), 4259A.] Examines *Gawain* in terms of other medieval romances in order to demonstrate how and why the *Gawain*-poet deviates from romance conventions and punctures romance ideals, especially in his conception of Gawain as a flawed human being and in his treatment of the tension between appearance and reality. Discusses the duality of vision (romance milieu versus ironic humor) in important structural motifs—time, journey, castle episode, and the "Perilous Chapel."

24   MOON, DOUGLAS M. "The Role of Morgain la Fée in *Sir Gawain and the Green Knight." Neuphilologische Mitteilungen,* 67, no. 1:31-57.

Claims that Morgan the enchantress (old woman) erroneously believed Guinevere to be Gawain's mistress and that Morgan as seductress (Bercilak's wife) attempted to humiliate Gawain, to test the glory of Camelot, and to precipitate Guinevere's death (either from fear of the exposure of her adultery or from the knowledge of Gawain's death). Contends that Morgan was imperceptive, for Gawain's adventures trumpeted the renown of Camelot and shamed the enchantress.

25   NAGANO, YOSHIO. "Old Icelandic Loan-Words in *Sir Gawayne and the Grene Knight." Studies in English Literature and Language* (Kyushu University,

Fukuoka, Japan), No. 16 (June), pp. 51-70.

[Part II of the article. *See also* 1962.14.] Presents a schematized arrangement of the loan-word vocabulary in *Gawain* in order to direct attention to the effects of "linguistic interaction . . . when the foreign element is brought into contact with the native under such peculiar circumstances as the mixture of two races" (p. 51). Categorizes the loan-words (five distinct classes) and arranges the vocabulary according to parts of speech; the largest number of loan-words are nouns (37%) and verbs (37%), whereas adjectives constitute 17% of the vocabulary.

26   OLSZEWSKA, E. S. *"Wylyde Werke: Sir Gawain and the Green Knight 2367."* Notes and Queries, New Series, 13 (December), 451-452.

Interprets *wylyde werke* as "sexual intercourse."

27   SALTER, ELIZABETH. "The Alliterative Revival: I." *Modern Philology*, 64 (November), 146-150.

[*See also* Salter (1967.24).] Contends that fourteenth-century alliterative poems (English) are associated with aristocratic households in the north and west of England and that no real conflict existed between the barons and English monarchy from 1350 on. Suggests that the Cotton Nero poems "with their varied background in the bible and Patristic literature, rhetorical treatises, and French romance" (p. 150) may be traced, perhaps, to the libraries of some well-known patrons, such as Thomas III of Berkeley, for whom clerks paraphrased into alliterative verse significant foreign works.

28   SAN JUAN, EPIFANIO, JR. "Technique of Description in *Sir Gawain and the Green Knight.*" *Diliman Review* (University of the Philippines, Quezon City), 14 (July), 249-257.

Contends that the descriptive details, particularly the depiction of nature (Gawain's journey to Hautdesert), may represent the external manifestations of Gawain's psychological struggle: ". . . a figurative correspondence or analogy exists between external setting and spiritual or internal state" (p. 253). Maintains that setting (Green Chapel scene) foreshadows Gawain's ultimate trials and emphasizes the clash between natural forces and the urbane manners of the court. Emphasizes the winter landscape (1998-2007) and the poet's indebtedness to rhetorical *topoi.*

29   SAVAGE, HENRY L.   *"Fare,* Line 694 of *Sir Gawain and the Green Knight,"* in *Studies in Language and Literature in Honour of Margaret Schlauch.* Edited by Mieczyslaw Brahmer, Stanislaw Helsztyński, and Julian Krzyżanowski. Warsaw: Polish Scientific Publishers, pp. 373-374.

Argues against Conley's interpretation (1957.3) of *fare* as "going, way." Contends that *fare* means "food" because *hym byfore* (1. 694) refers to "the food placed before him for his consumption."

30   SCOTT, P. G. "A Note on the Paper Castle in *Sir Gawain and the Green Knight." Notes and Queries,* New Series, 13 (April), 125-126.

Claims that the image of the paper castle (11. 800-802), somewhat analogous to an image in *Purity* (11. 1407-1408) and in Chaucer's *Parson's Tale* (X[I] , 445), may foreshadow Gawain's temptations and imminent peril for him.

31   SPEARING, A. C.   *"Patience* and the *Gawain*-Poet." *Anglia,* 84, nos. 3-4:305-329.

[Reprinted (in part) in Fox (1968.6).] Perceives a common world view in the Cotton Nero poems; each poem focuses on "a confrontation between a human being and some more than human power" (p. 306). Notes that the hero—essentially a weak, flawed human being—lashes out fruitlessly against the supernatural force which recognizes the frailties of human flesh. Discusses the role of the Green Knight and the testing of *Gawain*—a trial which comically shrinks Gawain's heroic character (especially in the temptation scenes).

32   SUZUKI, EIICHI. "Poetic Synonyms for 'Man' in Middle English Alliterative Poems." *Essays and Studies in English Language and Literature* (Tohoku Gakuin University, Sendai, Japan), 49-50:209-227.

[Covers all four Cotton poems and numerous other alliterative poems.] Employs August Brink's (1920.1) concept of alliterative ranking of words as a yardstick for gauging the quality and function of alliterative synonyms for "man":

burne, freke, gome, haþel, lede, renk, schalk, segge, tulk, and
wyȝe. Notes that all of these "elevated" synonyms appear in
Gawain and that these synonyms, often oral formulas, were
understood easily by the medieval audience—an audience
familiar with alliterative conventions and oral delivery of
poetry.

33   TUTTLETON, JAMES W. "The Manuscript Divisions of
Sir Gawain and the Green Knight." Speculum, 41
(April), 304-310.
Argues that Madden's division of *Gawain* into four fits is
substantiated by manuscript evidence. Notes, however, that
the nine capitals in the manuscript (the four oversized capitals
—fit markers—at lines 1, 491, 1126, and 1998 *plus* the five
small capitals) delineate sections which represent "a coherent
narrative validity" (p. 309) and call attention to sub-sections
operating within the major four-part structure.

1967

1   BAUGH, ALBERT C. "The Middle Ages," in his *A Literary History of England.* Second edition. Vol. 1.
New York: Appleton-Century-Crofts, 190, 236-238.
[Revised edition of 1948.1. The text is the same as that
of the first edition, but a bibliographical supplement (#233,
235-236), listing recent critical studies of *Gawain,* has been
provided.]

2   BENSON, LARRY D. Review of the Kottler-Markman
Concordance to the Cotton Nero poems and *Erkenwald. Speculum,* 42 (April), 382-384.
[*See also* 1966.17.] Notes the inconsistent use of Middle
English words and their modern English equivalents in the
classification of vocabulary as well as the inconvenient grouping of head words in the *Concordance.* Suggests that the *Concordance* may assist scholars in resolving the problem of single
or multiple authorship of the Cotton Nero poems.

3   BORROFF, MARIE, trans. "Introduction," in *Sir Gawain and the Green Knight: A New Verse Translation.* New York: Norton, pp. vii-xiii.

[Reprinted: 1968 and all subsequent editions of the *Norton Anthology of English Literature,* Vol. 1. "The Metrical Form" (pp. 55-62) includes basic and extended forms (in translation) as well as variant forms of the alliterative line, samples of the bob and wheel, and specimen scansions of *Gawain.*]

Discusses the manuscript—its history and poetic works; the ideal of chivalric conduct at the heart of *Gawain;* the fusion of three motifs—"beheading game," temptation, and "exchange of winnings"—in the poem; the parallels between the three hunts and the three temptations; and the formulaic style of the alliterative poetic tradition.

4   BREWER, D. S. "The *Gawain*-Poet: A General Appreciation of Four Poems." *Essays in Criticism,* 17 (April), 130-142.

[Examines all 4 Cotton Nero poems. For a reply to this essay, *see also* Samson (1968.26).] Notes that the Cotton Nero poems were probably composed by one author. Claims that a thematic pattern, tension between selfishness leading to destruction of the spirit and ideal courtesy, is woven into the Cotton peoms; in *Gawain,* self-centeredness takes the form of "sexual desire, worldly self-regard, fear of death" (p. 131). Emphasizes the sophisticated humor suffusing the temptation scenes in *Gawain* as well as the spirited description of winter's harshness, the courtly life and Yuletide festivities, and the "breaking of the deer." Argues that the *Gawain*-poet employs the narrative primarily "to provide strong situations to show how good a knight Gawain is" (p. 137) and that Christian virtue molds relationships between individuals.

5   CHAMPION, LARRY S. "Grace versus Merit in *Sir Gawain and the Green Knight.*" *Modern Language Quarterly,* 28 (December), 413-425.

Contends that Gawain's attempt to preserve his life—either by simply trusting in God's mercy and grace or by molding his salvation through acceptance of the girdle—mirrors a central theological debate during the fourteenth century, "whether salvation is achieved by divine grace or by human merit" (p. 415). Argues that Gawain's struggle to shape his fate is abortive and that the girdle is ultimately emblematic of his need for divine grace.

6   DAVIS, NORMAN, ed. "Introduction," in his edition of
     Sir Gawain and the Green Knight. Edited by J. R. R.
     Tolkien and E. V. Gordon. Revised second edition.
     Oxford: Clarendon Press, pp. xi-xxvii.
         [*See also* (1925.8). Contains an "Appendix" (pp. 132-
     52) on language and meter and a select bibliography (pp. 153-
     156).] Discusses the Cotton Nero manuscript—its appearance,
     foliation, scribal hand, history, divisions, illustrations, and
     locale—as well as the analogues and sources of the challenge/
     beheading game, temptation, and exchange of winnings motifs.
     Comments upon the *Gawain*-poet's sensitive use of color, light,
     and motion and claims that the poem's force springs not from
     magic, but from the poet's comprehension of humanity.
     Traces the relationship between *Gawain* and the other Cotton
     works, *Erkenwald,* and alliterative poetry generally. Examines
     the date and place of composition of *Gawain.*

7   EVANS, W. O. " 'Cortaysye' in Middle English." *Media-
     eval Studies,* 29:143-144, 148, 150-151, 156-157.
         Suggests that *cortaysye* normally connotes Christian vir-
     tue (kindness, fidelity, valor, consideration) rather than court-
     ly love unless the literary context demands the latter. Notes
     that *cortaysye* is linked with *amour courtois* in the temptation
     episodes of *Gawain* and that Bercilak's wife's conception of
     courtesy (adultery) deviates sharply from Gawain's true
     cortaysye. Emphasizes that *cortaysye*—flowing from God—
     allows men "to live life as it is lived in Heaven, to live in such
     a way as to help and please others" (p. 156).

8   EVANS, WILLIAM W. "Dramatic Use of the Second-
     Person Singular Pronoun in *Sir Gawain and the Green
     Knight.*" *Studia Neophilologica,* 39, no. 1:38-45.
         [*See also* Evans (1959.5).] Claims that in *Gawain,* "the
     pronoun *you* [as opposed to *thou,* the historical singular] is
     the normal second-person singular to superiors and between
     equals" (p. 39), whereas *thou* is employed by superiors when
     they are addressing inferiors. Contends that the *Gawain*-poet
     uses *thou* to delineate characters and their attitudes toward
     each other as well as to dramatically represent unstated aims
     and attitudes.

9   GROSS, LAILA. "Time in the Towneley Cycle, *King*

Horn, Sir Gawain and the Green Knight, and Chaucer's *Troilus and Criseyde.*" Ph.D. dissertation, University of Toronto.

[*See Dissertation Abstracts,* 29 (1969), 3097A.] Suggests that *Gawain* depends, in part, upon a division of time, frequently "with dependence on biological time and its inferred recurring motion, into scenes of action in time"—brief scenes during which time is precisely marked.

10   HARGEST-GORZELAK, ANNA. "A Brief Comparison of the *Knight's Tale* and *Sir Gawain and the Green Knight.*" *Roczniki Humanistyczne* (Lublin, Poland), 15, no. 3:91-102.

Focuses on the tone, aims, and rhetoric of the *Knight's Tale* and *Gawain.* Discovers that Chaucer's romance is primarily a rhetorically balanced work in which form outweighs all other elements, whereas *Gawain* bears the imprint of a creative imagination.

11   HAWORTH, PAUL. "*Warthe* in *Sir Gawain and the Green Knight.*" *Notes and Queries,* New Series, 14 (May), 171-172.

Claims that *warthe* (1. 715), perhaps a variant form of *wath,* means "crossing place, ford."

12   HIEATT, CONSTANCE, trans. *Sir Gawain and the Green Knight.* Illustrated by Walter Lorraine. New York: Thomas Y. Crowell, 48 pp.

[Children's version of *Gawain. See also* Utley (1969.31).]

13   JOHNSTON, EVERETT C. "The Signification of the Pronoun of Address in *Sir Gawain and the Green Knight.*" *Language Quarterly* (University of South Florida), 5, nos. 3-4 (Spring-Summer), 34-36.

Examines the pronoun of address, both the familiar form (*þou, þe*) and the polite form (*yow, you*). Contends that Bercilak and his wife frequently switch from one form to the other when they address Gawain, perhaps suggesting that in any new friendship "there is liable to be an early period where the two friends alternate between formality and informality" (p. 36). Claims that Gawain, except for two lapses (1. 2379 and 1. 1802), adheres to the proper mode of address, thereby underscoring his reputation as the "perfect knight."

14   JONES, R. T. "The Gome in the Grene." *The Oxford Review*, 5 (June), 53-61.
       [Review of Burrow (1965.6).] Claims that *Gawain*, a brilliant poem, attempts to question through the hero's quest the values of chivalry and courtesy. Links the Green Knight, especially because of his bush-like beard and holly bob, with vegetation.

15   KEAN, P. M. *The Pearl: An Interpretation.* New York: Barnes & Noble, pp. 14, 48-49, 64, 97n, 116, 186n, 189, 229-230, 238-241.
       Claims that the five-fold nature of the pentangle as well as its endlessness signalize perfection. Emphasizes the visual manner of depicting Hautdesert and the realistic visual details in portraying Gawain's jewels and embroidered figures (11. 608 ff). Interprets the concept of *courtesy*—"nobility and generosity of conduct" (p. 189) as well as courtly manners, especially in the service of *amour courtois.* Compares the disillusionment of Gawain and the dreamer in *Pearl* and examines the term *destiné* or *wyrd* in *Gawain* as well as Gawain's faithless rejection of his destiny and the will of Providence.

16   LONGO, JOSEPH A. "*Sir Gawain and the Green Knight*: The Christian Quest for Perfection." *Nottingham Mediaeval Studies*, 11:57-85.
       Views Gawain as an Everyman figure, a Christian knight who acknowledges and atones for pride of life and *cupiditas* and who ultimately puts on robes of love and humility. Identifies Gawain, especially in the three temptations and hunts, with Adam and the *felix culpa* theme. Employs many exegetical works in order to elucidate the Green Knight's holly bob and ax, Hautdesert, the three animals hunted at Bercilak's castle, the circumcision motif, the Knight's association with the devil, and color symbols—especially green, gold, red, and white.

17   MEHL, DIETER. *Die mittelenglischen Romanzen des 13. und 14. Jahrhunderts.* Anglistische Forschungen, No. 93. Heidelberg: Carl Winter Universitätsverlag, pp. 160-172, and as indexed.

[In German. *See* 1969.18.]

18   MOORMAN, CHARLES. *A Knyght There Was: The Evolution of the Knight in Literature.* Lexington, Kentucky: University of Kentucky Press, pp. 5, 58-75, and as indexed.

[Parts of "The Stained Knight: *Sir Gawain and the Green Knight*" (pp. 58-75) appeared previously in Moorman's article (1956.8).]

Contends that "the hero-quest, *rite de passage,* withdrawal-return pattern" (p. 5) is integral to *Gawain.* In comparing and contrasting *Gawain* and *Troilus and Criseyde,* notes that both poems emphasize the tragic effects of courtly love—the inability of *amour courtois* to produce true happiness and the ultimate failure of courtly ideals and morality. Depicts Gawain's quest as partly spiritual in nature; mythically, his quest represents "a *rite de passage* by which Gawain is initiated into a full understanding of himself and his code of values and . . . to an understanding of the true nature of the chivalry" (p. 62) of Camelot.

Suggests that Camelot and Hautdesert represent two disparate grades of chivalry and that Bercilak's court is more closely tied to the chivalric ideal. Views Morgan's role in *Gawain* as that of a prophetess, disclosing two possible evils—disloyalty and sexual infidelity—which may destroy the chivalric fabric of Camelot in the future. Claims that "the tragedy of the Round Table, and of the secular society which it symbolizes, was inevitable, given its basis in *fin amor*" (p. 73) and that such a tragedy germinated even during the Yuletide revelry at Camelot (as depicted in *Gawain*).

19   NEWSTEAD, HELAINE. "Arthurian Legends," in *A Manual of the Writings in Middle English, 1050-1500.* Edited by J. Burke Severs. Vol. 1, Romances. New Haven: Connecticut Academy of Arts and Sciences, 54-57, 238-243.

[Contains a "Commentary" (pp. 54-57) and a comprehensive bibliography (pp. 238-43) of the scholarly and critical studies of *Gawain.* "Intended to be complete for all serious studies down through 1955 and to include all important studies from 1955 to the present [1966]." *See also* Hamilton, "The *Pearl* Poet," in Vol. 2 of the *Manual* (1970.10).]

"Commentary": Discusses the Cotton Nero manuscript—
its works, dialect (Northwest Midland), and date (1375-1400)
—as well as the possible sources of and motifs (beheading
game, temptation, and exchange of winnings) underlying
Gawain. Emphasizes *Gawain*'s careful use of suspense, sharp
contrast between the outdoor scenes (nature) and the courtly festivities indoors, the hunting and temptation episodes, and
the poem as a "comedy of manners."

20   PACE, GEORGE B. "Physiognomy and *Sir Gawain and
the Green Knight.*" *English Language Notes,* 4
(March), 161-165.

Interprets Morgan le Fay's "black brows" (1.961) physi-
ognomically as an emblem of lechery. Claims that Bercilak's
wife and Morgan in their seductive advances represent, "tropo-
logically, opposite sides of the same coin, aspects of the same
whole" (p. 164).

21   ROBBINS, ROSSELL HOPE. "Middle English Misunder-
stood: Mr. Speirs and the Goblins." *Anglia,* 85:273,
275-278.

Attacks Speirs (1949.9 and 1957.12) for his myth-and-
ritual interpretation of *Gawain* because he offers unsubstan-
tiated statements as conclusive evidence and a "primitivistic"
view of medieval poetry.

22   ROSENBERG, BRUCE A. "The Morphology of the Middle English Metrical Romance." *Journal of Popular
Culture,* 1 (Summer), 67-68.

Employs "morphological analysis" in order to discern the
narrative structure in *Gawain.* Suggests that *Gawain* involves
the "test and reward" pattern, for after being tested by the
Green Knight, he is viewed as the exemplar of chivalry.

23   RYAN, J. S. "The *Ubi Sunt* Theme and *Sir Gawain and
the Green Knight.*" *Journal of the Faculty of Arts*
(Royal University of Malta), 3, no. 3:211-213.

Suggests that it is questionable whether the other knights
of the Round Table will mirror Gawain's courtly and Christian
behavior. Inasmuch as the poet signalizes a fall from the past
ideal behavior at Camelot, perhaps an elegiac note is sounded
in *Gawain.*

24   SALTER, ELIZABETH. "The Alliterative Revival: II."
      Modern Philology, 64 (February), 233-237.
      [*See also* Salter (1966.27).] Focuses on the type of cul-
      tural milieu which may have left its imprint both on the
      Gawain-poet and his alleged patron, John of Gaunt, who pos-
      sessed many estates and castles in the North and in the Mid-
      lands. Notes that John of Gaunt's frequent journeys both to
      London and to the outlying districts where he owned lands
      attests to a clear link between London and the "alliterative
      country"; although alliterative verse is rooted in regional dia-
      lect and metre, such poetry is imbued with a sophisticated
      tone and style—one which would appeal to a cultured audi-
      ence.
          Notes parallels between elements in *Gawain* and objects
      owned by Gaunt (as specified in Gaunt's *Registers*) and con-
      tends that the *Gawain*-poet was, at least, a member of "a
      household maintained by a lord of considerable standing"
      (p. 235).

25   SHEDD, GORDON M. "Knight in Tarnished Armour:
      The Meaning of *Sir Gawain and the Green Knight.*"
      Modern Language Review, 62 (January), 3-13.
          Views *Gawain* as a critical appraisal of the knightly code
      and of man's flawed quest for perfection. Interprets Ga-
      wain's temptation at Hautdesert, "a repetition of the Behead-
      ing Game" (p. 5), as a test of his bravery, honor, fidelity, and
      courtesy. Claims that Gawain does not recognize his human
      failings and the limitations of the knightly code until the
      Green Chapel scene, whereas Arthur's court, marred by a
      myopic vision of human nature, never achieves Gawain's self-
      knowledge.

26   SHUTTLEWORTH, JACK M. "On 'Gawain's' Hagiolo-
      gy." *Discourse,* 10, no. 3 (Summer), 348-351.
          Attempts to emphasize the Christian tone of *Gawain*
      through an examination of the invocation of saints—Peter,
      Julian the Hospitaller, Giles, and John the Baptist. Notes
      parallels between the saints and their legends and the themes
      and narrative events in *Gawain.*

27   SILVERSTEIN, THEODORE. "Allegory and Literary
      Form." *Publications of the Modern Language Asso-*

ciation of America, 82 (March), 30-32.

Argues for a literal interpretation of *Gawain*, "a superb serious comedy" (p. 32), and contends that an allegorical interpretation of this romance is unwarranted.

28   SKLUTE, LARRY MARTIN. "The Ethical Structure of Courtly Romance: Chrétien de Troyes' *Yvain* and *Sir Gawain and the Green Knight.*" Ph.D. dissertation, Indiana University.

[*See Dissertation Abstracts,* 28 (1968), 3648A.] Discusses the influence of the conflicting aims of the Christian, feudal, and courtly codes upon courtly romance and the hero. Examines the opening tableau at Camelot; Gawain's character; Gawain's dilemma and error; and the conclusion of the adventure. Suggests that an "ironic" pattern—a pattern in which the poet claims that no blending of conflicting ethical systems is possible—is interwoven in *Gawain.*

29   SOSNOSKI, JAMES J. "The Methodology of Kenneth Burke's Literary Criticism as Applied to *Sir Gawain and the Green Knight.*" Ph.D. dissertation, Pennsylvania State University.

[*See Dissertation Abstracts,* 29 (1968), 275A.] Discusses Burke's "pentad structure of action: scene, act, agency, agent, and purpose" and applies Burke's method to *Gawain.* Analyzes *Gawain* for its use of games and games within games.

30   SUZUKI, EIICHI. "The Green Knight as Enigma." *Essays and Studies in English Language and Literature* (Tohoku Gakuin University, Sendai, Japan), 51-52: 99-116.

Offers a critical review of the scholarship on the identity and symbolic greenness of the Green Knight. Emphasizes the ambiguous nature of the Green Knight/Bercilak as a game-like element of dramatic suspense.

*31   WEBB, P. H. *"Sir Gawain and the Green Knight."* Unisa English Studies, 1:29-42.

[Unlocatable. Cited in *Modern Language Association Annual Bibliography* (1968).]

32   WEIDHORN, MANFRED. "The Anxiety Dream from

Homer to Milton." *Studies in Philology,* 64 (January), 79.

Compares Gawain's restless sleep and dream prior to his meeting with the Green Knight to the troubled mental state of Wolfram von Eschenbach's Parzival when he sleeps in the grail castle. Claims that Gawain's dream "is yet a delicate touch that humanizes the knight."

33   WILLIAMS, MARGARET. "Introduction," in her translation of *The Pearl-Poet: His Complete Works.* New York: Random House, pp. 3-18, 45-62, 92-98.

[Includes background discussions and translations of all four Cotton poems plus *Erkenwald;* appendices on the manuscript (transcriptions, divisions, and illustrations), language, and prosody (pp. 323-31); a selected bibliography of *Gawain* criticism (pp. 332-337); and annotated charts.] Examines the Cotton Nero manuscript—its language and author—as well as the alliterative movement and possible sources of the *Pearl*-poet's works. Reviews, likewise, many aspects of *Gawain,* including its vocabulary, alliterative style, sources and analogues, anticourtly love motif, comedy, structure and symmetry, and symbolism (color, number, pentangle, animal, girdle, and the Green Knight). Emphasizes the significance of order in the works of the *Gawain*-poet—an order which is rooted in medieval aesthetic and theological ideals.

1968

1   ACKERMAN, ROBERT W. "Sir Frederic Madden and the Study of Medieval Literature," in *Medieval Drama: A Collection of Festival Papers,* Vol. 3, ed. William A. Selz. Vermillion, South Dakota: University of South Dakota Press, pp. 69-77.

Emphasizes Madden's role as a pioneer editor of Middle English texts, especially his collection of Gawain-romances (*see* 1839.1). "The notion of preparing such a book was quite likely provided by Madden's experience of working with the manuscripts of Sir Robert Cotton which survived the fire at Ashburnham House in 1731, for in Manuscript Cotton Nero A.x. he read *Sir Gawain and the Green Knight* for the first time." Notes the significance of Madden's letters (British

Museum Library) and his private journal (Bodleian Library, Oxford) spanning (43 volumes) the period from 1819 to 1872.

2   ACKERMAN, ROBERT W. *"Sir Gawain and the Green Knight* and Its Interpreters," in *On Stage and Off: Eight Essays in English Literature.* Edited by John W. Ehrstine, John R. Elwood, and Robert C. McLean. Pullman: Washington State University Press, pp. 66-73.

Provides a critical appraisal of selected *Gawain* scholarship (articles and books) published during the 1960's (through 1967). Categorizes interpretations of the theme of *Gawain* into three major classes: those which emphasize the importance of *trawþe* and courtesy, those which scrutinize the romance genre and the chivalric code, and those which pinpoint parallels between *Gawain* and *La Queste del Saint Graal.*

3   DAVID, ALFRED. "Gawain and Aeneas." *English Studies,* 49 (October), 402-409.

Contends that *tulk* (1. 3), in the opening description of the fall of Troy, refers to Aeneas, not Antenor. Suggests that the historical cycle in *Gawain*—applicable to both kingdoms and individuals—is reflected in the moral parallels between Aeneas and Gawain.

4   EADIE, JOHN. "Morgain la Fée and the Conclusion of *Sir Gawain and the Green Knight." Neophilologus,* 52 (July), 299-304.

Suggests that the Green Knight's final reference to Morgan as the force underlying the poem's narrative hints at future events in *Gawain.* ". . . when Gawain rides away from Arthur's court, he is leaving the historical world where all moral choices are only potentially good or bad, and going to an enclosed world [Hautdesert] where the consequences of one's moral choices are almost immediately apparent" (p. 301). Contends that the Knight's allusion to Morgan reminds the audience that Gawain must return to the historical world of Camelot, the setting for the recurring conflict between good and evil.

5   EVANS, W. O. "Gawain's New Pentangle." *Trivium,* 3 (May), 92-94.

Interprets þe *pentangel nwe* (1. 636) on Gawain's shield. Claims that the poet gives Gawain a new symbol, the pentangle, rather than the conventional eagle or griffin in order to suggest a new image for the hero and to establish the true meaning of *cortaysye*—Christian "concern and consideration for others" (p. 93).

6   FOX, DENTON, ed. "Introduction," in his *Twentieth Century Interpretations of Sir Gawain and the Green Knight: A Collection of Critical Essays.* Englewood Cliffs, New Jersey: Prentice-Hall, pp. 1-12.

[Contains reprints (mainly excerpts) of Everett (1955.3); Benson (1965.1); Burrow (1965.6); Howard (1964.6); Borroff (1962.1); Mathew (1948.5); Whiting (1947.3); Speirs (1949.9); Zimmer (1948.8); Donaldson (1962.4); Lewis (1962.10); Spearing (1966.31); Clark (1966.8); and Elliott (1958.4).]

"Introduction": Focuses, in part, on the "alliterative revival," *Gawain's* use of the alliterative tradition, and the flowering of English as a literary language. Comments upon the Cotton Nero manuscript, the other Cotton poems, the possible background of the *Gawain*-poet, and the folk motifs underlying *Gawain*. Surveys various critical interpretations of *Gawain*, especially analyses of Bercilak/Green Knight, and emphasizes "the alternation between contrasting scenes—and some of its most important themes—mutability, and the interplay between nature and civilization" (p. 8). Examines the turning of the seasons, emblematic of natural flux; the pentangle, a token of perfection; the bedroom and hunting scenes at Hautdesert; and the paradoxes which infuse the poem.

7   HIEATT, A. KENT. "*Sir Gawain*: Pentangle, *Luf-Lace,* Numerical Structure." *Papers on Language and Literature,* 4 (Fall), 339-359.

[Reprinted in Fowler (1970.12).] Contends that the theme of *Gawain*, troth versus untroth, is signalized by two main symbols—the pentangle and the green girdle (*luf-lace*); "the relationship of these two objects is that of a balanced, two-part symbolic structure rather than that of an isolated construct (the pentangle) to a mere narrative motif (the *lace*) to which significance has been arbitrarily attached" (p. 340). Examines the greenness (inconstancy in love) of the

knotted lace, an emblem of imperfection, and its etymological
links with "noose" or "snare" in the chase or in the game of
love; contrasts the *luf-lace* with the protective qualities offered
by the "endless knot" of the pentangle, a symbol of perfection. Analyzes the symbolic connection between 1. 2525 of
Gawain and the five of the pentangle as well as the general
role of number symbolism in the poem.

8   HOWARD, DONALD R. and CHRISTIAN ZACHER,
     eds. "Preface," in their *Critical Studies of Sir Gawain
     and the Green Knight.* Notre Dame, Indiana: Univer-
     sity of Notre Dame Press, pp. ix-xii.
          [Contains reprints of L. H. Loomis (1959.11); Bloomfield
     (1961.3); Lewis (1962.10); Bowers (1963.1); Mills (1965.16);
     Renoir (1962.16); Howard (1964.6); Silverstein (1964.15);
     Kiteley (1962.8); White (1965.27); Delany (1965.8); Malarkey
     and Toelken (1964.10); Carson (1963.3); Bercovitch (1965.3);
     Solomon (1963.15); Manning (1964.11); Gardner (1966.11);
     Hills (1963.8); and Burrow (1964.2).
          Contains excerpts from Benson (1965.1); Borroff
     (1962.1); and Spearing (1964.16).] "Preface": Traces the his-
     tory of the Cotton Nero manuscript from its cataloguing by
     Thomas Smith (1696) through its "discovery" by Frederick
     Madden in the 1830's. Discusses the scribal hand (early fif-
     teenth century), the date and dialect of *Gawain*, and the au-
     thorship question (common or multiple authors).

9   HUSSEY, S. S. "*Sir Gawain* and Romance Writing."
     Studia Neophilologica, 40, no. 1:161-174.
          Argues that the central concerns of *Gawain* may be
     elucidated through an examination of medieval romances and
     romance conventions. Analyzes the significance of ambiguous
     phraseology and word play, especially in the employment of
     gomen and in the courtly love bantering of the temptation
     episodes (another type of "play"). Focuses on the central
     position of *trawpe* in *Gawain* and other contemporary ro-
     mances and asserts that Gawain's quest involves "a questioning
     of traditional romance values" (p. 174).

10   IKEGAMI, TADAHIRO. "Courtesy in *Sir Gawain and
     the Green Knight.*" *Eigo-bungaku-sekai* (*The World
     of English Literature*), 3, no. 11:38-41.

[In Japanese.   Annotation provided by the author.]
Focuses particularly on the third fitt. Discusses the subtle
and comic difference between Gawain and the lady's concept
of courtesy; her outlook on courtesy signalizes the decline and
illusory nature of chivalry in the late Middle Ages.

11   KENNEDY, SALLY PITTS. "Vestiges of Rule Ritual in
     Sir Gawain and the Green Knight." Ph.D. disserta-
     tion, University of Tennessee.
        [*See Dissertation Abstracts,* 29 (1968), 1513A. The au-
     thor's name is now Sally K. Slocum.]   Focuses on the two
     fundamental methods of governing society—the male's rule
     through power and achievement and the female's rule through
     "blood ties and inheritance."   Emphasizes the conflict be-
     tween the male (Arthur and Camelot) and the female (Morgan
     and Hautdesert) principles in *Gawain,* resulting in a compro-
     mise as well as a comic conclusion for the poem.

12   LUCAS, PETER J. "Gawain's Anti-Feminism." *Notes
     and Queries,* New Series, 15 (September), 324-325.
        Claims that Gawain's "anti-feminist" diatribe is "strictly
     relevant to the means [the acceptance of the girdle from the
     lady] through which he acquired his fault" (p. 325). Suggests
     that the Old Testament *exempla* (11. 2416-19) buttress Ga-
     wain's argument that he was emotionally and spiritually blind.

13   McNAMARA, JOHN FRANCIS. "Responses to Ock-
     hamist Theology in the Poetry of the *Pearl*-Poet,
     Langland, and Chaucer." Ph.D. dissertation, Louisi-
     ana State University.
        [Covers all four Cotton Nero poems and *Erkenwald. See
     Dissertation Abstracts,* 29 (1969), 3148A-49A.] Discusses the
     influence of the fourteenth-century nominalist-realist debate
     (grace versus merit) upon *Gawain.* Contends that Gawain is
     guilty of serious sin; yet, at the end, he reconciles himself
     with God by accepting His grace.

14   MATHEW, GERVASE. *The Court of Richard II.* Lon-
     don: John Murray, pp. 53, 116-118, 123-125, 166.
        Comments upon the Cotton Nero manuscript—its nature,
     contents, and provenance—which "was bound into its present
     volume . . . by Sir Robert Cotton [and] . . . had come into his

possession from that of the Yorkshire antiquarian Henry Savile of Bank (1568-1617)" (p. 116), thereby calling attention to a northern origin. Claims that the poet of *Gawain* may have been a knight in some lord's household and conjectures that the lost *original* manuscript may have been a "repertory book" sponsored by an affluent nobleman. Links the crude manuscript illuminations with the experimental portrayals of scenery and architecture found in French court art (late fourteenth and early fifteenth centuries).

Views *franchyse,* part of the language of chivalry, as a type of magnanimity of spirit, whereas courtesy (good manners in behavior or in speech) frequently manifested itself in service to the lady (Bercilak's wife, for example). Concludes by noting that Sir John Stanley, an influential lord from southwest Lancashire, was, perhaps, the *Gawain*-poet's patron; alludes to the dialect of *Gawain* as well as to the reference to the Order of the Garter and contends that ". . . at this period Sir John Stanley was the only knight of the Garter in southwest Lancashire" (p. 166).

15   MATHEWSON, JEANNE T. *"Sir Gawain and the Green Knight* and the Medieval Comic Tradition." Ph.D. dissertation, Stanford University.

[*See Dissertation Abstracts,* 29 (1969), 2678A-79A.] Analyzes the medieval comic tradition in order to demonstrate the link between *Gawain* and the fall of Adam. Suggests that *Gawain,* a comedy fittingly tied to the Christmas season, emphasizes Gawain's lesson of humility and his acceptance of human limitations.

16   MATTHEWS, WILLIAM, ed. *Old and Middle English Literature.* Goldentree Bibliography. New York: Appleton-Century-Crofts, pp. 61-62.

[Brief select bibliography of editions, translations, and scholarly studies of *Gawain.*]

17   MILLS, DAVID. "An Analysis of the Temptation Scenes in *Sir Gawain and the Green Knight." Journal of English and Germanic Philology,* 67 (October), 612-630.

Attempts to examine the comic tone and "moral tension" evoked by the three temptations. Argues that the comedy

underlying the first temptation springs from the sudden shift
of conventional chivalric diction and motifs to a highly sexual-
ized bedroom setting. Contends that the second temptation
focuses on the contrast between Gawain's behavior and idealized chivalric behavior and that the third temptation highlights
the emotionally charged interplay between Gawain and Bercilak's wife, culminating in Gawain's victory and his anti-
climactic acceptance of the girdle.

18   MOORMAN, CHARLES. *The Pearl-Poet.* Twayne's Eng-
     lish Authors Series, No. 64. New York: Twayne, pp.
     19-34, 88-117.
     [Contains a select (briefly annotated) bibliography (pp.
     131-135, 138-141) of editions; authorship, cultural, and
     linguistic studies; and scholarly studies of *Gawain.*] Examines
     the historical and cultural milieu, including the "alliterative
     revival," in which the *Gawain*-poet wrote and discusses the
     possible identity of this poet, the "unity of authorship" of·
     the Cotton Nero poems, and the dating and locale of the
     Cotton poems. Views *Gawain* in terms of its versification,
     plot, structure and symmetry, analogues and sources of its
     three Celtic motifs (challenge/beheading game, temptation,
     and exchange of winnings), mythic elements, and morality.
     Contends that all four Cotton poems focus on "the relation
     of sexual morality [and/or] . . . loyalty to one's code of con-
     duct, both secular and religious" (p. 115).

19   NEALE, ROBERT. *"Sir Gawain and the Green Knight."*
     The Use of English, 20, no. 1 (Autumn), 41-46.
     Claims that critics frequently pay inordinate attention to
     linguistic elements in *Gawain* or to the poem's literary and
     mythic sources. Discusses the poem's cyclical structure—the
     reference to the fall of Troy at the beginning and ending of
     Gawain; the contrasts and parallels between Camelot and
     Hautdesert; the relationship between the hunts and tempta-
     tions; the poetic employment of specific, concrete details; the
     ambiguous nature of the Green Knight's moral challenge to
     Arthur's court and to Gawain; and the comic aspects of
     Gawain, including the Knight's humor and "gusto."

20   NEWSTEAD, HELAINE, ed.   "Introduction" to her
     Chaucer and His Contemporaries: Essays on Medi-

eval Literature and Thought. Greenwich, Connecticut: Fawcett Publications, pp. 9, 10, 16-17.

[This book, likewise, reprints L. H. Loomis (1959.11) and Brewer (1966.6).] Briefly discusses the Cotton Nero manuscript—its date (1400), dialect, and meter—and calls attention to the *Gawain*-poet's delight in symmetry and acquaintance with the life of the aristocrats.

21   NOSSEL, MARGARET A. "Christian Commitment and Romance Ideals in *Sir Gawain and the Green Knight.*" Ph.D. dissertation, Cornell University.

[*See Dissertation Abstracts,* 29 (1969), 4464A.] Focuses on the conflict between Gawain's chivalric ideals and spiritual ideals as represented by the pentangle. Views *Gawain* as a kind of "typological game designed to show Gawain the necessity for a constantly renewed baptismal commitment to Christ by allowing him to repeat in his own experience the general pattern of salvation history."

22   OAKDEN, J. P. *Alliterative Poetry in Middle English: The Dialectal and Metrical Survey.* Vol. 1. Hamden, Connecticut: Shoe String Press (Archon Books), 72-89, 154-156, 177, 179-180, 251-255, 257-263, and passim.

[Reprint of 1930.4.]

23   OAKDEN, J. P. *Alliterative Poetry in Middle English: A Survey of the Traditions.* Vol. 2. Hamden, Connecticut: Shoe String Press (Archon Books), 46-48, 89-93, 167-168, 179-181, 183-193, 263-312, passim, 381-391, passim, 392-399.

[Reprint of 1935.3.]

24   OWEN, D. D. R. "Burlesque Tradition and *Sir Gawain and the Green Knight.*" *Forum for Modern Language Studies,* 4, no. 2 (April), 125-145.

Argues that the *Gawain*-poet employed two French romances—*Le Chevalier à l'épée* and *La Mule sans frein*—as his main literary sources and that he used the"burlesque tradition," a tradition often linked with Gawain in the earliest romances, in *Gawain.* Contends that the seduction scenes in *Gawain,* scenes which hint at but do not highlight Gawain's

reputation as a lover in French romances, represent the apex
of the burlesque tradition in *Gawain.*

25   PIERLE, ROBERT C. *"Sir Gawain and the Green
      Knight*: A Study in Moral Complexity.*" The South-
      ern Quarterly,* 6 (January), 203-211.
      Notes the conflict in *Gawain* between the poet's essential-
      ly Christian viewpoint and the romance elements he depicts.
      Emphasizes the use of contrasts in *Gawain,* especially the con-
      flict between man's body and spirit.

26   SAMSON, ANNE. *"Sir Gawain." Essays in Criticism,* 18
      (July), 343-347.
      [Reply to Brewer (1967.4).] Emphasizes the artistic
      fusion of narrative parallels in order to achieve structural unity
      in *Gawain.* Argues against Brewer's view of Hautdesert as the
      earthly counterpart of heaven. Maintains that testing, especial-
      ly the testing of the essential worth of chivalric ideals, is the
      thematic undercurrent running throughout *Gawain.*

27   SCHILLER, ANDREW. "The Gawain Rhythm." *Lan-
      guage and Style,* 1 (Fall), 268-294.
      Attempts to analyze the rhythmic pattern, including both
      meter and alliteration, of *Gawain.* Employs musical notation
      in his analysis and claims that the *Gawain* stanza includes "an
      indefinite number of lines of the pattern ¼ plus 3 plus ¾; a
      bob of the pattern of ¼ plus ¾; four wheel lines of the pattern
      ¼ plus one plus ¾—and the bob and wheel together rhymed
      ababa" (pp. 275-276). Views *Gawain* as "isochronic verse"
      and as "organically alliterative" in pattern. Argues that the
      rhythm of *Gawain* may be linked with the music of the *ars
      nova,* a fourteenth-century musical style of great complexity.
      Claims that the rhythmic unit in *Gawain* is the stanza and that
      Gawain employs the structure of the *chanson de geste.*

28   SUZUKI, EIICHI. "The Aesthetic Function of the Syn-
      onyms for 'Man, Knight': A Case in *Sir Gawain and
      the Green Knight." Essays and Studies in English
      Language and Literature* (Tohoku Gakuin University,
      Sendai, Japan), 53-54:15-31.
      Refutes Benson's view (1965.1) that the alliterative poets
      vary synonyms for "man" and "knight" in order to define

character roles and suggests that Benson overlooks the stylistic significance of "archaic synonyms and oral formulas" in alliterative poetry. Maintains the "dominant" position of the Green Knight, especially in the Green Chapel scene, and analyzes the aesthetic function of ten synonyms [*see also* Suzuki (1966.32)] for "man, knight," all of which normally appear in alliterating position in *Gawain*. "The primary function of these nouns corresponds to the alliterative poets' intention to idealize and typify their subject matters, and as a result they are endowed with traditional and familiar associations" (p. 30).

1969

1   ANTTILA, RAIMO. *"Sound Preference in Alliteration."* *Statistical Methods in Linguistics* (Stockholm), 5:44-48.

Contends that alliterative poetry is a helpful element in determining sound preference. Uses *Gawain* as a test case to ascertain whether sound preference may be evaluated statistically. Suggests that his method may be employed to resolve the authorship problem surrounding the Cotton Nero Poems.

2   BARTON, ROBERT JOYCE. "A Figural Reading of *Sir Gawain and the Green Knight.*" Ph.D. dissertation, Stanford University.

[*See Dissertation Abstracts,* 30 (1970), 3423A.] Contends that *Gawain*, like the other Cotton Nero poems, belongs to the poetic tradition of Christian meditation and that the comic spirit informing *Gawain* is ultimately Christian. Examines the fall of Troy frame, the recurring allusions to laughter, the illusory nature of the romance world, and the image clusters in *Gawain*. Discusses, likewise, the use of color symbolism and Gawain's pentangle, an ironic emblem of Gawain's fault.

3   BLOOMFIELD, MORTON W. "Some Notes on *Sir Gawain and the Green Knight* (Lines 374, 546, 752, 1236) and *Pearl* (Lines 1-12, 61, 775-776, 968)," in *Studies in Language, Literature, and Culture of the Middle Ages and Later.* Edited by E. Bagby Atwood and Archibald A. Hill. Austin: University of Texas

Press, pp. 300-301.

Interprets difficult words, including *byden* (1. 374) as "await (forever)"; *cost* (1. 546), derived from the Old French *cost*, as "what's at stake" or "price"; *baret* (1. 752) as "woe"; and *tale* (1. 1236) in the sexual sense of "tail."

*4   CAVALLO, SIMONETTA. *"Sir Gawain and the Green Knight."* Ph.D. dissertation, Università del Sacro Cuore, Facoltà di Magistero, Milan.

[Citation provided by Professor Carl Berkhout.]

5   COFFEY, JEROME EDWARD. "The Evolution of an Oral-Formulaic Tradition in Old and Middle English Alliterative Verse." Ph.D. dissertation, State University of New York at Buffalo.

[Partly on *Gawain*. See *Dissertation Abstracts,* 30 (1969), 2477A-78A.] Contends that the Germanic long line in English alliterative poetry is closely tied to an oral tradition in both Anglo-Saxon and Middle English verse. Scrutinizes *Gawain* (11. 130-50) for its formulaic and prosodic features and concludes that *Gawain,* although it reflects the influence of literary conventions, bears the imprint of oral tradition.

6   COMO, FRANK THOMAS. *"Sir Gawain and the Green Knight*: A Normalized and Glossed Text." Ph.D. dissertation, Arizona State University.

[Contains Middle English text with English introduction and notes. See *Dissertation Abstracts,* 30 (1969), 2512A.] Discusses the Cotton Nero MS, the verse form of *Gawain,* and the Northwest Midland dialect.

7   COTTLE, BASIL. *The Triumph of English, 1350-1400.* New York: Barnes and Noble, pp. 30, 34, 42-44, 46, 96-98, 109, 149, 164, 259, 261, 276, 279-285, 287-288.

Comments upon the appropriate invocation of saints in *Gawain* as well as upon the realism of the castle belonging to Bercilak. Treats of the distinction between *þou* (thou), the pronoun employed by superiors to inferiors and by familiar social equals, and *ȝe* (you), the appelation used by inferiors toward superiors. Focuses on the use of these pronouns at Camelot, Bercilak's castle, during the journey with the guide to the Green Chapel, and finally, at the Chapel.

8   CRANE, JOHN KENNY. "The Four Levels of Time in *Sir Gawain and the Green Knight.*" *Annuale Mediaevale,* 10:65-80.

Perceives four distinct levels of time operating in *Gawain* —cosmic time, the foundation of all conceptions of time; historical time, a linear arrangement of narrative events; psychological time, the ordering of events as they appear to Gawain; and sacred time, a representation of Camelot's efforts to render powerless the corrosive effects of time upon the Christian life. Demonstrates how and why these four levels of time are interlocked in *Gawain* and how a knowledge of time helps to elucidate the behavior of the characters in this romance.

9   GROSS, LAILA. "Telescoping in Time in *Sir Gawain and the Green Knight.*" *Orbis Litterarum,* 24, no. 2: 130-137.

[*See also* 1967.9.] Argues that the *Gawain*-poet weaves into his narrative a technique involving "the narrator's establishing an historical period and then carving up the period into progressively smaller temporal sections until he reaches an important event. Then the temporal indications stop" (p. 130). Examines the opening of *Gawain,* the historical cycle depicting the fall of Troy and its legendary link with Britain and finally zeroes in on Arthur, the descendant of the Trojans, and his Yuletide festivities at Camelot. Claims that the use of telescoped time as a narrative technique generates suspense, rivets the audience's attention to the scene or action, and enhances the realistic elements in the story.

10   HALVERSON, JOHN. "Template Criticism: *Sir Gawain and the Green Knight.*" *Modern Philology,* 67 (November), 133-139.

Attacks some critics of *Gawain* for misinterpretation or distortion of the poetic text in their eagerness to discern the "meaning" of this difficult romance. Debunks the notion of profound "spirituality" embedded in *Gawain,* and rejects other kinds of "template criticism"—mythic and psychological —because they are reductive and frequently ignore the poem itself.

11   ISAACS, NEIL D. "Royal Robes and Regicide: A Preliminary Study of Literary Vestiges of Rule Rituals." *Folklore,* 80 (Autumn), 214.

Notes that "symbolic robing as a possible royal investiture of a sacral king" may be illustrated by *Gawain,* a poem which contains many allusions to rule ritual. Claims that Gawain's girdle is an emblem of "his worthiness to undergo a ritual sacrifice as king-surrogate."

12   JENSEN, ELISABETH N. "Uoverensstemmelserne i Gawains karakter belyst ud fra *Sir Gawain and the Green Knight* og Sir Thomas Malory's *Morte d'Arthur.*" *Extracta,* 2:196-201.

[Abstract of a work in Danish.] Traces the poet's depiction of the hero in *Gawain* and contrasts that characterization with Malory's treatment of Gawain in the *Morte d'Arthur.* Focuses, primarily, on how the two works delineate the relationship between Gawain and Arthur and portray Gawain's outlook on religion and women.

13   JONES, EDWARD TROSTLE. "The Sound of Laughter in *Sir Gawain and the Green Knight.*" *Mediaeval Studies,* 31:343-345.

Examines Gawain's return to Camelot in order to demonstrate that the court's laughter almost suggests a "comedy of manners," a humorous reaction to Gawain's overserious self-judgment. Claims that the laughter of Arthur and his court preserves Gawain from guilt.

14   KER, W. P. *Medieval English Literature.* Oxford: Oxford University Press, pp. 75-78, and as indexed.

[Reprint of 1912.2, with "Bibliographical Notes" (pp. 136-40) by Pamela Gradon.]

15   LAMBA, B. P. and R. JEET. "*Sir Gawain and the Green Knight,* 800-802." *The Explicator,* 27, no. 6 (February), no. 47.

Associates the paper castle image in *Gawain* with the paper table decoration in *Purity* (11. 1498-1499) and with the paper castle allusion in Chaucer's *Parson's Tale* (*Canterbury Tales* X(I), 44), a denunciation of pride and waste. Views the paper castle image in *Gawain,* then, as a "court metaphor," a foreshadowing of Gawain's imminent danger at Hautdesert.

16   LOOMIS, ROGER SHERMAN. *Wales and the Arthurian Legend.* Folcroft, Pennsylvania: Folcroft Press, pp. 20, 77-90, 100, 163, 216.
[Reprint of 1956.6.]

17   MANSON, H. W. D. "Postscript" to his *The Green Knight.* Cape Town: Human & Rousseau, pp. 75-83.
[*The Green Knight* represents a dramatic reinterpretation of *Gawain.*] Claims, first of all, that his play was inspired by Speirs's article (1949.9). Maintains, furthermore, that the original *Sir Gawain* involves a challenge by a natural "civilization" or vibrancy itself (Green Knight) against the urbane, yet artificial, values of Camelot, and, perhaps, of Christianity. Emphasizes Gawain's quest as a personal experience and the threatening nature of the temptation scenes. Views the lady's girdle as an emblem of human love: "In accepting the green girdle, Gawain accepts the woman's love and her body as the token of this love" (p. 81).

18   MEHL, DIETER. *The Middle English Romances of the Thirteenth and Fourteenth Centuries.* London: Routledge & Kegan Paul, pp. 193-206, and as indexed.
[Revised English version of 1967.17. Published in 1969, for 1968.] Argues that *Gawain* is analogous to other Middle English romances in its references to past English history (fall of Troy and the founding of Britain), its artistic structure, and its metrical control. Yet *Gawain* is in many respects "quite unique in Middle English literature and can be compared with very few of the other romances." Comments on the *Gawain*-stanza (especially the wheel); the symmetrical elements (the fall of Troy, the Yuletide season, the fusion of the temptation motif and the "beheading game," and the indoor-outdoor hunting scenes); the dramatic significance of the turning of the seasons passage; and the poet's narrative art.

19   MERTENS-FONCK, PAULE. "Morgan, Fée et Déesse," in *Mélanges offerts à Rita Lejeune.* Vol. 2. Gembloux: Éditions J. Duculot, 1067-1076.

[In French.]   Points out that the action in *Gawain* un-
folds in a supernatural atmosphere.   Claims that the two epithets assigned to Morgan le Fay—fairy and goddess—are
reminiscent of the Celtic goddess Morrígu.   Inasmuch as Morrígu often assumes the form and coloring of a crow, the allusion in *Gawain* to Morgan's black chin (1. 958) and eyebrows
(1. 961) may symbolically identify Morgan with Morrígu.

20   MOORMAN, CHARLES.   "Communication: the *Pearl*-
      Poet Concordance." *Chaucer Review* 3, no. 4:304-
      308.
            Examines the merits and weaknesses of *A Concordance to*
      Five Middle English Poems (1966.17).

21   MOORMAN, CHARLES. "The Origins of the Alliterative
      Revival." *The Southern Quarterly,* 7 (July), 345-371.
            [Provides background information.]   Traces the origins
      of the "alliterative revival" (1350-1450), actually the blossom-
      ing of a tradition which is rooted in Old English literature and
      which remained vibrant through oral poetic forms in the
      Anglo-Norman age.   Maintains that the "revival" springs from
      the anti-French, anti-monarchy views of the English barons,
      noblemen who wished to cultivate the Anglo-Saxon verse
      forms and traditions as well as the provincial dialects.   Notes
      the parallels in phraseology (hunting) and description between
      Gawain and *Parlement of the Thre Ages.*

22   PACE, GEORGE B. "Gawain and Michaelmas." *Traditio,*
      25:404-411.
            Notes that Michaelmas, the feast of St. Michael and the
      Angels which is celebrated on September 29, is mentioned in
      lines 531-534 of *Gawain.*   Suggests that *Meȝelmas mone*
      (1. 531) does not mean "harvest moon," but may be identi-
      fied with a "quarter day," an appointed time for settling ac-
      counts; for Gawain, then, Michaelmas is a reminder of the
      wynter wage (1. 532), the "wage" of his beheading, to be paid
      to the Green Knight on New Year's Day.

23   SKINNER, VERONICA L. "The Concept of 'Trawþe' in
      Sir Gawain and the Green Knight." *Massachusetts*
      Studies in English, 2 (Fall), 49-58.
            Argues that *trawþe* and its affiliated qualities—faith,

loyalty, truth—play a significant role in *Gawain*. Examines *trawþe* in all its various senses and explores how these meanings function in *Gawain*.

24   STEELE, PETER. *"Sir Gawain and the Green Knight*: The Fairy Kind of Writing." *Southern Review* (University of Adelaide), 3:358-365.

Claims that *Gawain* is a fairy poem, a work which contains the "impulse which is most at home with the exact seen as the gratuitous" (p. 358). Focuses on the core of *Gawain*, an imaginative fusion of the real and the marvelous, and argues that the Green Knight's role in the poem is that of game player.

25   STEPHANY, WILLIAM A. "A Study of Four Middle English Arthurian Romances." Ph.D. dissertation, University of Delaware.

[Partly on *Gawain*. *See Dissertation Abstracts*, 30 (1969), 1537A.] Offers a structural analysis of *Gawain* in order to illuminate the poem's theme, "the reaffirmation of the value of an individual's growth of self-awareness in the midst of a society ruled by Fortune and destined to fall." Notes the significance of the *felix culpa* motif in *Gawain*.

26   SUZUKI, EIICHI. "Middle English *Molde*." *Studies in English Literature* (English Number), 45, no. 3:79-82, 85-86.

Applies the oral-formulaic theory, especially Donald K. Fry's modifications of the theory, to the word *molde* ("earth"). Notes the unconventional use (*Gawain*, 1. 964) of *on molde* to delineate a woman rather than a man (*man on molde*).

27   SUZUKI, EIICHI. "The Temptation Episode in *Sir Gawain and the Green Knight*." *Journal of the English Institute* (Sendai, Japan), 1:1-31.

[In Japanese. Annotation provided by author.] Emphasizes that the Lady of the Castle follows the code of courtly love and that the central concern here, as viewed from the total structure of the poem, is Gawain's loyalty.

28   SUZUKI, EIICHI. "Two Notes on *Sir Gawain*." *Essays*

and Studies in English Language and Literature
(Tohoku Gakuin University, Sendai, Japan), 55:63-
80.
[In Japanese. Annotation provided by author. *See also*
Suzuki (1977.15).] Suggests that the meaning of *hyghe*
(1. 844) is "advanced in age, old" (for a more detailed discussion, see my "A Note on the Age of the Green Knight,"
NM, 78 (1977), 27-30) and that a kind of flattery may be per-
ceived in Gawain's address to the Green Knight as *hende* where
hathel would seem more appropriate.

29   TAMPLIN, RONALD. "The Saints in *Sir Gawain and the
      Green Knight.*" *Speculum*, 44 (July), 403-420.
          Argues that the poet's allusions to five saints—the Virgin
      Mary, St. Peter, St. John the Evangelist, St. Giles Aegidius,
      and St. Julian the Hospitaller—are shaped by the contexts in
      which such references appear in *Gawain* and by the legendary
      or literary background and traditions associated with the in-
      dividual saints. Claims that when the porter of Hautdesert
      swears (1. 813) by Peter, the patron saint of porters, this oath
      probably represents a note of reassurance. Links Gawain's re-
      ference to Julian (11. 774-76), when Arthur's knight first
      sights the castle, with the important motifs of hunting, hospi-
      tality, and penitence. Suggests that Bercilak invokes Giles
      (1. 1644) because of the saint's traditional identification with
      merchants, contrition, and hunting. Contends that allusions
      to Mary and John appear in the temptation scenes in order to
      signalize Gawain's need for chastity.

30   TAYLOR, P. B. " 'Blysse and blunder': Nature and Ritu-
      al in *Sir Gawain and the Green Knight.*" *English
      Studies*, 50 (April), 165-175.
          Claims that the chivalric ritual which Gawain follows is
      patterned after Nature and represents an imperfect imitation
      of the divine. Discusses the function of nature as a setting for
      the narrative action and as "a force contrasting with and acting
      upon Gawain's courtly ritual" (p. 166). Demonstrates that
      Gawain veers toward worldly pleasures, ignores spiritual
      duties, and falls prey to the Green Knight's deception.

31   UTLEY, FRANCIS LEE. "The Strategies of Transla-
      tion." *Journal of Aesthetic Education*, 3, no. 4

(October), 137-141.

[Review article: a commentary upon the value of translations.]   Analyzes Constance Hieatt's (1967.12) children's version of *Gawain*. Contends that this version excises the language and mood of *amour courtois* and emphasizes psychological elements rather than the Christian underpinnings of *Gawain*.

1970

1   ACKERMAN, ROBERT W. "Castle Hautdesert in *Sir Gawain and the Green Knight*," in *Mélanges de langue et de littérature du Moyen Âge et de la Renaissance offerts à Jean Frappier—par ses collègues, ses élèves et ses amis. PRF*, No. 112. Vol. 1. Geneva: Librairie Droz, 1-7.

[Includes some comments on *Pearl*.]   Suggests parallels between Gawain's view of Castle Hautdesert and Perceval's outlook on the castle of the Rich Fisher King, as depicted in Chrétien de Troyes' *Roman de Perceval*. Claims that the *Gawain*-poet's descriptive technique—employment of "the beholder's viewpoint"—may be indebted to established literary tradition, "a tradition in which the beholder is struck by the splendor but more importantly the suggestion of mystery as he surveys from a distance a vast structure which he longs . . . to enter."   Such a tradition may be rooted in St. John's vision (*Apocalypse*) of the New Jerusalem.

2   BLOOMFIELD, MORTON W. "Episodic Motivation and Marvels in Epic and Romance," in his *Essays and Explorations: Studies in Ideas, Language, and Literature.* Cambridge, Massachusetts: Harvard University Press, pp. 109-110.

[This book also reprints (pp. 131-57) Bloomfield's survey of *Gawain* scholarship (1961.3).]   Examines "backward motivation" in *Gawain*, specifically the murky explanation by the poet of the Green Knight's challenge to Arthur's court.

3   BOSSY, MICHEL-ANDRÉ RAOUL. "The Prowess of Debate: A Study of a Literary Mode, 1100-1400." Ph.D. dissertation, Yale University.

[Partly on *Gawain*. *See Dissertation Abstracts*, 31 (1971), 6540A-41A.] Discusses the debates between Gawain and Lady Bercilak—debates which signalize the tension between courtesy and physical prowess and call attention to the ambivalence pervading *Gawain*.

4   CARRIÈRE, JEAN LOUISE. *"Sir Gawain and the Green Knight* as a Christmas Poem." *Comitatus*, 1 (December), 25-42.

[Pages 40-42 represent Professor William Matthews' "Appendix" to Carrière's essay.] Discusses various Christmas elements in *Gawain*—Yuletide merriment and games as well as colors (red, green, and gold) and setting. Contends that Gawain and the other members of Arthur's court must learn the true meaning of Christmas and the need for Christian perfection and grace. Depicts in the "Appendix," however, the significance of the manuscript illustration of the appearance of Bercilak's wife to the sleeping Gawain. Contends that the figure represented on the pillar behind Gawain is Bercilak, an allegorical emblem of Christ, that Lady Bercilak symbolizes Eve, and Gawain represents Adam.

5   DAVIS, NORMAN. *"Sir Gawain and the Green Knight* 2073." *Notes and Queries*, New Series, 17 (May), 163-164.

Interprets *Gef hym God and goud day* ("gave him God and good day") as a truncated version of the conventional "farewell" phrase, "betaught him to God and gave him good day."

6   DENDINGER, LLOYD N. "The Dynamic Structural Balance of *Sir Gawain and the Green Knight*," in *Essays in Honor of Esmond Linworth Marilla*. Edited by Thomas Austin Kirby and William John Olive. Baton Rouge: Louisiana State University Press, pp. 367-378.

Uses Randall's schematic representation (1957.11) of the three-part structure of *Gawain* as a starting point for his discussion of the poem's narrative structure. Maintains that the *Gawain*-poet "has taken the materials of *two* plots [Challenge and Temptation], combined them in a basic *three*-part structure and produced a *single* harmonious whole" (p. 373). Finds dynamic structural balance in the poem, especially in "Gawain's two preparations for departure" (p. 375) and in the first and third hunt/temptation tableaux "adorned by the relatively heavy deer-breaking scene and the drama and the color of the gift of the green girdle" (p. 376).

7   DIAMOND, SARA ARLYN. "A Study of the Middle English Alliterative Romances." Ph.D. dissertation, University of California, Berkeley.

[Partly on *Gawain*. *See Dissertation Abstracts,* 31 (1971), 3500A-01A.]   Investigates the alliterative romance tradition in order to shed light upon *Gawain*. Discusses (chap. 6) the theme, type-scenes, structure, and techniques employed in *Gawain*.

8   GALLANT, GERALD. "The Three Beasts: Symbols of Temptation in *Sir Gawain and the Green Knight.*" *Annuale Mediaevale,* 11:35-50.

Analyzes the hunting and the temptation scenes. Contends that "the animals [hunted] represent sinful modes of behavior . . . the way the temptress would like him [Gawain] to behave" (p. 36). Interprets the hart (a punning designation for "heart") as an emblem of passion, the boar as a symbol of the gluttony traditionally linked with the belly, and the fox as a representation of the cunning attributed to the human head.

9   GREEN, D. H. "Irony and Medieval Romance." *Forum for Modern Language Studies,* 6, no. 1 (January), 52-53, 58, 60-61, 63.

[Reprinted: 1971.16.]   Notes the *Gawain*-poet's use of verbal irony in the twofold meaning attached to "courtesy"—"love-making" as interpreted by Bercilak's wife and "gracious chivalric behavior" as viewed by Gawain. Claims that verbal irony in *Gawain* involves the undercutting of literary convention—the initial establishment (11. 625-30) of the pentangle, the emblem of Solomon, as a symbol of perfection and the subsequent allusion to Solomon's weaknesses (1. 2414 f.) once Gawain's imperfections have been disclosed. Finds dramatic irony, however, in the *Gawain*-poet's ability to keep his audience teetering between knowledge and ignorance and perceives "irony of values," especially in the conclusion of *Gawain*, for Gawain's shameful reaction to his fault sharply contrasts with the insensitive, albeit sportive, response of Camelot to Gawain's adventure. Concludes with a reference to "structural irony," Gawain's ignorance of the function and significance of the three temptations at Hautdesert.

10   HAMILTON, MARIE P.   "The *Pearl* Poet," in *A Manual of the Writings in Middle English, 1050-1500*. Edited by J. Burke Severs. Vol. 2. New Haven: Connecticut Academy of Arts and Sciences, 339-341, 503-516, passim.

[Contains a "Commentary" (pp. 339-41) on the Cotton Nero manuscript—its works, dialect, date—the problem of single or multiple authorship, and the stylistic features common to the *Pearl* poems *plus* a comprehensive bibliography (pp. 503-16), including occasional references to *Gawain*, of the scholarly and critical studies of *Pearl*, *Patience*, and *Purity*. *See also* Newstead, "Arthurian Legends," in Vol. 1 of the *Manual* (1967.19).]

11   HEYWORTH, P. L.   "Notes on Two Uncollected Middle English Proverbs." *Notes and Queries*, New Series, 17 (March), 87-88.

Analyzes the significance of "for the goodman is not at home," a proverb found in *Friar Daw's Reply* and ultimately derived from the Bible (*Prov.* vii.19). Finds a parallel between the proverb and Biblical reference and *Gawain*, especially the passage (11. 1531-34) in which Bercilak's wife views Gawain as sexual prey.

12   HIEATT, A. KENT.   "*Sir Gawain*: Pentangle, *Luf-Lace*, Numerical Structure," in *Silent Poetry: Essays in Numerological Analysis*. Edited by Alastair Fowler. London: Routledge & Kegan Paul, pp. 116-140.

[Reprint of 1968.7.]

13   HOFFMAN, DONALD L.   "*Renischsche Renkes* and *Runisch Sauez*." *Notes and Queries*, New Series, 17 (December), 447-449.

Views *runish* (OE. *rūn*) and *rennish* (OE. *brēoh*) as individual entities. Interprets *runish* in *Gawain* (11. 304, 432, 457) as "secret(ly), mysterious(ly)."

14   JACOBS, NICHOLAS. "Gawain's False Confession."
      English Studies, 51 (October), 433-435.
         Claims that a crucial test for Gawain is how to reconcile
      knightly courtesy with Christian ideals and precepts. Con-
      tends that once Gawain accepts and conceals the girdle (chival-
      ric duty) and makes a false confession, he makes the two ethi-
      cal systems collide.

15   KASKE, R. E. "Gawain's Green Chapel and the Cave at
      Wetton Mill," in *Medieval Literature and Folklore
      Studies: Essays in Honor of Francis Lee Utley.* Edit-
      ed by Jerome Mandel and Bruce A. Rosenberg. New
      Brunswick, New Jersey: Rutgers University Press, pp.
      111-121.
         Examines the topography of *Gawain,* specifically the
      topographical portrait of the Green Chapel. Identifies—
      through the use of photographs and critical-topographical
      commentary—the Chapel with the cave at Wetton Mill, a knoll-
      like structure located in northeastern Staffordshire.

16   LEHMAN, ANNE KERNAN. "Thematic Patterning and
      Narrative Continuity in Four Middle English Allitera-
      tive Poems." Ph.D. dissertation, Cornell University.
         [Partly on *Gawain. See Dissertation Abstracts,* 31 (1971),
      6558A.] Discusses the fusion of genres and disparate points
      of view as well as "disjunctive episodes" and their role in the
      thematic framework which shapes the meaning of *Gawain.*
      Analyzes the blending of symmetrical and parallel elements
      with the "progressive, linear character" of *Gawain.*

17   LEO, DIANA T. "The Concept of the Hero in the Mid-
      dle English Verse Romances." Ph.D. dissertation,
      University of Pittsburgh.
         [Partly on *Gawain. See Dissertation Abstracts Interna-
      tional,* 31 (1971), 6558A. The author's name is now Diana T.
      Childress.] Focuses largely upon the characterization of Ga-
      wain as a heroic type and upon his function in the British
      Gawain romances, including *Sir Gawain.* Notes that *Gawain*
      fails to depict the hero's physical features although his spring-
      like appearance suggests an idealized youthful beauty. Con-
      tends that Gawain is noted for his martial skills, courage (the
      Green Knight's challenge), humanity, courtesy, and scrupulous

conscience (when he feels shame at the end of *Gawain*).

18   LONG, CHARLES. "Arthur's Role in Morgan la Fay's Plan in *Sir Gawain and the Green Knight.*" *Tennessee Philological Bulletin*, 7, no. 1 (July), 3-10.

Contends that Morgan loves Arthur and that "Morgan's ulterior motive [in humiliating Camelot] may really be that of ridding herself of Guinevere and humbling Arthur, thereby regaining her scornful lover" (p. 6). Notes the ultimate failure of Morgan's scheme.

19   LOOMIS, ROGER SHERMAN. "More Celtic Elements in *Gawain and the Green Knight,*" in *Studies in Medieval Literature: A Memorial Collection of Essays.* New York: Burt Franklin, pp. 157-192.

[Reprint of 1943.2.]

20   LOOMIS, ROGER SHERMAN. "The Visit to the Perilous Castle: A Study of the Arthurian Modifications of an Irish Theme," in *Studies in Medieval Literature: A Memorial Collection of Essays.* New York: Burt Franklin, pp. 102-103, 105, 122-123, 125-126, 128-129, 133.

[Reprint of 1933.3.]

21   McALINDON, T. "Hagiography into Art: A Study of *St. Erkenwald.*" *Studies in Philology*, 67 (October), 475.

Suggests that *Gawain* and *Erkenwald* are linked through their use of the marvellous.

22   McGEE, ALAN VAN KEUREN. "The Geographical Distribution of Scandinavian Loan-Words in Middle English, with Special Reference to the Alliterative Poetry." Ph.D. dissertation, Yale University.

[Partly on *Gawain. See Dissertation Abstracts,* 31 (1970), 1785A.] Focuses on the number and the percentage of Scandinavian loan-words in *Gawain.* Compares the diction of the Cotton Nero poems with the diction of the Fairfax MS of *Cursor Mundi.*

23   MILLER, HELEN HILL. *The Realms of Arthur.* Lon-

don: Peter Davies, pp. 105, 195-200.

Contends that the geography noted in *Gawain* may probably be traced to an area near Leek, Staffordshire—especially the terrain around Dieulacres Abbey.

24 MILLS, DAVID. "The Rhetorical Function of Gawain's Antifeminism?" *Neuphilologische Mitteilungen,* 71, no. 4:635-640.

Argues that Gawain's criticism of women (11. 2414-28) serves as a counterpoise to his intemperate response (11. 2369-88) to the Green Knight's unraveling of the narrative events. Suggests that once the Knight laughs and speaks in a controlled manner, Gawain's normal courtesy returns and his "attack on women," a balanced, unemotional speech, is a rhetorical representation of an essentially comic tone.

25 PATCH, HOWARD ROLLIN. *The Other World, According to Descriptions in Medieval Literature.* New York: Octagon Books, pp. 292, 318.
[Reprint of 1950.10.]

26 PERÉNYI, ERZSÉBET. "*Sir Gawain and the Green Knight* and the Traditions of Medieval Art." *Annales Universitatis Scientiarum Budapestinensis de Rolando Eötvös nominatae, Sectio Philologica Moderna,* 1:101-107.

Notes the humor in *Gawain*, especially the parody of courtly love in Fitt 3, which resembles fabliau motifs ("exchange motif" and "the revenge of the deceived husband"). Suggests that the Green Knight is an allegorical representation of the life force or the "Natural Man." Emphasizes the artistic texture and design of *Gawain*, particularly the winter landscaped contrasted with the warmth and comfort of indoor life as well as the gradual geometric progression of episodes in succeeding Fitts.

27 RAFFEL, BURTON. "Introduction," in his translation of *Sir Gawain and the Green Knight.* Afterword by Neil D. Isaacs. New York: New American Library (Mentor Book), pp. 9-41.
[*See also* Blanch (1973.3).]
"Introduction": Outlines (pp. 40-41) the methodology

employed in his translation and discusses *Gawain* as a literary masterpiece—its delicacy, its graphic descriptions, its alliterative prosody and "visual particularity," and its juxtaposition of high drama with comedy. Concludes with a lengthy commentary upon some recent critical studies of *Gawain.*

"Afterword" (pp. 127-44): Discusses the unmagical nature of the girdle and the *Gawain*-poet's sophisticated use and ironic undercutting of romance materials and conventions. Examines the authorship problem and the alliterative style of and traditions underlying *Gawain.* Attempts to pinpoint *Gawain*'s festive tone and employment of comic elements and to evaluate select scholarly studies of the poem.

28   SHEPHERD, GEOFFREY. "The Nature of Alliterative Poetry in Late Medieval England." *Proceedings of the British Academy,* 56:58-59, 65.

[Delivered (January 21, 1970) as the "Sir Israel Gollancz Memorial Lecture."] Examines the hunting scenes in *Gawain,* graphic examples of "memorable instruction" for an audience basically interested in the chase. Claims that alliterative poetry is largely mnemonic in structure and ideas.

29   SPEARING, A. C. *The Gawain-Poet: A Critical Study.* Cambridge, England: Cambridge University Press, pp. 1-2, 6-10, 15, 21-22, 29-30, 34, 36, 38, 41, 65, 79, 98, 163, 166, 171-236.

Discusses the Cotton Nero MS—its poems, dating (1400), and scribal hand—as well as the "alliterative revival," the aristocratic life depicted in *Gawain, Gawain*'s indebtedness to French courtly romance and to formulaic patterns, pearl imagery, and the style of *Gawain.* Analyzes various aspects of *Gawain,* including the story; the intermeshed plots (beheading game, temptation, and exchange of winnings); the "psychological realism" permeating the poem; the sexual temptation of the hero at Hautdesert; the interlocking virtues of the pentangle and their dependence upon the endlessness of the endless knot; the values of *cortaysye* and chastity; the juxtaposition of the hunts with the temptations; Gawain's fault and the moral perspective of the poem; and the ambiguous Green Knight.

30   SPENDAL, RALPH JAMES, JR. "Narrative Structure in

Five Middle English Poems." Ph.D. dissertation, University of Oregon.

> [Discusses all four Cotton Nero Poems and *Erkenwald. See Dissertation Abstracts*, 31 (1971), 5376A-77A.] Argues that a common structural device ("protoplot"), involving both a movement "of the human spirit, and of a corresponding transcendent response," binds together the five poems. Discusses Gawain's two acts of *trawpe* in terms of the seasonal setting (Birth of Christ and Circumcision). Examines the poem's rhetorical style and the cyclical patterns.

31   TAYLOR, PAUL BEEKMAN. "Icelandic Analogues to the Northern English Gawain Cycle." *Journal of Popular Culture*, 4 (Summer), 93-106.

> Notes that *Gawain, Sir Gawain and the Carl of Carlisle*, and *The Turk and Gawain* are rooted in the same folk traditions, especially a "magical beheading" and a number of ritual duties assigned to the hero. Suggests that both traditions involve a meeting between Gawain and an otherworld giant, frequently a shape-shifter, and that the "beheading game" motif in *Gawain* may spring from *Caradoc*.
>
> Interprets *arʒe* (1. 241) as "frightened out of one's nature" and stresses the psychological role of magic in *Gawain*—diversion of the audience's and Gawain's attention from the crucial bedroom temptations. Focuses especially on the identification of Gawain with Thor (Eilif Goðrunarson's tenth-century poem, *þórsdrápa*, and the exploits of Thorstein in *þórsteins þáttr Baejarmagns*) and on the influence of Thor myths upon *Gawain*.

32   TESTER, SUE K. "The Use of the Word *Lee* in *Sir Gawain and the Green Knight*." *Neophilologus*, 54 (April), 184-190.

> Contends that *lee* (1. 1893), denoting "shelter," "refuge," and "peace and calm," is employed ironically, for Hautdesert is designed to form in Gawain the illusion of security. Claims that *lee* (1. 849) is ironically rooted in Old English *hleo* ("protector"); ". . . Bertilak does not turn out to be a protector of men, but instead a tester and a tempter . . ." (p. 189).

33   THIÉBAUX, MARCELLE. "Sir Gawain, the Fox Hunt,

and Henry of Lancaster." *Neuphilologische Mitteilungen,* 71, no. 3:469-479.

Points out parallels between Bercilak/Green Knight as
hunter/confessor in *Gawain* and Henry of Lancaster's confessional work, *Le Livre de Seyntz Medicines* (1354); Henry's
allegorical piece employs the central figure of the fox-hunt in
order to portray foxes as human sins which covertly attack the
hearts of men. Traces the significance of the Fox's moral
qualities, the stripping of the fox's pelt, the character of the
hunter/confessor, and the penitential employment of *three* in
both Henry's work and in *Gawain.* Claims that Henry may
serve as a prototype for the humane Bercilak and that *Gawain*
represents, perhaps, a literary tribute to Henry.

*34   THOMPSON, RAYMOND H. "Sir Gawain and Heroic
       Tradition: A Study of the Influence of Changing
       Heroic Ideals upon the Reputation of Gawain in the
       Medieval Literature of France and Britain." Ph.D.
       dissertation, University of Alberta (Canada).
       [Cited in *Comprehensive Dissertation Index, 1861-1972.*
       Vol. 29 (Language and Literature). Ann Arbor: Xerox Univer-
       sity Microfilms, 539.]

35   WALDRON, R. A., ed. "Introduction," in his edition of
       Sir Gawain and the Green Knight. York Medieval
       Texts, edited by Elizabeth Salter and Derek Pearsall.
       London: Edward Arnold, pp. 1-27.
       [Contains a select bibliography (pp. ix-xii) of editions,
       translations, and textual notes plus important books and criti-
       cal essays on *Gawain.*]
       "Introduction": Argues that *Gawain* poses numerous
       moral questions through the instrument of romance fiction.
       Emphasizes the poem's descriptive techniques, including point
       of view, as well as the conflicting demands imposed upon
       Gawain by his chivalric ideals, the significance of Gawain's
       pentangle and the concepts of *cortaysye* and *covetyse,* the
       moral ambiguity coloring the poem, and the elements of
       gomen and irony in *Gawain.*

36   WESTON, JESSIE L. "Preface," in *Sir Gawain and the
       Green Knight: A Middle-English Arthurian Romance
       Retold in Modern Prose.* New York: AMS Press,

pp. v-xii.
[Reprint of 1905.3.]

37   WILLIAMS, D. J. "Alliterative Poetry in the Fourteenth
and Fifteenth Centuries," in *The Middle Ages*. Edited by W. F. Bolton. History of Literature in the English Language, Vol. 1. London: Barrie & Jenkins,
143, 148-152.

Notes that the Cotton poems, aimed at a courtly audience, were written sometime between 1360 and 1400. Suggests that the opening of *Gawain*—the historical focus on the
fall of Troy and on Felix Brutus—thematically frames the
narrative events of the poem, the emphasis on loyalty and
treachery, conflict and joy. Concentrates on the stanza form
of *Gawain* as well as on its symmetry and "circular" design.
Suggests that courtly ideals are analyzed critically and that
romance conventions are represented ambivalently. Contends
that the poet presents "in Christian and aristocratic romance
terms, a comment on human limitation and the relation between ideal and real" (p. 151).

38   WILLIAMS, SISTER MARGARET.   "Oriental Back-
grounds & the *Pearl*-Poet." *Tamkang Review*, 1, no.
1 (April), 93-107.

[Traces oriental influences, including *The Travels of
Marco Polo,* upon the works of the *Pearl*-poet.] Suggests
that the oriental influences upon *Gawain* are more oblique, involving the color and texture of rich robes, gems and tapestries as well as the use of magic talismans (the pentangle) and
number symbolism (five, the emblem of perfection). Notes
the mythic elements in the poem, especially the use of the
Beheading Game.

39   WIMSATT, JAMES I. *Allegory and Mirror: Tradition
and Structure in Middle English Literature*. New
York: Pegasus, pp. 17, 122, 194-196, 198-202, 204,
210, 212-214, 216.

Scrutinizes Gawain's five-pointed pentangle as a representation of knightly ideals and emphasizes the significance of
chastity and courtesy in *Gawain*. Analyzes the temptation
scenes, episodes which reflect the congruence between Christian values and courtesy.

1971

1   ALLEN, JUDSON BOYCE. *The Friar As Critic: Literary Attitudes in the Later Middle Ages.* Nashville: Vanderbilt University Press, pp. 145-149.

Notes the double vision within *Gawain*—the blend of romance elements and realism, of Celtic motifs and Christian concerns. Emphasizes the identification of the lord of Hautdesert with the Green Knight: "Bercilak and the Green Knight are doubles; they exist over against one another, in parallel. As such, they exist as the two halves of an identity which can best be understood as figural" (p. 146). Views the ending of the poem as a "spiritual allegory," for Gawain now perceives how his experience at the Green Chapel is intertwined with the temptation-hunts at Hautdesert and, more significantly, how human existence parallels "its spiritual and moral value and meaning" (p. 147). Concludes by claiming that the multileveled *Gawain* is an example of a "transspiritual" poem.

2   BARBER, R. W. *Arthur of Albion: An Introduction to the Arthurian Literature and Legends of England.* London: Boydell Press, pp. 71, 85, 95-107, 111, 119, 121.

[Reprint of 1961.1.]

3   BEATIE, BRUCE A. "Patterns of Myth in Medieval Narrative." *Symposium: A Quarterly Journal in Modern Foreign Literatures,* 25 (Summer), 110.

Suggests that on a mythic level the Arthurian court always reflects an eternal spring or summer; in *Gawain* and *Parzival,* however, snow blankets "Arthur's world."

4   BLACK, NANCY B. "The Hero's Fight with a Dragon or Giant Adversary in Medieval Narrative." Ph.D. dissertation, Columbia University.

[Partly on *Gawain.* See *Dissertation Abstracts,* 32 (1971), 3243A.] Contends (Chap. 5) that the old dragon or giant adversary in medieval narrative (*Beowulf*) is metamorphosed, frequently through the shapeshifting motif, into "a man turned monster" (Green Knight).

5   BLOOMGARDEN, IRA.   "Northern Middle English

Arthurian Romance and Its Historical Background."
Ph.D. dissertation, City University of New York.

[Partly on *Gawain*. *See Dissertation Abstracts*, 31 (1971), 6539A-40A.] Offers an explanation of how the northern Middle English Arthurian romances are unique literary creations and why they are aligned with the historical background of the North. Examines the courtly qualities of Gawain as well as the structure of and the shaping power of Northern topography upon *Gawain*; views *Gawain* against the backdrop of the rising power of the Northern barons.

6   BURROW, JOHN A. *Ricardian Poetry: Chaucer, Gower, Langland and the Gawain Poet.* London: Routledge & Kegan Paul, pp. 1-3, 5, 8-9, 24-28, 33, 41-43, 46-47, 51, 56, 58-61, 64-65, 68-75, 83, 86-87, 94-96, 99-101, 103, 105-109, 111, 113-114, 120-122, 127-129, 133-134, 137-140.

Attempts to examine the "common characteristics" of the four major poets of the "Ricardian" age (the reign of Richard II, 1377-99). Notes the *Gawain*-poet's proud use of alliterative verse (11. 27-36), his dramatic employment of oral narrative—his minstrel-like address to the audience (11. 1994-97)—and the style, in general, of *Gawain*. Comments, in part, upon the *Gawain*-poet's use of irony, his description of the seasons, and his focus upon narrative events.

Emphasizes the Ricardian poets' preoccupation with structural divisions—the suspenseful "fitt"-units of *Gawain*, the link between line 2525 of *Gawain* and the numerological meaning of the pentangle, and the "circular" form (verbal repetition at the beginning and close) reminiscent of the pentangle's "endless knot." Claims that Ricardian poetry, including *Gawain*, does not extol the virtues of warfare and offers an unheroic representation of humanity. Focuses, finally, on the confession scenes in *Gawain*, its comic aspects, and its artistic use of similes.

7   CHISNELL, ROBERT EMMETT. "Unconventionality and Irony: A Reading of *Sir Gawain and the Green Knight.*" Ph.D. dissertation, Auburn University.

[*See Dissertation Abstracts*, 32 (1971), 910A.] Attempts to examine *Gawain* within its cultural milieu and to explain why the romance conventions in *Gawain* are employed unconventionally. Suggests that the *Gawain*-poet creates a new moral vision, a romance composed as irony in order "to keep his material simultaneously under the eye of comedy and the eye of moral judgment."

8   CHRISTOPHERSEN, PAUL. "The Englishness of *Sir Gawain and the Green Knight,*" in *On the Novel: A Present for Walter Allen on His 60th Birthday from His Friends and Colleagues.* Edited by B. S. Benedikz. London: J. M. Dent, pp. 46-56.

Traces, at first, the nature, scope, and conventions of the medieval romance—the forerunner of the novel. Claims that *Gawain,* a poem in the mainstream of the fourteenth-century "alliterative revival" in western England, "continues—almost certainly not as a revival of something dead but as a re-emergence in written form of something which had never been allowed to die in that part of the country—a tradition with its roots in the earliest Anglo-Saxon literature" (p. 48). Contends that *Gawain* is linked with Anglo-Saxon poetry in metrical patterns, diction, and depictions of nature—especially the uniquely English portrayal of winter landscapes. Such graphic descriptions of winter contrast sharply with the ordinary "—foreign-inspired—convention in Middle English verse, where illustrations of nature most often present a picture of an April or May morning with joyous bird-song and gaily coloured flowers" (p. 50).

Argues, likewise, that Gawain is an untypical medieval romance, for this poem minimizes the other-worldly milieu, portrays Gawain as the chivalric knight *par excellence,* places "the whole complex of knightly virtues on trial" (p. 53), and carefully fuses various continental motifs so as to impart "a meaning and a tone and a setting that are more English" (p. 55).

9   CLARK, CECILY. *"Sir Gawain and the Green Knight:* Its Artistry and Its Audience." *Medium Aevum,* 40, no. 1:10-20.

Attempts to examine the impact of the diction in *Gawain* upon its audience. Demonstrates how the poet's use of unornate, simple words, colloquialisms, regionalisms and technical vocabulary (hunting and architecture) contributes to the "realism" of *Gawain* and counterpoises its formal literary language. Analyzes, likewise, the poet's use of oral-formulaic technique in order to suggest through verbal echoes the interlaced pattern in *Gawain*. Interprets ȝe ar welcum to my cors (1237) as an impersonal seductive advance by Bercilak's wife; cors may connote "body" or "corpse."

10   DEAN, CHRISTOPHER. "The Temptation Scenes in *Sir Gawain and the Green Knight.*" *Leeds Studies in English*, New Series, 5:1-12.

Analyzes the crucial temptation scenes in order to prove that Gawain is beguiled and ultimately defeated by Bercilak's wife. Claims that ȝe ar welcum to my cors (1. 1237) is a blunt sexual offer by the lady, a form of amorous entanglement employed so as to overshadow the real temptation—the promise of life through acceptance of the girdle. Contends that the lady tracks down Gawain through her stratagem of placing so much importance on the process of seduction that Gawain loses sight of truly noble and loyal behavior.

11   EDWARDS, A. S. G. "*Sir Gawain and the Green Knight,* 250-252 and 2239-2240." *The Explicator*, 29, no. 9 (May), no. 73.

Notes the poet's use of an oral formula in order to interlace the Green Chapel episode with the opening Yuletide festivities at Camelot. Suggests that the Green Knight's greeting to Gawain at the Chapel ironically echoes and contrasts with Arthur's courteous greeting to the Knight at Camelot.

12   FIELD, P. J. C. "A Rereading of *Sir Gawain and the Green Knight.*" *Studies in Philology*, 68 (July), 255-269.

Examines the penance motif and Gawain's confession. Uses the writings of John Myrc, Thomas Aquinas, and others to substantiate his view that Gawain commits a venial sin in breaking his promise to Bercilak (acceptance and concealment of the girdle).

13   FLETCHER, P. C. B. "Sir Gawain's Anti-Feminism." *Theoria: A Journal of Studies in the Arts, Humanities, and Social Sciences*, 36 (May), 53-58.

Examines Gawain's verbal assault on women (11. 2414-2428) in order to link this attack with a significant theme, the conflict within Gawain between two types of chivalry—an older "masculine" ideal emphasizing devotion to God and a newer "feminine" ideal involving protection of and service to ladies. Views Gawain's acceptance of the girdle as a rejection of the "masculine" ideal and his tirade against women as a realization that true courtesy demands the safeguarding of women, not submission to them.

14   GOLLANCZ, ISRAEL.   "Introduction" to his *Pearl, Cleanness, Patience and Sir Gawain: Reproduced in Facsimile from the Unique MS. Cotton Nero A.x. in the British Museum.*   Early English Text Society, Original Series #162.   London: Oxford University Press, pp. 7-11.
       [Reprint of 1923.3.]

15   GRADON, PAMELA.   *Form and Style in Early English Literature.*   London: Methuen, pp. 131-139, 237-238.
       [Contains discussions of *Cleanness* (pp. 119-24) and *Pearl* (pp. 194-211).] Examines structure and symmetry in *Gawain,* including the three temptations and hunts. ". . . each hunting scene is used as a kind of frame for the equivalent temptation scene. Thus we find the episode of the first kiss inserted into the first hunt, dividing it into two parts and so with the other two. The rendering of the kiss in each case is accompanied by festivities" (pp. 131-32).
       Contrasts the loose episodic structure of *Beowulf* with the "interlaced" episodes of *Gawain:* "The structure of *Beowulf* is that of a folk-tale, of *Gawain* that of a *virelai* or *ballade.* It thus appears that the links which, in *Beowulf,* are purely thematic, are, in *Gawain,* part of a space-time continuum, and the episodes are linked by a pattern of causation as well as by a simple symmetry of arrangement" (p. 133).
       Emphasizes the "ironic reversals" in *Gawain,* especially the Green Knight's metamorphosis from brusque challenger to a humanized "confessor." ". . . the circular structure serves to emphasize the psychological evolution of the characters. . ." (p. 138).

16   GREEN, D. H.   "Irony and Medieval Romance," in *Arthurian Romance: Seven Essays.*   Edited by D. D. R. Owen.   New York: Barnes & Noble, pp. 52-53, 58,

60-61, 63.

[Reprint of 1970.9.]

17   GUNN, ALAN M. F. "The Polylithic Romance: With Pages of Illustrations," in *Studies in Medieval, Renaissance, [and] American Literature: A Festschrift Honoring Troy C. Crenshaw, Lorraine Sherley, [and] Ruth Speer Angell.* Edited by Betsy F. Colquitt. Fort Worth: Texas Christian University Press, pp. 1-18.

Argues that the medieval romance signalizes "complexity in form, . . . multivalence in meaning" (p. 1), without sacrificing structural unity. Terms *Gawain* a "Romance of Wonder, Faërie, the Marvelous, and the Supernatural" (p. 3), a "Tightly Organized" (p. 4) Romance, a "Comic Romance" (p. 4), an " 'Educational' Romance (i.e., youth's *l'enfances,* initiation, 'growing-up')" (p. 4), and a "Christian Romance" (p. 5), thereby making this poem "polylithic."

Enumerates the genre-patterns (pp. 12-14) operating in *Gawain,* especially Gawain's quest as an "adventure," a sophisticated "comedy of manners" (part of Fitt Two and all of Fitt Three), and as an illustration of "psychological fiction." Emphasizes the *Gawain*-poet's fusion of romance and realism in his description of nature and the poem as a narrative of "mystery . . . suspense . . . surprise" (p. 15). Concludes by claiming that "Gawain's quest has its roots in pagan *mythoi* and in the lore of still quasi-pagan folk and at least a surface resolution in a quasi-Christian penitence. Its dominant tonalities are those of romance and comedy, yet the tragic mode is present in threatening shape. The prevailing comic and romantic modes verge at times upon the tragic, at times upon the ironic. . . ." (p. 18).

18   HAINES, VICTOR YELVERTON. "Morgan and the Missing Day in *Sir Gawain and the Green Knight.*" *Mediaeval Studies,* 33:354-359.

Suggests that the poet playfully uses magic, somewhat like Morgan le Fay, to create the illusion of eliminating December 28 from *Gawain.* Claims that when Gawain bids "good day!" (1029) to Bercilak, it is December 28th, and Gawain sleeps for the remainder of the day. Views the *Gawain*-poet's manipulation of time in the poem as another example of a game by a "fairy poet."

19   HERZOG, MICHAEL B. "The Development of Gawain
      as a Literary Figure in Medieval German and English
      Arthurian Romance." Ph.D. dissertation, University
      of Washington.
          [Partly on *Gawain. See Dissertation Abstracts,* 32 (1972),
      6377A-78A.] Discusses the honor displayed toward Gawain,
      the knight *par excellence,* in *Gawain* although some criticism
      of his character is offered.

20   HOWARD, DONALD R. *"Sir Gawain and the Green
      Knight,"* in *Recent Middle English Scholarship and
      Criticism: Survey and Desiderata.* Edited by J. Burke
      Severs.   Pittsburgh: Duquesne University Press, pp.
      29-54.
          Extends Bloomfield's evaluation (1961.3) of critical
      treatments, editions, and translations of *Gawain* through 1968
      and offers *desiderata* for future *Gawain* scholarship. Discusses
      articles and books on various aspects of *Gawain,* including its
      structure, style, Christian elements and symbolism, humor,
      theme, and social background.

21   HUGHES, DEREK W. "The Problem of Reality in *Sir
      Gawain and the Green Knight." University of Toron-
      to Quarterly,* 40 (Spring), 217-235.
          Examines the tension between the tinsel values of Came-
      lot and Christian ideals. Maintains that "artifice imagery,"
      including an emphasis on games, rituals, trappings, and theatri-
      cal illusions, is employed to represent Camelot as devoted to
      insubstantial ideals alien to Christianity.

22   KINDRICK, ROBERT L.   "The Unknightly Knight:
      Anti-Chivalric Satire in Fourteenth and Fifteenth
      Century English Literature." Ph.D. dissertation, Uni-
      versity of Texas (Austin).
          [Partly on *Gawain. See Dissertation Abstracts,* 32 (1972),
      5742A.] Uses the concepts of humor and tone in elucidating
      anti-chivalric satire. Contends that the *Gawain*-poet employs
      chivalric ideals as ethical norms in his criticism of romance
      conventions; *Gawain* is termed an anti-romance.

23   KITELEY, JOHN F.   " 'The Endless Knot': Magical
Aspects of the Pentangle in *Sir Gawain and the Green
Knight.*" *Studies in the Literary Imagination,* 4, no.
2 (October), 41-50.

Notes that the representation of the pentangle as Gawain's
heraldic emblem is completely untraditional and that the
poet's explanation of the pentangle's significance focuses on
the moral implications of that device. Attempts, however, to
examine the magical aspects of the pentangle, its employment
as protection against "evil spirits"—a traditional use well-
known to the medieval audience; analyzes the meaning of
five, a perfect number, and its link with magic.

Contends that magic *per se* may not overpower another
type of magic and suggests that Gawain would have been tri-
umphant if he had adhered to the moral virtues residing in the
pentangle.

24   LASATER, ALICE E.   "Hispano-Arabic Relationships to
the Works of the *Gawain*-Poet." Ph.D. dissertation,
University of Tennessee.

[*See Dissertation Abstracts,* 32 (1972), 4570A-71A.]
Notes the influence of Arabic literary traditions upon *Gawain,*
particularly the Green Knight as a reflection of "al-Khadir,
'the green one,' of Islamic lore who had evolved as a combined
vegetation and religious figure whose mission as a noble representative of divine knowledge was frequently to appear in
court with a challenge."

25   MARKUS, MANFRED.   *Moderne Erzählperspektive in
den Werken des Gawain-Autors.*   Sprache und Literatur: Regensburger Arbeiten zur Anglistik und Amerikanistik, Vol. 3, ed. Karl Heinz Göller. Regensburg:
Verlag Hans Carl, 236 pp.   [Doctoral dissertation,
Regensburg.]

[In German, with an abstract in English (pp. 234-236).
Extensive notes (pp. 177-207) and bibliography (pp. 208-27),
but no index.]   Attempts to elucidate the modern narrative
style (perspective, composition, tone, and syntax) and the
artistic value of the works of the *Pearl*-poet through an examination of their respective points of view.   Point of view includes "(1) the narrator's temporal relation to the events of
his story, (2) his distance to the places described in his story

and the spatial surroundings of the characters, and (3) the psychic relation of the narrator to his *personae*" (p. 234).

26   MATONIS, ANN. *"Gawain and the Green Knight*: Flux and the Fayntyse of the Flesche." *Journal of Narrative Technique,* 1 (January), 43-48.

Analyzes *Gawain,* especially two passages—11. 491-531 and 1998-2008, in terms of the poet's commentary upon cyclical and temporal patterns within nature. Argues that the strategic positioning of these passages links human activities with "the natural laws of flux and mutability" (p. 44). Suggests that the first passage, the turning of the seasons, represents the transitory nature of human life, and the second passage—the description of Gawain's awakening prior to his meeting with the Green Knight—emphasizes the turbulence within nature and Gawain's soul as the meeting with the Green Knight draws near.

27   MATSUI, NORIKO. "Allegory of Courtesy in *Pearl* and *Sir Gawain and the Green Knight." Studies in English Literature* (English Literary Society of Japan), 47, no. 2 (March), 123-124, 132-140.

[Synopsis of article found on pp. 165-167 of the English Number for 1971.] Views Christian courtesy as informing the theme of *Gawain*—the testing of Gawain's chivalric mettle. Notes the ambivalent nature of the concept of "courtesy" because the *Gawain*-poet fuses a courtly ideology with a celestial ideology.

28   METCALF, ALLAN A. "Sir Gawain and *You." Chaucer Review,* 5 (Winter), 165-178.

Contends that *thou* was the normal form of address in the *Gawain*-poet's time and that *you,* a formal, polite term directed at nobility, social superiors, and the objects of veneration, is employed often in *Gawain.* Analyzes the *Gawain*-poet's subtle shifts from *thou* to *you,* especially in the scenes at Hautdesert, and suggests that such pronouns of address highlight "the nuances of interaction among the characters" (p. 178).

29   MILLER, J. FURMAN. "The *Gawain* Poet's Possible Indebtedness to Jesus' Temptation." *Newsletter-Con-*

ference on Christianity and Literature, 21, no. 1-2: 27-29.

[Actual date of publication is listed as 1971-72.] Contends that the hunts and temptations in *Gawain* may spring from St. Mark's account (1:3) of Jesus's temptation—the Scriptural narrative which suggests that wild animals live with Christ in the wilderness. Discusses the identification of the hunt with the devil; the symbolic tripartite animalistic temptation of humanity (lust of the flesh, concupiscence of the eyes, and pride of life); and the connection between the animals hunted by Bercilak and the three seduction scenes.

30   REICHARDT, PAUL F. "A Note on Structural Symmetry in *Gawain and the Green Knight.*" *Neuphilologische Mitteilungen*, 72, no. 2:276-282.

Contends that the structural symmetry (parallels and contrasts) of *Gawain* may be discerned in the ways Morgan le Fay and the Virgin Mary shape the narrative events. Suggests that Mary, Gawain's chaste protector, is identified with the shield, pentangle, and spiritual ideals, whereas her foil and Gawain's antagonist, Morgan the enchantress, is associated with the girdle and subservience to the flesh (self-preservation and unchastity).

31   ROSENBERG, JAMES L. "Introduction," in *Sir Gawain and the Green Knight: The Original Middle Text as Edited by A. C. Cawley, and a Modern Verse Translation, with an Introduction, by James L. Rosenberg.* Illustrated by Cyril Satorsky. New York: Printed for Members of the Limited Editions Club, pp. vii-xiii.

[The Cawley text is a reprint of 1962.3; the Rosenberg translation is a reprint of 1959.9.] Suggests that the *Pearl*-poet, perhaps a cleric, resided in the Northern Midlands in the vicinity of Chester. Comments upon the flowering of poetic achievement in the late fourteenth century and upon the "muscular and kinetic onomatopoeia" (p. viii) penetrating the diction of *Gawain.*

Emphasizes the poet's use of suspense, playful ambiguity, and deft manipulation of his audience through withholding crucial information or riddling his narrative with misleading clues. Discusses the "cinematic" techniques employed in the temptation and hunting scenes; the mythic pattern in

Gawain—the progress of the hero from youth to maturity through a type of *rite de passage;* the poem's structure, especially the use of threes; the balance between the urbane world of the court and the dynamism of nature; and Gawain's humanized character in the realm of comedy.

32 SCHELP, HANSPETER. "Gestaltung und Funktion des Auftakts in der mittelenglischen alliterierenden *Morte Arthure.*" *Archiv für das Studium der neueren Sprachen und Literaturen,* 207 (April), 421-422, 427, 429, 435-438.

[In German.] Reveals that the opening lines of the alliterative *Morte Arthure* (26-242) closely parallel parts of *Gawain,* especially in their common use of the Arthurian feast motif.

33 SHIPPEY, T. A. "The Uses of Chivalry: *Erec* and *Gawain.*" *Modern Language Review,* 66 (April), 241-250.

Suggests that both Chrétien de Troyes's *Erec et Enide* and *Gawain* in their emphasis upon joy and play offer a possible resolution to the vexing question of the social aims of chivalry. Contends that a vein of seriousness runs throughout the games in *Gawain;* "good cheer," however, veils the characters' fears and underlies Gawain's courteous behavior.

34 TAYLOR, P. B. "Commerce and Comedy in *Sir Gawain.*" *Philological Quarterly,* 50 (January), 1-15.

Examines *Gawain* as a type of "ledger of Gawain's worldly accounts" (p. 13). Discusses the significance of *chepez* (1941), *prys* (1379), *costes* (2360), debts, exchanges, and promises in *Gawain* as well as the meaning of the axe and girdle. Concludes that Gawain remains in debt to Bercilak and implies that Gawain's spiritual account may be disordered.

35 VANTUONO, WILLIAM. "*Patience, Cleanness, Pearl,* and *Gawain*: The Case for Common Authorship." *Annuale Mediaevale,* 12:37-69.

Attempts to present a cogent case for common authorship through thematic links (the importance of accepting humbly God's will and of ablution through penance); imagery (nature); diction (word-play); similar phraseology; paraphrases for God; analogous methods of introducing a poem; and the repetition of lines at the beginning and end of a poem (verbal echoes). Emphasizes the significance of humility, fidelity to one's pledged word, and purity in *Gawain*.

36 WHITEBOOK, BUDD BERGOVOY. "Individuals: Eccentricity and Inwardness in English and French Romance, 1170-1400." Ph.D. dissertation, Yale University.

> [Partly on *Gawain*. See *Dissertation Abstracts*, 32 (1971), 3275A-76A.] Emphasizes the delineation of psychological awareness in *Gawain*, especially in the temptation scenes, and the hero's inability to communicate his insight to Arthur and his court.

1972

1 ACKERMAN, ROBERT W. "Sir Frederic Madden and Medieval Scholarship," in *Studies Presented to Tauno F. Mustanoja on the Occasion of His Sixtieth Birthday, Neuphilologische Mitteilungen*, 73, nos. 1-2:1-14.

> [Traces Madden's career as a pioneer editor of Middle English texts and as an officer of the British Museum (Department of Manuscripts).] Notes the significance of Madden's diary (MS. hist. C. 140-82) in the Bodleian Library, Oxford. Emphasizes his restoration and accurate cataloguing of the Cottonian Library—those manuscripts not completely destroyed by the October, 1731 fire at Ashburnham House. "The results of his labors he [Madden] recorded in the margins of Joseph Planta's catalogue of that collection, published in 1802 and still today the only complete guide to the Cotton manuscripts" (p. 7). Claims that Madden corrected the faulty description by Planta and earlier cataloguers of the nature and scope of MS. Cotton Nero A.x. although Richard Price, "the editor of the 1824 edition of Thomas Warton's *History of English Poetry*" (p. 8), was, perhaps, the first scholar to refer explicitly to *Sir Gawain*.

2 BURROW, J. A., ed. *Sir Gawain and the Green Knight*. Baltimore: Penguin, 176 pp.

[Contains a brief "Introduction" (pp. 7-9) on the syntax, diction, and orthography of *Gawain;* the text of *Gawain;* "Notes" (textual and explanatory); "Manuscript Readings"; and a "Glossary."

3   BURROW, J. A. "Two Notes on *Sir Gawain and the Green Knight."* *Notes and Queries,* New Series, 19 (February), 43-45.

Alludes to *Pearl* (1. 563), especially the words *Fyrre* and *plete,* in order to explain the legalistic implication of *And fire* ["further"] ; *lest he displese yow, so plede hit no more*: "And do not continue to press your claims in this way any further, lest he incur your displeasure." In the second note, emends *lordes and ladis* ("ladies") to *lordes and ledes* ("knights").

4   BUTTURFF, DOUGLAS R. "Laughter and Discovered Aggression in *Sir Gawain and the Green Knight."* *Literature and Psychology,* 22, no. 3:139-149.

Examines the dualism in *Gawain,* the function of the balance between the comic and the menacing, and calls attention to the undercutting of humorous scenes through an emphasis on cruelty; ". . . the effect of such a technique is to force us to feel more intensely the horror and suffering the work's hero experiences and to compel us to identify more closely with him" (p. 139). Focuses on the ambivalent nature of the Green Knight, the games the Knight plays with Gawain, and the meaning of Camelot's laughter at the conclusion of the poem.

5   DOVE, MARY. "Gawain and the *Blasme des Femmes* Tradition." *Medium Aevum,* 41, no. 1:20-26.

Discusses Gawain's verbal attack upon women (11. 2414-28) by noting the traditional link between Gawain and the *blasme des femmes* motif in French, English, and Anglo-Norman literature (twelfth century on). Claims that the *Gawain*-poet fuses two particular roles assumed by Gawain— the most courteous of knights and the reviler of women—in order to suggest the tension between and the ultimate reconciliation of civilized values and qualities of natural man.

6   DUNN, THOMAS P. "Comic Effect in *Sir Gawain and the Green Knight."* Ph.D. dissertation, University

of Cincinnati.

[*See Dissertation Abstracts*, 33 (1973), 3581A.] Considers each fitt as a separate entity and investigates the comic episodes and concepts in all four fitts. Emphasizes the game-like festivities at Camelot (Fitt 1); the badinage between Gawain and Bercilak's wife in the temptation scenes (Fitt 3); and the comic underscoring of Gawain's foibles and ultimate self-knowledge (Fitt 4).

7   GOLDBECK, HELEN J. "The Gawain Puzzle: A Study of MS. Cotton Nero A.x." Ph.D. dissertation, University of Oklahoma.

[*See Dissertation Abstracts*, 33 (1972), 1142A.] Perceives *Cleanness* and *Gawain* as a compound poem because of common thematic, tonal, stylistic, and syntactic links. Contends that *Cleanness/Gawain* focuses on the role of justice and will in the social world of humanity.

8   GREENWOOD, ORMEROD. "The Endless Knot." *The Friends' Quarterly*, 17, no. 5 (January), 233-239.

[General appreciation of *Gawain*.] Identifies the theme of *Gawain* with keeping faith (*trawþe*) and with "the difficulties of being a man of principle" (p. 233). Views the girdle as a symbol of shame and human weakness and the endless knot of the pentangle as an emblem of truth and life.

9   HALPERN, R. A. "The Last Temptation of Gawain: 'Hony Soyt Qui Mal Pence'." *American Benedictine Review*, 23 (September), 353-384.

Contends that the Green Knight's praise of Gawain's essential virtue at the conclusion of the Green Chapel episode is speciously attractive both to Gawain and to the audience and that the Knight's explanation of events represents "a temptation to vainglory and carnal understanding" (p. 358). Maintains, moreover, that Gawain has violated the spirit of the law, a transgression which he ultimately acknowledges when, as a true soldier of God, he returns to Camelot and offers the girdle as a penitential emblem; once Gawain resists the Knight's final temptation, Arthur's court views and wears the green girdle as a sign of Camelot's glory—a false interpretation which is interlocked with the scribal comment, "Hony Soyt Qui Mal Pence."

10   HARRIS, VERONICA. "Bertilak the Fox: A Reassess-
       ment of the Character of the Green Knight." *Studies
       in English* (University of Cape Town), 3 (December),
       1-18.
            Suggests that the *Gawain*-poet is deliberately ambiguous,
       for the meaning of *Gawain* springs from an emblematic "knot"
       or game intertwined with the poem's theme. Contends that
       Bercilak is an unconscious cheater who fails to comprehend
       the meaning of fair play, especially in his dealings (as the
       Green Knight) with Gawain at the Green Chapel; claims that
       green, the color of the Knight and of the girdle, is a symbol of
       untruth (p. 6). Comments on the seasonal allegory pervading
       the poem as well as on the emblematic significance of the
       animals tracked down by Bercilak. Views Bercilak, then, as
       "the complete human fox—cowardly, covetous, wily, treacher-
       ous" (p. 15)—an animalistic man incapable of comprehending
       his deceit or of feeling remorse.

11   HEYWORTH, P. L. "Sir Gawain's Crossing of Dee."
       Medium Aevum, 41, no. 2:124-127.
            Investigates the *Gawain*-poet's use of topography, espe-
       cially *þe fordez by þe forlondez* (1. 699), and claims that
       Gawain fords the unstable lower Dee estuary somewhere near
       Blacon Point, a headland located near Chester.

12   HILL, ARCHIBALD A. "The Green Knight's Castle and
       the Translators." *Canadian Journal of Linguistics,*
       17, no. 2:140-158.
            Focuses on lines 794-802, the passage which depicts Ga-
       wain's initial view of Bercilak's castle. Examines, then, numer-
       ous translations of the castle passage in order to determine
       which translations accurately convey the meaning of the pas-
       sage. Notes the concrete nature of the "iconic" vocabulary
       in the castle description and interprets *clambred* (1. 801) as
       "climbed [upward]" or (possibly) as "clamped together";
       and *pared out of papure* (1. 802) as an image of costliness,
       whiteness, and strength.

13   JONES, R. T., ed. "Introduction" to his *Sir Gawain and
       the Grene Gome: A Regularized Text.* London:
       Heinemann Educational Books, pp. 1-8.
            [Revised version of 1960.3.] Contains a critical evalua-

tion of scholarly books on and editions of *Gawain*. Claims that the poem focuses on "the testing of Sir Gawain as the representative of the ideal of Christian chivalry and 'cortaisie,' the ideal embodied imaginatively in mediaeval treatments of the legends of King Arthur and his knights and of a past that was generally regarded as the good old days—the standard by which the decay of morals and manners was measured." Emphasizes the greenness of the Green Knight although it notes circumspectly the Knight's link with vegetation and the Jack-in-the-green figure.

14   KELLOGG, ALFRED L. "The Identity of the Green Chapel in *Sir Gawain and the Green Knight,*" in his *Chaucer, Langland, Arthur: Essays in Middle English Literature.* New Brunswick, New Jersey: Rutgers University Press, pp. 6-10.

    [Reprint, with slight revisions, of Kellogg (1966.16).]

15   LEVITSKY, STEVEN E. "The Discovery of *Sir Gawain and the Green Knight.*" Ph.D. dissertation, Johns Hopkins University.

    [*See Dissertation Abstracts,* 33 (1972), 1689A.] Traces the history of *Gawain* from its discovery (1824) and first printing (1839.1) through its true discovery (1950's) as an artistic work. Suggests that the New Critics finally stimulated critical interest in the literary merits of *Gawain*.

16   LOGANBILL, DEAN. "The Medieval Mind in *Sir Gawain and the Green Knight.*" *Bulletin of the Rocky Mountain Modern Language Association,* 26:119-126.

    [Presented to the Classical and Medieval Literature section of the Rocky Mountain Modern Language Association meeting (October 21-22, 1972) at Tucson.]

    Claims that *Gawain* fuses mythic and modern patterns of thinking, thereby representing "the transitional nature of the medieval mind" (p. 120). Examines the mythic origins of the supernatural castle in *Gawain* and its affinity with Curoi's castle in *Bricriu's Feast* and notes the parallels between Gawain and Cuchulinn as well as between Bercilak/Green Knight and Curoi, a representative of deities of death. Suggests the *Gawain*-poet's modern sensibilities—his perception of himself as a poetic creator and his use of psychology.

17   MACRAE, SUZANNE HAYNES. "A Study of Ideal
      Kingship in the Middle English Romances." Ph.D.
      dissertation, University of North Carolina (Chapel
      Hill).
        [Partly on *Gawain*. *See Dissertation Abstracts,* 33 (1973),
        4353A.] Discusses the ideals of kingship—including the ruler's
        physical characteristics, his courtly nature, his ritual qualities,
        and his depiction as the just king—in her characterization of
        King Arthur.

18   MARTIN, JOHN W. "*La Mule sans frein*: A New Ap-
      proach to *Sir Gawain and the Green Knight.*" Ph.D.
      dissertation, University of Rochester.
        [*See Dissertation Abstracts,* 33 (1972), 319A.] Calls at-
        tention to the numerous contrasts between the hero of *Gawain*
        and Gauvain, the protagonist of *Mule,* in order to suggest the
        artistry and originality of *Gawain.* Argues that Gawain is
        linked through his fault with Adam and that Gawain is a type
        of Everyman, a figure who learns that grace is the *sine qua non*
        for salvation. Contends that Gawain is a Christ figure.

19   MOORMAN, FREDERIC W. *The Interpretation of Na-
      ture in English Poetry from Beowulf to Shakespeare.*
      New York: AMS Press, pp. 95-102, and as indexed.
        [Reprint of 1905.2.]

20   MUSCATINE, CHARLES. *Poetry and Crisis in the Age
      of Chaucer.* University of Notre Dame Ward-Phillips
      Lectures in English Language and Literature, Vol. 4.
      Notre Dame, Indiana: University of Notre Dame
      Press, 34-35, 41-45, 51, 55-69, 71, 108, 125.
        Claims that the *Gawain*-poet focuses on impurity (Ga-
        wain's departure from *trawpe*) and imperfection since "he is
        always aware of the ideal: the pure, the perfect" (p. 42). Em-
        phasizes the interlocking of words through sound in *Gawain* as
        well as the poem's circularity, number symbolism (pentangle),
        symmetrical patterns, and contrasts. Contends that "the inter-
        play between formal unity and variation is at the core of both
        the style and the meaning" (p. 45) of *Gawain.* Discusses the
        poem's rich descriptive details, images and diction suggestive
        of movement and energy, "variational style," the festive spirit
        of game permeating *Gawain* (the hunts and temptations), and
        the poem as artifice.

21   OWEN, D. D. R. "The *Gawain*-Poet." *Forum for Mod-
      ern Language Studies,* 8 (January), 79-84.
           [Review article on Spearing's *The Gawain-Poet: A Critical
      Study* (1970.29).] Suggests that a thorough study (compara-
      tive) of the ironic implications of the "would-be hero" would
      be welcome and notes the significance and scope of source
      studies in interpreting *Gawain* and other medieval works. Con-
      tends, moreover, that two particular sources—*Le Chevalier
      à l'épée* and *La Mule sans Frein*—represent the main sources
      of *Gawain* and demonstrates how the *Gawain*-poet uses these
      sources to shape the figures of the guide and the Green Knight.

22   PATRICK, MICHAEL. "Racy Relevance in *Sir Gawain*
      and *The Graduate.*" *Missouri English Bulletin,* 29:30-
      32.
           In order to deflate the skeptical attitudes of students to-
      ward Gawain's reactions to the lady's temptations and to
      demonstrate that *Gawain* is relevant today, compares Gawain's
      temptation to Mrs. Robinson's sexual advances to Benjamin
      in *The Graduate.* Contends that the male characters in both
      works initially reject the temptation because it represents a
      "violation of propriety" and that Gawain and Benjamin's
      brooding response to their "fall" is realistically attributable
      to guilt feelings.

23   ROBINSON, IAN. *Chaucer and the English Tradition.*
      Cambridge, England: Cambridge University Press, pp.
      131, 194, 202, 219-233, 286, 288-289.
           Examines the "difficulties" in *Gawain,* including the color
      and nature of Green Knight (human or a member of the fairy
      world) as well as his link with Bercilak; the significance of the
      Knight's challenge, his boastful testing of Camelot (civiliza-
      tion); the lady's temptations; and the poem's theme—loyalty.
      Interprets the meaning of words in lines 1770-71, particular-
      ly *depresed* ("subdued" or "freed"); and *Nurned* ("offered").

24   SOUCY, ARNOLD F. "Linear Pattern Within the Cycli-
      cal Patterns of *Sir Gawain and the Green Knight.*"
      Ph.D. dissertation, University of Minnesota.
           [*See Dissertation Abstracts,* 33 (1973), 3613A-14A.]
      Identifies the linear pattern in *Gawain* with Gawain's progress
      from pride to humility and represents the cyclical patterns as

the setting at Camelot for the beginning and conclusion of the poem ("narrative structure") as well as "seasonal, liturgical and historical cycles." Notes the hero's metamorphosis—the only real change of character delineated in Gawain; the poet's criticism of the values of Camelot; and the Green Knight's link through his greenness with fertility, fairies, and wild man figures.

25   STEVENS, MARTIN. "Laughter and Game in *Sir Gawain and the Green Knight.*" *Speculum,* 47 (January), 65-78.

Employs Johan Huizinga's *Homo Ludens* as a point of departure for his reflections upon the play and game elements in *Gawain.* Attempts to delineate "the types of play and the juxtaposition of games as a formal narrative framework within which to re-evaluate the world of literary romance" (p. 67) in *Gawain.* Examines the phraseology of play, the Beheading Game and the temptation motif, and the links between hunting and seduction. Concludes with a discussion of the girdle.

26   SUZUKI, EIICHI. "Oral-Formulaic Theme Survival: Two Possible Instances and Their Significance in *Sir Gawain and the Green Knight.*" *Studies in English Literature* (English Number), 48:15-31.

Attempts to find Old English oral-formulaic themes, particularly the themes of "Exile" and "Hero on the Beach," in *Gawain.* Claims that *Gawain* involves the motif of exile, for the hero is separated from his rightful lord, King Arthur, and makes a winter journey in order to find the Green Knight, the new lord. Claims that the "Hero on the Beach" motif in *Gawain* (11. 2069-90), implicit in Gawain's journey from Hautdesert to the Green Chapel, suggests a victorious outcome for Arthur's knight; Gawain's subsequent humiliation comes as a shock to his audience. Concludes by noting that Gawain's journey or quest should be viewed "*primarily* as chivalric rather than allegorical or mythical" (p. 29).

27   VON ENDE, FREDERICK A. C. "The Prosody of the *Pearl*-Poet: A Technical Analysis of the Poems in MS Cotton Nero A.x." Ph.D. dissertation, Texas Christian University.

[Discusses all four Cotton Nero poems. *See Dissertation*

Abstracts, 33 (1973), 3605A-3606A.] Investigates various prosodic aspects of *Gawain,* including rhythm, meter, alliteration, line groups, and stanza units. Argues that the Cotton Nero poems were composed by one person, that the poet's familiarity with the native alliterative verse form was limited, and that *Gawain* may have been written "in stages."

28   WESTON, JESSIE L. *The Legend of Sir Gawain: Studies upon its Original Scope and Significance.* New York: AMS Press, pp. 85-102.
[Reprint of 1897.3.]

29   WHALEY, HELEN R. *"Sir Gawain and the Green Knight* and Biblical Tradition: The Scriptural Pattern of the Work of the *Gawain*-Poet." Ph.D. dissertation, State University of New York (Buffalo).
[Covers all four Cotton poems. *See Dissertation Abstracts,* 33 (1973), 4370A-71A.] Contends that the thematic focus in each poem involves "the nature of man in the fallen world and his coming to know an immanent, omniscient God who punishes with brutal vengeance and rewards with Grace." Examines key enclosure images in *Gawain* (Gawain's armor, the bed curtains at Hautdesert, green girdle) which encircle, interlock, and surround.

Investigates the Scriptural traditions embracing David and Solomon and identifies Gawain with Christ and St. Peter, and especially, with David. Links the Green Knight with Satan (hunter, game-player) and with the values of Saturn.

1973

1   BARBER, RICHARD. *King Arthur in Legend and History.* Ipswich, England: Boydell Press, pp. 103, 107-117.
[Reprint of 1961.1.]

2   BARRON, W. R. J. "French Romance and the Structure of *Sir Gawain and the Green Knight,*" in *Studies in Medieval Literature and Languages in Memory of Frederick Whitehead.* Edited by W. Rothwell, W. R. J. Barron, David Blamires, and Lewis Thorpe. Man-

chester, England: Manchester University Press, pp. 7-25.

Criticizes source studies which employ preconceptions in order to determine the *Gawain*-poet's thematic framework. Focuses on the interlaced structure and theme of *Gawain*, especially the triadic pattern of hunts and temptations at the castle and the "ambivalent duality" of the *forwarde* itself; notes the contrast between Bercilak who naturally plays his role as hunter and the lady who unnaturally stalks Gawain in the bedroom tableaux.

Emphasizes the significance of the third hunt/temptation —how the fox hunt and the characteristics of the fox mirror Gawain's behavior, his ignobility, slyness, and cowardice—as well as structural parallelism juxtaposed with "ironic variation." Contends that two kinds of time (linear and cyclic) pervade this romance; *Gawain*, "though linear in narrative sequence, is cyclic in structure" (p. 22), particularly because of the allusions to the fall of Troy and to Felix Brutus at the beginning and end of the poem.

3   BLANCH, ROBERT J. Review article on Burton Raffel's translation of *Gawain*. *Archiv*, 210, no. 1 (June), 185-189.

[*See also* 1970.27.] Calls attention to Raffel's distortion of the idiom, rhythm, and alliterative metrical pattern of *Gawain*. Offers a lengthy commentary upon Raffel's "Introduction" to his translation of *Gawain*, especially his interpretation of the poem and his attack against many critics of *Gawain*.

4   BREWER, ELISABETH, trans. "Introduction," in *From Cuchulainn to Gawain: Sources and Analogues of Sir Gawain and the Green Knight*. Cambridge, England: D. S. Brewer, pp. 1-5.

[Contains extracts from various sources and analogues of the "beheading game" and temptation motifs in *Gawain* as well as two later stories from the English Gawain cycle—*The Green Knight* and *Sir Gawain and the Carl of Carlisle*.] Notes that such sources and analogues point to medieval methods of narration and emphasize the *Gawain*-poet's artistry in using traditional episodes and adding new material to his romance. Discusses the symmetrical structure of *Gawain*—its careful blending of beheading, temptation, and exchange of winnings themes—as well as the poem's psychological sensitivity and use of repetition and variation.

5　BURNLEY, J. D. *"Sir Gawain and the Green Knight, lines 3-7." Notes and Queries,* New Series, 20 (March), 83-84.

Alludes to a syntactic parallel in *Purity* (11. 977-84) in order to clarify þe *tulk* (1. 3) and þe *trewest on erthe* (1. 4) in *Gawain.* Claims that the courtly tradition of Aeneas and his perfidious treatment of Dido would be germane to *Gawain,* a narrative depicting the hero's faithlessness.

6　BURNLEY, J. D. "The Hunting Scenes in *Sir Gawain and the Green Knight." Yearbook of English Studies,* 3:1-9.

Notes two types of "expectation" stirred up in a perceptive audience, the conventions of "exemplary narrative" and the interlacing of allusions within a medieval poem, and proceeds to call attention to examples of each in *Gawain.* Contends that the link between the three hunts and temptations may be found in "the audience's reaction conditioned by the familiar motifs and techniques employed there" (p. 2). Suggests an increase in moral intensity as each temptation ensues and an association between the immediacy and threatening nature of the hunts and the moral dangers implicit in the temptations. Views the first hunt/temptation as orderly yet emotionally remote; the second hunt/temptation as a fierce struggle ending in victory for Gawain; and the third hunt/temptation as suggestive of the audience's "anxiety" and "disappointment" when Gawain departs from his "pentagonal" virtues.

7　BURROW, J. A. "Bards, Minstrels, and Men of Letters," in *Literature and Western Civilization: The Mediaeval World.* Edited by David Daiches and Anthony Thorlby. London: Aldus Books, pp. 357-359, 367.

Notes that *Gawain,* composed for delivery to a listening audience, bears the imprint of a minstrel style. Discusses the use of alliteration, especially double alliteration, and the "middle style" of *Gawain*—the development of a fluent narrative, graphic, individualized details in description, and disparate tones in conversation.

8   DAVENPORT, W. A. "Sir Gawain's Courteous 'Whoa!'."
      English Language Notes, 11 (December), 88-89.
         Interprets line 2330, especially *hoo* and *hende.* Cites
      medieval romances and manuals of chivalry in order to prove
      that *hoo* is a word conventionally used for stopping combat.
      Claims that *hoo* and *hende* thus represent Gawain's signal to
      the Green Knight to behave in a gentlemanly manner.

9   EVANS, W. O.   "The Case for Sir Gawain Re-opened."
      Modern Language Review, 68 (October), 721-733.
         Contends that belief in the magical power of gems and
      other items like the green girdle is not inconsistent with Chris-
      tian teaching and that Gawain's fault consists of spiritual
      blindness, a lack of self-awareness as suggested by his accep-
      tance of the girdle. Notes that the circumstances surrounding
      the "exchange of winnings" agreement are essentially game-
      like and that Gawain's confession to the priest is genuine and
      complete.   Suggests that Gawain's self-accusation (covetous-
      ness) is riveted to "the requirements for a knight on a spiritual
      quest" (p. 729): once Gawain accepts the girdle, he is guilty
      of *covetyse* and is catapulted into violating his promise of
      loyalty to his host, Bercilak.

10   FIGGINS, ROBERT H. "The Character of Sir Gawain in
      Middle English Romance." Ph.D. dissertation, Uni-
      versity of Washington.
         [Partly on *Gawain. See Dissertation Abstracts,* 34 (1973),
      2556A.] Notes that Gawain is traditionally renowned for his
      courtesy, loyalty, and valor; yet chivalric weaknesses in Ga-
      wain's character are represented in numerous romances. Sug-
      gests that Gawain's loyalty in *Gawain* is compromised when
      his life is threatened and that his courtesy is tested in his con-
      frontations with Lady Bercilak and the Green Knight. Per-
      ceives, moreover, "ambiguous or ironic implications regarding
      Gawain's character," as he is represented in *Gawain.*

11   HAMBRIDGE, ROGER A.   *"Sir Gawain and the Green
      Knight:* An Annotated Bibliography, 1950-1972."
      Comitatus, 4:49-84.
         [Selected annotated bibliography (objective appraisals)
      of articles, critical books, editions, and translations of *Gawain*
      (1950-1972).]

Uses three main sources—the *PMLA Annual Bibliography*, the Utley-Schroeder checklist, and the annual bibliography in the *Bulletin bibliographique de la Société internationale Arthurienne*—for his bibliography. Does not represent an "exhaustive" list, for no systematized investigation of foreign language journals has been conducted. Contains brief annotations and lists 246 items, 47 of which were not seen and/or read.

12   JAMBECK, THOMAS J. "The Syntax of Petition in *Beowulf* and *Sir Gawain and the Green Knight.*" *Style,* 7, no. 1 (Winter), 21-29.

Claims that the *Gawain*-poet employs "syntactical variation" when Gawain implores Arthur that he be permitted to respond to the Green Knight's challenge; such an elaborate and varied use of syntax reveals Gawain to the audience as a worldly-wise chivalric knight. Notes parallels between Beowulf's petition to Hrothgar and Gawain's request and suggests that the *Gawain*-poet may have adapted from *Beowulf* the artistic use of syntax for the psychological development of character.

13   JOHNSON, LYNN S. "Poetic Structure and Christian Doctrine: A Reinterpretation of the Works of the *Gawain*-Poet." Ph.D. dissertation, Princeton University.

[Covers all four Cotton poems. *See Dissertation Abstracts,* 34 (1974), 6592A-93A.] Employs the Bible and Scriptural commentaries, especially those composed by Bede, Rabanus Maurus, Hugh of St. Victor, St. Bernard, and Pierre Bersuire, in order to shed light upon the "transcendent meaning" of *Gawain.* Examines the focal theme of penance in *Gawain* as well as the structure and important images.

14   McCLURE, PETER. "Gawain's *Mesure* and the Significance of the Three Hunts in *Sir Gawain and the Green Knight.*" *Neophilologus,* 57 (October), 375-387.

Suggests that Gawain's courtesy toward Bercilak's wife during the first two temptations indicates that he refrains from behaving like the deer (timid, cowardly) and the boar (overbold, sexually aggressive). Contends, further, that Gawain's quest represents, in part, "a test . . . of his self-control or *mesure*" (p. 375) and the animals tracked down by Bercilak may be identified with the human flaws which Gawain must control. Claims that the three animals are individualized through their reactions to the imminence of death and perceives parallels between the three hunting episodes and Gawain's preparations (concluding in Fitt 4) for his inevitable death at the Green Chapel.

15   MARTIN, JOHN W. "The Knight who Stayed Silent through Courtesy." *Archiv,* 210 (June), 53-57.

Interprets *sum* (*sum for cortaysye*) of line 247, a line following Camelot's reaction (11. 237-45) to the sudden appearance of the Green Knight, as "one"—an allusion to Gawain. Suggests that such a reading of *sum* prepares the audience for Gawain's involvement in the narrative.

16   MEDCALF, STEPHEN. *"Piers Plowman* and the Ricardian Age in Literature," in *Literature and Western Civilization: The Mediaeval World.* Edited by David Daiches and Anthony Thorlby. London: Aldus Books, pp. 644, 650, 654-665, 671-674, 677, 680.

Discusses the fusion of two worlds in *Gawain*—the artistic blend of Norman French words and Old English/Norse diction as well as the mélange of chivalric ideals and manners (French) and the voice of a native Midlander who revels in heroic tales (alliterative) pulsating with the rhythms of nature—and the parallels in phraseology between the opening lines of *Gawain* and *Wynnere and Wastoure;* the beginning of *Gawain,* however, spotlights "a sense of time contained in time" (p. 656) as well as the crushing effects of conflict and the instability of peace, echoed later in the changing of the seasons. Focuses on Gawain's arming; his pentangle (the interlocking five fives); topography (Dee to the Wirral) and the severe winter; the audience's identification with Gawain; and the thematic concern with penitence.

17   OWEN, D. D. R. *Two Old French Gauvain Romances. Part II: Parallel Readings with Sir Gawain and the Green Knight.* New York: Harper and Row, Barnes & Noble Import Division, pp. 159-208.

[Contains "Introduction" (pp. 159-70), "Commentary" (pp. 171-202), and "Conclusions on the *Gawain*-Poet's Techniques" (pp. 203-208).] Attempts to show parallels in situation, details, and phraseology between *Le Chevalier à l'épée,* *La Mule sans frein,* and *Sir Gawain*—particularly to demonstrate that the *Gawain*-poet consciously employed these two French romances as the main sources for his work. Praises the *Gawain*-poet for his carefully structured narrative pace, his use of irony, and his evocation of dramatic tension. Concludes by delineating the differences between the amorous knight-errant, Gauvain, in the French romances and the spiritually mature hero of *Gawain.*

18 PEARSALL, DEREK. "The Story and Its Setting," in *Literature and Western Civilization: The Mediaeval World.* Edited by David Daiches and Anthony Thorlby. London: Aldus Books, p. 404.

Suggests that *Gawain*'s idealized portrait of courtly society and ideals and the hero's basically unreal quest are hallmarks of romance; yet the dilemmas which Gawain faces and his ultimate failure sever the poem's ties with the romance mode and aligns *Gawain* with "realistic 'low-mimetic' fiction."

19 PEARSALL, DEREK and ELIZABETH SALTER. *Landscapes and Seasons of the Medieval World.* Toronto: University of Toronto Press, pp. 45, 135, 147-154, 167, 179-180, 201.

Claims that *Gawain,* especially its winter indoor settings, is linked with January and February Calendar patterns and emphasizes the thematic parallel between the New Year festivities at Camelot (*Gawain*) and the depiction of January in the *Très Riches Heures* painted for Jean, duc de Berri. Focuses also on the graphic images of winter in *Gawain,* suggesting the hero's suffering and impoverished state, and on the dramatic role played by seasonal change and landscape, and thus underscoring the mutability of human life.

20 SANDERLIN, GEORGE. " 'Thagh I were burde bryghtest'—*GGK,* 1283-1287." *Chaucer Review,* 8 (Summer), 60-64.

Suggests that the original MS reading (1. 1283)—"Thagh I were burde bryghtest the burde in mynde hade"—should be retained even though it signalizes a shift in point of view (from Gawain to Lady Bercilak). Claims that Bercilak's wife as

temptress and as Morgan's companion would be aware of Gawain's meeting with the Green Knight at the Green Chapel
and that lines 1283-87 reveal to the audience both Lady Bercilak's modest demeanour and Gawain's character as viewed by
his antagonist.

21   STEVENS, JOHN. *Medieval Romance: Themes and Ap-
      proaches.* London: Hutchinson and Company, pp.
      21, 57-58, 75-77, 89, 91, 101, 105, 117, 149, 166,
      168-174, 188-190, 192, 206, 233, 236.
         [Reprinted: 1974.27.] Discusses the courtly merry-
      making of the Christmas festivities and the idealized lifestyle
      and urbane manners depicted in *Gawain* as reserved for the
      high-born. Focuses, likewise, on Gawain's loneliness upon his
      return to Camelot, a factor which reflects his soaring beyond
      the chivalric values of Arthur's court. Emphasizes the "mar-
      velous" humanity of the Green Knight; the perfection of
      Gawain, the chivalric knight; the realism and courtesy de-
      picted; the parallels between *Gawain* and Jehan Renart's *Le
      Lai de l'Ombre;* and the gracious bantering (*luf-talkyng*) as
      well as Gawain's polished repartee in the temptation scenes.

22   WASWO, RICHARD. "Parables of Civilization: *Sir Ga-
      wain and the Green Knight* and *The Tempest.*"
      Genre, 6 (December), 448-461.
         Claims that language, especially language linked with the
      nature and significance of civilization, is an integral part of
      both *Gawain* and Shakespeare's *The Tempest.* Views Gawain,
      the exemplar of chivalry, as undergoing a quest and a testing.
      Suggests, moreover, that Gawain's quest involves a disclosure
      and criticism of the values of Camelot as well as a "deadly
      game"; the references to Troy in *Gawain* intimate the destruc-
      tion of Camelot because of immorality. Notes that the "par-
      able of civilization" found in *Gawain* involves "the necessity
      of accommodating the irrational into a rationally ordered view
      and conduct of life, of acknowledging its claims and controll-
      ing it" (p. 451).
         Focuses on a number of important matters, including the
      Christmas feast; the three temptations and hunts ("sports"),
      which "bring natural forces under control by creating rules to
      be observed in the exercise of that control, rules which make
      the exercise a matter of . . . skillful and elegant performance"

(p. 454); the vitality of the Green Knight; and the ending of *Gawain*.

23   ZIMMERMANN, RÜDIGER. "Verbal Syntax and Style in *Sir Gawain and the Green Knight.*" *English Studies*, 54 (December), 533-543.

Attempts to demonstrate that "the poet's shifting from preterite to perfect [tenses] or to narrative present, from the active to the passive voice, and from the indicative to the subjunctive mood" (p. 533) is structurally significant in *Gawain*. Notes that the perfect tense is employed primarily in direct discourse although this tense may serve as a signpost in narrative parallels.

Maintains that narrative present is used to describe central characters or to contrast individuals and groups as well as to introduce dramatic elements, especially "simultaneity" of scenes. Suggests that mood serves to delineate character traits and that the ending of *Gawain* emphasizes the intellectual myopia of Camelot and Gawain's "complete isolation."

1974

1   BARRON, W. R. J., ed. "Introduction," in his edition and prose translation of *Sir Gawain and the Green Knight.* Manchester Medieval Classics, edited by G. L. Brook. Manchester, England: Manchester University Press, pp. 1-24.

Explicates the history, nature, and scope of the romance—its conventions and materials—and the chivalric code; demonstrates how and why *Gawain*'s departure from such conventions, even though the poem adheres to them in numerous ways, creates an aura of ambiguity. Discusses, moreover, numerous aspects of *Gawain*—fitt by fitt—including the ambivalent nature of the Green Knight; the ironic description of the turning of the seasons; the pentangle symbol; the hunts and temptations; and the important roles played by ambiguity and irony.

*2   BERTI, I. "Traduzione e introduzione al poemetto medio-inglese *Ser Galvano e il Cavaliere Verde.*" Ph.D. dissertation, Università di Pisa, Facoltà di lingue e letterature straniere.

[Citation provided by Professor Carl Berkhout.]

3 CHRISTMAS, PETER. "A Reading of *Sir Gawain and the Green Knight.*" Neophilologus, 58 (April), 238-247.

Argues that Gawain passes three distinct tests—courage in his confrontation with the Green Knight, exemplary behavior in his dealings with Bercilak's wife, and the acceptance of the green girdle—and thus is innocent of any major fault. Claims that the Green Knight emphasizes in the chapel tableau Gawain's victory and notes the significance of a serious view and use of the chivalric code in *Gawain* as opposed to Chaucer's *Knight's Tale*. Suggests that Gawain is justified in his reluctance to share the laughter of Arthur's court, for he perceives that laughter may explode the chivalric code which imparts meaning to his existence.

4 ELLIOTT, RALPH W. V. "Some Northern Landscape Features in *Sir Gawain and the Green Knight*," in *Iceland and the Mediaeval World: Studies in Honour of Ian Maxwell*. Edited by Gabriel Turville-Petre and John Stanley Martin. Clayton, Victoria, Australia: Wilke and Company, pp. 132-143.

Attempts to focus on topographical diction and its artistic influence upon *Gawain;* claims that two different landscapes—the conventional "romantic" descriptions with their dependence upon rhetorical techniques and alliterative formulas; and the second type, the "realistic" *topos* with its emphasis upon terrain which can be easily visualized and upon unusual Norse vocabulary—appear in *Gawain* (pp. 132-134).

Interprets a number of words, derived from Old Norse, in the "realistic" vein, including *bonk* (11. 2077, 2082) as "hillside, slope, bank of a river" (pp. 133-34); *forlondez* (1. 699), derived from *forlendi* ("the land between sea and hills"), as applied to terrain near the Dee "with appropriate fording places attested by place-names containing the element *ford* [1. 699, *fordez*]" (p. 134); *ker(re)*, derived from *kjarr* ("brushwood"), as "bog, marsh" (p. 135); *knot* (11. 1431, 1434), perhaps derived from *knǫttr* ("a ball"); *rasse* (1. 1570), rooted in *rás* ("water-course, channel"), as "river bed" (p. 137); *forȝ* (1. 2173), derived from *fors* ("waterfall"), as "waterfall" (pp. 138-139); *scowtes* (1. 2167), derived from *skúti*, as "a cave formed by jutting rocks"; *wro* (1. 2222), stemming from *vrá* ("a corner"), as "nook" (p. 139); and *strothe* (1. 1710), derived from *storð* ("a young wood, plantation"), as "a wood . . . possibly on marshy ground" (p. 140).

Suggests that such realistic Norse words in *Gawain* offer "a topographical distinctiveness within the 'realistic geography' of the poem that points beyond the poet's eclecticism of diction to the names of real places" (p. 142), especially in Cheshire, Derbyshire, and Staffordshire.

5   FOLEY, MICHAEL M.   "A Bibliography of *Purity* (*Cleanness*), 1864-1972." *Chaucer Review,* 8, no. 4: 324-334.

Contains a list of editions of *Gawain* and references to books, articles, and dissertations which analyze *Gawain*.

6   FOLEY, MICHAEL M. "Gawain's Two Confessions Reconsidered." *Chaucer Review,* 9 (Summer), 73-79.

Suggests that Gawain's acceptance and concealment of the green girdle is not a mortal sin but a minor violation of the chivalric code, a fault which is aptly revealed in a secular "confession" to a knight (Green Knight). Claims that Gawain does not violate an oath (*untraw þe*) but fails to abide by the rules of a courtly *gomen.* Contends that "in his attempt to live by two parallel moral codes, the Christian and the knightly, Gawain falls slightly short of perfection in the latter" (p. 77).

7   GANIM, JOHN M. "Mutable Imagination: Time, Space and Audience in Medieval English Narrative." Ph.D. dissertation, Indiana University.

[Partly on *Gawain. See Dissertation Abstracts,* 35 (1974), 2221A.] Discusses the influence of style, particularly the poet's conceptions of time and space, upon the meaning and the audience of *Gawain.* Emphasizes the jarring effect of the style of *Gawain*, springing from "subtle disorientation and confusion . . . as well as formal perfection."

8   GROSS, LAILA. "Gawain's Acceptance of the Girdle." *American Notes and Queries,* 12, nos. 9-10 (May-June), 154-155.

Alludes to medieval historical evidence, "Letter from

Thomas Duke of Gloucester and Constable of England to King Richard II. Concerning the Manner of Conducting Judicial Duels," in order to prove that Gawain violated the chivalric code—a code which expressly forbade "a knight in single combat . . . to have any magical objects on his person" (p. 155).

9   HAINES, VICTOR YELVERTON. "Allusions to the Felix Culpa in the Prologue of *Sir Gawain and the Green Knight.*" *Revue de l'Université d'Ottawa,* 44, no. 2 (April-June), 158-177.

[*See also* Haines (1975.11).] Views the opening of *Gawain,* especially the paradoxical references to the fall of Troy, Aeneas, Felix Brutus, and *blysse and blunder* (1. 18), as a "veiled allusion" to the *felix culpa* motif. Links Gawain's antifeminist tirade, particularly the mention of Adam's Edenic fall because he was beguiled by Eve, with Gawain's fall from grace. Claims that the historical frame for *Gawain* prepares the audience for the action of the poem as well as for the conventional association of Adam's fall and the Redemption. Concludes by examining the *felix culpa* traditions underlying Camelot and by raising the question, "Is Camelot to be admired for a relatively high standard of achievement in wholesome freshness or criticised for the imaginary innocence of playing real life as a game and forgetting their fallen state?" (p. 177).

10   HARK, INA RAE. "Gawain's Passive Quest." *Comitatus,* 5:1-13.

Suggests that the conventional romance quest, a form which stresses success and accomplishment, is undercut in *Gawain,* for Gawain "directs all his actions toward placing himself in a position of ultimate submission" (p. 1). Discusses the conflict between the quest convention and the objectives of the contemplative life, thereby calling attention to the disparity between Gawain's vision of himself and society's view of Gawain. Views Gawain's quest, then, as an initiation into self-knowledge, insight which demands that Gawain acknowledge the imperfections of humanity; emphasizes, likewise, game and play in *Gawain,* especially the festive affirmation of mankind.

11   HIEATT, CONSTANCE B. "The Rhythm of the Alliterative Long Line," in *Chaucer and Middle English*

Studies in honour of Rossell Hope Robbins. Edited by Beryl Rowland. Kent, Ohio: Kent State University Press, pp. 119-130.

Employs Borroff's study (1962.1), specifically her elucidation of the "chief syllables," in order to disclose "the boundaries of each metrical unit, or 'measure' " in *Gawain*. Substitutes for Borroff's "*C* and *c* the symbols used in scanning Old English," essentially "[´] . . . , for *C*, a *lift*, or 'major chief syllable,' and [`] . . . for *c*, a *half-lift*, or 'minor chief syllable'," in a scanning of 11. 842-849 of *Gawain*. Finds variegated "patterns of relationship between lift and half-lift, but also in the use of caesural pause and anacrusis." Concludes by nothing "that all the Old English type patterns *except* the hypermetric can be observed" in Middle English poetry although "Old English hypermetric verses [perhaps] . . . did have some influence on the alliterative patterns" of *Gawain* and other works.

12   HILL, JOHN M. "Middle English Poets and the Word: Notes Toward an Appraisal of Linguistic Consciousness." *Criticism,* 16 (Spring), 153-154, 158-160, 162-164.

States that *Gawain* and *Pearl* represent "a thematic elaboration of the ways in which language—or the word—can fail us" (p. 153). Contends that Gawain misconstrues the Green Knight's desire for a *gomen* and that an exchange of blows does not demand beheading. Suggests, further, that Gawain's comprehension is limited, for he does not really listen to the Green Knight's playful challenge.

13   HOWARD, DONALD R. "Renaissance World-Alienation," in *The Darker Vision of the Renaissance: Beyond the Fields of Reason.* Edited by Robert S. Kinsman. UCLA Center for Medieval and Renaissance Studies Contributions, Vol. 6. Berkeley: University of California Press, 64-72.

Focuses on the medieval concept of *contemptus mundi*, especially as expounded by Pope Innocent III. Selects *Gawain,* especially *Fer floten fro his frendez fremedly* (1. 714) and succeeding passages, as a graphic illustration of world-alienation; notes that the famous winter passage (11. 726-32) illustrates Gawain's removal from the world and initiation into "direct confrontation with external nature and (perhaps) with his own animal side, his fallen nature" (p. 65). Views Bercilak's castle with its late fourteenth-century architecture and ornamentation as an emblem of the world—comfortable, extravagant, yet illusory and "morally questionable" (pp. 66-69). Concludes by suggesting that Gawain's quest may represent worldly life itself and that "the world cannot ever be wholly escaped, except in death" (p. 69).

14   KÄSMANN, HANS. "Numerical Structure in Fitt III of *Sir Gawain and the Green Knight,*" in *Chaucer and Middle English Studies in Honour of Rossell Hope Robbins.* Edited by Beryl Rowland. Kent, Ohio: Kent State University Press, pp. 131-139.

Postulates, first, that the number 2525 in *Gawain* leads the reader "to the pentangle, which is of central importance as a symbol of Gawain's *trawþe* . . ." (p. 131). Claims that the *Gawain*-poet employs numerological patterns as a structural device, not as a symbolic element (p. 133), in order to create symmetry: on the first day, the two sections on the deer-hunt are identical (46 lines per section), and these two sections—combined with the second castle section (47 lines)—constitute 139 lines "as opposed to 140 for the temptation scene" (p. 137). Argues, moreover, that on the second day the two hunting sections (57 and 58 lines, respectively), when added to the "evening in the castle" scene (69 lines), equal 184 lines—"exactly twice the number of the lines of the second temptation scene (92 lines)" (p. 137). Cannot perceive, however, any definite numerological pattern underlying the depiction of the events of the third day.

15   LASATER, ALICE E. *Spain to England: A Comparative Study of Arabic, European, and English Literature of the Middle Ages.* Jackson, Mississippi: University Press of Mississippi, pp. 168-196, and as indexed.

Views *Gawain* as a courtly romance, a Christian poem infused with a festive spirit of humor. Discusses the symmetrical structure of the poem as well as the verse-arrangement, a combination of four-stress alliterative long lines and a bob and wheel (often used for dramatic suspense). *Gawain* may represent an example of *chante-fable,* an Arabic genre which alternates recitation and song. Comments upon the festive elements (Yuletide celebrations and games) and the religious aspects (testing, confession and penance) as well as the roles played by Morgan le Fay and the tradition of courtly love in *Gawain;* contends that the courtly love role-reversal here may not be a satirical device, for "the woman's taking the initiative [in wooing] is a Celtic custom" (p. 179).

Examines the various sources and analogues of the challenge/beheading game, temptation, and exchange of winnings and contends that Gawain's pentangle, a magical and Semitic emblem identified with Solomon, became a well-known figure (pp. 184-185, 187-188, 195) in the twelfth century when numerous scientific and magical works were disseminated through translation into Spanish. Summarizes the various critical interpretations of the Green Knight, especially the significance of his greenness (winter, vegetation, death, literary green man or wild man, devil, and Otherworld creature), and identifies the Knight with the Persian and Islamic al-Khadir—" 'the Green One,' who is associated with ancient vegetation myths, who is both frightening and benevolent, and who is a noble and religious figure" (p. 188); al-Khadir, a character in the *Qur'ān* (12th century) and in the *Arabian Nights,* often proposes a challenge to the court and fails to disclose his identity.

16   LEE, JENNIFER A. "MS Cotton Nero A.x.: A Study of the Illustrator and Translator as Primary Critics of the Middle English *Pearl, Cleanness, Patience* and *Sir Gawain and the Green Knight.*" Ph.D. dissertation, State University of New York (Stony Brook).

[*See Dissertation Abstracts International,* 35 (1974), 407A.] Discusses the four illustrations of scenes from *Gawain.* Claims that the illustrator was familiar with the poetic texts in the Cotton MS and with manuscript illumination conventions and that he viewed the texts largely as moral poems. Evaluates, finally, translations of *Gawain.*

17   LEIGHTON, J. M. "Christian and Pagan Symbolism and Ritual in *Sir Gawain and the Green Knight.*" *Theoria: A Journal of Studies in the Arts, Humanities, and Social Sciences,* 43 (December), 49-62.

Attempts to interpret the meaning of the Green Knight, particularly the significance of his greenness, axe, and holly bob. Argues that the Knight's challenge of Arthur represents "a re-enactment of a coronation ceremonial . . . appropriate for a time when the king holds formal court" (p. 51). Criticizes the fertility myth theories (green as a vegetation symbol) and notes that green is the color of ecclesiastical vestments worn at Epiphany (January 6), a time of joy, faith, rebirth, and revelation. Contends, moreover, that the *Gawain*-poet has reshaped the elements of pagan ritual underlying the poem into a truly Christian structure, for Gawain must perceive through the experience of a test the significance of Christian ideals.

18   LUPACK, ALAN C. "Structure and Tradition in the Poems of the Alliterative Revival." Ph.D. dissertation, University of Pennsylvania.
      [Partly on *Gawain. See Dissertation Abstracts,* 36 (1975), 323A.] Emphasizes the artistic structure, theme, and style of *Gawain,* a romance which fuses thematically two narrative sections.

19   MARKUS, MANFRED, ed. and trans. "Epilogue" to *Sir Gawain and the Green Knight/Sir Gawain und der Grüne Ritter* (English and German).   Stuttgart: Philipp Reclam jun., pp. 181-191.
      [In German. Contains German prose translation and Middle English text on facing pages (pp. 6-165) plus critical/textual notes (pp. 169-79) and a select bibliography (pp. 193-196).] Focuses on the authorship problem; the "alliterative revival"; the sources of *Gawain;* the poem's use of rhetorical figures and point of view; the "bob and wheel"; and feasible interpretations of *Gawain.*

20   MARKUS, MANFRED. "Some Examples of Ambiguity in *Sir Gawain and the Green Knight." Neuphilologische Mitteilungen,* 75, no. 4:625-629.
      Specifies three illustrations of verbal ambiguity which disclose the link between individual words or phrases and the poetic context in which they appear. Interprets *þat þer stod and stalked hym nerre* (1. 237), especially *stalked* ("to pursue game by the method of stealthy approach, esp. by the use of a stalking-horse . . . for concealing oneself from the view of the hunted animal" or "to walk with stiff, high, measured steps,

like a long-legged bird," suggesting haughtiness), as an object phrase referring to the Green Knight. Claims, however, that lines 955, 968, and 1273 are sexually ambiguous, and finally, that lines 1263-67 reveal Gawain playing the role of "the inno-cent by comparing her [Bercilak's wife] liberality to the generosity of the other inhabitants of the castle" (p. 627).

21   MEIER, HANS HEINRICH. "Middle English Styles in Action." *English Studies,* 55 (June), 196-204.

Focuses on the conclusion (lines 1719-32) of Bercilak's fox hunt: claims that the "passive without agent expressed" and concrete verbs play important roles here. Contrasts the style ("painterly," "atectonic," "open form," "continuity," "excited," and "committed") of Þe Wohunge of Ure Lauerd (ca. 1225) with the style ("linear," "tectonic," "closed form," "calm," and "detached") of *Gawain.* Suggests that *Gawain* discloses the concept of sport, employs the passive voice to "stabilize" movement, and uses contrast and sharply drawn images in order to evoke the poet's "linear vision."

22   MERCER, MARY ELLEN. "A Violent Order: Moral Vision in Late Arthurian Romance, 1215-1500." Ph.D. dissertation, Syracuse University.

[Partly on *Gawain.* See *Dissertation Abstracts,* 36 (1976), 6708A.] Examines "high chivalric" ideals, including the con-cept of courtesy, in *Gawain.*

23   MOSELEY, C. W. R. D. "Chaucer, Sir John Mandeville, and the Alliterative Revival: A Hypothesis Concern-ing Relationships." *Modern Philology,* 72 (Novem-ber), 182-184.

Notes that the *Pearl*-poet used Mandeville's *Travels* (1356) as one of his literary sources and claims that only "northern" poets and Chaucer (writing for an audience famil-iar with *Gawain*) seem to have their works shaped, in part, by *Travels,* probably because Mandeville's work was disseminated among the highly sophisticated poets of the "alliterative re-vival" and among John of Gaunt's household. Conjectures that John of Gaunt's household may be the common intellec-tual bond tying Chaucer and the *Pearl*-poet.

24   OIJI, TAKERO. "Catholicism in *Sir Gawain and the*

Green Knight." Studies in English Literature (English
Literary Society of Japan), 51, nos. 1-2 (November),
5-21.

[In Japanese. English synopsis of article found on pp.
161-162 of the English Number for 1975.] Suggests that Gawain's pentangle and the image of Mary on his shield point to
him as the ideal Catholic knight. Contends that Gawain's
spiritual rebirth following "contrition, confession, and penance" emphasizes the *Gawain*-poet's Catholic position and that
penance (sacrament) is an integral part of the concluding sections of this poem.

25   OLSZEWSKA, E. S. "ME. *Brittene & Brenne." Notes
       and Queries,* New Series, 21 (June), 207-209.

Interprets *brittened and brent* (*Gawain*, 1. 2), a phrase
rooted in Norse vocabulary, as "destroyed (demolished) and
burned."

26   SPEARING, A. C. and J. E. SPEARING, eds. *Poetry of
       the Age of Chaucer.* London: Edward Arnold, pp.
       2-5, 9-14, 16-18, 21-22, 24, 27-28, 33, 35, 39, 80-87.

Discusses, in the "General Introduction," various aspects
of and elements in *Gawain*—the romance as court poetry;
suspense; connection with the audience; alliterative tags;
similes, especially those which identify the Green Knight with
nature and the courtly milieu; cinematic quality of the descriptive passages; onomatopoeic diction; vocabulary (Norse,
French, and English); alliterative verse; romance conventions;
courtesy; and second-person pronouns (*thou* and *you*).

Examines, in the "Introduction" to the excerpt (most of
Fitt I) from *Gawain,* the Beheading Game and Temptation
motifs; the ironic juxtaposition of Gawain's reputation as a
lover with his traditional role of courteous knight; the Knight's
ambiguous greenness, emblematic of the devil, the fairy world,
nature, the new year; the Knight's testing of Camelot's renown; and the ironic depiction of Arthur and his court.

27   STEVENS, JOHN. *Medieval Romance: Themes and Ap-
       proaches.* New York: Norton, pp. 21, 57-58, 75-77,
       89, 91, 101, 105, 117, 149, 166, 168-174, 188-190,
       192, 206, 233, 236.

[Reprint of 1973.21.]

28   STONE, BRIAN, trans. *Sir Gawain and the Green Knight.* Second edition. New York: Penguin Books, 185 pp.

[Revised edition of 1959.17. Revised introduction (pp. 9-20), revised verse translation, condensed background material, more extensive notes (pp. 163-85) than in the first edition, select bibliography and reference suggestions (pp. 159-62), and three new essays—"The Common Enemy of Man," "Gawain's 'Eternal Jewel'," and "The Poem as a Play."] Comments in his Introduction upon the alliterative verse employed by poets of the west and northwest of England; the *Gawain*-poet's use of Norse vocabulary and northern culture; the poem's sources, including *Bricriu's Feast* (the Beheading Game motif), *Le Livre de Caradoc,* and *Yder* (Temptation motif); the framework of *Gawain* as a "game of truth"; the significance of elements from pagan ritual and Christianity; the poem's use of patterning and parallelism, including the interlacing of the hunts and temptations; the nature of Bercilak/ Green Knight; and Gawain's courtesy.

Compares the Green Knight, in "The Common Enemy of Man," to a jovial devil who tempts Gawain for God's ends. Comments upon some of the qualities and figures linked with the Knight's greenness: death, vegetation, youth, earthiness, the wild man, and the green man, but views the Knight's color and ax primarily as symbols of truth. In "Gawain's 'Eternal Jewel'," however, notes that Gawain abandons "truth" when he conceals the girdle from Bercilak—an act of disloyalty to his host. Deals in "The Poem as a Play," the final essay, with the Christmas production (theatrical) of *Gawain* at Newcastle.

29   SZÜCS, CLARA A. "Visual Experience in *Sir Gawain*: A Method of Discovering Depictive Techniques." Ph.D. dissertation, University of Michigan.

[*See Dissertation Abstracts International,* 35 (1975), 4470A-71A.] Suggests that the *Gawain*-poet consciously molds his narrative so as to create a visual impression for the audience. ". . . in descriptive passages the poet always describes his subject twice, first giving a general structural image showing size and shape, then individuating qualities of color, ornament, and sometimes material substance." Argues that in episodes, however, the poet skillfully employs the elements of repetition and variation to produce a desired visual effect (hunting scenes), whereas some episodes—the temptation scenes—are consciously blurred in order to emphasize the inflated ideals and diction of courtly love as contrasted with the clarity and energy of the real world.

30   TAITT, PETER S. "The Quest Theme in Representative English Works of the Thirteenth and Fourteenth Centuries." Ph.D. dissertation, University of British Columbia (Canada).

[Partly on *Gawain. See Dissertation Abstracts International*, 35 (1974), 3703A.] Contends that *Gawain*—through the quest motif—mirrors "uncertainties and doubts about the lasting values of the chivalric ethic and the efficacy of dogma which earlier generations seem to have taken for granted."

31   TAYLOR, P. B. "Gawain's Garland of Girdle and Name." *English Studies,* 55 (February), 6-14.

Contends that the trials in *Gawain* are shaped so as to force Gawain and Camelot to prove their essential worth. Suggests that the lady's three temptations represent an attack on Gawain's name, his courtesy, and that, in a similar vein, the Green Knight verbally assaults Gawain's heroic reputation (Green Chapel scene): once Gawain admits his flaws, however, the Green Knight "re-invests him with a name" (p. 12), the name of truth. Concentrates, finally, upon Gawain's intellectual myopia once he returns to Camelot.

32   THIEBAUX, MARCELLE. *The Stag of Love: The Chase in Medieval Literature.* Ithaca: Cornell University Press, pp. 71-88.

[*See also* Richter (Add. 28). Views *Gawain* as an "instructive chase."] Depicts the hunting scenes at Bercilak's castle: "One of the principal effects to proceed from the instructive hunting of the host is the young hero's enlarged self-awareness." With the advent of Fitt 3, the audience perceives Gawain's inner feelings—fears, doubts, imperfections. Concentrates upon the enigmatic character of Bercilak, especially the lord's attempt to make Gawain his unwary quarry by urging him to remain idle (lounging in bed); employs references to hunting manuals—*De Arte Bersandi, The Master of Game,* and Henry of Lancaster's *Livre des Seyntz Medicines*—to show the conflict between hunting and idleness. Maintains that the *Gawain*-poet links hunting, especially the fox-chase, with "teaching and the correction of sin." Concludes with an analysis of hunting terms, especially verbs, in *Gawain.*

33   VALAITIS, KRISTINA A. "The Narrator of *Sir Gawain and the Green Knight.*" Ph.D. dissertation, Northern Illinois University.

[*See Dissertation Abstracts International,* 35 (1974), 2957A.] Discusses *Gawain* in the context of Arthurian romance in order to disclose the poem's comic irony. Contends that the narrator of *Gawain,* "a raconteur-romancer," achieves aesthetic distance from his material, Gawain and his quest, in order to produce ironic effects. Claims, moreover, that the conclusion of *Gawain* is consciously ambiguous so as to force the audience to participate in Gawain's predicament, to comprehend the meaning of human limitations.

34   WATSON, GEORGE, ed. *The New Cambridge Bibliography of English Literature.* Vol. 1, 600-1660. Cambridge, England: Cambridge University Press, cols. 400-406, 547-549.

[Comprehensive bibliography of editions, translations, and scholarly studies of *Gawain. See also* Bateson (1941.1).]

*35   WILSON, A. D. "Medieval Romance Seen as Story." Ph.D. dissertation, University of Birmingham (England).

[Cited in Derek Brewer (1976.4). *See also* Wilson (1976.36).]

36   WRIGHT, THOMAS L. "Sir Gawain *in vayres.*" *Philological Quarterly,* 53 (Summer), 427-428.

Contends that the bob *in vayres* (1. 1015) simultaneously denotes "in truth" and suggests the vair (Old French *vair*) pattern in heraldry. Claims that vair as an emblem of heraldic design signalizes "the patterned variety of the feast and the pairing of companions at table, particularly Gawain and the lady. . . . In a field *vairé* (*in vayres*), Gawain is enclosed in membership with the company: he is thus both captive and guest" (p. 428).

1975

1 BARBER, RICHARD. *The Knight and Chivalry.* Second edition. Totowa, New Jersey: Rowman and Littlefield, p. 131.

Emphasizes *Gawain*'s portrayal of knighthood as the greatest human achievement. Links *Gawain* with *Parzival*, for both poems involve a quest for "earthly perfection."

2 BILLINGS, ANNA HUNT. *A Guide to the Middle English Metrical Romances Dealing with English and Germanic Legends, and with the Cycles of Charlemagne and of Arthur.* Folcroft, Pennsylvania: Folcroft Library Editions, pp. 160-168.

[Reprint of 1901.1.]

3 CAMPBELL, ALPHONSUS M. "The Character of King Arthur in the Middle English Alliterative Poems." *Revue de l'Université d'Ottawa,* 45, no. 1 (January-March), 26-30, 40.

Examines the opening stanzas of *Gawain* and notes that Arthur is depicted as a happy, buoyant chivalric leader.

4 COFFER, KARIN B. "Myth, Code, Order: Transformations in the Narrative Structure of Courtly Romance." Ph.D. dissertation, University of Colorado.

[Partly on *Gawain*. See *Dissertation Abstracts,* 36 (1976), 5273A.] Applies structuralist and post-structuralist critical theories to *Gawain*. Contends that *Gawain* is a conscious fictional exercise, a free-flying romance which does not purport to mirror reality. ". . . *Gawain* makes its own fictionality . . . an issue in its own 'plot'."

5 COURTNEY, CHARLES R. "The *Pearl* Poet: An Annotated International Bibliography, 1955-1970." Ph.D. dissertation, University of Arizona.

[Covers all four Cotton Nero poems and *Erkenwald*. See *Dissertation Abstracts International,* 37 (1976), 327A.] Examines, in the "Introduction" (32 pp.), the problem of authorship; the Cotton Nero MS; the various editions (before 1955) of the Cotton Nero poems and *Erkenwald;* and recent important critical approaches to the works of the *Pearl*-poet.

In the bibliography, attempts to include "all editions, translations, and modernizations of the works of the *Pearl*-poet from 1955 through 1970 as well as all published essays, books, and unpublished doctoral dissertations." Lists under the category of *Gawain* studies all editions, translations, general studies, and collected essays as well as interpretations of the poem's comic and Christian qualities, images, language, sources and background, and style.

6   CURLEY, MICHAEL J. "A Note on Bertilak's Beard." *Modern Philology*, 73 (August), 69-73.
    Claims that Bertilak's beaver-colored beard (1. 845) suggests, as found in *Physiologus*, the acquisition of spiritual freedom through payment of debts (renounced sins) to Satan. Perceives this spiritual meaning for "beaver-hued" through an interpretation of the beaver's self-castration in *Physiologus*.

7   FARLEY-HILLS, DAVID. "John Massy as the *Pearl*-Poet." *Review of English Studies*, New Series 26 (November), 451.
    [Letter of reply to Thorlac Turville-Petre (1975).] Reiterates his claim that Thomas Hoccleve's Massy was a poet and argues that his view represents a supplement to Greenwood's hypothesis (1956.4) that Massy was the *Pearl*-poet's name.

8   FRY, NANCY M. "A Study of Play and Festivity in Literature: Four Essays." Ph.D. dissertation, Yale University.
    [Partly on *Gawain. See Dissertation Abstracts*, 36 (1976), 8032A.] Explores *Gawain*, a dramatic version of festive play, in terms of modern game and play theories. Views the Yuletide *gomen* underlying *Gawain* as a ritualistic device which allows the hero to comprehend more fully both his religious beliefs and man's mortality.

9   GOETINCK, GLENYS. *Peredur: A Study of Welsh Tradition in the Grail Legends.* Cardiff: University of Wales Press, pp. 213, 235, 255, 263-264.
    Notes some similarities between the temptation scenes in *Gawain* and the story of Peredur, the Miller, and the Empress

in *Peredur.* Notes, likewise, parallels between *Gawain* and *The Champion's Bargain.*

10   GREEN, DENNIS H. *"Alieniloquium*: Zur Begriffs-bestimmung der mittelalterlichen Ironie," in *Verbum et Signum.* Vol. 2. Edited by Hans Fromm, Wolf-gang Harms, and Uwe Ruberg. Beiträge zur mediävis-tischen Bedeutungsforschung. Studien zu Semantik und Sinntradition im Mittelalter. Munich: Wilhelm Fink, 133-134, 146-148.

     [In German.] Discusses the ironic implications of Ga-wain, frequently depicted as a lover in medieval literature, and the Lady's seductive advances in the Hautdesert tempta-tions; analyzes the meaning of *cors* (1. 1237). Examines the ironic connection between Solomon, the Biblical character ensnared by love, and Gawain, for Gawain wears the pentangle —Solomon's token of truth.

11   HAINES, VICTOR YELVERTON. *"Sir Gawain and the Green Knight* as *Figura* of the Felix Culpa." Ph.D. dissertation, McGill University (Canada).

     [*See Dissertation Abstracts,* 36 (1976), 6703A-04A; *see also* Haines (1974.9).] Uses figural art and Christian typology in order to demonstrate Gawain's identification with Adam, particularly Adam's fortunate fall (*felix culpa*). Views the nar-rative of *Gawain* as "a unique part of history which partici-pates in the felix culpa."

12   HUNT, TONY. "Gawain's Fault and the Moral Perspec-tives of *Sir Gawain and the Green Knight."* *Trivium,* 10 (May), 1-18.

     Focuses on Gawain's *faute,* a venial sin, and emphasizes the poet's concern with the themes of integrity and tempta-tion. Depicts in detail the third bedroom scene involving Ga-wain's acceptance of the girdle as well as the Green Chapel epi-sode. Analyzes the meaning of *unleuté, couetyse,* and *cowar-dyse,* Gawain's self-accused weaknesses, and concludes that the *Gawain*-poet especially calls attention to "the conduct of the Christian life of the knight" (p. 17).

13   KIRK, ELIZABETH D. "Chaucer and His English Con-temporaries," in *Geoffrey Chaucer: A Collection of*

Original Articles. Edited by George D. Economou.
Contemporary Studies in Literature. New York:
McGraw-Hill, pp. 111, 118-123, 126.

Contends that the *Pearl*-poet composed his works for "an
aristocratic court in the northwest Midlands" (p. 118). Comments upon the style and verse form of the alliterative tradition, especially that of the Cotton Nero poems, and notes that
the *Pearl*-poet's elaborate concern with artistic form mirrors
his perception of the tension between the divine ideal and
human limitations. Views *Gawain,* finally, as a festive poem,
a sophisticated comedy which reconciles conflicting serious
elements without repudiating them.

14   KJELLMER, GÖRAN. *Did the "Pearl Poet" Write Pearl?*
Gothenburg Studies in English, No. 30. Göteborg:
Acta Universitatis Gothoburgensis, 105 pp.

Examines past authorship investigations and both internal
and external evidence in order to determine the author(s) of
the Cotton Nero poems and *St. Erkenwald.* Ranks the five
poems according to linguistic variables—"Lexical Frequency,"
"Clause Length," "Sentence Length," "Clause Linkage
Types," "Subordinator Types," "Passive Forms," and "Alliteration"—and finds that *Pearl* swerves away from the linguistic norm. Contends, moreover, that *Gawain* is the most "representative" of the five poems, that the case for multiple
authorship is still open, and that the *Pearl*-poet probably did
not compose *Pearl.*

15   KNAPP, PEGGY ANN. "Nature is a Woman," in *The
Roles and Images of Women in the Middle Ages and
Renaissance.* Edited by Douglas Radcliff-Umstead.
University of Pittsburgh Publications on the Middle
Ages and Renaissance, Vol. 3. Pittsburgh: Center for
Medieval and Renaissance Studies, pp. 62-67.

Claims that *Gawain* is "a document central to late fourteenth-century English culture, and the most sophisticated
surviving attempt to investigate the duties of man to God and
to society in that period" (p. 62). Notes that the poem re-
volves about the opposition between nature and culture,
especially in the tableau depicting the Green Knight's arrival
at the Yuletide banquet: "The knight is green though outside
it is winter; his bushy hair and wild eyes suggest both the

Green Man (vegetation god of pagan folklore) and the Wild Man (degenerate forest recluse who attacks knights in romances)" (p. 63). Traces the imprint of nature, the emblem of mutability, in Fitt Two: ". . . the cyclic operation of the seasons is contrasted with the linear progression of Gawain's life" (p. 63).

Concludes by examining the roles of women in *Gawain*: Mary, a figure of grace and "the unchanging image of nature redeemed" (p. 63); Guinevere, a representation of culture and courtly sophistication; Bercilak's wife, "the benevolent face of nature" (p. 65), albeit illusory; and Morgan le Fay, the master puppeteer behind the action. Views Gawain's antifeminist harangue essentially in the tradition of *Contemptus mundi* and the antagonists in this romance as Mary and Morgan, with "Guinevere and the lady the agents of their contest" (p. 66).

16   LEYERLE, JOHN. "The Game and Play of Hero," in *Concepts of the Hero in the Middle Ages and Early Renaissance*. Edited by Norman Burns and Christopher Reagan. Albany, New York: State University of New York Press, pp. 49-82.

Aligns the concept of hero with a literary game—half-serious and half-fun—observing set rules. Views the poetic "nucleus" of *Gawain* as a type of game-playing (*gomen*), involving a number of Yuletide games—challenge/beheading game; temptation (game of love); hunting, "the game" in the Middle Ages; and the exchange of winnings bargain.

17   LOGAN, BETTY Y. B. "A Study of Isolation in Selected Old and Middle English Alliterative Poems." Ph.D. dissertation, University of Southern Mississippi.

[Partly on *Gawain*. See *Dissertation Abstracts International*, 36 (1975), 2221A.] Examines the role of Gawain in the universe created by the poet: "Gawain is sure of his identity within the court of Camelot but once he must venture out of the confines of Camelot and into the real world beyond, he finds himself confronted by a universe . . . totally alien to his former concept of himself and his identity."

Analyzes Gawain's gradual perception of and reconciliation with his isolation as well as the "shifting narrative focus" employed by the poet to heighten Gawain's sense of isolation.

18	LONG, CHARLES. "Was the Green Knight Really Merlin?". *Interpretations: Studies in Language and Literature*, 7, no. 1:1-7.

Claims that the Green Knight may be identified with Merlin and that Morgan le Fay used "Arthur's own trusted supernatural force" (p. 6), Merlin, in order to humiliate Arthur.

19	MARINO, JAMES G. A. "Game and Romance: A Discussion of the Game-Like Structure of Certain Middle English Metrical Romances." Ph.D. dissertation, University of Pittsburgh.

[Partly on *Gawain*. *See Dissertation Abstracts*, 37 (1976), 1538A-39A.] Argues that *Gawain*, an ironic romance, does not offer a completely ludic vision, for the hero evaluates the game he plays, thereby shattering, in part, the play world. Contends that an "anti-ludic" poem is created by "an ironic double vision resulting partly from a contrast between the game as Gawain sees it and the game as it really is, and partly from Gawain's breaking of the game circle by cheating in the central exchange of gifts."

20	MATTHEWS, WILLIAM. *"bi lag mon:* A Crux in *Sir Gawayn and the Grene Kny3t." Medievalia et Humanistica*, New Series, 6:151-155.

Interprets *bi lag mon* (1. 1729) as "cunningly" or "like a lawyer."

21	MORSE, RUTH, ed. "A Note on Authorship," in *St. Erkenwald*. Cambridge, England: D. S. Brewer, Limited, pp. 45-48.

Notes that nineteenth-century scholars often attributed *Erkenwald* "to the hand of the man who had written the four poems in Cotton Nero A.x. . . . though the hand was assumed to be trembling slightly with age" (p. 45). Claims that the author of *Erkenwald* is unknown, that the *Gawain*-poet and the poet of *Erkenwald* focus on different theological problems, and that "It is possible, though extremely unlikely, that the man who wrote the *Gawain*-poems also wrote the poem in Harley 2250" (p. 48).

22	RICE, NANCY H. "Beauty and the Beast and the Little Boy: Clues about the Origins of Sexism and Racism from Folklore and Literature." Ph.D. dissertation, University of Massachusetts.

[Partly on *Gawain*. *See Dissertation Abstracts,* 36 (1975), 875A.] Discusses Gawain's unjustified verbal attack against women (Beauty).

23   SANDERLIN, GEORGE. "Lady Bercilak of Haut-desert." *Studies in the Humanities* (Indiana University of Pennsylvania), 4, no. 2 (February), 21-26.

Analyzes the complex character of Lady Bercilak and her ties with the structure and theme of *Gawain*. Reveals her empathy toward Gawain (11. 1283-87), her regret over her temptation of the hero (1550), and her love for Gawain (1733). Suggests that Lady Bercilak is both playing a role (temptress) and delighting in Gawain's company, resulting in emotional conflicts for her.

24   SIMS, JAMES H. "Gawayne's Fortunate Fall in *Sir Gawayne and the Grene Knight.*" *Orbis Litterarum,* 30, no. 1:28-39.

Traces the *felix culpa* motif in *Gawain*—the "fortunate fall" through which Gawain and the other knights at Camelot experience self-knowledge and thus spiritual rebirth (the wearing of the green baldric). Claims that Gawain's fall springs from pride, a human weakness which leads him to cowardice and covetousness.

25   SVEINSSON, EINAR ÓLAFUR. "Herra Valvin og Karlinn grái," in his *Löng er För.* Studia Islandica, Vol. 34, edited by Sveinn Skorri Höskuldsson. Reykjavík: Bókaútgáfa Menningarsjóds, 128-139.

[In Icelandic. English summary on pp. 167-169.] Suggests that some lost literary piece, perhaps written in England, is the source for the Icelandic *Sveins Saga Múkssonar,* a work which forms the foundation of the seventeenth-century *Sveins-rímur Múkssonar.* Notes parallels between the *rímur,* especially *ríma* 13-17, and the Beheading Game in *Gawain.*

26   TAITT, PETER. "Sir Gawain's Double Quest." *Revue de l'Université d'Ottawa,* 45, no. 4 (October-December), 508-517.

Perceives two quests in *Gawain*—"the first a structurally

exterior and literal progress, the second an interior and ambiguous revelation" (p. 508). Contends that Gawain's "interior quest" represents the audience's insights into and involvement with Gawain's thought-patterns—his ruminations on
impending doom, chivalric and spiritual responsibilities (temptation scenes), and personal safety. Notes Gawain's humbling
self-awareness at the end of the poem and his absurd penitential reaction to his shortcomings; claims that wearing the girdle
may be emblematic of pride, not humility.

27   TAJIMA, MATSUJI. "The *Gawain*-Poet's Use of *Con* as
      a Periphrastic Auxiliary." *Neuphilologische Mit-
      teilungen*, 76, no. 3:429-438.
         [Focuses on all four Cotton Nero poems.] Claims that
      the poet's employment of "the periphrastic auxiliary *con* with
      an infinitive as the equivalent of the simple verb" (p. 429), a
      characteristic of Northern language forms, appears frequently
      in the rhymed lines of *Gawain* as a metrical technique "to
      place the infinitive in rhyming position" (p. 433) and appears
      infrequently in the unrhymed alliterative long lines of *Gawain*.

28   TOLKIEN, J. R. R., trans. "Introduction" to *Sir Gawain
      and the Green Knight, Pearl and Sir Orfeo*. Edited by
      Christopher Tolkien. Boston: Houghton Mifflin, pp.
      13-17.
         [This book also contains a verse translation (pp. 25-88) of
      Gawain and comments (pp. 142-146) upon *Gawain*'s allitera-
      tive verse-form.] Comments briefly upon the Cotton MS, the
      Gawain-poet, and the verse of the "alliterative revival." Discus-
      ses the interlacing of the three hunts with the lady's tempta-
      tions; Gawain's Christian chivalry rooted in divine *cortaysye*;
      Gawain's repudiation of courtly love with its earthly "courte-
      sy"; and the humanity of Gawain, the most perfect knight of
      Camelot.

29   VANTUONO, WILLIAM. "A Name in the Cotton MS.
      Nero A.x. Article 3." *Mediaeval Studies*, 37:537-542.
         Notes that the name J. Macy, perhaps John de Masey of
      Sale, Rector of Ashton-on-Mersey (1364-1401), appears in
      an illuminated folio of *Gawain* and of *Purity*. Contends that
      Macy may be identified with the illuminator although it is
      possible that Macy may represent the *Pearl*-poet or the family
      for whom the Cotton manuscript was written.

30   WILSON, JANET.   "A Note on the Use of the Word
      kny3t in Fitt 4 of *Sir Gawain and the Green Kny3t.*"
      Parergon, No. 13 (December), p. 49.
          Suggests that the word *kny3t,* a term normally applied to
      noblemen, is used in the Green Chapel scene to suggest the
      sharp difference between the chivalric ethos of Camelot and
      the values of the natural world and of the Green Knight.

31   WOODS, WILLIAM F.   "The Hero in Search of Himself:
      The Ethical Development of the Hero in *Yvain, Par-*
      zival and *Sir Gawain and the Green Knight.*"   Ph.D.
      dissertation, Indiana University.
          [*See Dissertation Abstracts International,* 36 (1975),
      2803A.]   Demonstrates how Gawain achieves ethical develop-
      ment through an "alter ego," the Green Knight.   Contends
      that Gawain's response to the Knight's challenge nourishes the
      "selfish ambition" inherent in the Knight's proud boast and
      that Gawain is blind to both courtly ideals and his *trawþe.*
      Claims that at the end of the poem Gawain admits his human
      frailties and achieves redemption.

32   YERKES, DAVID.   *"Sir Gawain and the Green Knight*
      211: 'Grayn'.*"   Notes and Queries,* New Series, 22
      (January), 4.
          Alludes to the poem *John de Reeue* in the Percy Folio for
      further proof of "spike" as the meaning of *grayn.*

1976

1   ACKERMAN, ROBERT W.   "Madden's Gawain An-
      thology," in *Medieval Studies in Honor of Lillian*
      Herlands Hornstein.   Edited by Jess B. Bessinger, Jr.
      and Robert R. Raymo.   New York: New York Uni-
      versity Press, pp. 5-18.
          Notes the scholarly significance of the publication of Mad-
      den's *Syr Gawayne: A Collection of Ancient Romance-Poems*
      (1839.1), thereby vaulting him into the position of "foremost
      Arthurian of the nineteenth century."   Contends—based upon
      an examination of Madden's unpublished Diary in the Bod-
      leian Library, Oxford (MS hist. C. 140-82)—that he gave *Sir*
      Gawain and the Green Knight its title when he first saw the

MS of the romance (July 9, 1829). Claims, further, that the sources of *Gawain* may be found in *Roman de Perceval, Le Chevalier à l'Épée,* and *La Mule sans Frein.*

2   BEALE, WALTER H. *Old and Middle English Poetry to 1500: A Guide to Information Sources.* American Literature, English Literature, and World Literatures in English Information Guide Series, Vol. 7. Detroit: Gale Research, 345-347, 353-357.

[Selected (annotated) primary and secondary bibliography.]

3   BLANCH, ROBERT J. "Games Poets Play: The Ambiguous Use of Color Symbolism in *Sir Gawain and the Green Knight." Nottingham Mediaeval Studies,* 20: 64-85.

Examines, first, the disparate "mythic" appraisals of *Gawain,* particularly the "mythic" interpretations of the Green Knight, and second, the elements of play, game, and ambiguity in *Gawain.* Contends that the *Gawain*-poet employs color symbolism, "suggestive of literary convention, ironic reversal of tradition, and poetic ambiguity" (p. 68), in order to fool his audience, increase dramatic suspense, reinforce "the elaborate symmetrical design and game-like tone of the poem" (p. 85), and trace slyly, especially through his manipulation of Christmas green, gold, red, and white, Gawain's fate at the Green Chapel.

4   BREWER, DEREK. "The Interpretation of Dream, Folktale and Romance with Special Reference to *Sir Gawain and the Green Knight." Neuphilologische Mitteilungen,* 77, no. 4:569-581.

Applies psychological terms and themes employed in the analysis of folktales and dreams to the plot and characters of *Gawain.* Views the plot, then, as a kind of *rite de passage,* a symbolic rendering of the young adult's efforts to rebel against his parents and to assume his own mature identity. Identifies Bercilak/Green Knight with an ambivalent father-figure, Bercilak's wife with the alluring aspects of the mother-figure, and Morgan le Fay with the pernicious aspects of the mother-figure. Claims that *Gawain* depicts sex as death and "self-inhibition" as the path to life and maturity.

5   CAWLEY, A. C. "Introduction" to *Pearl, Cleanness, Patience, Sir Gawain and the Green Knight.* Edited by A. C. Cawley and J. J. Anderson. Everyman's University Library, No. 346. London: Dent, pp. vii-viii, xxi-xxvi.

[Reprint of Cawley (1962.3). Contains Anderson's new select bibliography of editions, translations, and book-length studies of *Gawain* plus collections of essays on *Gawain.*]

6   COOPER, HELEN. "Magic that Does Not Work." *Medievalia et Humanistica,* New Series 7:144-145.

Claims that *Gawain* represents "the only instance in romance where one assumes that the magic [green girdle] does not work, even that it is not magic at all, and where the lingering question at the back of one's mind afterwards is that perhaps it may have been magic, after all" (p. 144). Suggests that the magical girdle is employed ironically, for the *luf-lace,* not the object of Gawain's absolute trust, is the cause of his wound. Notes that the talisman in *Gawain* is emblematic of human weakness, not "his attainment of the superhuman absolute" (p. 144).

7   DIAMOND, ARLYN. "*Sir Gawain and the Green Knight*: An Alliterative Romance." *Philological Quarterly,* 55 (Winter), 10-29.

Argues that *Gawain* should be viewed in the context of the numerous Middle English alliterative romances known by the author and his audience. Contends that the *Gawain*-poet fused two disparate romance traditions—the courtly (tone and content) and the alliterative (emphasis on heroism and honor) —in order to elucidate the tension between style and subject matter, a significant thematic concern of this poem.

8   DUNCAN, PATRICIA J. "From Folklore to Archetype: Analyses of Four Middle English Romances." Ph.D. dissertation, State University of New York (Albany).

[Partly on *Gawain. See Dissertation Abstracts,* 37 (1976), 3606A.] Employs Northrop Frye's archetypal criticism in order to demonstrate that the thematic core of *Gawain* is initiation—the hero's evolution from youth, innocence, and immaturity to an awareness of his human weaknesses.

9   GANIM, JOHN M. "Disorientation, Style, and Consciousness in *Sir Gawain and the Green Knight.*" *Publications of the Modern Language Association of America,* 91 (May), 376-384.

Demonstrates how and why the style of *Gawain* is inextricably linked to a process of disorientation—a process which frequently balloons the audience's expectations and then swiftly deflates such presuppositions through veering to an entirely different frame of reference. Claims that the *Gawain*-poet's methodology often intimates "how a specific and concrete situation can also be ambiguous and to throw the audience off balance, forcing it to search for some rule . . . to orient itself, which he graciously provides" (p. 380). Analyzes the founding of Britain (11. 20-36), Gawain's wintry journey over frozen terrain (11. 713-39), and Gawain's antifeminist commentary (11. 2411-28).

10   GILBERT, A. J. "A New Analogue for *Sir Gawain and the Green Knight.*" *Neuphilologische Mitteilungen,* 77, no. 3:365-368.

Claims that *Karlamagnus saga ok kappa hans* (ca. 1400), rooted in a thirteenth-century Norwegian collection of episodes focusing on Charlemagne, supplies an important analogue to various incidents and themes in *Gawain,* including Gawain's journey to Bercilak's castle, the link between the chastity and temptation motifs, the exchange of winnings, and Gawain's disloyalty through concealment of the girdle.

11   HAINES, VICTOR YELVERTON. "When Gawain Sins?" *Revue de l'Université d'Ottawa,* 46, no. 2 (April-June), 242-246.

Focuses on Gawain's confession to the priest and on the nature of both Gawain's "sin" and intention (his possible use of the green girdle). Notes that Gawain is garbed in blue (1928), an ironic emblem of truth, constancy, and "a bluecoat servant . . . unfaithful" (p. 243), at the conclusion of the third hunt. Views Gawain's confession as true and valid and his subsequent guilt as disloyalty (violation of his promise to Bercilak) and pride.

12   HALPERN, RICHARD A. "Spiritual Vision and the City of God in *Sir Gawain and the Green Knight.*"

Ph.D. dissertation, Princeton University.

[*See Dissertation Abstracts International,* 37 (1977), 6471A-72A.] Contends that the thematic roots of *Gawain* include "spiritual vs. carnal vision, life according to the spirit or according to the flesh." Employs St. Augustine's concepts of the City of God and the City of Man (Camelot) in order to explicate the meaning of the poem.

13   HENRY, AVRIL. "Temptation and Hunt in *Sir Gawain and the Green Knight.*" *Medium Aevum,* 45, no. 2: 187-199.

Analyzes the relationship between the hunts as a unit and the temptations. Argues that "a steady diminution in the scale" (p. 188) of the chase signalizes Gawain's increasing concern with himself and his worldly reputation. Examines the scene of Gawain's return to Camelot and claims that the hunts —specifically the "exchange of winnings" at Hautdesert—blur the true meaning of gain and loss and suggest the ambiguity of the Green Knight's motive in testing Arthur and his court.

14   HIEATT, A. KENT. "Symbolic and Narrative Patterns in *Pearl, Cleanness, Patience,* and *Gawain.*" *English Studies in Canada,* 2 (Summer), 125-126, 130-131, 134-143.

Examines the motif of clothing or adornment which links *Gawain* and *Pearl,* especially the parallels between the "endeleʒ" (11. 629-30) pentangle depicted on Gawain's shield and embroidered on his surcoat (637, 2026) and the "endeleʒ rounde" pearl of *Pearl.* Notes that Gawain's pentangle is represented "as the 'endeleʒ knot' because it, like the pearl, has neither beginning nor end but is enclosed by a continuous line. . . . Also, as the pearl presents a hard, enduring surface, so the pentangle is locked into shape by its triangulating geometry. . . . Its five points relate to Gawain's five-times-five excellences, and its firm endlessness, with no crack or cranny, relates to his apparently impermeable moral armour" (p. 134). Discusses the *luf-lace* worn by Gawain (11. 2026-36) as he prepares for his journey to the Green Chapel. Claims that while the greenness of the girdle suggests inconstancy, the *lace* itself signifies "a noose with a sliding knot with which a hunter may catch game" (p. 135)—Lady Bercilak's method of ensnaring Gawain in a false sense of security. Calls attention to the contrast between the "endless knot" of the pentangle and the knotted noose—containing a beginning and an end—of the *luf-lace* (p. 136). Analyzes the character of Gawain; the central role of Hautdesert in the poem; and the numerical patterns in *Gawain*, particularly stanza 33 as a possible reference to the traditional duration of Christ's life.

15   HUNT, TONY. "Irony and Ambiguity in *Sir Gawain and the Green Knight.*" *Forum for Modern Language Studies*, 12, no. 1 (January), 1-16.

Claims that the poet has informed the romance conventions of *Gawain* with irony and ambiguity, thereby apparently deflating the honored traditions. Focuses on the prologue of *Gawain* (the references to Aeneas and Felix Brutus); the Yuletide festivities at Camelot; the intrusive entrance of the Green Knight; the passing of the seasons; and the temptations and hunts at Hautdesert. Contends that the *Gawain*-poet employs irony and ambiguity in order to forestall hasty conclusions by the audience and that the typical romance fusion of "individual identity and formal social identity" (p. 15) in the hero cannot be found in *Gawain* (see the ending of the poem).

16   IKEGAMI, TADAHIRO. "King Arthur and Arthurian Legend." *Eigokyoiku* (*English Education*), 25, no. 1:56-57.

[In Japanese. Annotation provided by the author.] Provides a short survey of the development of Arthurian legend—from history to romance—in the Middle Ages.

17   KANE, GEORGE. "Some Reflections on Critical Method." *Essays and Studies by Members of the English Association*, New Series 29:23-38.

[Compares techniques employed in evaluating Shakespeare's *Venus and Adonis* and *Gawain.*] Evaluates the methodology and limitations of critical interpretations of *Gawain*. Suggests that subjective appraisals may be curbed somewhat by appealing directly to the text of *Gawain* and by employing precise critical terminology and accurate, logical arguments. Concentrates especially upon the tone and moralistic implications of the temptation scenes.

18   KIRKPATRICK, HUGH. "The Bob-Wheel and Allied

Stanza Forms in Middle English and Middle Scots Poetry." Ph.D. dissertation, North Texas State University.

[Partly on *Gawain*. *See Dissertation Abstracts*, 37 (1976), 3608A.] Examines the influence of Latin verse technique upon the bob-wheel form and notes that the bob-wheel stanza, probably the first regular Middle English stanzaic form, developed first in the Southern areas of England, not the North. Praises *Gawain* for its skillful fusion of unrhymed alliterative stanzas and its bob-wheel stanzas.

19　LEONARD, FRANCES M. "The School for Transformation: A Theory of Middle English Comedy." *Genre*, 9 (Fall), 185-188.

Notes that "transformational comedy" includes a tutor and a pupil. Suggests that Gawain, the teacher of chivalric and Christian precepts, is metamorphosed into a student by the end of *Gawain*—a confused, ignorant pupil who must "confess" his weaknesses to the Green Knight as tutor.

20　LESTER, G. A. "Gawain's Fault in Terms of Contemporary Law of Arms." *Notes and Queries*, New Series, 23 (September), 392-393.

Cites Thomas Woodstock's fourteenth-century ordinance, *The Ordenaunce and Fourme of Fightyng within Listes*, in order to prove that Gawain's concealment of the girdle was expressly forbidden. Suggests that Gawain's apparent reluctance to put complete faith in God is emblematic of covetousness.

21　METCALF, ALLAN A. "Silent Knight: 'Sum for Cortaysye'?" *Archiv für das Studium der neueren Sprachen und Literaturen*, 213, no. 2:338-342.

[Contains references to the use of *some* in *Patience, Pearl,* and *Purity*.] Contends that *sum* ("some") is employed only as a plural pronoun in other selections of *Gawain* and *sum* in this instance (lines 246-47) refers to "some" of Arthur's knights, not Gawain alone.

22　METCALF, ALLAN A. "Supplement to a Bibliography of *Purity* (*Cleanness*), 1864-1972." *Chaucer Review*, 10 (Spring), 367-372.

Includes, in "Studies Containing Discussion of *Purity*," some items which focus partially on *Gawain*.

23   MOODY, PATRICIA A. "The *Childgered* Arthur of *Sir Gawain and the Green Knight.*" *Studies in Medieval Culture*, 8-9:173-180.

Points out the *Gawain*-poet's employment of paradox and parallelism, especially artistic ambiguity, in the historical introduction (Felix Brutus, fall of Troy). Notes that *childgered* may mean "boyish, merry" as well as convey the sense of "restlessness." Claims that *childgered* is laced with ambiguity, one of the characteristics of *Gawain*. "In a poem that abounds in games and humor, the poet makes gentle fun of romance and romance convention, of a court and a hero that take themselves too seriously, but he does so humanely, with good nature and gentle tolerance of the discrepancy between real and ideal" (p. 179).

24   NAKAO, SISTER BERNADETTE SETSUKO. "Sir Gawain's Confessions Reconsidered: A Catholic View." *Studies in English Literature* (English Literary Society of Japan), 53:3-25.

[Synopsis of article found on pp. 215-216 of the English Number for 1977.] Analyzes Gawain's acceptance of the girdle and his confession to the priest in terms of traditional Catholic views of sin and the sacrament of penance. Suggests that Gawain's acceptance of the girdle does not constitute a mortal sin and that Gawain's confession was valid despite the penitential overtones of Gawain's subsequent "confession" to the Green Knight.

25   NEAMAN, JUDITH S. "Sir Gawain's Covenant: Troth and *Timor Mortis.*" *Philological Quarterly*, 55 (Winter), 30-42.

Offers a liturgical interpretation of *Gawain*, particularly religious feasts and rituals which demarcate the significant episodes of *Gawain*. Examines the thematic thread binding together All Souls' Day and New Year's Day (Circumcision of Christ) in order to illustrate the poem's emphasis on human frailty and mortality, redemption through penitence, fear of death, and the need for "keeping troth."

26 POLLARD, WILLIAM F., JR. "Franciscan Exemplarism in *Gawain and the Green Knight.*" Ph.D. dissertation, Duke University.

[*See Dissertation Abstracts International,* 37 (1977), 7766A.] Analyzes *Gawain* in terms of Exemplarism, the theological perspective taught by St. Bonaventure and others, and employs many allusions to St. John's *Revelations* and apocalyptic iconography in his discussion. Claims that the *Gawain*-poet focuses primarily on "the operations of grace in the spiritual itinerary of the individual." Identifies parts of the opening scene at Camelot and of the Green Chapel tableau with the *visio pacis,* especially the throne of the Lamb of God (*Apoc.* 22:1-3).

27 SCHOTTER, ANNE H. "The Sacramental and Satirical Use of Formulas of Luxury in Middle English Alliterative Poetry." Ph.D. dissertation, City University of New York.

[Partly on *Gawain. See Dissertation Abstracts International,* 37 (1977), 4344A.] Analyzes the sacramental use of formulas of luxury—formulas which visually depict the kingdom of God through courtly images (feasts, garments, and buildings)—in *Gawain* and other Cotton Nero poems.

28 SPEARING, A. C. *Medieval Dream-Poetry.* Cambridge, England: Cambridge University Press, pp. 1, 65, 111.

Examines the use of hunting scenes in *Gawain* and in Chaucer's *Book of the Duchess.* Views the three temptations in *Gawain* as a type of hunt and analyzes the structural link, "a threefold repetition of the same formal pattern (hunt begins, bedroom scene, hunt ends" (p. 65), between the hunts and Lady Bercilak's visits to Gawain.

29 SPENDAL, R. J. "The Fifth Pentad in *Sir Gawain and the Green Knight.*" *Notes and Queries,* New Series, 23 (April), 147-148.

Claims that the fifth pentad, including the virtues of *fraunchyse, felaȝschyp, clannes, cortaysye,* and *pité,* springs from Thomas Aquinas's concept of justice. Contends that Gawain's "ethic" as well as the pentangle, Beheading Game, and "exchange of winnings" underscore the poet's preoccupation with the notion of justice.

30   STILLINGS, JUSTINE T. "A Generative Metrical Analy-
      sis of *Sir Gawain and the Green Knight.*" *Language
      and Style,* 9 (Fall), 219-246.

      Notes that *Gawain* employs two separate stanza forms—
unrhymed stanzas composed of long alliterative lines (probably derived from Anglo-Saxon poetry), and rhymed stanzas
(the bob and wheel) apparently composed in iambic trimeter.
Inasmuch as modern theories of metrics do not illuminate the
Gawain meters, offers a "generative theory of meter" in order
to determine how the iambic lines operate in *Gawain.*

      Claims that *Gawain* is composed in "syllabotonic meter":
"The short rhymed lines are written in iambic feet and the
long alliterative lines in anapestic feet" (p. 241); suggests that
the bob and wheel stanza includes a fixed number of metrical
feet and of syllables for each foot, whereas the alliterative long
lines contain "a free number of feet per line, ranging from two
to five or six" (p. 241) along with a set number of syllables
for each foot.

31   THOMPSON, RAYMOND H. " 'Muse on þi mirrour . . .':
      The Challenge of the Outlandish Stranger in the Eng-
      lish Arthurian Verse Romances." *Folklore,* 87, no.
      2 (November), 201-202, 208.

      Contends that most Middle English Arthurian romances
include a bizarre character who challenges and discloses the
weaknesses of Arthur's court. Notes that the Green Knight,
the challenger in the Beheading Game, is a shape-shifter and
focuses upon Gawain's faults—disloyalty, discourtesy, cowardice, and imperceptiveness. Claims that the conclusion of
Gawain's quest is a bitter reminder of "man's flawed nature"
despite humanity's attempts to soar toward splendid ideals.

32   TRISTRAM, PHILIPPA. *Figures of Life and Death in
      Medieval English Literature.* London: Elek Books,
      pp. 28-34, 91-92, 111-113, and as indexed.

      [Discusses *Pearl* in another section.] Emphasizes the test-
ing of Christian *gentilesse* and civilization by natural dangers
within and without, and identifies the courtly Gawain and
Camelot with Youth (pp. 28-31); Bercilak, in part, is linked
with Middle Age. Maintains that images of life and death—
the start of Winter, the New Year, saints' festivals, and the
passage of the seasons—permeate *Gawain* (pp. 111-112). The

turning of the seasons, especially, "comes to reflect the passage of life, and mirrors in the temporal world both the uncertainties and the assurance of the eternal" (p. 112).

*33 TSUCHIYA, TADAYUKI, ed. *Sir Gawain and the Green Knight Annotated by OED and MED.* Tokyo: Author, 185 pp.

[Not for sale. Cited in the 1976 *Modern Language Association International Bibliography*, Vol. 1.]

34 TURVILLE-PETRE, JOAN. "The Metre of *Sir Gawain and the Green Knight.*" *English Studies*, 57 (August), 310-328.

Attempts to formulate some alternative approach to analyzing the metre of *Gawain*, an approach which does not employ the precepts of Old English metre. Examines the link between syntactic patterns and metrical patterns (accentuation and alliteration) in *Gawain*.

35 WEISS, VICTORIA L. "Gawain's First Failure: The Beheading Scene in *Sir Gawain and the Green Knight.*" *Chaucer Review*, 10 (Spring), 361-366.

Interprets the Green Knight's challenge (lines 285-90, 297-98) as an exchange of blows, not a "beheading game." Argues that Gawain's decapitation of the Green Knight, then, points to the hero's inordinate concern with chivalric values rather than with the Christian concept of the sanctity of human life; in the Green Chapel scene, however, Gawain finally comprehends what true knightly behavior involves.

36 WILSON, ANNE. *Traditional Romance and Tale: How Stories Mean.* Ipswich, England: D. S. Brewer; Totowa, New Jersey: Rowman & Littlefield, pp. 1-3, 5-6, 80-83, 96-107, and as indexed.

Argues, first of all, that *Gawain* and other narratives create for their audiences an extraordinary "time out of time . . . an artificial world in which we can temporarily live" (p. 6); in such a playworld, the audience can experience strong emotions as separate entities, "and as we isolate each feeling, we heighten and transfigure it" (p. 6). Examines the imagery permeating the scenes at Bercilak's castle and finds "a consistent sequence of images expressing the hero's conflicting feelings about his desire for the lady" (p. 82).

Claims, moreover, that *Gawain*—its characters and narrative events (including the sudden appearance of the Green Knight)—is a product of the hero's creative mind (p. 97). "The hero's own wishes and other feelings impel the story while leaving him without a sense of full control over what is to happen next" (p. 98). Notes that the Green Knight, evoked by Gawain's imagination, represents the hero's desire to punish or test himself (p. 107) and that the greenness of the Knight suggests "that he cannot exist in nature; he cannot exist in the outer world of reality" (p. 105).

37   WILSON, EDWARD. *The Gawain-Poet.* Medieval and Renaissance Authors, edited by John Norton-Smith and Douglas Gray. Leiden: E. J. Brill, pp. 25, 48-50, 60, 63, 65, 72, 78, 85, 113-131.

[Contains a select bibliography (pp. 132-134)—mainly books—of editions, reference works, bibliographies, and critical studies of *Gawain.*] Examines the topographical allusions in *Gawain* and the hero's journey from a romance world to the unknown dangers of a "real" world. Emphasizes the elements of game and play, especially in the hunting and temptation scenes at Hautdesert, as well as Gawain's isolation at the end of the poem.

*38   ZUCCHI, M. R. *"Sir Gawain e il Cavaliere Verde."* Ph.D. dissertation, Università di Torino, Facoltà di Magistero.

[Citation provided by Professor Carl Berkhout.]

1977

1   ANDERSON, J. J., ed. "Introduction," in *Cleanness.* Manchester, England: Manchester University Press, pp. 1-2, 5.

Comments upon the Cotton Nero manuscript, the dialect (Northwest Midland), and the date of composition (last half of the fourteenth century); contends that the Cotton Nero poems were composed by one poet. Notes that in all of the Cotton Nero poems "a small slanting double line appears regularly in the left-hand margin" (p. 2) and that the marginal notation in *Gawain* marks the start of a new stanza. Emphasizes the significance of cleanness in the Cotton Nero poems and views cleanness as "an aspect of 'trawþe' in *Sir Gawain*" (p. 5).

2   BLENKNER, LOUIS. "Sin, Psychology, and the Structure of *Sir Gawain and the Green Knight.*" *Studies in Philology,* 74 (October), 354-387.

Emphasizes the significance of the manuscript divisions in determining the structure of *Gawain* and views Gawain's tests as tests of valor (*fortitudo*), mental acuteness (*sapientia*), and chastity. Claims that a "corporeal-spiritual-divine triad, operative in the major divisions of the romance [*Gawain*] as Nature, Human Society, and Grace" (p. 359) represents the structural core of *Gawain;* examines in this light, then, the beheading agreement, the "exchange of winnings," the temptation and hunting scenes, and Gawain's flaws—cowardice, covetousness, and *untrawþe.* Analyzes, likewise, the numerological and theological significance of the five fives of the pentangle and claims that the pentangle is not emblematic of divine truth, but of a fallible human truth.

3   BURROW, JOHN, ed. *English Verse 1300-1500.* Longman Annotated Anthologies of English Verse, Vol. 1. London: Longman, 46-47, 76-78.

[Introductory commentary on the *Gawain*-poems.] Discusses the *Gawain*-poet (manuscript, authorship, dates of composition for the four poems, and reputation) as well as *Gawain* (its theme and meaning, metre, style, structure, sources, and editions).

4   DAVENPORT, W. A. "The Word *Norne* and the Temptation of Sir Gawain." *Neuphilologische Mitteilungen,* 78, no. 3:256-263.

Analyzes the use of the rare verb *norne* ("say," "declare," "reveal") in *Gawain, Purity,* and *Erkenwald* and claims that *norne* may still convey suggestions of magic and secrecy. Examines in particular the employment of *norne* (1. 1771) in the third temptation scene of *Gawain* as well as the sexual ramifications of lines 1760-72 and contends that editors of *Gawain* erroneously gloss *mare* (1. 1769) as a form of "Mary" and emend *prynce* (1. 1770) to *prynces.*

5 DUGGAN, HOYT N. "Strophic Patterns in Middle English Alliterative Poetry." *Modern Philology,* 74 (February), 223, 225, 236.

Contends that many alliterative poems written during the fourteenth century have been lost and questions whether the four poems attributed to the *Gawain*-poet constitute his total literary output.

6 FRIEDMAN, ALBERT B. and RICHARD H. OSBERG. "Gawain's Girdle as Traditional Symbol." *Journal of American Folklore,* 90, no. 357 (July-September), 301-315.

Attempts to discern the nature and significance of the girdle, an object which plays a crucial role in the temptation scenes at Hautdesert, in the Green Chapel episode, and in Gawain's return journey to Arthur's court. Views the magical girdle, moreover, as a sexual emblem—a talisman whose power is activated once Gawain wears it openly over his surcoat as he prepares for his meeting at the Chapel. Interprets the girdle as baldric with its decorative knot placed at Gawain's left hip as a ceremonial object, a reminder of Gawain's shameful adventure. Discusses, finally, the artificiality of the "endless knot" of the pentangle.

7 GALLAGHER, JOSEPH E. "*Trawþe* and *Luf-Talkyng* in *Sir Gawain and the Green Knight.*" *Neuphilologische Mitteilungen,* 78, no. 4:362-376.

In his examination of the temptation scenes, contends that Gawain's *luf-talkyng* is as erotic as the phrases employed by Bercilak's wife, thereby reinforcing Gawain's traditional role as a lover. Argues, however, that Gawain preserves his chastity by refusing to translate amorous overtures into sexual intercourse, for *luf-talkyng* as overt sexuality transgresses the "pentagonal" ideal of *trawþe*.

8 KNAPP, PEGGY A. "Gawain's Quest: Social Conflict and Symbolic Mediation." *Clio: An Interdisciplinary Journal of Literature, History, and the Philosophy of History,* 6, no. 3 (Spring), 289-306.

Claims that the structure of *Gawain* involves the symbolic reconciliation of two polar extremes—"chivalric nationalism and penitential Christianity" (p. 289), both of which are mythic systems underlying fourteenth-century society. Suggests that the fall of Troy passage which opens and closes *Gawain* is significant, for it signalizes the pattern of cyclic time which informs this romance. Identifies the Green Knight, especially his greenness, with "cyclic nature" (p. 295), ambivalently depicted both as potential destroyer of man and as provider (p. 297). Views Bercilak and his environment, however, as linked with comfort, warmth, and ordered civilization. Perceives Gawain, another "mediating figure," as both master of nature and lowly servant to nature's bidding (pp. 298-299).

Contends, moreover, that the girdle is an emblem of "natural man" and that the Green Chapel is, simultaneously, a symbol of initiation into fairyland and of Christian penance and spiritual rebirth (pp. 302-303). Concludes by noting that the final lines of *Gawain* point to a double ending—an artistic fusion of Christian epiphany and chivalric triumph (pp. 303-304).

9   LAVERS, NORMAN. "How Gawain Beat the Green Knight." *Publications of the Arkansas Philological Association,* 3, no. 3 (Summer), 17-23.

Expands Speirs's account (1949.9) of *Gawain* in order to explain the meaning of the poem. Identifies the Green Knight with "the force of Nature" (p. 19), both as a cornucopia and as a potential source of devastation (pp. 19-20), and links Bercilak, especially his autumnal hues, with nature at harvest-time. Views the green girdle, moreover, as an emblem of life resurgent and "sexual fertility" (p. 21) and Bercilak's wife as the "feminine creative principle" (p. 22). Claims, finally, that Gawain—enveloped by a girdle of fertility—wins because the Green Knight cannot kill him at the Green Chapel.

10   MARGESON, ROBERT W. "Structure and Meaning in *Sir Gawain and the Green Knight.*" *Papers on Language and Literature,* 13 (Winter), 16-24.

Views the symmetrical structure of *Gawain* in terms of circularity, for Gawain leaves and ultimately returns to Camelot; other circular patterns include the cycle of the seasons and the historical cycle involving the fall of Troy and the founding of Britain. Examines, moreover, the circular and linear structures in *Gawain* and how they operate; "Gawain sees the

shape of his quest as linear, but the court insists that it has
been circular" (p. 16).

11   MOORMAN, CHARLES, ed. "Introduction" to his edition, *The Works of the Gawain-Poet.* Jackson,
Mississippi: University Press of Mississippi, pp. 10-16,
18-22, 26-27, 37-45.

> [Contains medieval texts of *Gawain, Pearl, Purity,* and
> *Patience;* a selected bibliography (pp. 52-62); and a limited
> glossary.] Describes the manuscript (Cotton Nero A.x.); the
> characteristics of the "alliterative revival"; the authorship,
> date, and place of composition; the sources of *Gawain;* and the
> artistic qualities of *Gawain*—the parallels between the hunts
> and the temptations, the mythic elements, the comedy, and
> the use of the courtly love convention.

*12 PALAZZI, ANNALISA. *"Sir Gawain and the Green
Knight* in rapporto alla tradizione celtica e alla letter-
atura medievale." Ph.D. dissertation, Università di
Bologna, Facoltà di lettere e filologia.

> [Citation provided by Professor Carl Berkhout.]

13   PEARSALL, DEREK. *Old English and Middle English
Poetry.* Routledge History of English Poetry, Vol. 1.
London: Routledge & Kegan Paul, 153, 156, 158,
160-162, 165, 170, 172-176, 186, 188, 250, 262,
310, 321, 323.

> Discusses the "revival" of unrhymed alliterative poetry
> in the fourteenth century and the relationship of *Gawain*
> to aristocratic patronage and alliterative verse techniques,
> particularly formulas and idealizing phrases. Examines, fur-
> thermore, the *Gawain*-poet's use of the bob and wheel "for
> ironic comment, summary anticipation and recapitulation
> and . . . for abbreviated rapid narration" (p. 174); structure,
> symmetry, and anti-romance elements in *Gawain;* the isolation
> of the hero; the extravagance of some recent interpretations of
> *Gawain;* and the *Gawain*-poet's artistic use of language in
> description and in an evocation of the evanescent nature of
> earthly joy.

14   SILVERSTEIN, THEODORE. "Sir Gawain in a Dilemma, or Keeping Faith with Marcus Tullius Cicero."

Modern Philology, 75 (August), 1-17.

Analyzes the temptation and confession scenes, Gawain's shield, and the significance of *couetyse* in order to disclose the moral and psychological narrative of *Gawain.* Employs Cicero's *De officiis,* especially his concept of *fides,* in order to demonstrate that the pentangle, an emblem of *trawþe,* is linked with the keeping of a promise. Argues that *Gawain* is essentially a comedy of manners, the plot of which ultimately shifts to Christian virtue and "social principle."

15   SUZUKI, EIICHI. "A Note on the Age of the Green Knight." *Neuphilologische Mitteilungen,* 78, no. 1: 27-30.

Suggests that the *Gawain*-poet makes two contradictory allusions to the Green Knight's age—a reference to the lord's maturity (1. 844) and a reference to Bercilak as an old lord (1. 1124). Resolves the critical problem by interpreting *hyghe* (1. 844, *of hyghe eldee*) as "old, advanced in years," a gloss which may be substantiated by an analogous use of the word in 1. 656 of *Purity.*

16   TURVILLE-PETRE, THORLAC. *The Alliterative Revival.* Cambridge, England: D. S. Brewer, pp. 29-30, 32-34, 37, 39, 45-46, 51-59, 62, 66-69, 72-73, 75-77, 81, 83, 86-91, 96, 137, and as indexed.

Analyzes many aspects of *Gawain,* including its meter, manuscript, structure, style, bob and wheel stanzas, date, dialect, and "grammetrical" units.

17   WEISS, VICTORIA L. "Knightly Conventions in *Sir Gawain and the Green Knight.*" Ph.D. dissertation, Lehigh University.

[*See Dissertation Abstracts International,* 38 (1977), 2110A.] Elucidates *Gawain* within the framework of fourteenth-century concepts of chivalry (military and religious) and courtesy. Claims that the Green Knight's challenge is bizarre, that Lady Bercilak's aggressive behavior is unorthodox, and the ambiguity coloring *Gawain* stems "from the fact that the knightly code offered little guidance about how Gawain ought to behave."

1978

1   ANDREW, MALCOLM and RONALD WALDRON. "In-
     troduction," in their edition of *The Poems of the
     Pearl Manuscript: Pearl, Cleanness, Patience, Sir Ga-
     wain and the Green Knight.* London: Edward
     Arnold, pp. 15-17, 21-22, 36-43.
        [Contains a helpful select bibliography (pp. 5-7, 10-13) of
     works—editions, translations, textual notes, and criticism—
     dealing with *Gawain*.]   Examines the Cotton Nero poems in
     terms of the native alliterative tradition, the theory of com-
     mon authorship, the recurring thematic patterns (courtesy,
     purity, humility), and the underlying Christian and chivalric
     foundations.
        Discusses *Gawain* as a chivalric romance, a poem which
     raises moral and psychological questions through irony and
     fictional detachment.   Emphasizes, further, *Gawain*'s descrip-
     tive and dramatic force; its narrative technique of allowing the
     audience to share Gawain's predicament; its focus on the inter-
     locked religious and knightly virtues of chivalry—especially
     cortaysye, chastity, and *trawþe*; and its symbolism (pent-
     angle).

2   DAVENPORT, W. A. *The Art of the Gawain-Poet.* Lon-
     don: Athlone Press (University of London), pp. 1-6,
     136-194, 198-207, 209-210, 213-218.
        Assumes that the Cotton Nero poems were composed by
     one man and discusses the poetic and artistic effects of these
     four works.   Emphasizes the "literary sophistication" of
     Gawain—the ironic objectivity of the narrator, the artistic use
     of structure and symmetry (101 stanzas—"completeness com-
     bined with continuity" (p. 137), the poet's highly original
     fusion of traditional romance conventions and motifs) the
     blend of the comic and serious as well as of the illusory and
     the real, and the interweaving of the romance world and the
     real world.
        Examines, furthermore, the nature and significance of the
     ambivalent Green Knight/Bercilak and Castle Hautdesert and
     discusses the carefully shaped structure of the hunting and
     temptation episodes.   "The hunting scenes both expose and
     make up for the essentially passive nature of the hero's own
     role in the poem.   The poem needs these [hunting] passages

. . . to set off the play of wits between Gawain and the lady and also the ingenuity of the structure into which they are fitted" (p. 163). Scrutinizes, finally, the guide, the Knight as "judge" in the Green Chapel tableau, and the ironic ending of *Gawain,* wherein the hero recognizes his human imperfection.

3   IKEGAMI, TADAHIRO. *"Gawain-*Poet," in "Gothic Literature" (chap. 3) from *An Introduction to English Literature—Society and Literature.* Edited by Bishu Saito. Tokyo: Chukyo Shuppan Publishing Company, pp. 49-52.

[In Japanese.   Annotation provided by the author.] Traces the works of the *Gawain-*poet and supplies a critical analysis of *Gawain* and *Pearl.*

4   REID, WENDY M. "The Drama of *Sir Gawain and the Green Knight." Parergon,* no. 20 (April), pp. 11-23.

In emphasizing the dramatic nature of *Gawain* and its parallels with mumming and folk rituals, points out the theatrical qualities of the beheading episode, the impersonation techniques employed at Hautdesert, the use of dramatic suspense, the dramatic function of dialogue and symbolism (ring, shield, girdle, and clothing), and the juxtaposition of parallel episodes.

ADDENDA

Add. 1   ANDERSON, HEATHER JERRIM. "The Terrestrial Paradise: A Study in the 'Intermediacy' and Multi-Levelled Nature of the Medieval Garden of Eden." Ph.D. dissertation, State University of New York at Buffalo, 1973.

[Partly on *Gawain. See Dissertation Abstracts International,* 34 (1974), 5830A.] Contends that a "geographical understanding of the three overlapping divisions of Eden [the Garden of Eden, the Pre-Paradise, and the Celestial Paradise] . . . leads to a fuller interpretation of the landscape and meaning" of *Gawain.*

Add. 2   BARRON, W. R. J. "A propos de quelques cas d'écorchement dans les romans anglais et français du Moyen Age," in *Melanges de littérature: Du moyen âge au XXe siècle.* (Coll. de l'Ecole Normale Supérieure de Jeunes Filles 10). Offerts à Mademoiselle Jeanne Lods, professeur honoraire de littérature médiévale à l'Ecole Normale Supérieure de Jeunes Filles, par ses collègues, ses élèves et ses amis. Paris: Ecole Normale Supérieure de Jeunes Filles, 1978, pp. 49-51, 64.

[Focuses on treason and its punishments in medieval law, history, and literature.] Discusses the medieval judicial penalty—flaying alive—for treason, particularly the flaying of the fox in *Gawain* as linked with the knight's potential sexual treason. Suggests that if Gawain had surrendered to the Lady's sexual advances, he would have been guilty of treason and that failure in one's sworn faith, a violation of the chivalric code, usually results in death.

Add. 3   BARRY, PETER. "*Sir Gawain and the Green Knight.*" *Explicator,* 37, no. 1 (Fall, 1978), 29-30.

Suggests that *desert* (as in the Green Knight's name,

Bercilak de Hautdesert) connotes "the dwelling place of a
hermit." Claims that both of the Knight's names/identities
—the Knight of the Green Chapel and Bercilak de Hautdesert—are invested with mystery.

Add. 4   BENNETT, H. S. "Medieval Literature and the Modern Reader." *Essays and Studies by Members of
the English Association,* 31 (1945), 14-15.

Focuses upon the *Gawain*-poet's use of descriptive details and upon his artistic manipulation of chivalric elements.

Add. 5   BLAKE, NORMAN. *The English Language in Medieval Literature.* London: J. M. Dent, 1977, pp. 90,
128, 130-132, 134, and as indexed.

Discusses the prisoner image pervading the lady's temptation (1208 ff.) as well as the poet's use of dramatic suspense and ironic themes. Examines in some detail Gawain's
antifeminist harangue, the theme of amazement (the
Knight's disruption of Camelot's Yuletide feast), and the
ironic application of "eulogistic epithets" to Gawain once
he accepts the green girdle.

Add. 6   BLENKNER, LOUIS. "The Three Hunts and Sir Gawain's Triple Fault." *American Benedictine Review,* 29 (September, 1978), 227-246.

Maintains that the delineation of the three blows at
the Green Chapel evokes memories of the deer, the boar,
and the fox, thereby linking the hunting and temptation
scenes. Identifies the deer with the irascible power of the
soul, the boar with concupiscence, and the fox with ra-
tionality and interlaces the animals' actions with Gawain's
faults, cowardice, covetousness, and *untrawþe.* Emphasizes
the poet's employment of symmetry and artistic design
(narrative, thematic, and symbolic structure).

Add. 7   BRASWELL, MARY FLOWERS. "Confession and
Characterization in the Literature of the Late Middle Ages." Ph.D. dissertation, Emory University,
1978.

[*See Dissertation Abstracts International,* 39 (1978),
2246A.] Focuses, in part, on the concept of the sinner in

the Cotton Nero poems. Contends that the Cotton poems emphasize the sin of pride and the need for humility and claims that Gower, Chaucer, Langland, and the *Pearl*-poet employ "the device of the confession, the surrogate priest, the form and content of the penitential manuals, the egotistical sinner who has a lesson to learn."

Add. 8   CAMPBELL, BERNARD R.   "An Advertiser's Lost Stanza of *Sir Gawain and the Green Knight.*" *CEA Critic*, 29, no. 5 (February, 1967), 7.

[Brief poetic parody purporting to explain why Gawain resisted Lady Bercilak's temptations.]

Add. 9   CLARK, S. L. and JULIAN N. WASSERMAN.   "The Pearl Poet's City Imagery." *The Southern Quarterly: A Scholarly Journal of Studies in the Humanities and Social Sciences*, 16 (July, 1978), 297-309.

Examines the apocalyptic judgment theme and the significance of city imagery, including the poet's convergence of spatial (inclusion and exclusion) and temporal (linear and cyclical time) motifs in the Cotton Nero poems. Emphasizes the importance of the historical cycle in *Gawain*, including Gawain's real insights into his nature and the moral fabric of Arthur's court.

Add. 10   COOK, JAMES RHODES.   "Aesthetic and Religious Symbolism in *Sir Gawain and the Green Knight.*" Ph.D. dissertation, Georgia State University, 1977.

[*See Dissertation Abstracts International*, 39 (1978), 277A.] Emphasizes the influence of Scripture upon five symbol patterns: color, fire, arming, typological elements, and grouping of details (sensory impressions and numerological images). Claims that ethical and religious elements pervade *Gawain* and that the poet employs Scripture to shape his narrative and characters.

Add. 11   DYKSTRA, TIMOTHY EUGENE.   "Humor in the Middle English Metrical Romances." Ph.D. dissertation, Ohio State University, 1975.

[Partly on *Gawain*. *See Dissertation Abstracts International*, 36 (1976), 5313A.] Perceives a "paradoxical" humor occasionally operating in *Gawain*, for "the audience cannot automatically share the point of view of the laugher." Claims that a comprehension of this type of humor may elucidate the paradoxes underlying this romance.

Add. 12   FITZPATRICK, JOHN FRANCIS. "Courtly Love and the Confessional in English Literature from 1215 to John Gower." Ph.D. dissertation, Indiana University, 1978.

[*See Dissertation Abstracts International*, 39 (1978), 895A.] Contends that *Gawain* fuses the traditions of penance and *amour courtois* through two confession scenes which signalize the tension between Christian ideals and courtly love.

Add. 13   GARDNER, JOHN. *The Life and Times of Chaucer.* New York: Knopf, 1977, pp. 10, 14, 15, 56, 93-94, 192, 204, 214.

Identifies the *Gawain*-poet with John Massey. Contends that the Cotton Nero poems explore the medieval motifs of purity and patience. Comments briefly upon the lush imagery in *Gawain*, Gawain's pride and humanity, and the motto of the Order of the Garter.

Add. 14   GRIFFITH, RICHARD R. "Bertilak's Lady: The French Background of *Sir Gawain and the Green Knight*," in *Machaut's World: Science and Art in the Fourteenth Century.* Edited by Madeleine Pelner Cosman and Bruce Chandler. Annals of the New York Academy of Sciences, Vol. 314. New York: New York Academy of Sciences, 1978, pp. 249-266.

Suggests that the thirteenth-century Vulgate *Merlin* by Robert de Boron and an anonymous sequel to this prose account constitute two important sources for *Gawain*, particularly for the concept of Lady Bercilak as a type of "false Guinevere" and for the name and characterization of Bercilak.

Add. 15   HAMILTON, GAYLE KATHLEEN. "Chaos and Conclusion in Late Middle English Romance." Ph.D. dissertation, University of Rochester, 1977.

[*See Dissertation Abstracts International,* 39 (1978), 1538A.] Claims that late ME romances mirror contemporary historical issues, particularly the origins and nature of both authority and a "healthy community." Notes that Gawain's inability to found a healthy community mirrors the cyclical swing from bliss to blunder in *Gawain.*

Add. 16 HANNA, RALPH, III., ed. "Introduction," in his edition of *The Awntyrs off Arthure at the Terne Wathelyn.* Old and Middle English Texts, gen. ed. G. L. Brook. Manchester, England: Manchester University Press, 1974, pp. 11, 14-15, 38-39, 43-48, 52.

Compares the wheel of *Awntyrs* (unsyllabic verse) with the wheel (a kind of syllabic verse) of *Gawain.* Discusses the traditional poetic vocabulary and formulas found in *Gawain* and *Awntyrs* A. Examines the parallels in diction and descriptive detail between the hunting scene in *Awntyrs* A and the deer-hunt in *Gawain* and notes the circular form of both *Awntyrs* A and the Cotton Nero poems. Links Gawain's predicament in the first Hautdesert temptation with the deer's plight in the first hunt; suggests that the breaking of the deer episode may be connected with the unraveling of Gawain's pentangle-shield.

Add. 17 HARWARD, VERNON J., JR. *The Dwarfs of Arthurian Romance and Celtic Tradition.* Leiden: E. J. Brill, 1958, pp. 2-3, 84.

Notes the influence of *Bricriu's Feast* and of Welsh tradition upon *Gawain.* Identifies Bercilak with an Arawn figure.

Add. 18 HEATHER, P. J. "Colour Symbolism: Part IV." *Folklore,* 60 (September, 1949), 321, 324-326.

Emphasizes the symbolic use of green and gold, particularly *Gawain*'s links with magic and fairyland.

Add. 19 HIEATT, A. KENT. "Numerical Structures in Verse: Second-Generation Studies Needed (Exemplified in *Sir Gawain* and the *Chanson de Roland*)," in *Essays in the Numerical Criticism of Medieval Literature.* Edited by Caroline D. Eckhardt. Lewisburg,

Pennsylvania: Bucknell University Press, 1980, pp. 66-70.

> [This annotation is based upon page proof graciously provided by Professor Caroline D. Eckhardt.] Analyzes Käsmann's numerical study (1974.14), a work which criticizes, in part, Hieatt's numerological proposals (1968.7). Comments upon the numerical significance of 12 in *Pearl* and upon the symbolic use of 25, especially the 5 x 5 virtues of Gawain and his pentangle. Focuses on the differences between the school of "aesthetic symmetries" (numerical) and the school of "symbolic symmetries."

Add. 20 HOMANN, ELIZABETH R. "Chaucer's Use of 'Gan'." *Journal of English and Germanic Philology*, 53 (July, 1954), 396.

> Suggests that the auxiliary verb 'gan' is frequently "tucked into the short lines [of *Gawain*] where a simple preterit would do as well." Analyzes the various examples of *gan* (*con, can*) in the poem.

Add. 21 IKEGAMI, TADAHIRO. "*Cortaysye* and *Trawþe* in *Sir Gawain and the Green Knight*." *Gengobunka-Ronshu* (*Studies in Languages and Cultures*), University of Tsukuba, No. 6 (March, 1979), 1-13.

> [In Japanese. Annotation provided by the author.] Employs *cortaysye* and *trawþe* as pivotal concepts in his discussion of Gawain's humanity and the religious aspects of this romance.

Add. 22 JENNINGS, ELIZABETH. *Christianity and Poetry.* London: Burns & Oates, 1965, pp. 30-32, 37.

> Praises *Gawain* for its luminous descriptive passages, its dynamic portraits of hunts and castle scenes, and its rhythm.

Add. 23 JONES, GWYN. *Kings* [,] *Beasts and Heroes*. London: Oxford University Press, 1972, pp. 103-105, 110.

> Comments briefly on Bercilak and on the boar-hunt in *Gawain*.

Add. 24 McKEE, JOHN DeWITT. "Three Uses of the Arming

Scene." *Mark Twain Journal,* 12, no. 4 (Summer, 1965), 18-19, 21.

[Examines the arming scene in *Gawain,* Chaucer's *Sir Thopas,* and Twain's *A Connecticut Yankee in King Arthur's Court.*] Discusses the arming of Arthur's knight and the pentangle-shield symbolism in *Gawain,* a possible source for the depiction of Hank Morgan's arming in *Yankee.*

Add. 25 METCALF, ALLAN. "Gawain's Number," in *Essays in the Numerical Criticism of Medieval Literature.* Edited by Caroline D. Eckhardt. Lewisburg, Pennsylvania: Bucknell University Press, 1980, pp. 141-155.

[This annotation is based upon page proof graciously provided by Professor Caroline D. Eckhardt.] Discusses the connection between the pentangle, especially its numerical structure of symbolic fives and twenty-fives, and Gawain's character. Claims that "the form of . . . *Gawain,* the poetic framework, is fundamentally a matter of 5s and 25s" (p. 143); analyzes the significance of line 2525 as an echo of line 1, similar numerical parallels in *Pearl,* the role of the five-line bob and wheel, and the average stanza length (25 lines), a poetic means of suspense.

Add. 26 PERRYMAN, JUDITH. "Decapitating Drama in *Sir Gawain and the Green Knight.*" *Dutch Quarterly Review of Anglo-American Letters,* 8, no. 4 (1978), 283-300.

Examines the element of ambiguity (the greenness of the Knight, the tension between game and horror) as well as the shattering of audience expectations. Suggests that the Green Knight might be "an actor wearing a false head" (p. 286) in the beheading drama and that this romance may have been visualized by the poet as a type of dramatic production.

Add. 27 PETERSON, CLIFFORD, ed. "Introduction," in his edition of *Saint Erkenwald.* Haney Foundation Series, Vol. 22. Philadelphia: University of Pennsylvania Press, 1977, 9-10, 15-23.

[Reviewed by Robert J. Blanch, *Studies in the Age of*

Chaucer, 1 (1979), 193-197.] Presents the various critical opinions on the question of authorship. Contends that *Erkenwald* and the Cotton Nero poems may have been composed by the same author, perhaps John Massey of Cotton.

Add. 28 RICHTER, MARCELLE THIÉBAUX. "The Allegory of Love's Hunt: A Medieval Genre." Ph.D. dissertation, Columbia University, 1962.
[*See* Thiébaux (1974.32).]

Add. 29 RONEY, L. Y. *"Sir Gawain and the Green Knight." Explicator,* 37, no. 1 (Fall, 1978), 33-34.
Notes that the hunting scenes disclose Bercilak's seasoned control of events at Hautdesert; if the hunts did not exist, Bercilak would be viewed as a fool. Claims that the actions of Bercilak and those of his retainers during the hunts illuminate his extraordinary managerial talents.

Add. 30 SANDERLIN, GEORGE. "Two Transfigurations: Gawain and Aeneas." *Chaucer Review,* 12, no. 4 (Spring, 1978), 255-258.
Claims that Gawain's transformation in lines 864-68, including the interpretation of *ver* (866) as "spring," may have been inspired by the transformation of Aeneas, prior to a love adventure, in Virgil's *Aeneid* (I. 588-93). Interprets *visage* (*Gawain,* 1. 866) as "face."

Add. 31 SAPORA, ROBERT WILLIAM, JR. "A Theory of Middle English Alliterative Meter with Critical Applications." Ph.D. dissertation, University of Connecticut, 1976.
[Discusses *Gawain, Purity, Patience,* and *Erkenwald. See Dissertation Abstracts International,* 36 (1976), 7395A. *See also* Sapora (Add. 32).] Proposes a partially new theory of ME alliterative meter and applies this theory to the entire text of *Gawain.* Appendices include "A Brief History of Commentary on the Authorship of the *Gawain*-group," "A Catalogue of Occurrences of the Various Line Types in the . . . Poems," and "An Annotated List of Problematic Lines."

Add. 32 SAPORA, ROBERT WILLIAM, JR. *A Theory of Middle English Alliterative Meter with Critical Applications.* Speculum Anniversary Monographs, Vol. 1. Cambridge, Massachusetts: Mediaeval Academy of America, 1977, 1-5, 17-29, 32-35, 39, 42-45, 51-52, 57-58, 62, 64, 68-78, 83-91, 115-116.

> [Discusses *Gawain, Purity, Patience,* and *Erkenwald. See also* Sapora (Add. 31). Employs the latest linguistic research in his partially new theory of ME alliterative meter and clarifies the distinction as well as the link between meter and rhythm. Applies his theory (pp. 51-52) to the complete text of *Gawain* and lists the metrical form (pp. 83-91) and the problematic lines (pp. 115-116) of *Gawain.* Offers a stylistic analysis of the temptation scenes (pp. 71-75) and alludes briefly to the authorship problem.

Add. 33 SOUCY, A. FRANCIS. "Gawain's Fault: 'Angardez Pryde'." *Chaucer Review,* 13, no. 2 (Fall, 1978), 166-176.

> Examines the "exchange of winnings" agreement, the temptation scenes, and the Green Chapel episode in order to disclose Gawain's acknowledgment and confession of his most serious fault, his inordinate pride in his knightly reputation. Contends that the green girdle, a symbol of Gawain's *untrawþe,* is worn in order to avoid future sins of pride.

Add. 34 TAJIMA, MATSUJI. "Additional Syntactical Evidence against the Common Authorship of MS. Cotton Nero A.x." *English Studies,* 59 (June, 1978), 193-198.

> Offers a syntactical analysis of *hit* (as a plural noun, as a determinative, as an equivalent of Modern English preparatory *there,* and as a genitive) in *Gawain* and the other Cotton Nero poems in order to refute the common authorship theory.

Add. 35 TURVILLE-PETRE, THORLAC. "Two Notes on Words in Alliterative Poems." *Notes and Queries,* New Series, 25 (August, 1978), 295-296.

> Interprets *tried* (4), a word equivalent to *treid* in *The Wars of Alexander* (3439), as "exposed," for the *Gawain-*

poet alludes to Aeneas's treachery as narrated in Guido de Columnis's *Historia Destructionis Troiae.*

Add. 36 WALSH, EDWARD MICHAEL. "The Meaning of Rhythmic Changes in Fourteenth-Century English Poetry." Ph.D. dissertation, Southern Illinois University, 1974.

[Partly on *Gawain. See Dissertation Abstracts International,* 35 (1975), 7883A.] In his investigation of alliterative meter and rhythm, analyzes the initial one hundred lines of *Gawain, Parlement of the Thre Ages,* and *Siege of Jerusalem.* Contends that *Gawain* employs "complex and dynamic" rhythms.

Add. 37 WARD, MARGARET CHARLOTTE. "French Ovidian Beasts in *Sir Gawain and the Green Knight.*" *Neuphilologische Mitteilungen,* 79, no. 2 (1978), 152-161.

Contends that the hunts of Venus and Diana in medieval French versions of Ovid, the continental "bestiaries of love," and *Les Échecs amoureux* are thematically analogous to *Gawain.* Interlaces the hunts and temptations of *Gawain* through an analysis of the Ovidian beasts, the deer, the boar, and the fox.

Add. 38 WEISS, VICTORIA L. "The Medieval Knighting Ceremony in *Sir Gawain and the Green Knight.*" *Chaucer Review,* 12, no. 3 (Winter, 1978), 183-189.

Explores the connection between the three axe strokes at the Green Chapel and the chivalric dubbing ritual of the accolade (neck-blow). Views the "beheading game" episode as Gawain's initiation into knighthood, the green girdle as the Knight's dubbing gift to Gawain, the chapel as an appropriate fourteenth-century setting for dubbing, and the conclusion of the poem as a revelation of Gawain's spiritual growth and humanity as well as the limitations of mankind.

Add. 39 WILSON, EDWARD. "*Sir Gawain and the Green Knight* and the Stanley Family of Stanley, Storeton, and Hooton." *Review of English Studies,* New Series, 30 (August, 1979), 308-316.

Suggests a potential patronage or even authorship link between *Gawain* and the Stanley family of Stanley (Staffordshire) and of Storeton and Hooton (Cheshire). Examines the dialect and topography of *Gawain,* especially the reference to Wirral (701-702), and claims that the Green Knight's holly bob represents a token of peace as well as a Stanley of Hooton crest (derived from the arms of the Silvesters of Storeton). Perceives connections between Bercilak/Green Knight and the Wirral Stanleys.

INDEX

Ackerman, Robert W., 1957.1;
  1958.1; 1966.1; 1968.1, 2;
  1970.1; 1972.1; 1976.1
Aeneid, 1945.1; Add. 30
Akkartal, T., 1953.1
Aljubouri, A. H., 1966.2
allegory, 1961.15; 1965.16;
  1966.11; 1967.27; 1970.33;
  1971.1; 1972.10, 26; Add. 10;
  Add. 28
Allen, Judson Boyce, 1971.1
"alliterative revival" (verse), 1824.1;
  1876.1; 1878.1, 2; 1882.1;
  1893.2; 1895.1; 1899.3; 1900.1,
  2; 1901.2, 3, 6; 1905.2; 1908.2,
  3; 1909.1, 2; 1911.1; 1914.3;
  1917.3; 1920.1, 3; 1921.4;
  1925.2; 1926.4; 1929.1; 1930.1,
  4; 1931.5, 8; 1933.4; 1935.3;
  1944.3; 1949.1; 1952.5; 1953.8;
  1956.4, 11; 1957.4, 13; 1958.7;
  1959.11, 12; 1961.7; 1962.1, 3,
  14, 15; 1965.1, 10, 28; 1966.19,
  27, 32; 1967.6, 24, 33; 1968.6,
  18, 27; 1969.1, 5, 21; 1970.27,
  28, 29; 1971.6, 8; 1972.27;
  1973.7; 1974.11, 15, 19, 26, 28;
  1975.13, 14, 27, 28; 1976.18,
  30, 34; 1977.11, 13, 16; 1978.1;
  Add. 31; Add. 32; Add. 36
ambiguity, 1933.3; 1963.3; 1964.11;
  1965.1, 23; 1966.15; 1967.30;
  1968.9, 19; 1970.3, 35, 37;
  1971.27, 31; 1972.4, 10; 1973.2,

  10; 1974.1, 20, 26, 33; 1975.26;
  1976.3, 9, 13, 15, 23; 1977.8,
  17; Add. 26
ambivalence, *see* ambiguity
Amours, F. J., 1899.1
Anderson, Heather Jerrim, Add. 1
Anderson, J. J., 1976.5; 1977.1
Andreas Capellanus, 1961.10
Andrew, Malcolm, 1978.1
Andrew, S. O., 1929.1, 2; 1930.1
antifeminism, 1934.2; 1962.7;
  1966.6; 1968.12; 1970.24;
  1971.13; 1972.5; 1974.9;
  1975.15, 22; 1976.9; Add. 5
Anttila, Raimo, 1969.1
Arthur, King, 1920.2; 1925.9;
  1959.15, 17; 1960.5, 7; 1961.6,
  15; 1963.7; 1965.11; 1968.11;
  1969.12; 1970.18; 1971.11, 36;
  1972.17, 26; 1975.3, 18;
  1976.16, 23; Add. 9
Augustine, Saint, 1961.15; 1965.13;
  1966.7; 1976.12
authorship controversy, 1864.1;
  1869.1; 1876.1; 1878.2; 1882.1;
  1883.1; 1886.2; 1888.1; 1889.2,
  3; 1891.1; 1893.1; 1901.4;
  1902.1, 4; 1904.1; 1905.1;
  1906.3; 1910.1; 1914.1; 1921.4;
  1922.4; 1926.4; 1928.2; 1930.4;
  1932.2, 6; 1936.2; 1940.1;
  1941.2; 1946.3; 1948.6; 1949.2,
  11; 1950.4, 5, 6; 1951.3; 1952.4;
  1955.3; 1956.4, 10; 1958.3, 9;

1959.11, 12, 17; 1962.3, 9;
1965.2; 1966.12; 1967.2;
1968.8, 18; 1969.1; 1970.10,
27; 1971.35; 1972.27; 1974.19;
1975.5, 14, 21; 1977.1, 5, 11;
1978.1, 2; Add. 13; Add. 27;
Add. 31; Add. 32; Add. 34;
Add. 39; *see also* biography

Baker, Ernest A., 1924.1; 1950.1;
1957.2
Baker, Sister Imogene, 1937.1
baldric, *see* Green Girdle
Baldwin, Charles Sears, 1914.1;
1922.1
Banks, Theodore Howard, Jr.,
1929.4
Barber, R. W., 1961.1; 1971.2;
1973.1; 1975.1
Barnet, Sylvan, 1956.2
Barron, W. R. J., 1973.2; 1974.1;
Add. 2
Barry, Peter, Add. 3
Barton, Robert J., 1969.2
Bateson, F. W., 1941.1
Baugh, Albert C., 1948.1; 1967.1
Baughan, Denver Ewing, 1950.2
Bayley, A. R., 1936.7
Bayley, John, 1950.3
Bazire, Joyce, 1952.1
Beale, Walter H., 1976.2
Beatie, Bruce A., 1971.3
Becker, P. A., 1931.1
Beheading Game, 1905.3; 1906.5;
1907.2, 3; 1912.1, 2, 4;
1915.2; 1916.4; 1917.3;
1923.8; 1925.1, 4, 8; 1929.1;
1932.1; 1933.3; 1937.4;
1938.5; 1940.1; 1944.2;
1946.3; 1949.1, 6; 1950.2;
1951.6, 8; 1952.4; 1953.6, 7;

1956.2, 4, 11; 1957.9; 1958.8,
10; 1959.7, 9, 11; 1960.2, 8;
1961.1, 2, 17; 1962.3, 4;
1964.9, 16; 1965.7, 26;
1967.6, 19; 1968.18, 19;
1969.18; 1970.2, 6, 17, 29,
31, 38; 1971.24; 1972.23, 25;
1973.4; 1974.12, 15, 17, 26,
28; 1975.9, 16, 25, 31;
1976.29, 31, 35; 1977.2, 17;
1978.4; Add. 26; Add. 38
Belshazzar, 1957.1; 1959.15
Bennett, H. S., Add. 4
Benson, Larry D., 1959.1; 1961.2;
1965.1, 2; 1966.3; 1967.2;
1968.6, 8
Beowulf, 1971.4, 15; 1973.12
Bercilak de Hautdesert, *see* Green
Knight
Bercovitch, Sacvan, 1965.3;
1968.8
Berry, Francis, 1949.1; 1959.2
Berti, I., 1974.2
Bible,
—*Apocalypse,* 1956.4; 1970.1;
1976.26
—*Mark,* 1971.29
—*Proverbs,* 1970.11
bibliography, 1926.4; 1940.1;
1941.1; 1946.3; 1948.7;
1959.11; 1960.10; 1961.3,
17; 1962.3; 1966.1; 1967.1,
6, 19, 33; 1968.2, 16, 18;
1969.14; 1970.10, 35; 1971.20,
25; 1973.11; 1974.5, 19, 28,
34; 1975.5; 1976.2, 5, 22, 37;
1977.11; 1978.1
Billings, Anna Hunt, 1901.1;
1965.4; 1975.2
biography, 1889.1; 1891.1;
1901.1; 1906.5; 1907.2;
1913.6; 1917.3; 1921.4, 5;

1925.8; 1929.4; 1930.4;
1931.9; 1932.2; 1935.1;
1938.8; 1940.1; 1944.3;
1946.3; 1949.11; 1955.3;
1956.1, 10; 1957.4; 1961.4;
1964.9; 1965.10; 1966.27;
1967.24, 33; 1968.6, 14, 18;
1971.31; 1974.23; 1975.7, 13,
28, 29; 1977.13; Add. 13;
Add. 39; *see also* authorship
controversy
Black, Nancy B., 1971.4
Blake, Norman, Add. 5
Blanch, Robert J., 1966.4; 1973.3;
1976.3
Blenkner, Louis, 1977.2; Add. 6
Bloomfield, Morton W., 1961.3;
1968.8; 1969.3; 1970.2
Bloomgarden, Ira, 1971.5
"bob and wheel," 1906.4; 1907.2;
1916.2; 1930.4; 1931.8; 1949.3;
1955.3; 1959.7; 1962.15;
1964.9; 1965.7, 10; 1967.3;
1968.27; 1974.15, 19; 1976.18,
30; 1977.13, 16; Add. 16;
Add. 20; Add. 25
Bonjour, Adrien, 1951.1
Borroff, Marie, 1956.3; 1962.1;
1967.3; 1968.6, 8
Bossy, Michel-André R., 1970.3
Bowen, E. G., 1944.1
Bowers, R. H., 1963.1; 1968.8
Braddy, Haldeen, 1952.2
Bradley, Henry, 1888.1
Brandl, Alois, 1893.1
Branford, William, 1964.1
Braswell, Mary Flowers, Add. 7
Brett, Cyril, 1913.1; 1915.1;
1918.1; 1919.1; 1927.1
Breuer, Rolf, 1966.5
Brewer, D. S., 1948.2; 1966.6;
1967.4; 1968.20; 1976.4

Brewer, Elisabeth, 1973.4
Brink, August, 1920.1
Brink, Bernhard ten, 1877.1;
1889.1; 1899.2
Broes, Arthur T., 1965.5
Brook, G. L., 1963.2
Brown, Carleton F., 1904.1
Brown, J. T. T., 1902.1
Bruce, J. Douglas, 1903.1; 1923.1;
1928.1; 1958.2
Brunner, Karl, 1961.4
Bruten, Avril, 1966.7
Buchanan, Alice, 1932.1
Burnley, J. D., 1973.5, 6
Burrow, J. A., 1957.4; 1959.3;
1964.2; 1965.6; 1966.4;
1968.6, 8; 1971.6; 1972.2, 3;
1973.7; 1977.3
Butler, Norbert P., 1930.2
Butturff, Douglas R., 1972.4

Campbell, Alphonsus M., 1975.3
Campbell, Bernard R., Add. 8
Cargill, Oscar, 1928.2
Carrière, Jean Louise, 1970.4
Carson, Mother Angela, 1962.2;
1963.3, 4; 1968.8
Cavallo, Simonetta, 1969.4
Cawley, A. C., 1962.3; 1971.31;
1976.5
Cebesoy, Ayşe, 1947.1
Challenge, *see* Beheading Game
Chambers, E. K., 1903.2
Chambers, R. W., 1907.1
Champion, Larry S., 1967.5
Chapman, Coolidge O., 1927.2;
1931.2; 1932.2; 1945.1;
1948.3; 1951.2; 1953.2
Chaucer, Geoffrey, 1894.2;
1918.1; 1928.3; 1955.1;
1974.23; Add. 7; Add. 24

—*Book of the Duchess,* 1976.28
—*Friar's Tale,* 1954.3
—*Knight's Tale,* 1967.10;
  1974.3
—*Parson's Tale,* 1957.1;
  1966.30; 1969.15
—*Squire's Tale,* 1947.3; 1953.2
—*Troilus and Criseyde,* 1965.10;
  1967.18
Chisnell, Robert E., 1971.7
chivalry, 1893.1; 1923.8; 1928.3;
  1933.2; 1947.2, 3; 1948.5;
  1949.5; 1951.4; 1955.3, 9;
  1956.8; 1957.10; 1960.3;
  1962.4, 5, 18; 1963.13, 14;
  1965.1, 3, 5, 8, 11; 1966.2,
  14; 1967.3, 14, 18, 23, 25;
  1968.2, 10, 14, 17, 21, 26;
  1969.30; 1970.9, 14, 17, 34,
  35, 37, 39; 1971.5, 6, 8, 13,
  21, 22, 27, 33; 1972.13, 24,
  26; 1973.8, 10, 16, 18, 21, 22;
  1974.1, 3, 6, 8, 9, 22, 30;
  1975.1, 12, 26, 28, 30, 31;
  1976.32; 1977.8, 17; 1978.1;
  Add. 2; Add. 4; Add. 38; Add.
  39
Christmas, Peter, 1974.3
Christophersen, Paul, 1971.8
Cicero, Marcus Tullius, 1956.12;
  1977.14
Clark, Cecily, 1955.1; 1966.8;
  1968.6; 1971.9
Clark, John W., 1941.2; 1949.2;
  1950.4, 5; 1951.3
Clark, S. L., Add. 9
Cleanness, see Purity
Clerk, Jayana J., 1965.7
Coffer, Karin B., 1975.4
Coffey, Jerome E., 1969.5
Colgrave, Bertram, 1938.1
color symbolism, 1883.1; 1912.1;

1913.2; 1915.2; 1916.1, 3, 4;
  1917.1; 1925.2; 1934.1;
  1938.4; 1946.3; 1948.8;
  1949.5, 9; 1950.14; 1953.7;
  1954.3; 1957.6; 1958.5, 7;
  1959.10; 1960.11; 1961.15,
  17; 1964.1, 11; 1965.1, 6, 10,
  13; 1966.16; 1967.16, 30, 33;
  1968.7; 1969.2; 1970.4, 6;
  1972.10, 23, 24; 1974.15, 17,
  26, 28; 1976.3, 11, 14, 36;
  1977.8; Add. 10; Add. 18;
  Add. 26
comedy, *see* game
Como, Frank T., 1969.6
confession, 1958.1; 1959.3;
  1963.8, 14; 1965.6; 1968.13;
  1969.29; 1970.14, 29, 33;
  1971.6, 12; 1973.9, 13, 16;
  1974.6, 15, 24; 1975.12;
  1976.11, 24, 25; 1977.8, 14;
  Add. 7; Add. 12; Add. 33
Conley, John, 1957.3
contemptus mundi, 1966.14;
  1974.13; 1975.15
Cook, Arthur Bernard, 1906.1
Cook, James Rhodes, Add. 10
Cook, Robert G., 1963.5
Coomaraswamy, Ananda K.,
  1944.2
Cooper, Helen, 1976.6
Cortaysye, see courtesy
Cottle, Basil, 1969.7
Cotton Nero MS A.x.,
  —contents of, 1864.1; 1869.1;
  1891.1; 1907.2; 1912.3;
  1917.3; 1921.4; 1922.3;
  1923.3; 1924.3; 1927.7;
  1929.4; 1938.6; 1940.1;
  1946.2; 1948.5, 7; 1956.4;
  1959.17; 1962.3; 1964.6;
  1966.33; 1967.3, 19, 33;

1968.14; 1970.4, 10, 29;
1974.16; 1977.1, 11
—date, 1839.1; 1891.1; 1901.1;
1912.4; 1913.2; 1918.1;
1921.4; 1923.3; 1925.8;
1929.1; 1938.6, 8; 1940.1;
1947.1; 1952.4; 1956.10;
1967.6, 19; 1968.8, 18;
1970.10, 29; 1977.1, 11, 16
—description of, 1839.1;
1864.1; 1869.1; 1891.1;
1907.2; 1921.4; 1923.3;
1924.3; 1925.8; 1940.1;
1946.2; 1967.6
—dialect, 1884.1; 1886.2;
1901.1; 1905.3; 1912.3,
4; 1918.1; 1921.6; 1922.5;
1925.8; 1927.7; 1929.1;
1930.4, 9; 1931.5; 1932.4;
1936.9; 1937.2; 1940.3;
1941.2; 1947.1; 1948.5, 7;
1952.4; 1958.9; 1959.17;
1962.3; 1963.2, 9, 10;
1967.6, 19; 1968.8, 14;
1969.6; 1970.10, 22; 1977.1,
16; Add. 39
—history of, 1891.1; 1921.4;
1923.3; 1925.8; 1933.5;
1948.5, 7; 1961.4; 1967.3,
6; 1968.1, 8, 14; 1972.1, 15;
1976.1
couetyse, see covetousness
courtesy, 1933.2; 1947.3; 1948.5;
1955.2; 1957.7; 1961.10;
1962.4, 7; 1963.13, 15;
1964.16; 1965.10, 21; 1966.6,
13; 1967.4, 7, 14, 15; 1968.2,
5, 10, 14; 1970.3, 9, 14, 17,
29, 35, 39; 1971.13, 27, 33;
1972.5, 13; 1973.10, 14, 15,
21; 1974.22, 26, 28, 31;
1975.28; 1976.29, 35; 1977.17;

1978.1; Add. 21
courtly love, 1925.2; 1949.5;
1951.8; 1955.3, 9; 1956.4;
1959.9, 16; 1961.10, 11;
1963.13; 1965.7, 10; 1967.7,
15, 18, 33; 1968.9; 1969.27,
31; 1970.9, 26; 1974.15, 29;
1975.28; 1977.11; Add. 12
Courtney, Charles R., 1975.5
covetousness, 1963.8; 1964.2;
1965.16; 1970.35; 1973.9;
1975.12, 24; 1976.20; 1977.2,
14; Add. 6
Crane, John K., 1969.8
C.[rawford], O. G. S., 1938.2
cruxes, *see* explanatory and textual notes
Curley, Michael J., 1975.6
Curry, Walter Clyde, 1916.1
Cursor Mundi, 1970.22
Cutler, John L., 1949.3; 1952.3

Dante,
—*Convivio,* 1936.9
—*Divine Comedy,* 1965.12, 13
D'Ardenne, S. R. T. O., 1959.4
Davenport, W. A., 1973.8; 1977.4;
1978.2
David, Alfred, 1968.3
Davies, R. T., 1948.4
Davis, Norman, 1966.9; 1967.6;
1970.5
Day, Mabel, 1919.2; 1923.2;
1940.1
Dean, Christopher, 1964.3;
1971.10
deBruyne, Edgar, 1946.1
deCoucy, Enguerrand, 1938.8;
1940.3; 1956.10
Delany, Paul, 1965.8; 1968.8
Dendinger, Lloyd N., 1970.6

description, 1948.1; 1951.5;
  1952.6; 1955.11; 1957.1, 9;
  1958.10; 1959.7; 1960.13;
  1963.13; 1964.13; 1965.1, 7;
  1966.12; 1967.15; 1970.1,
  27, 30, 35; 1971.26, 31;
  1972.20; 1973.7; 1974.26,
  29; 1976.27; 1977.13; 1978.1;
  Add. 4; Add. 16; Add. 22
—of nature, 1887.1; 1894.2;
  1900.4; 1905.2, 3; 1907.2,
  3, 4; 1913.6; 1929.3, 5;
  1931.8; 1935.3; 1946.4;
  1949.1, 9; 1950.8; 1951.4;
  1955.3, 11; 1956.11; 1957.5,
  9; 1958.5, 9; 1959.2, 11, 14;
  1960.3, 6; 1961.1, 5; 1962.3,
  19; 1963.12; 1964.7, 9, 15;
  1965.6, 7, 28; 1966.5, 28;
  1967.4, 19; 1968.6; 1969.18,
  22, 30; 1970.26; 1970.26;
  1971.6, 8, 17, 26, 31, 35;
  1972.10, 24; 1973.16, 19;
  1974.1, 4, 13; 1975.15;
  1976.9, 15, 32; 1977.10
Destruction of Troy, 1906.3
Diamond, Arlyn, 1976.7
Diamond, Sara A., 1970.7
Dickins, Bruce, 1934.1; 1966.10
diction, 1878.2; 1882.1; 1883.1;
  1886.1, 2; 1889.2; 1901.5;
  1902.2; 1909.1; 1910.1;
  1913.6; 1918.1; 1920.1;
  1923.1; 1925.2; 1926.4;
  1930.4; 1931.11; 1933.5;
  1935.3; 1937.3; 1939.1;
  1940.1; 1941.2; 1943.3;
  1949.2; 1950.4, 5, 12; 1951.3;
  1952.3, 5; 1955.3; 1956.4, 11;
  1957.13; 1958.3; 1959.5, 6,
  12, 17; 1961.5; 1962.1, 3, 6,
  14, 15; 1963.2, 9; 1964.5, 14;

  1965.2, 28; 1966.6, 8, 25, 32;
  1967.6. 8, 13, 33; 1968.9, 28;
  1969.7; 1970.13, 22, 32;
  1971.6, 9, 25, 28, 31, 35;
  1972.2, 12, 20, 25; 1973.3, 8,
  12, 16, 17, 22, 23; 1974.4, 7,
  12, 20, 21, 25, 26, 28, 29;
  1975.5, 30; 1976.9, 21; 1977.7,
  13; Add. 16; Add. 21
Dodgson, John McNeal, 1963.6
Donaldson, E. Talbot, 1962.4;
  1968.6
Donner, Morton, 1965.9
Dove, Mary, 1972.5
Dowden, P. J., 1949.4
Duggan, Hoyt N., 1977.5
Duncan, Patricia J., 1976.8
Dunn, Thomas P., 1972.6
Dykstra, Timothy Eugene,
  Add. 11

Eadie, John, 1968.4
Eagan, Joseph F., 1949.5
Ebbs, John Dale, 1958.3
Edward III, King, 1891.1; 1908.1;
  1913.2; 1928.3; 1938.8;
  1947.1
Edwards, A. S. G., 1971.11
Ekwall, Eilert, 1918.2
Elliott, Ralph W. V., 1958.4;
  1961.5; 1968.6; 1974.4
Embler, Weller B., 1964.4
Emerson, Oliver Farrar, 1916.2;
  1919.3; 1921.1, 2, 3; 1922.2,
  3; 1925.1; 1927.3
Engelhardt, George J., 1955.2;
  1965.24
Enkvist, Nils Erik, 1957.5
Evans, W. O., 1967.7; 1968.5;
  1973.9
Evans, William W., Jr., 1959.5;

1967.8
Everett, Dorothy, 1929.5; 1955.3;
1968.6
Exchange of Winnings, 1938.5;
1940.1; 1952.4; 1957.9;
1959.11; 1964.9; 1965.6;
1967.6, 19; 1968.18; 1971.34;
1973.4, 9; 1974.15; 1975.16,
19; 1976.10, 13, 29; 1977.2;
Add. 33
explanatory and textual notes,
1893.3, 4; 1894.1; 1897.1, 2;
1899.1; 1902.3; 1903.1;
1904.2; 1906.6, 7; 1908.1;
1913.1, 5, 6; 1915.1, 3; 1916.1;
1917.2; 1918.2; 1919.1, 2, 3;
1920.4; 1921.1, 2, 3; 1922.2,
5; 1923.2, 3, 4, 6, 7, 9; 1924.3,
4, 6, 7, 8. 9; 1925.1, 3, 6, 7;
1926.1, 2; 1927.1, 3, 5, 6, 8,
9; 1928.5; 1929.2, 6, 7, 8;
1930.1, 3, 6, 7, 9; 1931.6, 7,
10; 1932.3, 5, 6; 1933.1, 5, 6;
1934.3, 4; 1935.2, 3, 5, 6, 7;
1936.1, 11, 12, 13; 1937.3, 5,
6, 7; 1939.1; 1940.2; 1941.3,
4; 1942.1; 1943.1, 4; 1944.1;
1945.1, 2, 3, 4, 5; 1948.3, 6;
1949.7, 8; 1950.7, 13, 14;
1951.1, 7; 1952.1, 7; 1953.1,
5, 8, 9; 1954.2; 1955.1, 7, 8;
1956.4, 7, 9, 10; 1957.3, 5;
1958.6; 1959.8, 13; 1961.7, 9;
1962.12, 13, 20; 1963.2, 3;
1965.20; 1966.9, 10, 21, 26,
29; 1967.11; 1968.3; 1969.3,
26, 28; 1970.5, 11, 13, 32;
1971.9, 10, 11, 34; 1972.3, 12,
23; 1973.5, 8, 12, 15, 20, 23;
1974.4, 11, 20, 25, 36; 1975.10,
14, 20, 27, 30, 32; 1976.20,
21, 23; 1977.4, 15; Add. 20;
Add. 30; Add. 31; Add. 32;
Add. 34; Add. 35

Farley-Hills, David L., 1964.5;
1975.7
felix culpa, 1967.16; 1968.15;
1969.25; 1970.4; 1972.18;
1974.9; 1975.11, 24
Field, P. J. C., 1971.12
Figgins, Robert H., 1973.10
Fischer, Joseph, 1900.1; 1901.2,
3
Fisher, John H., 1961.6
Fitzpatrick, John Francis,
Add. 12
Fletcher, P. C. B., 1971.13
Foley, Michael M., 1974.5, 6
formulaic verse, 1824.1; 1876.1;
1886.1; 1906.3; 1925.8;
1933.6; 1935.3; 1937.5;
1957.5, 13; 1962.14; 1965.2;
1966.19, 32; 1967.3; 1968.28;
1969.5, 26; 1970.29; 1971.6,
9, 11; 1972.26; 1974.4, 26;
1976.27; 1977.13; Add. 16
Forse, Edward J. G., 1936.8
Förster, Max, 1924.2
F.[oster], T. G., 1897.1
Fox, Denton, 1968.6
Frankis, P. J., 1961.7
Friedman, Albert B., 1960.1;
1966.4; 1977.6
Fry, Nancy M., 1975.8
Frye, Northrop, 1957.6
Fuhrmann, Johannes, 1886.1

Gallagher, Joseph E., 1977.7
Gallant, Gerald, 1970.8
game (or play), 1931.6; 1933.7;
1935.6; 1937.4; 1951.8;

1952.7; 1953.6; 1955.2, 10;
1956.3; 1958.8; 1959.8, 9, 11;
1960.8; 1961.3, 16; 1962.4, 5,
20; 1963.1, 2, 5, 12; 1968.9,
11, 15, 17, 19, 24; 1969.2, 13,
24; 1970.4, 24, 26, 27, 35;
1971.6, 7, 17, 18, 20, 21, 22,
31, 33, 34; 1972.4, 6, 10, 20,
25, 29; 1973.9, 21, 22; 1974.6,
9, 10, 12, 15, 21, 28, 33;
1975.5, 8, 13, 16, 19; 1976.3,
19, 23, 36, 37; 1977.11, 14;
1978.2, 4; Add. 11; Add. 26
Ganim, John M., 1974.7; 1976.9
Gardner, John, 1965.10; 1966.11;
1968.8; Add. 13
Garrett, Robert Max, 1925.2
Gawain (character), 1891.1;
1905.3; 1913.2; 1917.3;
1921.4; 1924.1; 1926.3;
1927.4; 1930.5, 8; 1933.2;
1940.5; 1947.3; 1948.6;
1952.4; 1955.3, 9; 1956.5,
8; 1957.7, 10; 1959.7, 17;
1960.5, 7, 13; 1961.11, 17;
1962.4, 5, 8, 16; 1964.4, 7, 9,
11, 16; 1965.9, 22; 1966.2, 5,
6, 8, 15, 23, 28; 1967.16, 28,
32; 1968.24; 1969.12, 18;
1970.17, 31, 34; 1971.19, 31,
36; 1972.5, 16, 22, 24;
1973.10, 12, 14, 17, 20, 21,
22, 23; 1974.10, 13, 26, 31,
32; 1975.10, 17, 28, 31;
1976.4, 8, 14, 31, 32, 36;
1977.7; Add. 5; Add. 9; Add. 13;
Add. 21; Add. 25; Add. 30;
Add. 38
Geoffrey of Vinsauf, 1955.11;
1964.15
geography, *see* topography
Gerould, Gordon Hall, 1935.1;

1936.9; 1953.3
Gilbert, A. J., 1976.10
Giles, Saint, 1967.26; 1969.7, 29
Gillie, Christopher, 1965.11
glosses, *see* explanatory and
textual notes
Goetinck, Glenys, 1975.9
Goldbeck, Helen J., 1972.7
Goldhurst, William, 1958.5
Gollancz, Sir Israel, 1891.1;
1894.1; 1901.4; 1904.2;
1906.2; 1907.2; 1921,4, 5;
1922.4; 1923.3; 1928.3;
1931.3; 1940.1; 1950.6;
1955.4; 1971.14
Göller, Karl Heinz, 1963.7
Gordon, E. V., 1925.8; 1932.3;
1933.1; 1967.6
Gradon, Pamela, 1971.15
Gray, D., 1958.6
Green, D. H., 1970.9; 1971.16;
1975.10
Green, Richard Hamilton, 1962.5;
1965.24; 1966.4
Green Chapel, 1915.2; 1916.3;
1917.1; 1924.2; 1930.4;
1938.1, 2; 1944.1; 1948.2, 4;
1950.10; 1951.6; 1952.4;
1953.7; 1956.6; 1958.4;
1959.3; 1960.8, 13; 1961.5;
1962.16; 1963.3, 14; 1964.6,
10; 1965.13, 16; 1966.16, 23,
28; 1967.25; 1968.28; 1969.7;
1970.15, 24; 1971.11; 1972.9;
1973.14; 1974.3, 31; 1975.12,
30; 1976.3, 26, 35; 1977.6, 8;
Add. 3; Add. 6; Add. 33; Add.
38
Green Girdle, 1913.2; 1916.3;
1928.2; 1930.5; 1931.4;
1943.2; 1953.10; 1955.2;
1958.1, 8; 1960.1, 8; 1961.15;

1962.4; 1963.8, 15; 1964.2, 6,
10; 1965.13; 1966.7, 14;
1967.5, 33; 1968.7; 1969.11,
17; 1970.6, 27; 1971.13, 30,
34; 1972.8, 9, 25, 29; 1973.9;
1974.3, 6, 8, 28, 31; 1975.12,
24, 26; 1976.6, 14, 20, 24;
1977.6, 8, 9; 1978.4; Add. 5;
Add. 33; Add. 38
Green Knight, 1903.2; 1906.1;
1912.1; 1915.2; 1916.4;
1917.1; 1923.5; 1924.1, 2, 5;
1927.4; 1928.4; 1929.5;
1930.5; 1931.1; 1933.3;
1934.1; 1935.6; 1936.10;
1938.4; 1941.3; 1946.5;
1948.8; 1949.6, 9; 1950.14;
1952.2, 4; 1953.4, 7, 10;
1954.3; 1955.3, 11; 1956.4,
6, 11; 1957.6, 8; 1958.5, 8;
1959.2, 3, 4, 10, 17; 1960.2,
3, 6, 11, 13; 1961.15, 17;
1962.2, 3, 10, 19, 20; 1963.4,
14; 1964.1, 3, 8, 9, 11; 1965.1,
3, 10, 13, 14; 1966.15, 20, 31;
1967.14, 16, 30, 33; 1968.6,
28; 1969.17, 24; 1970.4, 26,
29, 31, 32, 33; 1971.1, 4, 15,
24; 1972.4, 10, 13, 16, 21, 23,
24, 29; 1973.2, 21, 22; 1974.1,
15, 17, 20, 26, 28, 32; 1975.6,
15, 18, 30, 31; 1976.3, 4, 13,
31, 32, 36; 1977.8, 9, 15;
1978.2; Add. 3; Add. 14; Add.
17; Add. 23; Add. 26; Add. 29;
Add. 38; Add. 39
Greenfield, Stanley B., 1961.17
Greenwood, Ormerod, 1956.4;
1972.8
Greg, W. W., 1924.3; 1932.4;
1941.3
Griffith, Richard R., Add. 14

Gringolet, 1906.2
Gross, Laila, 1967.9; 1969.9;
1974.8
guide, Gawain's, 1965.8, 19;
1968.8; 1969.7; 1972.21;
1978.2
Guidi, Augusto, 1958.7; 1959.6;
1966.12
Guinevere, 1950.2; 1965.11;
1966.24; 1970.18; 1975.15;
Add. 14
Gunn, Alan M. F., 1971.17

Habicht, Werner, 1959.7
Haines, Victor Yelverton, 1971.18;
1974.9; 1975.11; 1976.11
Halpern, R. A., 1972.9; 1976.12
Halstead, W. L., 1961.8
Halverson, John, 1969.10
Hambridge, Roger A., 1973.11
Hamilton, Gayle Kathleen, Add.
15
Hamilton, George L., 1908.1
Hamilton, Marie P., 1970.10
Hanna, Ralph, III., Add. 16
Hare, Kenneth, 1918.1; 1923.4;
1948.7
Hargest-Gorzelak, Anna, 1967.10
Hark, Ina Rae, 1974.10
Harris, Veronica, 1972.10
Harward, Vernon J., Jr., Add. 17
Hautdesert, 1913.2; 1915.2;
1930.4; 1945.3; 1957.1;
1958.4; 1960.12; 1961.5;
1962.2, 19; 1963.11; 1964.6;
1965.8, 10, 16; 1966.6, 23, 30;
1967.8, 15, 16, 18, 25; 1968.4,
19, 26; 1969.7, 15; 1970.1, 9,
29, 32; 1971.28; 1972.12, 16,
29; 1973.2; 1974.13, 14;
1975.10; 1976.14, 36, 37;

1978.2, 4; Add. 29
Haworth, Mary, 1959.8
Haworth, Paul, 1967.11
Heather, P. J., 1931.4; 1954.1;
     Add. 18
Heiserman, Arthur, 1966.13
Henderson, George, 1912.1
Henderson, Hamish, 1958.8
Henneman, John Bell, 1889.2
Henry, Avril, 1976.13
Henry, P. L., 1962.6
Herzog, Michael B., 1971.19
Heyworth, P. L., 1970.11; 1972.11
Hieatt, A. Kent, 1968.7; 1970.12;
     1976.14; Add. 19
Hieatt, Constance B., 1967.12;
     1974.11
Highfield, J. R. L., 1953.4
Hill, Archibald A., 1972.12
Hill, John M., 1974.12
Hill, Laurita Littleton, 1946.2
Hills, David Farley, 1963.8;
     1968.8
Hodgart, M. J. C., 1955.5
Hoffman, Donald L., 1970.13
Holthausen, Ferdinand, 1924.4
Homann, Elizabeth R., Add. 20
Hopper, Vincent Foster, 1938.3
Hoshiya, Goichi, 1951.4
Howard, Donald R., 1955.6;
     1964.6; 1966.4, 14; 1968.6, 8;
     1971.20; 1974.13
Hughes, Derek W., 1971.21
Huizinga, Johan, 1963.5; 1972.25
Hulbert, J. R., 1915.2; 1916.3;
     1921.6; 1923.5; 1925.3;
     1931.5
humor, *see* game
Hunt, Tony, 1975.12; 1976.15
hunts, 1900.4; 1902.4; 1903.1;
     1928.6; 1931.2; 1933.7;
     1937.7; 1938.7; 1946.5;

1948.6; 1951.6; 1952.4;
     1956.2, 10; 1957.11; 1958.7,
     10; 1959.11; 1960.8; 1961.17;
     1963.11; 1965.7, 10; 1966.10;
     1967.3, 4, 16, 19, 33; 1968.6,
     19; 1969.18, 29; 1970.6, 8, 28,
     29, 33; 1971.15, 29, 31;
     1972.10, 25; 1973.2, 6, 14, 22;
     1974.1, 14, 21, 28, 29, 32;
     1975.16, 28; 1976.11, 13, 14,
     15, 28, 37; 1977.2, 11;
     1978.2; Add. 2; Add. 6; Add.
     16; Add. 22; Add. 23; Add. 28;
     Add. 29; Add. 37
—in manuals of the chase,
     1903.1; 1938.7; 1956.10;
     1974.32
—parallels between *Gawain* and
     Parlement of the Thre Ages,
     1901.5; 1902.4; 1903.1;
     1907.2; 1955.3; 1969.21
—technical terms of, 1903.1;
     1929.7; 1931.10; 1935.5;
     1936.11; 1938.7; 1946.3;
     1948.6; 1950.9; 1951.9;
     1966.10; 1971.9; 1974.20,
     32; Add. 16
Hussey, S. S., 1968.9

Ikegami, Tadahiro, 1957.7; 1960.2;
     1962.7; 1964.7; 1968.10;
     1976.16; 1978.3; Add. 21
imagery,
     —commerce, 1971.34; 1976.13
     —fire, 1927.4; 1949.6; Add. 10
     —gem, 1931.4; 1971.21; 1973.9
     —metal, 1931.4; 1971.21; Add.
     10
     —pearl, 1883.1; 1970.29;
     1976.14
     —vegetation, 1936.10; 1946.4;

1949.1, 9; 1953.7; 1967.14;
1972.13; 1974.15, 17;
1975.15
—water, 1956.10; 1964.3
irony, 1953.6; 1959.9; 1960.8;
1962.4, 18; 1963.1, 3; 1964.6;
1965.5; 1966.14, 23; 1967.28;
1969.2; 1970.9, 27, 35; 1971.6,
7, 15, 17; 1972.21; 1973.2, 10,
17; 1974.1, 26, 33; 1975.10,
19; 1976.3, 6, 11, 15; 1977.13;
1978.1, 2; Add. 5
Isaacs, Neil D., 1969.11; 1970.27

Jackson, Isaac, 1913.2; 1920.2;
1950.7
Jacobs, Nicholas, 1970.14
Jambeck, Thomas J., 1973.12
James, Bridget, 1961.9
Jennings, Elizabeth, Add. 22
Jensen, Elisabeth N., 1969.12
John the Baptist, Saint, 1967.26
John the Evangelist, Saint, 1969.29
Johnson, Lynn S., 1973.13
Johnston, Everett C., 1967.13
Jones, Edward Trostle, 1969.13
Jones, Gwyn, 1944.1; 1952.4;
Add. 23
Jones, R. T., 1960.3; 1967.14;
1972.13
Jones, Shirley Jean, 1966.15
Julian the Hospitaller, Saint,
1967.26; 1969.7, 29

Kaluza, Max, 1891.2; 1909.1;
1911.1
Kane, George, 1951.5; 1976.17
Kaske, R. E., 1970.15
Käsmann, Hans, 1974.14
Kean, P. M., 1967.15

Kee, Kenneth O., 1956.5
Kelley, Gerald B., 1955.7
Kellogg, Alfred L., 1966.16;
1972.14
Kennedy, Sally P., 1968.11
Ker, W. P., 1907.3; 1912.2;
1969.14
Kindrick, Robert L., 1971.22
King, R. W., 1929.6; 1934.2
Kirk, Elizabeth D., 1975.13
Kirkpatrick, Hugh, 1976.18
Kirtlan, Ernest J. B., 1912.3;
1913.3
Kiteley, J. F., 1961.10; 1962.8;
1968.8; 1971.23
Kittredge, George Lyman, 1916.4;
1960.4
Kjellmer, Göran, 1975.14
Knapp, Peggy Ann, 1975.15;
1977.8
Knigge, Friedrich, 1885.1; 1886.2
Knott, Thomas A., 1915.3
Kobayashi, Atsuo, 1951.6
Kökeritz, Helge, 1942.1; 1943.1
Kottler, Barnet, 1966.17
Koziol, Herbert, 1932.5, 6
Krappe, A. H., 1938.4
Kreuzer, James R., 1959.9
Kuhnke, Bruno, 1899.3; 1900.2
Kullnick, Max, 1902.2

Lady Bercilak, 1891.1; 1905.3;
1916.3; 1948.8; 1955.11;
1956.6; 1961.10; 1962.2, 13;
1963.11; 1964.11; 1965.3;
1966.6, 24; 1967.7, 20;
1969.27; 1970.4, 11; 1971.10;
1973.2, 20; 1975.10, 15, 23;
1976.4; 1977.7, 9, 17; Add. 2;
Add. 5; Add. 14
Lamba, B. P., 1969.15

Lamba, R. Jeet, 1969.15
Lanham, Margaret, 1947.2
Lasater, Alice E., 1971.24;
    1974.15
Lass, Roger, 1965.12; 1966.18
Lavers, Norman, 1977.9
Lawrence, John, 1892.1; 1893.2
Lawrence, R. F., 1966.19
Leavis, Q. D., 1950.8
Lee, Jennifer A., 1974.16
legal terminology, 1901.6;
    1956.10; 1965.6; 1972.3;
    Add. 2
Lehman, Anne K., 1970.16
Leible, Arthur B., 1961.11
Leighton, J. M., 1974.17
Leo, Diana T., 1970.17
Leonard, Frances M., 1976.19
Leonard, William Ellery, 1920.3
Les Très Riches Heures, 1955.1;
    1973.19
Lester, G. A., 1976.20
Levitsky, Steven E., 1972.15
Levy, Bernard S., 1962.9; 1965.13
Lewis, C. S., 1962.10; 1964.8;
    1966.20; 1968.6, 8
Lewis, John S., 1959.10
lewté, see loyalty
Leyerle, John, 1975.16
Lippmann, Kurt, 1933.2
Logan, Betty Y. B., 1975.17
Loganbill, Dean, 1972.16
Löhmann, Otto, 1938.5
Long, Charles, 1970.18; 1975.18
Long, Clarence E., 1957.8
Longo, Joseph A., 1967.16
Loomis, Laura Hibbard, 1938.6;
    1957.9; 1959.11; 1962.11;
    1968.8, 20
Loomis, Roger Sherman, 1924.5;
    1927.4; 1928.4; 1933.3;
    1938.6; 1943.2; 1949.6;

    1956.6; 1964.9; 1969.16;
    1970.19, 20
loyalty, 1948.5; 1952.4; 1957.10;
    1963.15; 1965.8; 1968.18;
    1969.23, 27; 1970.37; 1972.23;
    1973.9, 10; 1974.28; 1975.12;
    1976.10, 11; Add. 2
Lucas, Peter J., 1968.12
luf-lace, see Green Girdle
Luick, Karl, 1889.3; 1905.1
Lupack, Alan C., 1974.18
Luttrell, C. A., 1951.7; 1955.8;
    1956.7; 1961.12; 1962.12
Lydgate Troy Book, 1938.6

McAlindon, T. E., 1961.13;
    1965.14, 15; 1970.21
McClure, Peter, 1973.14
Macdonald, Angus, 1935.2; 1954.2
McGee, Alan V., 1970.22
McIntosh, Angus, 1963.9; 1966.21
McKee, John DeWitt, Add. 24
McKeehan, Irene Pettit, 1925.4
McKisack, May, 1959.12
McLaughlin, Edward Tompkins,
    1894.2
McLaughlin, John C., 1961.14;
    1963.10
McNamara, John F., 1968.13
Macrae, Suzanne H., 1972.17
Madden, Sir Frederic, 1839.1
Magoun, Francis P., Jr., 1928.5;
    1937.3, 4
Malarkey, Stoddard, 1964.10;
    1968.8
Manning, Stephen, 1964.11;
    1968.8
Manson, H. W. D., 1969.17
Margeson, Robert W., 1977.10
Marino, James G. A., 1975.19
Markman, Alan M., 1955.9;

1957.10; 1964.12; 1966.4, 17
Markus, Manfred, 1971.25;
    1974.19, 20
Martin, John W., 1972.18;
    1973.15
Mathew, Gervase, 1948.5;
    1966.22; 1968.6, 14
Mathews, J. C., 1930.3
Mathewson, Jeanne T., 1968.15
Matonis, Ann T., 1966.23; 1971.26
Matsui, Noriko, 1971.27
Matthew of Vendôme, 1955.11;
    1961.5
Matthews, William, 1960.5;
    1968.16; 1970.4; 1975.20
Maynadier, Howard, 1907.4
Medcalf, Stephen, 1973.16
Mehl, Dieter, 1962.13; 1964.13;
    1967.17; 1969.18
Meier, Hans Heinrich, 1974.21
Melton, John L., 1955.10
Mennicken, Franz, 1901.3
Menner, Robert J., 1922.5;
    1924.6; 1926.1; 1931.6
Mercer, Mary Ellen, 1974.22
Mertens-Fonck, Paule, 1969.19
mesure, see moderation
Metcalf, Allan A., 1971.28;
    1976.21, 22; Add. 25
meter, 1878.1; 1889.3; 1891.1, 2;
    1895.1; 1900.1; 1901.1, 2;
    1905.1; 1908.3; 1909.1;
    1911.1; 1917.2; 1920.1, 3;
    1921.1; 1925.2; 1930.2, 4;
    1933.4; 1940.1; 1941.2;
    1944.3; 1952.1, 3, 4; 1956.3;
    1957.13; 1962.1, 15; 1964.14;
    1965.2; 1967.3, 33; 1968.18,
    27; 1969.6; 1972.27; 1973.3;
    1974.11; 1975.13, 27; 1976.30,
    34; 1977.16; Add. 31; Add. 32;
    Add. 36

Michael, Saint, 1969.22
Miller, Helen Hill, 1970.23
Miller, J. Furman, 1971.29
Mills, A. D., 1964.14
Mills, David, 1968.17; 1970.24
Mills, M., 1965.16; 1968.8
moderation, 1963.15; 1973.14
Moody, Patricia A., 1976.23
Moody, Philippa, 1960.6
Moon, Douglas M., 1965.17;
    1966.24
Moorman, Charles, 1956.8;
    1966.4; 1967.18; 1968.18;
    1969.20, 21; 1977.11
Moorman, Frederic W., 1905.2;
    1972.19
Morgan le Fay, 1903.3; 1923.5;
    1943.2; 1950.2; 1955.11;
    1956.6; 1959.17; 1960.1;
    1962.2; 1963.4; 1964.11;
    1966.15, 24; 1967.18, 20;
    1968.4, 11; 1969.19; 1970.18;
    1971.30; 1974.15; 1975.15,
    18; 1976.4
Morris, Richard, 1864.1, 2;
    1869.1, 2; 1965.18
Morse, Ruth, 1975.21
Morte Arthure (alliterative),
    1902.4; 1906.3; 1910.1;
    1913.2; 1951.5; 1971.32
Morte d'Arthur, 1969.12
Morton, A. L., 1960.7
Moseley, C. W. R. D., 1974.23
Mossé, Fernand, 1952.5
Muscatine, Charles, 1972.20
Musker, Francis, 1958.9
Mustanoja, Tauno F., 1959.13

Nagano, Yoshio, 1962.14; 1966.25
Nakao, Sister Bernadette Setsuko,
    1976.24

Napier, Arthur S., 1897.2; 1902.3

Neale, Robert, 1968.19

Neaman, Judith S., 1976.25

Neilson, George, 1901.5, 6;
1902.4

Newstead, Helaine, 1967.19;
1968.20

Newton, Humfrey, 1943.3;
1950.12; 1952.3

Nickel, Gerhard, 1965.19

Nitze, William A., 1936.10

Nossel, Margaret A., 1968.21

notes, *see* explanatory and textual
notes

number symbolism, 1938.3;
1946.1; 1956.2, 4, 10; 1959.17;
1962.5; 1963.11; 1965.6, 10;
1966.18; 1967.33; 1968.7;
1970.33, 38; 1971.6, 23, 29,
31; 1972.20; 1973.2; 1976.14;
1977.2; Add. 10; Add. 19;
Add. 25

numbers, 1936.3, 5, 6, 7, 8, 12;
1962.3; 1970.6; 1974.14;
1976.28, 29; 1977.2; *see also*
number symbolism

Oakden, J. P., 1930.4; 1933.4, 5;
1935.3; 1968.22, 23

Obrecht, Denise, 1938.7

Ohye, Saburo, 1962.15

Oiji, Takero, 1974.24

Olszewska, E. S., 1933.6; 1937.5;
1966.26; 1974.25

Ong, Walter J., 1950.9

Onions, C. T., 1923.6, 7; 1924.7,
8, 9; 1926.2; 1927.5, 6; 1931.7;
1932.3; 1933.1; 1953.5

Oppel, Ingeborg, 1960.8

Order of the Garter, 1891.1;
1902.4; 1906.5; 1907.2;

1908.1; 1913.2; 1916.3;
1921.4; 1928.2, 3; 1930.4;
1938.8; 1940.3; 1946.3;
1947.1; 1956.10; 1968.14;
Add. 13

Osberg, Richard H., 1977.6

Osgood, Charles Grosvenor,
1935.4

Owen, D. D. R., 1968.24; 1972.21;
1973.17

Owings, Marvin Alpheus, 1942.2;
1952.6

Pace, George B., 1967.20; 1969.22

Paganoni, Matilde, 1960.9

Palazzi, Annalisa, 1977.12

Paris, Gaston, 1888.2

Parlement of the Thre Ages,
1901.5; 1902.4; 1903.1;
1907.2; 1914.3; 1955.3;
1965.10; Add. 36

Patch, Howard Rollin, 1950.10;
1970.25

Patience, 1876.1; 1886.2; 1889.1,
3; 1891.1; 1893.2; 1905.1;
1908.3; 1909.1; 1914.3;
1919.2; 1925.8; 1927.7;
1930.4; 1932.5, 6; 1937.2;
1941.2; 1950.4, 5; 1951.3;
1957.13; 1958.3; 1964.5, 12;
1965.2; 1966.17, 31; 1967.4;
1970.30; 1971.25, 35; 1972.29;
1975.5, 14; 1976.21; 1977.11;
Add. 7; Add. 31; Add. 32;
Add. 34

Paton, Lucy Allen, 1900.3;
1903.3; 1960.10

Patrick, Michael, 1972.22

Pearce, T. M., 1963.11

Pearl, 1886.2; 1889.1; 1891.1;
1909.1; 1919.2; 1922.3;

1925.8; 1927.7; 1930.4;
1932.5, 6; 1937.2; 1939.1;
1941.2; 1946.3; 1950.5;
1951.3; 1956.4; 1958.3;
1961.6; 1964.5, 12; 1965.2;
1966.17, 31; 1967.4, 15;
1968.7; 1970.1, 30; 1971.15,
25, 35; 1972.3, 29; 1974.12;
1975.5, 14; 1976.14, 21;
1977.11; 1978.3; Add. 7; Add.
19; Add. 25; Add. 34
Pearsall, Derek A., 1955.11;
1973.18, 19; 1977.13
penitence, *see* confession
pentangle, 1893.3; 1913.2;
1916.3; 1928.2; 1933.2;
1938.3; 1943.2; 1946.1, 3;
1949.4; 1955.2; 1956.10;
1958.1, 7; 1959.4, 17; 1960.8;
1961.17; 1962.5; 1965.6, 10;
1966.6, 18; 1967.15, 33;
1968.5, 6, 7, 21; 1969.2;
1970.9, 29, 35, 38, 39; 1971.6,
23, 30; 1972.8, 20; 1973.16;
1974.1, 14, 15, 24; 1975.10;
1976.14, 29; 1977.2, 6, 14;
1978.1; Add. 16; Add. 19;
Add. 24; Add. 25
Perényi, Erzsébet, 1970.26
Perry, L. M., 1937.6
Perryman, Judith, Add. 26
Peter, Saint, 1967.26; 1969.7,
29; 1972.29
Peterson, Clifford, Add. 27
Pierle, Robert C., 1968.25
Piers Plowman, 1878.1; 1914.3;
Add. 7
Plessow, Gustav L., 1931.8
Pollard, William F., Jr., 1976.26
Pons, Emile, 1946.3; 1949.7;
1951.8
Price, Richard, 1824.1

Purity, 1876.1; 1886.2; 1889.1, 3;
1891.1; 1893.2; 1905.1;
1908.3; 1909.1; 1914.3;
1919.2; 1925.8; 1927.7;
1930.4; 1932.5, 6; 1937.2;
1941.2; 1949.2; 1950.4, 5;
1951.3; 1957.1, 13; 1958.3;
1959.15; 1964.5, 12; 1965.2;
1966.17, 30, 31; 1967.4;
1969.15; 1970.30; 1971.15,
25, 35; 1972.7, 29; 1973.5;
1975.5, 14, 29; 1976.21;
1977.4, 11, 15; Add. 7; Add.
31; Add. 32; Add. 34

Raffel, Burton, 1970.27
Randall, Dale B. J., 1957.11;
1960.11
Ray, B. K., 1926.3
Reichardt, Paul F., 1971.30
Reicke, Curt, 1906.3
Reid, Wendy M., 1978.4
Reinhold, Heinz, 1953.6
Renoir, Alain, 1958.10; 1959.14;
1960.12, 13; 1962.16; 1968.8
Rice, Nancy H., 1975.22
Richardson, M. E., 1941.4
Richter, Marcelle Thiébaux,
Add. 28
Ridley, M. R., 1944.3; 1950.11;
1962.17
Rigby, Marjory, 1956.9
Rix, Michael M., 1953.7
Robbins, Rossell Hope, 1943.3;
1950.12; 1967.21
Robertson, D. W., Jr., 1954.3
Robinson, Ian, 1972.23
Róheim, Géza, 1930.5
Roman de la Rose, 1964.5
romance, 1893.1; 1916.4; 1923.1;
1946.3; 1947.1, 2; 1949.5;

1951.6; 1957.6, 10; 1959.9;
1961.3; 1963.6, 13; 1965.1, 3,
5, 16; 1966.23; 1967.28;
1968.2, 9, 21, 24, 25; 1969.2,
18; 1970.7, 27, 29, 35; 1971.1,
5, 7, 8, 17, 22; 1973.8, 17, 18;
1974.1, 4, 10, 26, 33, 35;
1975.4, 19; 1976.7, 15, 16,
23, 37; 1977.13; 1978.1, 2;
Add. 15
Roney, L. Y., Add. 29
Rosenberg, Bruce A., 1967.22
Rosenberg, James L., 1959.9;
1971.31
Rosenthal, F., 1878.1
Ryan, J. S., 1967.23

Saint Erkenwald, 1882.1; 1886.2;
1889.3; 1893.1; 1902.1;
1905.1; 1914.3; 1922.4;
1926.4; 1932.6; 1935.3;
1940.1; 1941.2; 1950.4, 5;
1951.3; 1956.4, 10; 1964.12;
1965.2; 1966.17; 1967.6;
1970.21, 30; 1975.5, 14, 21;
1977.4; Add. 27; Add. 31;
Add. 32
Saintsbury, George, 1906.4
Salter, Elizabeth, 1966.27;
1967.24; 1973.19
Samson, Anne, 1968.26
San Juan, Epifanio, Jr., 1966.28
Sanderlin, George, 1973.20;
1975.23; Add. 30
Saperstein, J., 1962.18
Sapora, Robert William, Jr., Add.
31; Add. 32
Savage, Henry L., 1926.4; 1928.6;
1929.7; 1930.6; 1931.9, 10;
1933.7; 1934.3; 1935.5;
1936.11; 1937.7; 1938.8;

1940.2, 3; 1943.4; 1945.2, 3;
1946.4; 1948.6; 1949.8;
1951.9; 1952.7; 1956.10;
1965.20; 1966.29
Schelp, Hanspeter, 1965.21;
1971.32
Schiller, Andrew, 1968.27
Schlauch, Margaret, 1928.2;
1956.11; 1963.12; 1965.22
Schmittbetz, Karl Roland, 1908.2;
1909.2
Schnyder, Hans, 1959.15; 1961.15
Schofield, William Henry, 1906.5;
1914.2; 1921.7; 1925.5
Schotter, Anne H., 1976.27
Schroeder, Henry A., Jr., 1963.13
Schumacher, Karl, 1913.4; 1914.3
Schwahn, Friedrich, 1884.1
Scott, P. G., 1966.30
Scudder, Vida D., 1917.1
Secreta Secretorum, 1965.27
Self-Weeks, William, 1925.6
Serjeantson, Mary S., 1927.7;
1940.1
Shakespeare, William, 1900.4
  —*The Tempest,* 1973.22
  —*Venus and Adonis,* 1976.17
Shedd, Gordon M., 1967.25
Shepherd, Geoffrey, 1970.28
Shields, Ellis Gale, 1956.12
Shippey, T. A., 1971.33
Shuttleworth, Jack M., 1967.26
Silverstein, Theodore, 1964.15;
1965.23; 1967.27; 1968.8;
1977.14
Sims, James H., 1975.24
Sisam, Kenneth, 1927.8, 9;
1950.13
Skeat, W. W., 1893.3, 4; 1906.6
Skinner, Veronica L., 1969.23
Sklute, Larry M., 1967.28
Smith, John Harrington, 1934.4

Smith, Roland M., 1946.5
Smithers, G. V., 1950.14; 1953.8;
    1963.14
Snell, Beatrice Saxon, 1925.7
Solomon, 1916.3; 1938.3; 1949.4;
    1956.10; 1962.5; 1970.9;
    1972.29; 1974.15; 1975.10
Solomon, Jan, 1963.15; 1968.8
Sosnoski, James J., 1967.29
Soucy, Arnold F., 1972.24;
    Add. 33
sources (and analogues), 1883.1;
    1885.2; 1888.2; 1889.1;
    1893.1; 1897.3; 1901.1;
    1906.5; 1907.2, 3; 1912.1, 3,
    4; 1915.2; 1916.3, 4; 1917.1,
    3; 1920.2; 1923.5; 1924.1, 5;
    1925.4, 8; 1927.4; 1928.4;
    1929.1; 1931.1; 1932.1;
    1933.3; 1934.2; 1936.10;
    1938.5; 1940.1; 1943.2;
    1944.1, 2; 1945.1; 1946.5;
    1948.6; 1949.6; 1950.14;
    1952.4; 1953.8, 10; 1956.6,
    11, 12; 1957.9; 1958.8, 9;
    1959.9, 11; 1960.2, 12; 1961.1,
    2; 1963.11; 1964.9; 1965.1,
    22, 26; 1967.6, 19, 33; 1968.2,
    18, 24; 1969.19; 1970.1, 31,
    33, 38; 1971.8, 24, 29, 32, 33;
    1972.16, 18, 21, 26; 1973.2, 4,
    12, 16, 17, 21; 1974.15, 19, 23,
    28; 1975.5, 9, 25; 1976.1, 10;
    1977.11; Add. 14; Add. 17;
    Add. 30; Add. 37
Spearing, A. C., 1964.16;
    1966.31; 1968.6, 8; 1970.29;
    1974.26; 1976.28
Spearing, J. E., 1974.26
Speirs, John, 1949.9; 1950.15;
    1951.10; 1957.12; 1968.6
Spendal, Ralph J., Jr., 1970.30;

1976.29
Spenser, Edmund, 1894.2
    —*Faerie Queene*, 1921.4, 5
    —*Shepheardes Calender*, 1945.5
stanza, 1914.1; 1916.2; 1920.3;
    1924.3; 1930.4; 1949.3;
    1955.3; 1956.11; 1961.17;
    1968.7, 27; 1969.18; 1970.37;
    1971.6; 1972.27; 1976.18, 30;
    Add. 25; *see also* "bob and
    wheel"
Steele, Peter, 1969.24
Steinbach, Paul, 1885.2
Stephany, William A., 1969.25
Stephens, G. Arbour, 1940.4
Stevens, John, 1961.16; 1973.21;
    1974.27
Stevens, Martin, 1972.25
Stillings, Justine T., 1976.30
Stone, Brian, 1959.16, 17;
    1964.17; 1974.28
Strachan, L. R. M., 1936.12
structure (and symmetry), 1889.1;
    1923.8; 1931.8; 1946.2;
    1949.3, 10; 1951.6; 1952.4;
    1955.3; 1956.2; 1957.11;
    1958.7; 1959.11; 1961.3, 17;
    1963.15; 1964.6; 1965.1, 3, 6;
    1966.5, 14, 23, 33; 1967.22,
    26, 33; 1968.6, 7, 18, 19, 25,
    26; 1969.18, 25, 27; 1970.6, 7,
    9, 12, 26, 30, 37; 1971.5, 6, 9,
    11, 15, 17, 20, 25. 30, 31;
    1972.20, 25; 1973.2, 4, 6, 13,
    23; 1974.14, 15, 17, 18, 21,
    28, 29, 36; 1975.4, 13, 23, 26;
    1976.3, 23, 28; 1977.2, 8, 10,
    13, 16; 1978.2, 4; Add. 6;
    Add. 19; Add. 25
Stucken, Eduard, 1901.7
Sundén, K. F., 1920.4; 1929.8;
    1930.7

Suzuki, Eiichi, 1966.32; 1967.30; 1968.28; 1969.26, 27, 28; 1972.26; 1977.15

Sveinsson, Einar Ólafur, 1975.25

symbolism, 1916.3; 1930.5; 1938.4, 7; 1946.3; 1949.1, 4, 5, 6; 1956.4, 10; 1957.8; 1958.8, 9; 1961.5, 15; 1962.5, 10; 1964.1, 11; 1965.10, 11, 13, 17, 27; 1966.14, 15, 18; 1967.16, 20, 33; 1968.5, 7; 1969.11, 19; 1970.8, 9; 1971.20, 23, 29; 1972.9, 10; 1974.14, 17, 28, 36; 1976.4, 6, 14; 1977.6, 8; 1978.1, 4; Add. 6; Add. 10; Add. 25; *see also* color symbolism and number symbolism

Szücs, Clara A., 1974.29

Taitt, Peter S., 1974.30; 1975.26

Tajima, Matsuji, 1975.27; Add. 34

Tamplin, Ronald, 1969.29

Taylor, A. B., 1930.8

Taylor, Andrew, 1962.19

Taylor, Paul B., 1969.30; 1970.31; 1971.34; 1974.31

Taylor, Rupert, 1917.2

Temptation, 1905.3; 1906.5; 1912.4; 1916.4; 1917.3; 1923.8; 1925.8; 1929.1; 1932.1; 1933.2; 1938.5; 1940.1; 1946.3; 1949.6; 1950.2; 1951.6, 8; 1952.4; 1953.6; 1956.2, 6, 10, 11; 1957.9. 11; 1958.7, 8; 1959.9, 11; 1961.1, 10, 17; 1962.2, 3, 7, 13; 1963.11, 12, 14; 1964.9, 16; 1965.7, 16, 19; 1966.6; 1967.3, 4, 6, 7, 16, 19; 1968.6, 9, 10, 17, 18, 19, 24; 1969.17,

18, 29; 1970.3, 6, 8, 11, 29, 39; 1971.9, 10, 15, 29, 31, 36; 1972.6, 9, 22, 23, 25; 1973.2, 4, 6, 14, 20, 21, 22; 1974.1, 3, 14, 15, 20, 26, 28, 29, 31; 1975.9, 10, 12, 16, 23, 26, 28; 1976.10, 13, 15, 17, 28, 37; 1977.2, 4, 6, 7, 11, 14; 1978.2; Add. 2; Add. 5; Add. 6; Add. 16; Add. 32; Add. 33; Add. 37

Tester, Sue K., 1970.32

Thiébaux, Marcelle, 1970.33; 1974.32

Thomas, Julius, 1908.3

Thomas, Martha Carey, 1883.1

Thomas, P. G., 1913.5

Thompson, Raymond H., 1970.34; 1976.31

time, 1949.10; 1965.6; 1966.5, 14, 23; 1967.9; 1969.8, 9; 1971.15, 18, 25, 26; 1972.24; 1973.2, 16, 23; 1974.7; 1977.8; Add. 9

Toelken, J. Barre, 1964.10; 1968.8

Tolkien, J. R. R., 1925.8; 1967.6; 1975.28

topography, 1907.1; 1913.2; 1924.2; 1937.2; 1940.1; 1956.1; 1958.9; 1961.5; 1962.6; 1963.6; 1970.15, 23, 29; 1971.5; 1972.11; 1973.16; 1974.4; 1976.37; Add. 1; Add. 39

Trautmann, Moritz, 1876.1; 1878.2; 1882.1; 1895.1

Tristram, Philippa, 1976.32

Tsuchiya, Tadayuki, 1976.33

Turville-Petre, Joan, 1976.34

Turville-Petre, Thorlac, 1977.16; Add. 35

Tuttleton, James W., 1966.33

Twain, Mark, Add. 24

Utley, Francis Lee, 1960.14;
1969.31

Valaitis, Kristina A., 1974.33
Van der Ven-Ten Bensel, Elise
F. W. M., 1925.9
Vantuono, William, 1971.35;
1975.29
Vasta, Edward, 1965.24
Veitch, John, 1887.1
Virgin Mary, 1920.2; 1936.4;
1959.4; 1966.18; 1969.29;
1971.30; 1974.24; 1975.15
Vogel, Henry, 1940.5
Von Ende, Frederick A. C.,
1972.27
von Schaubert, Else, 1923.8

Waldron, Ronald A., 1957.13;
1962.20; 1970.35; 1978.1
Walsh, Edward Michael, Add. 36
Ward, Margaret Charlotte, Add. 37
Wars of Alexander, 1888.1;
1902.4; 1906.3; Add. 35
Warton, Thomas, 1824.1
Wasserman, Julian N., Add. 9
Waswo, Richard, 1973.22
Watson, George, 1974.34
Watson, John Gillard, 1951.11
Watson, Melvin R., 1949.10
Webb, P. H., 1967.31
Webster, K. G. T., 1917.3
Weichardt, Carl, 1900.4
Weidhorn, Manfred, 1967.32
Weiss, Victoria L., 1976.35;
1977.17; Add. 38
Weston, Jessie L., 1897.3; 1900.5;

1905.3; 1912.4; 1965.25;
1970.36; 1972.28
Whaley, Helen R., 1972.29
Whitbread, L., 1945.4
White, Beatrice, 1945.5; 1953.9;
1965.26
White, Robert B., Jr., 1965.27;
1968.8
Whitebook, Budd B., 1971.36
Whitehall, Harold, 1930.9
Whiting, B. J., 1947.3; 1968.6
Whiting, Ella Keats, 1931.11
William of Palerne, 1878.1
Williams, D. J., 1970.37
Williams, Sister Margaret, 1949.11;
1967.33; 1970.38
Wilson, A. D., 1974.35; 1976.36
Wilson, Edward, 1976.37; Add. 39
Wilson, Janet, 1975.30
Wilson, R. M., 1948.7
Wimsatt, James I., 1970.39
Wolfram von Eschenbach, 1933.3
—*Parzival,* 1933.3; 1959.14;
1961.1; 1964.9; 1967.32;
1971.3; 1975.1
Woods, William F., 1975.31
Wright, Elizabeth Mary, 1906.7;
1913.6; 1923.9; 1935.6, 7;
1936.13; 1939.1
Wright, Thomas L., 1974.36
Wynnere and Wastoure, 1914.3;
1973.16

Yamaguchi, Hideo, 1965.28
Yerkes, David, 1975.32
Ywain and Gawain, 1893.1

Zacher, Christian, 1968.8
Zesmer, David M., 1961.17
Zimmer, Heinrich, 1948.8;

1953.10; 1956.13; 1968.6
Zimmermann, Rüdiger, 1973.23
Zucchi, M. R., 1976.38